# Private Equity and venture Capital in Europe

# Private Equity and Venture Capital in Europe

## Markets, Techniques, and Deals

### Second Edition

Stefano Caselli

Giulia Negri

Academic Press is an imprint of Elsevier
125 London Wall, London EC2Y 5AS, United Kingdom
525 B Street, Suite 1800, San Diego, CA 92101-4495, United States
50 Hampshire Street, 5th Floor, Cambridge, MA 02139, United States
The Boulevard, Langford Lane, Kidlington, Oxford OX5 1GB, United Kingdom

**Notices**

Knowledge and best practice in this field are constantly changing. As new research and experience broaden
our understanding, changes in research methods, professional practices, or medical treatment may
become necessary.

Practitioners and researchers must always rely on their own experience and knowledge in evaluating
and using any information, methods, compounds, or experiments described herein. In using such
information or methods they should be mindful of their own safety and the safety of others, including
parties for whom they have a professional responsibility.

To the fullest extent of the law, neither the Publisher nor the authors, contributors, or editors, assume
any liability for any injury and/or damage to persons or property as a matter of products liability,
negligence or otherwise, or from any use or operation of any methods, products, instructions, or ideas
contained in the material herein.

**Library of Congress Cataloging-in-Publication Data**
A catalog record for this book is available from the Library of Congress

**British Library Cataloguing-in-Publication Data**
A catalogue record for this book is available from the British Library

ISBN: 978-0-12-812254-9

For information on all Academic Press publications
visit our website at https://www.elsevier.com/books-and-journals

Working together
to grow libraries in
developing countries

ELSEVIER   Book Aid International

www.elsevier.com • www.bookaid.org

*Publisher:* Candice Janco
*Acquisition Editor:* J. Scott Bentley
*Editorial Project Manager:* Susan Ikeda
*Production Project Manager:* Punithavathy Govindaradjane
*Cover Designer:* Mark Rogers

Typeset by SPi Global, India

# Contents

## PART 3    Managing a Private Equity Investment

# About the Authors

**Stefano Caselli** is vice rector for international affairs at Bocconi University where he is a full professor of banking and finance at Department of Finance and member of the board of directors of SDA Bocconi School of Management. He is also the founder and the director of the "Start-up Day" platform for Bocconi since 2015, devoted to facilitate the start-up process for Bocconi students and alumni. His research activities focus on the relationship between banking and industrial system, facing issues both of banking credit risk management and of corporate finance and capital structure. He is the author of numerous books and articles on the subject. His works have been published in *Journal of Financial Intermediation, Journal of Banking and Finance, European Financial Management, Journal of Financial Services Research, Journal of Applied Corporate Finance*, and *Economia & Management*, among others. He has got a long experience as independent director in several boards of corporations and financial institutions as well as advisor of investment committees (among them: SIAS S.p.A., Generali Real Estate, Santander Consumer Bank, Fondazione Cassa di Risparmio di Padova e Rovigo). He acts as columnist and opinion maker on "L'Economia del Corriere della Sera," as well radio and television programs. He is research fellow of BAFFI-CAREFIN (the research center for financial innovation of Bocconi University), member of the board of directors of ISBM (International School of Business Management) in the United Kingdom, and member of the Strategic Board of CEMS. He won several times the "Bocconi Teaching Award" and the "Bocconi Research Award" in 1997, 2004, and 2011.

**Giulia Negri** is research fellow of Corporate and Real Estate Finance Department at SDA Bocconi School of Management and a PhD candidate at The University of St. Gallen in Switzerland. Her field of interest concerns financial reporting, performance measurement, and the whole world of start-ups and private equity and venture capital. She conducts research about private equity, start-ups, and performance measurement systems. At the moment, she is working for the third consecutive year for the activity "Start-up Day" at Bocconi University that rewards the best Italian start-ups and that creates a marketplace among investors and startuppers. In the past, she has worked with J.P. Morgan, PwC, Assiteca (the largest Italian insurance broker), Assolombarda (the General Confederation of Lombardy), and Prysmian Group.

# Foreword by Michael Collins

The private equity industry has emerged strongly from the financial crisis thanks to its focus on building better and more valuable businesses. Not only do investors appreciate its ability to generate attractive returns for their portfolios, and company managers and employees welcome the operational expertise that accompanies investment, even policymakers also understand the industry's important role in European economic recovery. Together they are creating the tailwinds that will enable the industry to grow across Europe.

Private equity is a dynamic industry which plays an important role in the European investment landscape. Fund managers raise capital from investors to buy and invest in companies they believe have the potential to grow. They bring in new ideas and thinking, optimize operations, facilitate entry to new markets develop new products and services, and do whatever else it takes for the business to grow. When the time comes to exit, the businesses they have built can find willing buyers among corporate groups, public markets, and other private equity firms. Profits from disposals then flow back to investor, providing the capital that will allow the cycle of investment to begin again.

Venture capital follows essentially the same pattern, with some crucial differences. Investment is made into start-up and early stage enterprises, many of which are not yet registering profits, and some of which do not even have revenues. And that funding often goes in alongside other venture capital funds or investors in "rounds" to ensure a steady flow of finances for critical stages of the company development.

What unites private equity and venture capital and makes them different from many other asset classes is the alignment of interest between managers and investors. Fund managers, or general partners, put their own capital into funds alongside that of their investors, or limited partners. It is that unique alignment, combined with the potential for superior returns, that is increasing investor demand for private equity. Risks are shared, and so are the rewards.

The interest from investors and industry activity is reflected in the data that Invest Europe—the association representing private equity, venture capital, and infrastructure in Europe—collects from more than 1200 private equity firms managing assets of over €600 billion across Europe.

Private equity fundraising rose by 37% in 2016 to €74.5 billion, the highest level since 2008. Moreover, private equity funds raised some €240 billion in the 4 years from 2013 to 2016, more than double the amount that was raised in the four previous years. Meanwhile, private equity invested €53.7 billion in 2016 into almost 6000 companies. The mid-market, private equity's engine room in Europe has scope for activity and investment in small- and medium-sized enterprises (SMEs), accounted for 83% of companies backed. Completing the activity cycle, private equity exits amounted to some €38.9 billion in 2016. It was the third of the three strongest successive exit years on record, during which time disposals totaled €132 billion in former equity investments.

The data illustrate that not only is private equity an important asset class for investors, it is also an important source of funding, knowledge, and skills for growing companies. And it is the developer of better businesses, which can then attract strategic investors that need new growth divisions, public markets that want fresh companies to invest in, or other private equity firms ready to take companies to the next level. It is these contributions to the investment ecosystem in Europe that has attracted the attention of European policymakers. By investing in ambitious companies, private equity is helping the European Union to meet its own goals of backing innovation, accelerating economic growth, and creating new jobs.

Invest Europe has worked long and hard to explain these benefits—not only through public affairs activities, but also engaging events such as our Invest Week programme in Brussels and the provision of world-class data and statistics through our pan-European database initiative in collaboration with national private equity and venture capital associations. Policymakers are responding with measures that benefit the industry. Among the developments is a new €1.6 billion venture capital fund of funds that will be seeded with €400 million of EU capital with the aim of drawing in at least three times as much money from institutional investors. This fund of funds will then back venture capital funds across Europe, helping them to scale up and ultimately invest in more start-ups and early stage companies.

Another significant action is the amendment of the European Venture Capital Funds Regulation (EuVECA) to open up the existing legislation to more fund managers focused on SMEs. One crucial measure will lift the size of a qualifying investment under EuVECA regulation from 250 or fewer employees to under 499. It will enable more private equity fund managers who are focused on small- and mid-sized buyouts to qualify for the EuVECA designation, which in turn will allow them to access the passport permitting them to market their funds across the EU, helping investors access new funds and funds to invest in more businesses.

These are just two practical examples that include removing barriers to capital raising and reducing risk weightings on alternative investments. The regulatory agenda rarely stops and we are preparing for the planned review of the most significant piece of regulation regarding private equity in Europe—the Alternative Investment Fund Managers Directive (AIFMD). We are also watching and working on global issues, such as the taxation policy, including the OECD's Base Erosion and Profit Shifting (BEPS) program, which endeavors to close tax loopholes for industry and individuals around the world. It is essential that we fight for specific measures that will improve the operating environment for private equity, while remaining aware of actions that may cause detrimental impact or unintended consequences for the industry.

At the same time, private equity is taking a lead in industry standards, including environmental, social, and governance issues (ESG). Invest Europe's Handbook of Professional Standards is one of the most comprehensive documents of its kind and is updated regularly. Transparency, accountability, and responsible investment are areas on which institutional investors are increasingly focused, and we have responded with materials and training to help all private equity managers meet higher standards.

Private equity is also becoming more open. We recognize our obligations to promote the industry globally, not only to press and commentators, but also to politicians, investors and entrepreneurs—ultimately facilitating its activity globally. In addition, our events stimulate debate on all issues that are important to private equity and they cement the networks that professionals need in order to operate successfully.

Against all this, private equity does face challenges—as do other investment sectors—caused by recent political changes in the European landscape such as the UK's decision to leave the European Union. Invest Europe is helping managers and investors to think carefully about all the issues involved and prepare for the future. However, the industry also has qualities that play in its favor. Managers can generate some of their best returns when volatility creates dislocation in investment markets. They are agile and responsive, and so can pivot to the best opportunities across markets and sectors. And they have the experience to manage companies through difficult times, protecting and even growing market share. As a result, private equity has the ability to weather the potential challenges ahead.

It is clear from the appetite of investors, businesses, and eventual buyers of assets, as well as the development of new policy, that private equity is an industry with an important role to play in Europe. It is driving returns for institutions, performance for companies, and opportunities for corporate investors. It is aligning with policymakers' objectives to create innovation, jobs, and growth. And it is pushing forward advances that can make European private equity a leading light in industry's best practice and ethical investment. It is an industry on a growth trajectory and one that is the key to both the investment universe and the economy.

**Michael Collins**
*Chief Executive Officer*
*Invest Europe, Brussels, Belgium*

# Foreword by Josh Lerner

Private equity is an increasingly important part of the financial landscape. The global private equity sector grew from $870 billion in 2004 to $2.5 trillion in mid-2016.[1] Their enthusiasm of investors for this asset class is understandable: pension funds, government funds, and university endowments are in many cases facing financial shortfalls and are desperate for high returns.

The reasons why these investors have targeted private equity for investment are not hard to see. We all know about the spectacular returns that the investors in start-ups such as Amazon, Apple, Facebook, and Microsoft have enjoyed. But there have been many tremendous successes in private equity as well. For instance, Thomas H. Lee Company bought Snapple, the iced tea maker, for roughly $140 million. Eight months later, Lee took the company public. Only 2 years after the original acquisition, Lee sold Snapple to Quaker Oats for $1.7 billion.

Despite this growth, many questions about private equity remain unanswered, and many of its features continue to be mysterious. What do private equity groups really do? How do buyout funds create value—do they fundamentally transform the companies in which they invest, or is it all simply a financial "shell game?" What are the impact of these transactions on workers, the environment, and the society as a while? What kinds of returns have these funds generated? Maddeningly, private equity is just so…private!

In addition to questions about the day-to-day activities of these funds, the patterns of private equity fundraising and investment pose several puzzles. First, the level of activity today is far greater than in earlier decades—what explains this tremendous growth in these funds? Perhaps even more puzzling is the process of boom and bust that characterizes this industry. There were rapid increases in fundraising in the late 1960s, mid-1980s, late 1990s, mid-2000s, and mid-2010s, and precipitous declines in the 1970s, early 1990s, early 2000s, and the late 2000s. What explains the boom-bust cycles?

---

[1]Preqin, *2017 Global Private Equity Report*, London, 2017. This does not include private investments outside of funds, which are growing in volume.

Then there is the global dimension. Private equity originated in the United States and for much of its history, the industry was concentrated in that nation and the United Kingdom. Over the past 15 years, however, private equity has become much more global. Not only has the capital disbursed in continental Europe and Asia increased sharply, but also emerging markets are becoming far more important in the private equity landscape. This growth poses several questions. To what extent is the model, developed and refined over the past several decades, likely to be successfully translated to other countries? Will only buyout funds manage the transition or will other types of investments such as growth capital, also make the leap?

It is this exciting territory that the second edition of *Private Equity and Venture Capital in Europe* explores. The book examines how the industry grew in Europe, the obstacles it has faced, and its ongoing evolution. It highlights many of the institutional and regulatory challenges that are specific to European funds. As such, it should provide a portal into this frequently mysterious world, and should prepare many of the readers for careers in this exciting industry.

Good luck in your endeavors!

**Josh Lerner**
*Harvard Business School, Boston, MA, United States*
*Private Capital Research Institute, Allston, MA, United States*

# Acknowledgments

It's been a long time since the first edition of this book and many things have changed in the economic and financial environment. When writing the first edition of the book, the European Union had just been hit by the financial crisis and some European countries would have been about just to face bankruptcy. Seven years later, the European Union is slowly reprising from the financial crisis and yet many forces are trying to drive it apart.

It's been also a long time under a professional point of view, as I, and this is Stefano speaking, decided to get Giulia on board for this adventure.

Writing a book, and especially to write a second edition of it, is as twice as challenging and hence it cannot be done *solo*. As a team, Stefano and Giulia, need to thank the whole Bocconi University and SDA Bocconi School of Management environment.

In particular I, and this is Stefano speaking, would like to thank the colleagues and friends with whom I shared my researches and whose work has been of great inspiration for me. The very long list written in the first edition is still there and it represents the cradle for the beginning of the content of the book and its roots: I will never forget.

A special thank you is now devoted to colleagues and friends—from academia, the business world, and the media world—with whom I interacted a lot in the last years and who gave me ideas, suggestions, and new perspectives to analyze the ever-changing (and never sleeping) and fascinating world of private equity: Luisa Alemany, Luciano Balbo, Andrea Beltratti, Marina Brogi, Guido Corbetta, Leonardo Etro, Massimo Fracaro, Stefano Gatti, Gimede Gigante, Eugenio Morpurgo, Francesco Perilli, Alessandra Puato, Andrea Sironi, Andrea Tortoroglio, Veronica Vecchi, and Andrea Vismara. They were all so precious, bright, and smart and they enlightened every debate and brainstorming we had together, talking about the financial system and its evolution and transformation.

However, a special "thank you" is for two persons. Fabio Sattin, with whom I designed and launched (and still manage!) 15 years ago the "Private equity course" at Bocconi and I consider not only a great friend, but a leader in the private equity world. The second person that I would like to thank in a special way is Silvia Colombo, with whom I started from scratch the creative and exciting adventure of "Bocconi Start-up Day," a platform devoted to Bocconi students and Alumni to launch their own venture.

I, and now it is Giulia speaking, would like to thank all the people that stimulated me and guided me during my years at Bocconi University and SDA Bocconi and that led me to this adventure with Stefano. I am queuing on Stefano's thank you to each of the person listed above. However, I would like to add some people myself, running the risk to be redundant. In the first place, I would like to thank Angela Pettinicchio for being the first person to believe that I could fit in the academic world. I also would like to thank Andrea Dossi and Markus Venzin for being such strong leaders along my way. Both professionally and personally, I would like to thank Leonardo Etro and Matteo Vizzaccaro and my dear friend Claudia Marangoni for contributing to this project in giving insights on many different technical aspects. I also would like to thank the students that I have met so far, for each of them has left me a piece of theirs and each of their thoughts and ideas has contributed in enriching the content of this book.

I also would like to thank my colleagues at The University of St. Gallen, Philipp Engelhardt, Christina Gaupp, Felix Hermes, and Tobias Mueller for giving me different perspectives on the same topic and hence inspiring me in approaching the same subject under a different light. I also would like to thank my PhD supervisor, Professor Thomas Berndt, for making me explore different horizons during my PhD.

I also would like to thank the people from the professional world that helped me in approaching this topic from a hands on point of view. For this, I would like to thank Alberto Craici at Berrier Capital, Mauro Brunelli and Michele Fodde at Principia SGR, and Ezio Ravaccia at Solar Ventures. I also would like to thank Marzia Anelli at H-Farm and Andrea Tortoroglio at UniCredit for their work gave me more and more insights on the private equity and venture capital world.

I also would like to say a warm and honest "thank you" to the whole start-up environment that has been created around the Bocconi StartupDay initiative. Meeting such eager entrepreneurs and inventors gave me much enthusiasm in carrying on this project and each of them certainly gave to me a different standpoint on such a difficult topic as Private Equity is.

I also would like to sincerely thank Silvia Colombo as working with her undoubtedly broadened my horizon on the startup and the venture capital world, but also for being such a great and surely unique role model for me.

Last but certainly not least, I would like to thank Stefano, the co-author of the book. None of the achievements that I have reached so far would have been accomplished if it were not for him. I have to thank you, Stefano, for patiently mentoring me every day as I can only learn from someone at your level: thank you for bringing me on board on such a marvelous adventure, I surely owe you a lot.

We also would sincerely like to thank Michael Collins and Josh Lerner for writing for us the prefaces. We are honored to have such two exponents of the Private Equity world as preface writers.

We also would like to thank Noemi Azzolina, Valentina Todoro, and the whole then "BETA" center at Bocconi University (now called BUILT) for being the first partners in the adventure of "modernization" of the Private Equity and Venture Capital course in launching the Coursera MOOC course and helping us in "refreshing" some materials.

None of this would have realized without the constant help of the people from Elsevier: Scott Bentley, Executive Editor, and Susan Ikeda, the Editorial Project Manager who patiently guided us through this project. We also would like to thank another Project Manager at Elsevier, Punithavathy Govindaradjane for reviewing our drafts and for her constant help in the whole process.

But the most important "thank you," and this is Stefano speaking, is for the unique partners I had in my life: my wife Anna and my daughter and son Elisa and Lorenzo, who were kids when I wrote the first edition and who now aim to be young adults, and they challenge me anytime.

This book and all that I, Giulia, have completed at any level in my life so far would not have ever been possible without my Mum and Dad, Maria Cristina and Luciano, who never stopped believing in me. But my most sincere and silent thank you is for Andrea, whom I have to thank for constantly supporting me and for strengthening my eagerness towards everything I do every day.

# General Framework and Private Equity Deals

# CHAPTER 1

# The Fundamentals of Private Equity and Venture Capital

## 1.1 INTRODUCTION

This chapter presents the fundamentals of private equity and venture capital. The second section covers private equity and venture capital, underlining important differences between American and European approaches to funding start-ups and the typical characteristics of the business and presents specific characteristics of the business, in the end it describes why a company should address to a private equity investor. The third section explains how private equity finance is different from corporate finance, emphasizing the distinguishing elements. The fourth section analyzes private equity and venture capital from the entrepreneur's perspective, while the last section discusses the views of all types of potential investors. The chapter concludes with an overview of the private equity (PE) market in 2015.

## 1.2 DEFINITION OF PRIVATE EQUITY AND VENTURE CAPITAL

There is evidence that investing in the equity of companies started during the Roman Empire. However, the first suggestion of a whole structured organization that funded firms to improve and make their development easier was found during the 15th century, when British institutions launched projects dedicated to the increase and expansion of trade to and from their colonies.

From an institutional point of view, private equity is the provision of capital and management expertise given to companies to create value and, consequently, generate big capital gains after the deal. Usually, the holding period of these investments is defined as medium or long.[1]

Modern private equity and venture capital have been around since the 1940s when it started to be useful and essential for financial markets and companies'

---

[1] By a rule of thumb, a holding period larger than 12 months is considered as medium-long period.

**3**

Private Equity and Venture Capital in Europe. https://doi.org/10.1016/B978-0-12-812254-9.00001-2

development. Financing companies with private equity and venture capital has become ever since increasingly more important, both strategically and financially.

Because this type of business has been around for so long, and ever since the 1940s it evolved under many different aspects, one worldwide definition and classification for private equity and/or venture capital does not exist. However, it is clear that a broad definition does exist: *private equity is not public equity* because it includes investments realized outside the stock market only.

This provocative sentence means that private equity encompasses investments made by a financial institution in the equity of a company, whose shares are not listed.

As venture capital, which will be illustrated later in the book, was in fact born before the rest of private equity, many terms, definitions, and associations' names are named after it, even though they refer to both kind of deals, those in the first stages of life of the company and those in a mature age. This is why the company in which the private equity is investing is called "Venture-Backed Company" regardless the kind of deal that is being made. Hereinafter, the company in which the investment is made is called Venture-Backed Company or, simply, VBC. Besides the ultimate destination of the money injection (i.e., listed and unlisted shares), under three other aspects private equity differs from public equity (see Table 1.1):

- *Pricing*. As shares are publicly traded, in public equity the price is driven by the market fluctuations, either upwards or downwards. On the other hand, the price of a share of a private company is defined on the basis of the negotiation between the preexisting shareholders and the incoming shareholder, which is to say, the private equity investor.
- *Liquidity*. Publicly traded stocks are characterized by a high level of liquidity, whereas private equity stocks are illiquid. In fact, the selling of a private equity share corresponds to the exit of a private equity investor from an investment, where the private equity investor has to find another potential buyer for the stake.
- *Monitoring*. Investments in publicly traded stocks are strongly regulated by domestic and international laws and supervisors. On the contrary, investments in private equity are safeguarded by a contract between the parties (i.e., the preexisting shareholders and the private equity investor).

| **Table 1.1** Differences Between Public Equity and Private Equity | | | |
|---|---|---|---|
| | **Pricing** | **Liquidity** | **Monitoring** |
| Public equity | Market | High | Ad hoc laws |
| Private equity | Negotiation | None | • Civil code (Continental Europe countries) <br> • Common laws (Anglo-Saxon World) |

The definition provided earlier in this chapter, even if very broad, cannot be applied to the whole world, because operators' national associations (i.e., NVCA, Invest Europe, BVCA, AIFI, EVPA[2]), or central banks interpret the definition according to the countries in which they operate. For this reason, many definitions still exist. For instance, according to the American approach, venture capital is a cluster of private equity dedicated to finance new ventures. Therefore, venture capitalists fund companies in their initial phases of life or that are seeking for sources to expand and develop the operations, whereas private equity operators finance companies that have completed at least their first/fast growth process.

The European definition proposes that private equity and venture capital are two separate clusters based on the life cycle of the firm. Venture capitalists provide the funding for start-up businesses and early stage companies, whereas private equity operators are involved in deals with firms that find themselves in their mature age of the life cycle.

In recent years, the American definition has been adopted in the European context too. As such, in this book the American definition will be considered when mentioning private equity and venture capital, where the private equity label embeds the venture capital deals.

Regardless of the approach used for the main definition, in every deal of private equity it can be assessed that a strict relationship between the investor and the entrepreneur is created. This is a unique characteristic not found in any other financial institution. This is attributed to the typical characteristics of private equity and venture capital financing schemes:

- modification of shareholder composition (see Fig. 1.1) as a result of the investor investing in the equity of the VBC,
- knowledge and nonfinancial support, and
- predefined time horizon of the investment.

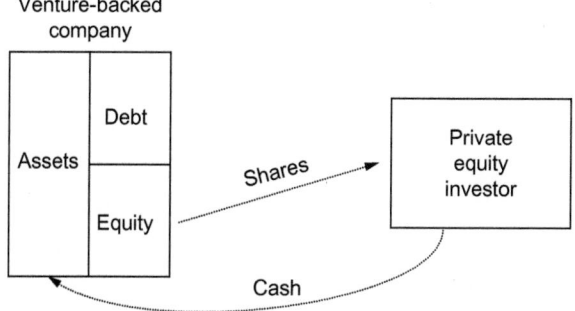

**FIG. 1.1** Basic representation of the functioning of a private equity investment.

---

[2]NVCA, National Venture Capital Association; BVCA, British Private Equity and Venture Capital Association; AIFI, Associazione Italiana Private Equity e Venture Capital; EVPA, European Venture Philanthropy Association.

As private equity investments are focused on private companies' equity for which no public data is available investors may also decide on the firm's strategy and on the day-by-day management. This participation, or the admission of a new shareholder in the share capital, generates a metamorphosis in the decision process. Additionally, a modification in the stability and symmetry of the organization and its consequences among original shareholders may be noted.

In fact, a private equity investment is not limited to simple money provision; the financial support comes from managerial activity consisting of advisory services and full-time assistance for the company's development. For young ventures or new business ideas, cooperation with financiers is very important, because reputation, know-how, networking, relationships, competencies, and skills are the nonfinancial resources provided by private equity and venture capital operators. Although difficult to measure, these resources are the true reason underlying the deal and important for firm growth. They may be defined as *benefits* or *effects* embedded within the money injection of the investor. In the private equity deals there is evidence of four benefits.

### 1.2.1   Certification Effect

For the law of the "lemons market"[3] only the companies in need of financial resources will ask the investors for a financing. This makes it very risky of an investor to decide to finance a business, where by definition, they will only find "lemons." Hence, it is relatively very rare for a private equity to accept finally to invest in a company; the investment is finalized only after a severe and detailed screening and only a few companies overcome such steps. It can then be gathered that the willingness of the private equity investor to invest in a specific company can be considered as a proxy of its high worthiness and potential.

### 1.2.2   Network Effect

As the investors gets involved in the day-by-day life of the company, they can share with the company a very strong network, in terms of, among others, suppliers, customers, and banks.

### 1.2.3   Knowledge Effect

A company can address to a private equity investor when it looks for specific competences, either hard or soft. While hard skills may support the company in the management of the business and these set of competences change with the company industry, soft skills passed down by the private equity may support the company in the management of the company regardless the industry in which it operates.

---

[3]The Market for Lemons: Quality Uncertainty and the Market Mechanism—George Akerlof.

### 1.2.4  Financial Effect

The last benefit is in fact a consequence of the previous three effects. From the moment in which the private equity invests, the rating of the company improves. Several researches proved that the cost of equity for companies with a private equity investor as a shareholder in comparison to other comparable companies. In addition, the rating enhancement positively affects the average cost of capital (usually measured with the Weighted Average Cost of Capital), which may ease in the future capital collection among the banking system.

If a company needs at least one of the following benefits, together with the money provision, they shall ask to a private equity firm to finance it.

Private equity and venture capital agreements always define the holding period and exit conditions of the financier. Even though financial institutions are active shareholders and engaged in the company management, they are not interested in taking over total control or transforming their temporary participation into long-term involvement. Venture capitalists and private equity operators, sooner or later, sell their stake; this is the most important reason for defining this type of investment as "financial" and not "industrial." The presence of a predefined time horizon for the investment makes private equity and venture capital useful for companies wanting quick development, managerial change, financial stability, etc.

> **TO SUM UP**
>
> **Why Should a Company Turn to a Private Equity Investor?**
>
> For at least one of the following benefits:
>
> 1. Certification effect
> 2. Network effect
> 3. Knowledge effect
> 4. Financial effect

## 1.3  MAIN DIFFERENCES BETWEEN CORPORATE FINANCE AND ENTREPRENEURIAL FINANCE

What is the difference between corporate finance and private equity finance (or entrepreneurial finance)? This is a very interesting question and the answer is not as easy as it may seem. The question can be answered in two different ways: institutionally and environmentally (see Table 1.2).

According to the institutional approach, where the standpoint of the financial institution is assumed, corporate finance, the most traditional way to fund firms, is more standardized, less flexible, and focused on debt. Expected returns are lower, if compared with private equity investments, and linked to the costs that financial institutions incur while collecting money from savers. The reference point for the valuation (i.e., costs, feasibility, etc.) is the whole company, independent of funded sources. Another interesting point is the

**Table 1.2** Corporate Finance vs Private Equity Finance—Institutional Approach

|  | Corporate Finance | Entrepreneurial Finance |
|---|---|---|
| Focus | Debt | Equity |
| Reference for the valuation | Whole company | Potential growth of the company |
| Collateral | Real estate | No guarantess → contracts to regulate it |
| Target return |  | High or very high |
| Exit | Settlement | Different options<br>1. Trade sale<br>2. Buy back<br>3. IPO or sale post IPO<br>4. Sale to other private equity investors<br>5. Write off |
| Holding period | Variable | From medium-long to long term |
| Financial institution involvement | No | Yes—The private equity investor is a shareholder and plays and active role in the company's day-by-day activities |
| Flexibility | Usually low | Very high |

financial institution's unwillingness to participate in the firm's decision framework.

Private equity finance is very flexible and the expected returns are higher (non-financial resources described in the previous section must be paid) than corporate finance. It is characterized by a medium-to-long time horizon, higher options available for the financial institution's exit strategy, and by its high profile in the decision process. The focus of private equity finance is the potential growth path of a company.

The institutional approach, even though it is able to distinguish between corporate and entrepreneurial finance, does not consider the environment companies deal with when they contemplate private equity as a financing option. The environmental approach does consider the environment and the situation faced by entrepreneurs during the financial selection process. Some aspects of the environmental approach are the same as the institutional approach, whereas some aspects better explain the consequences of entrepreneurial finance.

The elements in the following list distinguish private equity finance from corporate finance using the environmental approach, hence considering the environment in which the company operates:

- interdependence between investment and financing decision,
- managerial involvement of outside investors,

- information problem and contract design,
- value to entrepreneur, and
- legal and fiscal ad hoc rules.

With the institutional approach, private equity financing does not fund the whole company. In this scheme of financial and nonfinancial support, a specific project of the entrepreneur is targeted and financed. Because of this, a strong and effective interdependence between the firm's investment and financing must exist and must continue during the entire length of the deal.

Private equity operators and venture capitalists provide financial and nonfinancial sources. This generates the involvement of third parties (external investors) in the decision process and/or company management. It must be emphasized that only in private equity finance there is a decisive participation in the firm's administration.

The third issue seen in the environmental approach is that private equity operators support firms on risky projects. This increases conventional information problems occurring in all firm financing schemes. These problems lead to a lack of standardized agreements, so a special settlement is signed for every funded project.

The strong interdependence among companies and financial institutions generates problems in wealth and value distribution too. As private equity financiers become shareholders, a strong co-participation between the entrepreneur's desires and the financial institution's purposes exists. Private equity financiers support companies with their skills, competencies, know-how, etc. Because this creates value for funded firms, the investor allows the entrepreneur to take value from the funded idea. In most cases, without private equity or venture capitalists, the same company would not have been able to develop projects.

The special legal and fiscal framework for the investor and/or vehicle used to realize the deal is the last factor that sets private equity finance apart from venture capital. It will be shown throughout the following chapters that the private equity industry, needs special treatment regarding taxes and legal frameworks to develop and carry out investments as the investor simultaneously acts as entrepreneur/shareholder and financier.

In the private equity business, relationships between entrepreneur, shareholders, and external investors are intertwined. In large deals involving big corporations there is a clear convergence between the entrepreneur (and many times, the founding family) and the shareholders. This modifies the traditional perspective of corporate finance in which shareholders and managers are two separate blocks with different goals and tasks.

This is particularly true for venture capital. The smaller the firm or the earlier the life cycle, the more likely the entrepreneur is the shareholder and the manager. This makes it easier for the deal to be realized, developed, and carried out.

## 1.4    THE MAP OF EQUITY INVESTMENT: AN ENTREPRENEUR'S PERSPECTIVE

The development of the private equity and venture capital involvement starts when the entrepreneur or the management team realizes the need to be funded by external investors to support the expansion or the transformation of the company. Therefore, equity investment provides a firm's specific financial needs if not the finance necessary to actually start-up a company.

Firms need funding during sales development, which occurs during different stages for each firm. The drivers that measure the firm's need for funding are investment, profitability, cash flow, and sales growth. These four variables are strictly linked together, and should be evaluated from a long-term perspective. These four variables/drivers represent the stage the firm is in, which helps financiers define their strategy.

Analyzing the four drivers, typical stages of the firm used to classify financial needs can be identified. There are six different stages:

1. Development
2. Start-up
3. Early growth
4. Expansion
5. Mature age
6. Crisis and/or decline

These stages impact the four drivers—investment, profitability, cash flow, and sales growth—used when analyzing financial needs and equity capital demand of a firm as seen in Fig. 1.2 and Table 1.3.

During the first stage, the entrepreneur has to cope with development, the length of which depends on the business features and the entrepreneur's commitment. The objective is to define the most convenient structure for the project's progress. In this phase, sales do not exist and profitability and cash flow are negative due to the presence of unavoidable investments such as the completion of information memorandum, costs for legal and fiscal advisory, engineering development, etc.

The start-up stage consists of company creation and launch of firm activity. During this period, sales start, but the trend is not solid enough to support costs

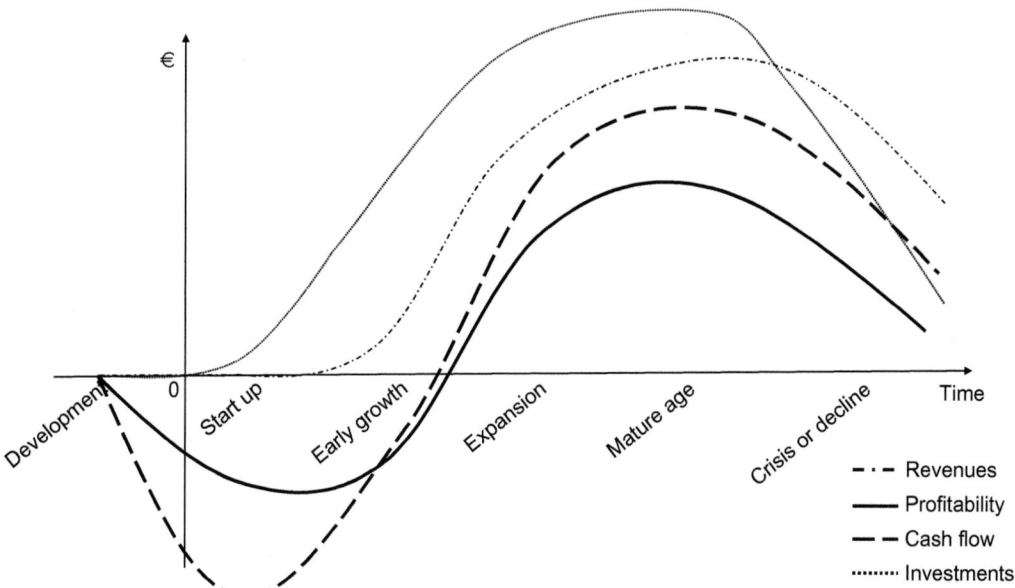

**FIG. 1.2** The flows of revenues, profitability, cash flow, and investment in the six stages of a company's life cycle.

**Table 1.3** The Characteristics of the Four Drivers in a Firm's Six Different Stages

|  | Investment | Profitability | Cash Flow | Sales Growth |
|---|---|---|---|---|
| Development | Concentrated to develop the idea | Negative | Negative | n.a. |
| Start-up | Concentrated to buy productive factors | Strongly negative | Strongly negative | Starting |
| Early growth | Limited to inventory | Negative but reducing | Negative but reducing | Positive and increasing |
| Expansion | Inventory and replacement | End of increasing | End of increasing | Close to zero |
| Mature age | Limited to inventory | Positive and increasing | Positive and increasing | Positive and increasing |
| Crisis or decline | Not possible to be identified | Plummeting | Plummeting | Negative |

incurred by sizeable and substantial investments related to the acquisition of productive factors. Consequently, cash flows and profitability are strongly negative.

The next stage, early growth, occurs just after start-up. Investments have been made and the firm's current needs are related to inventory, rather than working capital; the revenues realized by the company are increasing. There is a rise in profitability and cash flow, even though they remain negative. However, the whole trend is positive and stable and the negative value is slowly becoming greater than zero.

The next stage is expansion. The investments needed are the same as the early growth stage. In this period, sales are increasing but the growth trend is negative and cash flow and profitability are positive and increasing.

After the expansion stage, there is a period of maturity and firms enter the mature age phase. The sales growth tends to zero while profitability and cash flows level off. During this phase, investments are not just related to inventory and/or working capital but the replacement of ineffective or unused assets also must be taken into account. The last of the six stages is the crisis or decline phase. During this period, sales, profitability, and cash flow fall and the firm is unable to decide what investments should be completed to overturn the decline.

These stages create a demand for financial resources measured by the net cash flow produced by the firm. Demand for financial resources is satisfied by different players with different tools ranging from debt capital to equity capital.

## 1.5   THE MAP OF EQUITY INVESTMENT: AN INVESTOR'S PERSPECTIVE

Private equity operators and venture capitalists are just a sample of the groups in the financial system. They represent one of the various options that entrepreneurs consider to finance their business. At the same time, entrepreneurs must think about profitability, investment needs, sales growth, and cash flow to find the right counterparty.

Many potential investors are considered from both a debt and an equity perspective:

- Family and friends
- Other partners
- Business angels
- Private equity operators
- Banks
- Trade credit operators
- Financial markets

For equity investors it is critical to answer these questions:

1. What is the financial need?
2. What part can be satisfied through equity capital?
3. When will the firm be able to pay-off the equity investor?

The first question determines the size of resources required by the firm and the amount of resources that the financial institutions have to satisfy this need. The larger the amount the firm requires, the larger the size, reputation, and skills of the counterparty. The second question ascertains what sort of financial resources the firm needs; for example, venture capitalists and private equity operators tend to participate with equity, whereas banks are focused on debt. At the same time, the founder and his family and friends' will make an equity investment in the firm and trade credit counterparties only propose debt. The third question defines the time horizon and the capability of investors to wait and remain confident in their deals.

The answers to these questions help define profiles of investors with different levels of risk tolerance, chances to invest in equity, and the ability to support a shorter or longer payback period. The different profiles are related to different risk-return combinations and time horizons (Fig. 1.3).

The risk-return profile of the investors is strictly connected to the cash flow produced: the smaller the amount of sources generated by management, the greater the risk, and the larger the need for equity and the risk-taking profile of the investor.

If life-cycle stages and types of investors are considered simultaneously, the different risk-return profiles such as the ideal or potential size of investors create an interesting scheme of equity capital investment availability.

Fig. 1.4 illustrates the potential role of private equity and venture capital as the only financial institutions, which can support firms during all stages. In some

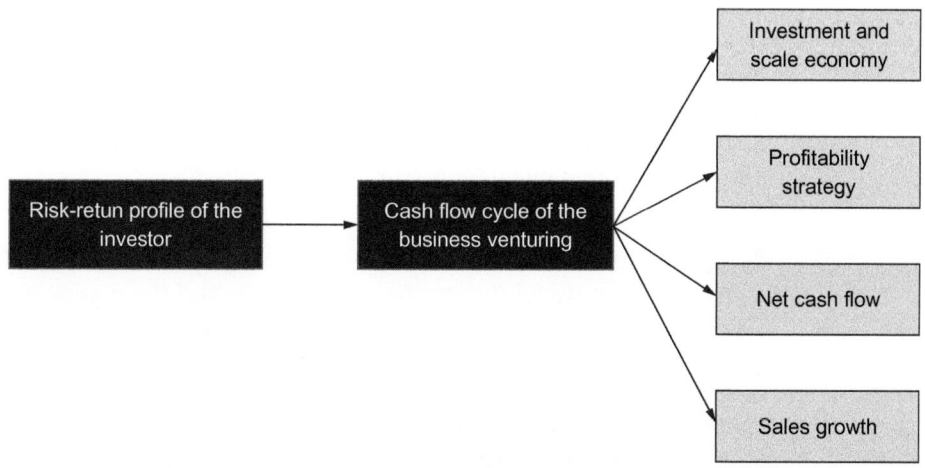

**FIG. 1.3** The relationship between risk-return profile and characteristics of the investment.

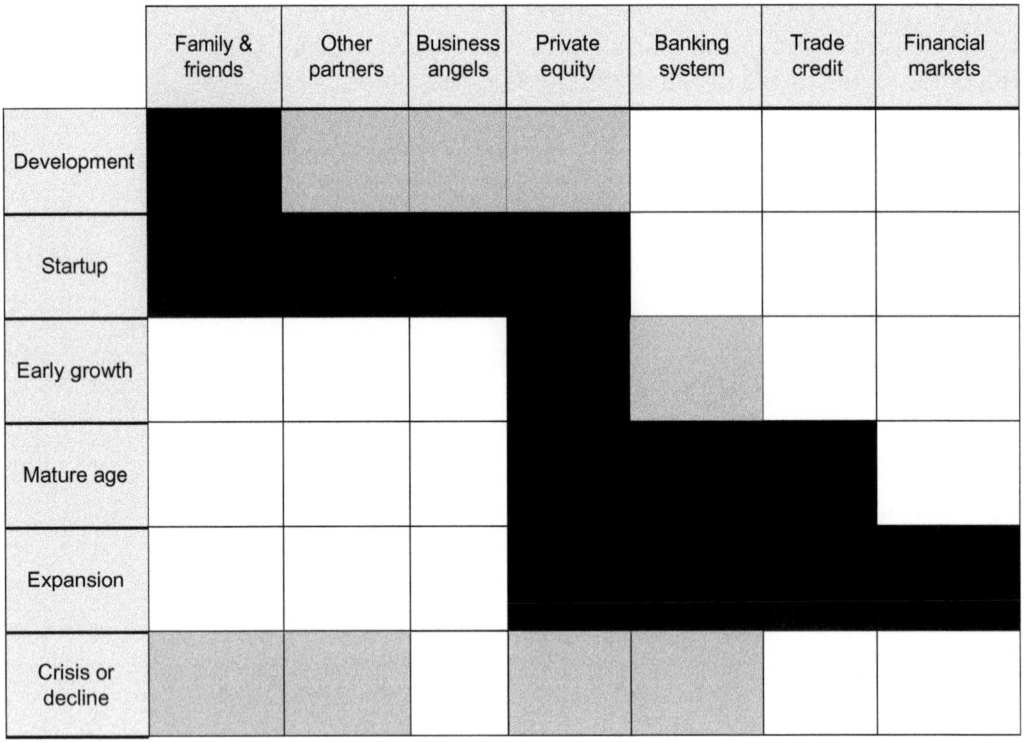

| | Family & friends | Other partners | Business angels | Private equity | Banking system | Trade credit | Financial markets |
|---|---|---|---|---|---|---|---|
| Development | ■ | ▒ | ▒ | ▒ | | | |
| Startup | ■ | ■ | ■ | ■ | | | |
| Early growth | | | | ■ | ▒ | | |
| Mature age | | | | ■ | ■ | ■ | |
| Expansion | | | | ■ | ■ | ■ | ■ |
| Crisis or decline | ▒ | ▒ | | | ▒ | ▒ | |

**FIG. 1.4** The different types of investors during the different stages.

stages the level of assistance can be very high (i.e., start-up or growth phases), while in other stages, such as the development phase or during the decline, the assistance may lessen. At the same time, it should be noted that private equity and venture capital are not the only financial institutions available for entrepreneurs. The Founders' resources along with family and friends are important during the riskiest and less stable phases such as development and start-up. At the same time, financial markets may be considered concrete options only during the more stable mature age.

According to Fig. 1.4, the banking system is a suitable counterpart for fully developed firms who have already gone through development and start-up. Banks are more useful during the rapid growth and the mature age periods. Similar conclusions may be reached for trade credit, which is most appropriate for firms in the rapid growth phase. Finally, there are Business Angels whose commitment can be compared with founders or family members, rather than "industrial" partners who help the entrepreneur develop the initial idea. Every kind of investor can help develop firms in any phase and entrepreneurs can find suitable investors to satisfy their financial needs.

## 1.6 THE PE MARKET IN EUROPE

In Europe, the Invest Europe organization each year presents a yearbook illustrating the situation of the private equity investments, divided by country and by cluster. Here the most important moments of the private equity activity (fundraising, investment, and divestment) are briefly presented.

Generally speaking, over the last decade the PE market in Europe reached its peak in the 3-year period 2006–08, right before the financial crisis hit Europe. Ever since 2009, private equity is slowly recovering and recording an overall increase with respect to the activity of 2014.

### 1.6.1 Fundraising Activity During 2015

In 2015, total fundraising reached €47.6bn (in 2014 it reached €48bn).

The number of funds decreased by 15% up to 274 compared with 2014, but it is still above the level of 2012 and 2013. Overall, European private equity and venture capital raised in the past 3 years (2013–15) was 70% more than in the years 2010–12, and this may be seen as a sign of recovery of the industry after the financial crisis years.

The largest single source of capital was represented by pension funds which contributed for nearly a quarter of funds raised from institutional investors. Funds of funds contributed for 18% of the funds raised, followed by government agencies (14%), sovereign wealth funds (13%), family offices, and private individuals (12%) and insurance companies (9%).

Out of a total of €47.6bn, €5.3bn was represented by Venture Capital reaching the highest level since 2008 and confirming a constant growth (+8% with respect to 2014). Government agencies contributed 31% of the funds raised, under the levels of the period 2010–12, in which more than one-third was attributed to this source. Government agencies are followed by funds of funds (23%), corporate investors (14%), and family offices and private individuals (12%). North American institutional investors contributed for 11%.

On the other hand, buyouts decreased by 7% to €33.6bn despite they still represent the largest part of the PE fundraising (70%). Pension funds are still the largest contributor (25%) in European buyout funds, followed by funds of funds and other asset managers (18%) and sovereign wealth funds (15%). North American institutional investors contributed more than a quarter.

The countries where funds were most raised were United Kingdom and Ireland, where around half of the funds have been raised (47%) linearly consistent with 2014 data (47%). The region of France and Benelux confirms as the second best in terms of fundraising (€11.9bn) outperforming 2014 performance

(€10.5bn). Third comes the Nordics region, which over the last 5 years kept itself stable in terms of funds raised (with the exception of 2012 where only €1.8bn were raised). In the Nordics, €7.8bn was raised.

## 1.6.2    Investment Activity During 2015

Following the fundraising activity and considering the investment analysis, the picture of the investment activity is a positive one, as the total amount of equity investment in European companies increased by 14% to €47.4bn. The amount of investment per company increased as the number of companies decreased by 11% to nearly 5000, which mostly are SMEs (86%) and for a third included cross-border investments equally distributed between private equity and venture capital deals.

Venture capital investment increased by 5% to €3.8bn. The amount invested was greater across all stages, led by seed investments with an increase of 18%. Later-stage venture increased by 5% and start-up investments by 4%. The larger equity amount invested in VBC is confirmed in venture capital deals as the number of companies decreased by 12% to 2836. Most capital was invested in life sciences (34%), computer and consumer electronics (20%), and communications (19%) sectors.

Buyout investments increased by 16% to €36.3bn (77%) reaching 944 companies. More than 60% of buyout investments concentrated in companies active in business and industrial products (18%), consumer goods and retail (15%), financial services (12%), and life sciences (11%).

Investments in private equity are mostly undertaken in the United Kingdom, where they account for 0.79% of the GDP. Even if the United Kingdom is the country with the highest rate of investments, this percentage is lower than the 2011–15 average (around 0.85%). As for fundraising, Nordics and France follow the United Kingdom in magnitude of PE deals. In 2015 in Denmark, investments accounted for 0.437% and in France, they did for 0.433%, followed by Sweden and Norway (0.388% and 0.332%, respectively).

## 1.6.3    Divestment Activity During 2015

Almost 2500 European companies were exited in 2015, representing equity divestments for €40.5bn. This amount matches the level of 2014, which was until then the highest reported exit volume to date for European private equity. Most investors exited via a trade sale (29%), followed by a sale to another private equity firm (27%), and sale of quoted equity (17%).

Venture capital accounted for €2.1bn representing 1005 companies. Within venture capital, half of the deal by amount occurred via trade sale, followed by a write off (14% by amount), which hit 23% of the companies involved in a deal. In all, 10% of the deals by amount took place by means of the sale to another private equity firm. IPO in venture capital is still quite a rare phenomenon, accounting for 2% of the deals by amount.

Buyouts are by far the largest cluster of equity divestment (€34.3bn), coherently with the data of investments illustrated above, including 797 companies. Trade sale and sale to another private equity firm alone account for more than a half of the exit amounts (27% and 28%, respectively). The sale of quoted entity is also one of the most prominent ways out in buyout deals (18%). In buyout, unlike in venture capital, IPO is less rare (8%).

# CHAPTER 2

# Theoretical Foundation of Private Equity and Venture Capital

## 2.1   INTRODUCTION

There are many theories explaining the birth and development of the private equity and venture capital industry and many schemes developed to help understand financing problems and their solutions. This chapter describes theories about financing selected by corporations; for example, whether debt or equity financing is (or should be) chosen. This is different from today's explanation about how venture capital and private equity works within companies.

## 2.2   THEORIES ABOUT CORPORATION FINANCING

Leading theories of capital structure attempt to explain the proportion of debt and equity on a corporation's balance sheet. Most research assumes that companies in need of financial sources are public, involved in nonfinancial business, and raise capital primarily from outside investors rather than from the firm's entrepreneurs, managers, or employees.

There is no universal theory of capital structure, and there are no reasons to expect one. There are useful conditional theories, but they differ in their relative emphasis on the factors that could affect the choice between debt and equity, such as agency costs, taxes, differences in information, and the effects of market imperfections, or institutional or regulatory constraints. These factors could dominate a firm or be unimportant for other corporations.

Leading theories of capital structure are

- *Capital-structure irrelevance.* This theory refers to the initial works of Modigliani and Miller from the mid-1950s. Their work states firm value and investment decisions are independent and not linked to financing decisions. The choice between debt and equity is not totally unimportant, but it indirectly effects real decisions.

**19**

Private Equity and Venture Capital in Europe. https://doi.org/10.1016/B978-0-12-812254-9.00002-4

- *Trade-off theory*. This idea follows the Modigliani and Miller framework, but focuses on fiscal consequences. Firms choose target debt ratios by trading off the tax benefits of debt against the costs of bankruptcy and financial distress. Actual debt ratios move toward the target.
- *Agency theory*. This approach was initially proposed by Jensen and Meckling. It theorizes that decisions have direct and real effects on firms and managerial behavior, because they change manager incentives and investment in operating decisions. Agency costs drive financing, or at least they explain the effects of financing decisions.
- *Pecking order theory*. According to Myers and Majluf and Myers, financing decisions mitigate problems created by differences between insiders (managers) and outside investors. The firm turns first to the financing sources where differences matter least.

These theories may be useful when explaining capital structures with data and findings that confirm they work.

Economic problems and incentives that drive these theories do not explain financing strategy, thus they offer only a partial understanding of the conditions under which each theory, or some combination of the theories, works. Zingales says that a "new foundation" for corporate finance is needed to understand effectively financing decisions. This new approach requires a deeper understanding of the motives and behavior of managers and employees of a firm. For example, all standard financing theories assume the manager pursues a simple objective. The manager's actual objectives depend on how he is rewarded for his actions. Managers used to be thought of as the agents of stockholders, but managers and employees also invest their human capital, which comes in the form of personal risk-taking and specialization. A general financial theory of the firm would model the co-investment of human and financial capital. In small and medium companies there is no difference between managers and shareholders as usually the entrepreneur represents both.

Because venture capital and private equity finance companies with both financial and nonfinancial capital, their motives cannot be explained through standard theories. Instead, a deeper analysis of the perspectives of the firms and financiers would lead to a more accurate motive that drives the private equity and venture capital decision process.

### 2.2.1    Remarks on the Approach of Modigliani and Miller

Modern theory of optimal capital structure starts with Modigliani and Miller (M-M) proving financing decisions do not matter in perfect capital markets. Their proof states the market values of the firm's debt and equity, $D$ and $E$, add up to total firm value, $V$. $V$ is a constant, regardless of the proportions of $D$ and $E$, provided that assets and growth opportunities on the left side of the balance sheet are held constant. Financial leverage or gearing ratio (i.e., the proportion of debt financing on equity capital) is irrelevant. This irrelevance results in a mix of securities issued by the firm. According to this approach, financial decisions are unable to increase or decrease the value regardless of who finances the deal.

For corporate finance, M-M propositions are benchmarks, not end results. Compared with investment and operating decisions, most financing decisions effect value: idiosyncratic financing decisions may not be harmful, and managers may not be able to discern the effects of financing on volatile stock market values.

M-M propositions are based on the perfect efficiency of capital markets and, consequently, on the perfect behavior of firms and the rational behavior of managers whose interests are aligned to those of the financier.

If this was a proven approach, private equity operators and venture capitalists would be no different from other financial institutions and would be considered only during reliable value growth of the left side of the balance sheet. Replacement and vulture financing could only be applied when the reorganization of financial sources generates an expansion of the firm's value.

## 2.2.2 Remarks on the Trade-Off Theory Approach

Trade-off theory changes M-M's proposition about the firm value. In this approach, the total value of a company is still the sum of equity financing and debt financing $(D+E)$, but these two elements must be considered:

1. Present value of future taxes saved because of interest tax deductions
2. Present value of costs of financial distress, that is, the present value of future costs attributable to the threat or occurrence of default

Firms choose the level of debt that maximizes the whole enterprise value; the optimum level requires the firm to borrow up to where the present value of interest tax shields and the present value of financial distress costs are equal at the margin.

Trade-off theory therefore explains moderate, cautious borrowing. It identifies firms that face high costs of distress; for example, firms facing higher business risk and firms with growth opportunities and mostly intangible assets. The trade-off theory predicts that firms or industries with these characteristics should be especially cautious and operate at low target debt ratios, as with the increasing of the level of indebtness, after a certain threshold the value of the company decreases as a result of the distress and bankruptcy costs.

These elements will be reprised and analyzed more in detail in Chapter 12 when dealing with the financial structure of the target company.

It must be emphasized that trade-off theory results are mostly qualitative; for example, lower borrowing for firms with valuable growth opportunities is predicted, but not the amount borrowed. At the same time, the theory does not specify financial distress probability as a function of leverage, nor does it quantify the costs of financial distress, except to say that these costs are important.

Trade-off theory explains the presence of venture capitalists and private equity operators among financial institutions, and how they help firms modify their value or their ability to calculate the probable costs of distress and/or their ability to support leverage. Trade-off theory also suggests that the private equity industry may represent a better solution for firms who are unable to use traditional financiers because of high financial risk or large amounts of intangibles and growth opportunities.

### 2.2.3   Remarks on Agency Theory

Agency theory describes the ever-present agency relationship in which one party (the principal) delegates work to another party (the agent) who performs the job. The fundamental idea is that the relationship is similar to a contract.

The following articles further explain agency theory:

- Jensen and Meckling explore the relationship between owners and managers and underline the way to align interests of all subjects.
- Fama discusses how efficiency of labor and capital markets plays an important role when monitoring the behavior of managers.
- Fama and Jensen conclude that an effective board may reduce management's opportunism.

Agency theory solves two sets of problems: difficulties in monitoring and attitudes toward risk. In the first case, agency theory tries to solve conflicts between the principal and agent or if there is a real problem verifying the agent's actions. In the latter case, agency theory proposes solutions when principal and agent act differently because of their risk preferences (see Table 2.1).

Agency theory offers an understanding of the relationship between financiers and existing shareholders. This becomes important if financiers are venture capitalists or private equity operators since they may also act as shareholders and managers.

During a deal entrepreneurs and private equity operators have information asymmetry: one party has more or better information than the other.

**Table 2.1** The Agency Theory Framework

| | |
|---|---|
| Cause | There is a difference among aims and goal of the principal and the agent, that is, among shareholders and managers, firm owners and firm financiers, companies and financial institutions, and majority shareholders and minority shareholders |
| Basic idea | the relationship between principal and agent may be improved and made more efficient |
| Role of information | Asymmetry information among the subject involved, information is a valuable item and becomes a clause in the agreement |
| Analyzed items | Contract between principal and agent |
| Contract problems | Moral hazard |
| | Adverse selection |
| | Monitoring and controlling |
| | Risk sharing |

This creates an imbalance of power which can cause transactions to go awry. Problems may manifest before, during, and after the deal.

The typical problem before the deal is adverse selection. This is a financial deal process where "bad" results occur when financiers and funded subjects have asymmetric information and the bad subjects are more likely to be selected. For example, a financial institution that sets one rate for all its products runs the risk of being adversely selected against by its low-balance, high-activity (and hence, least profitable) entrepreneurs.

A typical postdeal problem is moral hazard—a party insulated from the risk may behave differently than it would if it were fully exposed to the risk. For private equity operators and venture capitalists this a problem, because they do not know how entrepreneurs will use the financial sources they have been given.

During financing, problems can occur with the monitoring and controlling of a firm's performance. For venture capitalists and private equity operators, contracts must consider verification and disclosure costs. This is defined as the "costly state verification" (CSV) approach. Here the contract is designed so a lender has to pay a monitoring cost. The predeal contract structure specifies auditing and certification conditions. It must be emphasized that without an audit, the entrepreneur would be unable to raise money from investors because the financier anticipates the entrepreneur will falsify information about the company's performance.

Principal and agent, or entrepreneurs and private equity operators, are willing to take on different types of risk (the so-called risk-sharing problem) such as the type of financing (i.e., equity, debt, mezzanine), type of remuneration (i.e., interest, dividend, etc.), and the selection of a counterpart (i.e., new vehicle, existing company, etc.).

Previous theories are unable to explain why and how firms and institutions realize a deal, while agency theory states that entrepreneur's choices are not automatic and both parties emphasize that financiers are not just part of the financial support mechanism.

Deals between private equity operators or venture capitalists and a private company are usually more complicated than traditional financing contracts (e.g., mortgages), but their interests and opportunistic behaviors must be aligned or at least considered. Reputation is more important for venture capitalists and private equity operators than for traditional financiers because bad business behavior may reduce the future development opportunities.

According to the agency theory, private equity operators and venture capitalists represent a valuable counterpart for firms, but complicated agreements and specific clauses must be settled to realize the deal.

### 2.2.4   Remarks on Pecking Order Theory

The pecking order theory states that companies prioritize their sources of financing (from internal financing to equity) and consider equity financing as a last resort. Internal funds are used first, and when they are depleted, debt is issued. When it is not prudent to issue more debt, equity is issued. This theory maintains that businesses adhere to a hierarchy of financing sources and prefer internal financing when available, and debt is preferred over equity if external financing is required.

As noted by Berger and Udell, the hierarchy depends on the firm's size and level of development, because there is a particular level of information asymmetry and financial need for every phase of growth. This is also known as the "financial growth cycle."

During this cycle, venture capitalists and private equity operators may improve the efficiency of the entire financial system, because they tend to work with informationally opaque firms. For this reason, they represent the proper solutions for start-up because of the lack of information, the uncertainty of future results, and the organizational structure that is likely to develop. At the same time, firms that want to make strategic decisions linked to the governance or to the status of corporate finance decisions may find that the private equity industry is right for them.

According to this theory, private equity operators and venture capitalists revolutionized the pecking order system, because equity finance comes before debt financing in some cases. This occurs because of the need for more transparency and the reduction of information asymmetry among traditional financiers, such as banks and firms where the need for financial sources is just a part of the whole problem to be solved.

The pecking order theory explains the role of the private equity industry and, more important, highlights the reasons why it operates regardless of the level of development or size of a company. Different from traditional financiers that usually support firms only with money, the private equity industry brings management capabilities to the firms and information to the whole financial system. These elements set this industry apart from credit or banking institutions.

# CHAPTER 3

# Clusters of Investment Within Private Equity

## 3.1 INTRODUCTION

This chapter explains the different clusters of investment private equity opera-tors and venture capitalists put in place to meet a firm's needs. The second sec-tion illustrates two approaches explaining the relationship between investment and activity implemented by investors: traditional and firm-based. It concludes by explaining why investors choose the first approach. The third section iden-tifies the most important features of every cluster of investments: definition, risk-return profile, critical issues, and managerial involvement where the six different investment typologies are depicted. In this chapter, the different deals will only be briefly presented, while they will be deeply analyzed over in this chapter and Chapter 4, concentrated about venture capital and private equity, respectively.

## 3.2 PRELIMINARY FOCUS ON THE DIFFERENT CLUSTERS OF INVESTMENT

Different clusters of equity investment define the activity of the investor. There are two approaches implemented by investors explaining the relationship between investment and activity: traditional and firm-based (or modern approach). The traditional approach is based on the relationship between the firm's development and its financial needs. The firm-based approach, on the other hand, is a relatively new method of analysis. It evolved due to the competition and the great difficulty in matching a company's needs with the activities of the private equity investor.

According to the traditional approach, the stages of equity investment are:

- Seed financing (development)
- Start-up financing (start-up)
- Early stage financing (early growth)

**27**

Private Equity and Venture Capital in Europe. https://doi.org/10.1016/B978-0-12-812254-9.00003-6

- Expansion financing (expansion)
- Replacement financing (mature age)
- Vulture financing (crisis and/or decline)

where the first three clusters belong to the venture capital business.

A very close relationship exists between each stage and financial need. For example, during the development phase, the firm needs to fund the business idea, while during the start-up phase, the financial resources fund operations. The traditional approach is based on the firm's life cycle and the private equity investor.

The modern approach identifies three different investment categories based on private equity operator actions and involvement of the financial institutions:

1. Creation financing
2. Expansion financing
3. Change financing

*Creation financing* supports a new economic venture from the original idea. The need for private equity finance emerges when an entrepreneur looks for support when developing a new product, service, or renewing an existing production process. Usually, entrepreneurs approach financial sources to make the development faster and nonfinancial sources to define the competitive environment. According to the definition of venture capital presented above, creation financing includes all venture capital deals.

*Expansion financing* includes all deals aiming at addressing problems with growth and the increasing size of a firm. Firms follow three different paths to this growth:

- In-house growth path—Projects originate by sales development plans, rather than production capacity expansion. The support of private equity operators is primarily focused on financial sources, because firms have already developed their sales plans.
- External growth paths—Projects are linked to M&A deals. Private equity operators find their ideal partners or the best target company. International or supranational expertise represents a competitive advantage for financial institutions looking to operate in this business.
- Vertical or horizontal integration path—Projects create a holding that includes operative and complementary firms with similar supplied business areas, technologies, customers, etc. Private equity operators develop the holding's strategic issues, rather than the funding of the structure design (cluster venture).

*Change financing* funds operations that change a firm's shareholder composition.

With the exception of the expansion financing deals, the modern approach is based on the needs of the firm that are satisfied by private equity operators or venture capitalists. Because there is no clear relationship between financial need, stage of the firm, and type of financial institution, this approach relies on private equity operators.

The traditional approach creates a link between stage, financial needs, financial institution, and activities implemented during the investment phase, whereas the most modern approach proposes an easier way—focusing attention on the firm's needs and activities.

The modern approach is not innovative, but it is a newer, easier, and more firm-oriented way to look at private equity finance. Theoretically, the traditional approach is more precise. Moreover, the traditional approach better illustrates the investor's role and activities implemented to satisfy the needs of the entrepreneurs. In the following sections, these two approaches are presented in more detail.

## 3.3 THE MAIN ISSUES OF INVESTMENT CLUSTERS

Different clusters of equity investment have specific features that contribute to investor activity. Every cluster is classified by

- Definition
- Risk-return profile
- Critical issues
- Managerial involvement within business venturing

The first term, definition, describes the agreement between the entrepreneur and financial institutions. It explains the financing rationale and, indirectly, the firm's needs including why the firm is looking for money and how that money is used.

There are critical issues to manage at every stage in a company's growth. The most critical aspect is the matching of the right company that is being financed with the most appropriate financial institution.

Every stage is characterized by a risk-return profile related to the four drivers presented in Chapter 1: investment, profitability, cash flow, and sales growth. Every stage of the life of the company has risk measured as total or partial loss of invested sources, delays in project implementation, lower profits, etc., and an expected return usually measured as the internal rate of return (IRR).

The last term in the list, managerial involvement, identifies the financial institution's contribution to the growth of the firm and analyzes the decision process, rather than the percentage of shares owned. The managerial involvement can be either "Hands-On" or "Hands-Off". If the investor adopts a "Hands-On" approach, in addition to the money provision, he provides his concrete support under the forms of the four effects described in the first chapter and in addition, he operates together with the entrepreneur. On the contrary, a "Hands-Off" approach entails the mere provision of cash and the generation of at least one of the four effects, but he does not get involved in the day-by-day activity of the company and he does not give any additional support.

Hence, in private equity finance, a low-/high-level managerial involvement is not necessarily related to the number of shares held. On the contrary, it may be traced to the kind of deal in which the investor is involved, presented in the following sections.

## 3.4   PRIVATE EQUITY DEALS

Private equity deals are related to the company's life cycle as indicated in Fig. 3.1.

### 3.4.1   Seed Financing

Seed financing is necessary for the development of a new firm. Development indicates that the business idea or the development plan of a product that has not been created yet. During this type of financing, funded firms do not have an actual product or an output to sell and are unable to earn revenue. This is also called first round or initial financing.

The purpose of seed financing is to transform R&D projects into successful business companies or start-ups. Therefore, seed financing funded by financial institutions is used to create new ventures. The risk-return profile is very difficult to define, because risk is very high, while expected returns are impossible to calculate due to the uncertainty of R&D results and the difficulties with transforming R&D into business. Also, the huge risk and uncertainty derive from the fact that once the product is being produced it may not have a market, or worse, a marketability. This is particularly true for biotech and high-technology projects, which generate products that have a market but they do not have a marketability due to their complexity or high costs.

At this stage, equity-based financing is preferred to alternative debt-based instruments that beside in being sometimes more expensive, also require some collateral, which entrepreneurs cannot provide at this stage of the life cycle of their company. Entrepreneurs should also realize seed financing might be divided into preseed and seed capital finance. Preseed or "proof of concept" finance is generally provided from public sources and relates to basic research, while seed capital can be readily applied.

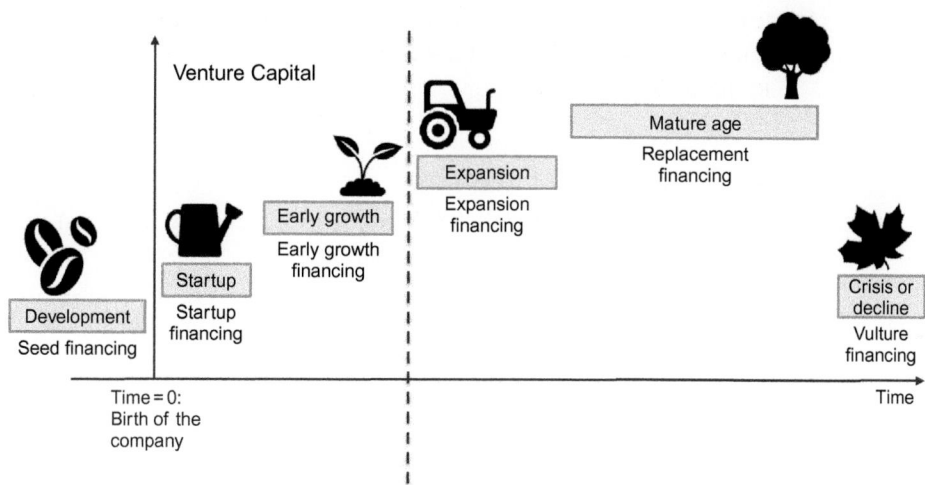

**FIG. 3.1** A company's stage of life and private equity deals.

Seed financing investors do not ask financiers to be managers because the project has just taken off. However, the role played by investors is not passive; on the contrary, they support research activities and translate the business idea into a production process. They support research activities, translate the business idea into a patent and production process, build the company team, and manage any sudden death risk. The most important elements financiers provide are the business plan preparation, analysis, and validation (see Table 3.1).

Because of the high risks, both public and private investors offer seed financing. There is no clear distinction between them, but the private sector provides the expertise required for efficient and effective management, even if the funding is (partly) provided by public authorities. Public authorities have a clear

| **Table 3.1**  Seed Financing | |
|---|---|
| Definition | Financing of a business idea or of a research activity to produce a business idea. In both cases, money is not actually used to create the new venture |
| Risk-return profile | Money is used to finance research. Risk is very high because of the uncertainty of the research activity and of the development of the business. It is very difficult to calculate the expected internal rate of return (IRR) |
| Critical issues to manage | Giving strong support to research, translating the business idea into a patenting process, building the team to support research, and managing the risk of sudden death |
| Managerial involvement | Very limited |

leadership role in development decisions, that is, deciding how to allocate public funding used to address shortcomings in seed capital provision and to develop the market.

### 3.4.2   Start-Up Financing

Seed financing transforms R&D into a business idea, and start-up financing converts the business idea into a real operating company. When in a start-up phase, the company exists but it is still at a very early stage of activity and operations. For this, the financing collected is used to set up projects and launch production. The funded sources are used to buy equipment, inventory, plants, and anything else useful to move the business idea to operations.

Even if the risk is lower than in seed financing, start-up financing is still a gamble for the financier. Although the investors think the business idea is worthwhile, they do not know if the market will support the idea transforming it into a profitable business. The risk-return profile of investors assumes high returns, measured as expected IRR, and high risks with possible delays in or the default of the project.

During seed financing, financiers are expected to be experienced in technical and engineering fields. In start-up financing, because the R&D stage has already been completed, financiers are expected to support the business plan, have an in-depth understanding of its nature and its assumptions, value the management team, and define the strategy used to implement proposals.

For this reason, private equity operators or venture capitalists are very involved in a firm's management and own a large number of shares. Their shares may be the majority of shares issued or make the financial operators the biggest shareholders (see Table 3.2).

| **Table 3.2** Start-Up Financing | |
|---|---|
| Definition | Financing a startup of a new venture that moves from its business idea to the initial operations, money is used to buy all that is necessary to start (e.g., equipment, inventory, building, etc.) |
| Risk-return profile | Money is used to finance a firm. Risk is very high because of the uncertainty of the future development of the business |
| | It is however possible to calculate the expected IRR even though the maturity of the investment can be very long |
| Critical issues to manage | Giving strong support to business plan, capability in deeply understanding the nature and the assumptions of the business plan, a strong valuation of the team |
| Managerial involvement | Very strong and related to all activities which are necessary to produce the business plan, the percentage of shares can also be very high |

### 3.4.3 Early Stage Financing

Early stage financing is essential when moving from the start-up to the real business life cycle. In this phase, sales and firm growth begin. The objective of early stage financing is to create a stable and permanent organization.

During this phase, all problems related to project, design, test, and launch have been resolved. Financial resources are used to fund a little developed company that needs equity to boost its growth. For financiers, this is the stage where financing really begins.

The risk-return profile at this stage is similar to earlier phases: there is more uncertainty within the market rather than technical items or feasibility questions. Because of this, financing during this phase is opened to investors new to the sector or the market.

The expected IRR and the relative risk are high, because investments are already made and there is no certainty about sales development. In this phase, financial institutions are asked to revise and strengthen the business plan. Private equity operators or venture capitalists are very involved in management and own a large numbers of shares. Realized and required activities range from assistance to strategic decisions to business plan certification to marketing and financial advice (see Table 3.3).

### 3.4.4 Expansion Financing

Expansion financing is for companies that need or want to expand their business activity. If the market conditions are right, it can be a great move; some businesses find they need expansion financing when fast business growth is possible.

**Table 3.3** Early Stage Financing

| | |
|---|---|
| Definition | Financing of the first phase of growth of a new venture that moves from the startup to sales. Money is used to buy inventory and to sustain the gap existing between cash flow and the money needed |
| Risk-return profile | Money is used to finance the first steps of a "baby firm." Risk is very high because of the uncertainty of the future development of the business. It is, however, possible to calculate the expected IRR and properly revise the previous business plan |
| Critical issues to manage | Giving strong support in the first steps of the firm (mentoring, advisory), capability of verifying if the assumptions of the business plan are realistic, strong assistance to strategic decisions |
| Managerial involvement | Very strong and related to all activities which are necessary to help the management not to do mistakes. The percentage of shares can also be very high |

Equity or debts are provided to support growing debt and inventories. The company is growing but may not be showing a profit at this stage. Funds may be provided for the major expansion of a company that has increasing sales volume and is breaking even or has achieved initial profitability. They are utilized for further plant expansion, marketing, and working capital or for development of an improved product, a newer technology, or an expanded product line. In addition to an organic growth scenario, there is the possibility for the company to grow through acquisitions and mergers in an external way.

For the investor, the risk in expansion financing is moderate and depends on the sector. Money is used to finance sales growth or to improve projects in known fields so there is no risk due to uncertainty. Returns should be lower at this stage.

Although firms are already operating, financial institutions also play a fundamental role during this phase. At this point they are asked to develop effective growth plans. Because of the size of a firm and the financier's need to diversify his portfolio, the percentage of shares held by private equity operators or venture capitalists during this phase is low. Expansion financing projects do not require specific technical skills or industrial abilities, so these deals may be funded by a very large number of financiers (see Table 3.4).

### 3.4.5 Replacement Financing

After the growth (rapid and slow) phase, the size of the firm becomes more stable and the company enters in a mature age. Although profitability and cash flows are stable, private equity finance still plays an important role. During the mature age, entrepreneurs modify their needs and, while almost all priorities were driven by sales development and size increasing, in this period the problems come from governance or corporate finance decisions.

| **Table 3.4** Expansion Financing | |
|---|---|
| Definition | Financing of the fast phase of growth of a firm that aims to consolidate its position in the market. Money is used only to sustain the (reducing) gap existing between cash flow and the money needed |
| Risk-return profile | Money is used to finance sales growth. Risk is moderate (and linked to the business) because the trend of development of the business is well known. It is possible to calculate the expected IRR |
| Critical issues to manage | Giving strong support to face the risks linked to a fast process of growth (i.e., accurate selections of the new markets to enter, inventory choices, etc.) |
| Managerial involvement | Mentoring (and sometimes advisory) for the right assumptions of strategic decisions on the main issue of growth. The percentage of shares is not very high and does not show a specific profile in this case |

Replacement financing—the typical support from private equity finance for firms in their mature age—funds companies looking for strategic decisions associated with the governance system and the firm's status, rather than the firm's approach to finance. This kind of investment may be realized in different ways:

- Listing on a stock exchange
- Substitution of shareholders
- Successions
- A new design for the company governance.

Replacement financing is never used to boost sales growth or to realize investment in plants. Instead it is used for strategic or acquisition processes. Replacement capital is the proper solution to fund spin-off projects, equity restructuring, shareholder substitution, IPOs, family buyin or family buyout, etc.

For investors the risk profile of these deals is moderate because:

- The firm business model is successful
- The firm governance is settled even though it is in a shifting phase
- Entrepreneurs usually remain and work for the company development
- The effective risk depends also on the whole sector/market risk and the quality of the process to be put in place.

Financial institutions operating in this environment could be used as just an investor or as an advisor and consultant. The role of the private equity operator is to support managerial strategic decisions and the implementation of the entire deal design.

At this point, the managerial involvement from the investor is extensive. When the financier acts as more than a financial operator, industrial knowledge, and previous expertise become very important. Entrepreneurs need to manage skillfully corporate governance issues and corporate finance deals.

In this case, private equity operators buy a large number of shares issued by the firm they are working with. This makes the whole plan easier to be implemented, and very often the private equity operators turn into prime shareholders. However, even though the investors hold the majority of the company's shares, they do not participate in the current management allowing the entrepreneur to retain the top management role.

Compared with the types of financing used by private equity operators and venture capitalists, replacement financing is the most independent from the actual business; instead it is related to the personal and private needs of entrepreneurs (see Table 3.5).

**Table 3.5** Replacement Financing

| | |
|---|---|
| Definition | Financing of a mature firm that wants to face strategic decisions linked to governance, status, corporate finance decisions. Money is used only to sustain the strategic process or the acquisition process |
| Risk-return profile | Money is not used to finance sales growth or investment. Risk is moderate and linked to the quality of the strategic process that is necessary to put in place. Examples are: IPO, turnaround, LBO, restructuring of family governance |
| | It is possible to calculate the expected IRR in depth. The business generally covers: acquisition, financing, and corporate governance deals |
| Critical issues to manage | Giving strong support to manage strategic decisions. The role of the private equity moves from a simple financer job to an effective consultant activity |
| Managerial involvement | Very high and qualified from a deep industrial knowledge and from a strong capability to manage corporate governance issues and corporate finance deals |

### 3.4.6   Vulture Financing

Even when firms are facing a decline or a crisis, private equity operators may be suitable partners. When a firm is financially distressed, private equity operators can offer what is named vulture financing. This is used to restructure companies to enable them to improve their financial performance, exploit new strategic opportunities, and regain credibility. In extreme situations, restructuring can make the difference between a company surviving or filing for bankruptcy.

There has been a great deal of research done on the causes and consequences of corporate restructuring, but little is known about the actual practice: this topic can be very difficult to analyze, because the issues involved are often politically and competitively sensitive. Moreover, many managers are reluctant to discuss the difficult decisions and choices made in these situations. It must be emphasized that the description of vulture investors in the press is often critical; similar to the description of corporate raiders in the context of hostile takeovers. The relevant issue, however, cannot be the public or personal perception of vulture investors, but rather the role they play in financially distressed firms.

For investors, vulture financing is very risky; there is no guarantee that the business will be revitalized by the survival plan. The risk is linked to the "nature" of the crisis: a business crisis is different from an audit fraud crisis because it is due to macroeconomic factors and not mismanagement of funds.

Vulture investors frequently gain control by purchasing senior securities, and they often become board members or managers of the target company. From this position they can propose a survival plan, implement it, and monitor the

| **Table 3.6** Vulture Financing | |
|---|---|
| Definition | Financing of a firm that faces crisis or its decline. Money is used to sustain the financial gap generated from the decline of growth |
| Risk-return profile | Money is not used to finance sales growth or new perspectives but to launch a survival plan. Risk is very high and linked to the nature of the crisis. Examples of different typologies of crises are: debt restructuring, turnaround, and/or failure. It is hard to calculate the expected IRR in depth |
| Critical issues to manage | Giving strong support to manage strategic decisions. The role of the private equity moves from a simple financer job to an effective entrepreneur |
| Managerial involvement | Very high and qualified from a deep industrial knowledge and from a strong capability to manage corporate governance issues and corporate finance deals. Entrepreneurial skills are necessary |

growth of the firm. Vulture financing serves to discipline managers of companies in financial distress (see Table 3.6).

Many skills are required of financial institutions operating in this environment, because their intervention forces them to act as advisor and consultant, or, more often, as entrepreneur. The fundamental role of the private equity operator is to support managerial strategic decisions and the implementation of the entire deal design. This requires deep industrial knowledge or the ability to manage corporate governance issues and corporate finance deals.

## TO SUM UP

| Deal | Shares Owned | | Approach | |
|---|---|---|---|---|
| | **Minority Stake** | **Majority Stake** | **Hands-On** | **Hands-Off** |
| Seed financing | X | | X | |
| Startup financing | X | | X | |
| Early growth financing | X | | X | |
| Expansion financing | X | | | X |
| Replacement financing | X | X | X | X |
| Vulture financing | | X | X | |

# CHAPTER 4

# Investing in the Early Stages of a Company: Venture Capital

## 4.1 INTRODUCTION

This chapter describes in detail the private equity deals involving companies at their earliest stages of life, which is to say venture capital deals. After an overview of the business, the chapter presents in detail the three clusters, their features, and motives leading a private equity to invest in a young company, where the three deals are:

- Seed financing
- Start-up financing
- Early growth financing.

## 4.2 GENERAL OVERVIEW OF EARLY STAGE FINANCING

Each entrepreneurial project is developed through several phases according to the life cycle time of a company (see previous chapters). It is easy to identify in which development phase a company finds itself by the problems that occur at different points in its structure and by the needs the private equity financing aim at filling in. In the first stages of life, the private equity investor, or better, the venture capitalist is considered more than a simple supplier of risk capital. As a matter of fact, in this phase, they support and work to improve the growth of the ventured-back company not only by providing money, but also by leveraging on the benefits deriving from their presence as a shareholder.

REMEMBER: There are four effects brought by the private equity investors.

How and why the venture capitalist decides to invest in a business idea, that has to be defined and planned before the company even exists, is reviewed in this chapter.

To understand the investment activity in the company's equity capital, it is necessary to analyze the key management process realized by the investor.

**39**

Private Equity and Venture Capital in Europe. https://doi.org/10.1016/B978-0-12-812254-9.00004-8

This analysis focuses on critical topics related to the relationship between the entrepreneur and the venture capitalist and all the steps necessary to organize the complex structure owned by the venture capitalist initiative. The classical approach to the venture capitalist investment, realized in the emerging entrepreneurial initiative, leads to the study of financing and managerial resources and their importance. The resources are destined to be used for highly innovative projects with good potential. These are matched with minority participation to reach capital gains because of the revaluation of the stakes and the opportunity to differentiate the risk.

It is therefore important to emphasize on those venture capitalists:

- operate with a preestablished and limited period of time, usually between 3 and 5 years,
- acquire only minority participation because of the entrepreneurial risk and difficulty selling the control participation,
- point out, from the first time with the target company, the importance of the return on the investment; their investment is in part remunerated during the holding period, by dividends and advisory fees, paid by the target company,
- manage their investment with a hands-in approach as they have to make sure that their investment will eventually yield a return,
- in the light of their investment profile, they usually protect themselves with some tools that decrease the likelihood of a write-off of the investment.

## 4.2.1   Seed Financing

Seed financing is defined as a participation in favor of a business idea for which the legal entity has not been founded yet. As there is not a company where the investor can actually invest in, the injection is made by using a special purpose vehicle (SPV) specifically meant for developing a research project. In this phase, there is a person or a team of researchers and the venture capitalist invests in them in order to develop a project that hopefully will produce a successful business idea (Fig. 4.1).

Industry sectors typically targeted for seed financing include information technology, pharmaceutical, chemical, telecommunication, and biomedical. Regarding the risk profile, it should be noted that investors have to consider that the management and the risk profile related to a good performance of the financed project is affected by the following three so-called "golden rules of seed financing".

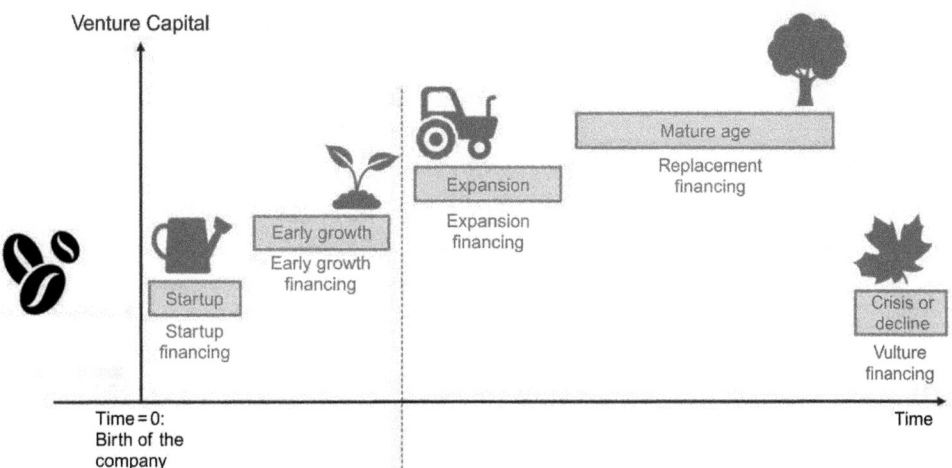

**FIG. 4.1** Seed financing within the life cycle of a company.

The golden rules of seed financing are:

- *100/10/1 rule.* In the business world, this rule describes the level of risk of investing in a company in its seed phase. On average, the investor has to screen 100 projects, finance 10 of them so that he will be lucky (and able) enough to find the one that will turn out to be successful. This activity is so risky that an investor must invest on many more than one project, as by the time the investors find the winning project they will have lost much of their beginning investment.
- *Sudden death risk.* Because this investment occurs before the company is even founded, the investors have to protect themselves in case the person owning the project's idea suddenly can no longer perform his job for whatsoever reason. On the other hand, the inventor in the very early stages of development of the idea is not much prone on sharing the ideas with other people. The solution to this tension is an Incubator Strategy, an ad hoc infrastructure in which the inventor can work without worrying about the ideas being stolen. In this protected environment, the investor may share the invaluable know-how with other persons.
- *Size of the market.* In being an extremely risky investment per se, the investors have to limit the possibility of the product/output that is being created by the inventors will not be sold. That is the reason why the venture capitalists tend to invest in seed financing only in the industries that they know best. Additionally, not only should they be able to recognize the possibility of a good investment in very difficult markets, but they also should be able to acknowledge the possibility of the marketability of the generated product. As a matter of fact, in this stage of

the investments, two are the levels of difficulty in the creation of the output:

- Will the team generate an output?
- If so, will there be a market for the output generated?

There are two strategies used to manage investment return: diversification, possible thanks to the large amount of resources divided between different business initiatives and mitigate the potential risk on the capital invested by having subproducts guaranteed by the project. There can be potential ethical problems with the second tool.

## 4.2.2   Start-Up Financing

This type of deal comes in the picture when the legal entity of a start-up company has already been set. In this phase not only is the legal entity founded, but there is a sound business plan. Nonetheless, the risk in investing in a company at this stage is still very high. The risk is based on launching a company built on a well-founded business idea and not on the gamble of discovering a new business idea (Fig. 4.2).

At this point in the business, risk depends on two variables: the total amount of the net financial requirement and the time necessary to reach the breakeven point of the activity financed. The risk is not strongly connected with the entrepreneur or the validity of his business idea, which are preconditions for the participation. What is really important is the potential growth of the industry in terms of capital intensity required and the forecasted trend of the turnover. The high level of risk is due to the investment realized at the time $(t_0)$ when it is uncertain whether the business will reach the breakeven point.

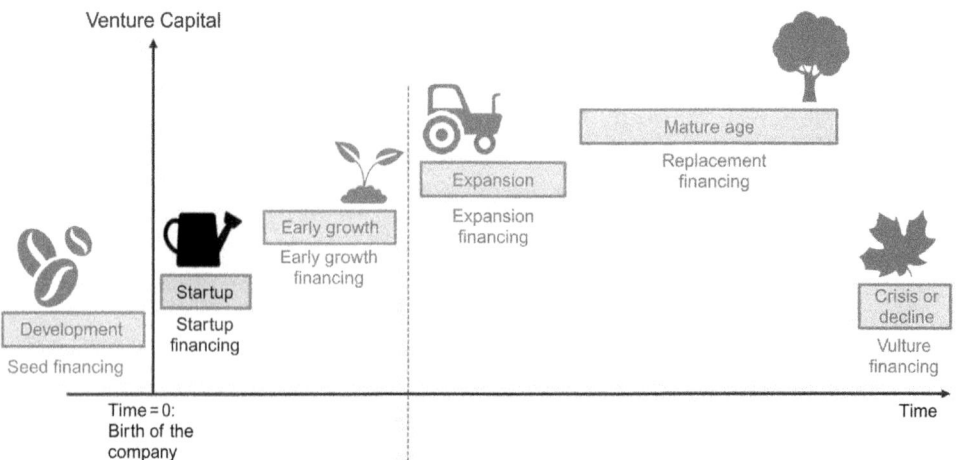

**FIG. 4.2** Start-up financing.

The performance profile of a private equity in a start-up initiative, in terms of IRR, is connected with the ability and capacity to re-sell the participation on the financial market. The track record and credibility of the private equity investor is a key factor in the success of the exit strategy when obtaining the desired return from the investment realized. The main investor's goal (a good and successful exit from the investment) can be facilitated by drawing up agreements with other private equity funds regarding their availability and commitment to buy the participation after a predefined period of time. Another solution is to sign a buy back agreement with the entrepreneur or other shareholders who agree to repurchase the venture capitalist's participation in the company after a predefined period of time (put option). However, the drawback of this possibility is that it assumes that the entrepreneur will have money enough to buy the stake back once the exit time will come. This is why the entrepreneur may be required to put some money in an escrow account. An alternative to a put option may be the pledge of some collaterals of the entrepreneurs. In the end, to create the right incentive for the entrepreneur to fully exploit the financing given by the investor is to grant him some stock options. In this way, the entrepreneur is incentivized to work to enhance the profitability of the company as much as possible.

### 4.2.3 Early Growth Financing

Early growth financing is the financing of the first phase of growth of a new company that has started generating sales (Fig. 4.3).

The founders' need of cash derives from the necessity to buy inventory to foster the company's growth and to bridge the gap existing between the level of cash

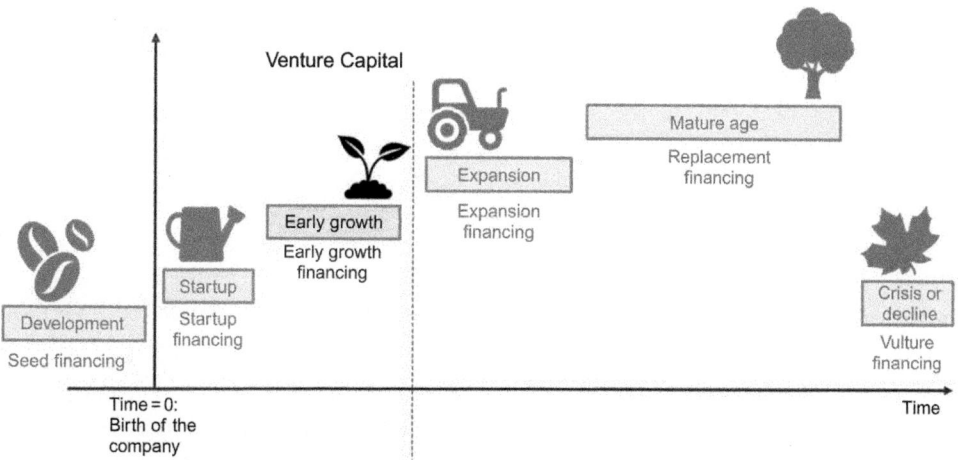

**FIG. 4.3** Early growth financing.

flow and the financial need. As a matter of fact, in this phase, the cash flow may still be very low, if not negative, even though the level of cash is enhancing with respect to previous stages of life of the company.

For an external investor, as the private equity, the risk in buying stakes of the equity of a company in this phase is still high as the venture is still very young and when the injection is made, the investors do not exactly know how the company will turn out. The hype in the company's revenues that characterizes this stage that dragged the company from a start-up phase to an early growth one may either be a bubble, or driven by a financial one, or a temporary phase.

In this phase, the investor has to adopt a hands-on approach. If the investor thinks that the company business model is based on a good idea, but the business plan is still not adequate, they help rewrite it (this is in fact a possible consequence of the knowledge effect).

For this reason, the private equity investor usually has a high amount of shares in the equity of the company when undertaking this kind of deal.

On average, this financing may occur until the end of the first 3 years after the start-up stage. In this kind of investment, the private equity may also not have any protections, due to the high stake in the equity of the company and due to the adoption of a hands-on approach that, combined, create a very powerful investment in the company.

## 4.3    OPERATION PHASES DURING EARLY STAGE FINANCING

Different stages of a company's development need different types of capital investment. From the origination to the implementation up to the exit strategy, each phase needs different capital and know-how. During the start-up phase, the venture capitalist has an intense and complex interaction with the entrepreneur to verify the necessary financial and managerial support. During the seed financing phase the technical validity of the product or service is still unproven, so the venture capitalist offers limited financial resources to support the development of the business idea and the preparation of the commercial feasibility plan. Consequently, there is huge risk faced by the investor.

Start-up financing provides the capital necessary to start operations without commercial validity of the product or service offered. During this stage, the entrepreneurial risk is huge, but there is also risk connected to the financial resources provided. This is usually higher than the ones invested during the seed phase.

Financing in the first stage of the life cycle of a company is linked to the improvement of production capacity after it is completed but the commercial validity of the business idea is still not totally verified. This requires a large amount of financial resources, but is less risky and managerial support is still limited.

Due to the high level of complexity that exists in the markets today, it is not easy to classify clearly these investments; it is more logical to classify them in relation to the potential emerging strategic needs of the company, industry problems, specific threats or opportunity, and final goals of the investor.

## 4.4 STRUCTURE OF VENTURE CAPITALISTS IN EARLY STAGE FINANCING

Financial markets are often unable to finance projects presented by companies; especially those with innovative, hence risky, initiatives. Because of this, the venture capitalist is an interesting and important opportunity to develop entrepreneurial projects. The specific remuneration structure of the venture capitalist is different when compared with a typical bank. The professional investor who invests risk capital wants to be reimbursed, but at the same time, the ultimate goal of the equity investment is to share the potential success of the business. On the contrary, a bank is uniquely interested in reimbursement.

On the other hand, for as much as the private equity is keen on bearing a high level of risk, they are however accountable to the investors, from whom they have to be able to pay off the capital invested and yet with the highest return possible. This is why two types of organization structures are typically used in venture capital operations during either seed or start-up initiative: Business Angels and corporate venture capitalists. A Business Angel is a private and informal investor who decides to bring risk capital to a small or medium firm during its start-up or first development phase. Business Angels are sustained by networks that match them with companies to meet the demand and supply of financial funds. This type of financial operator is common in the United States, but faces problems in Europe. Because of this situation, which directly affects new business, the European Strategy was launched in Lisbon in 2000. It defined the central role of Business Angels as concrete contributors to the improvement of European competitiveness and productivity.

Corporate venture capital is an investment in risk capital executed by very large industrial groups. The necessity to strengthen research and development to continue the high-tech evolution has created investment opportunities. Unfortunately, increasing investments is not linked with satisfactory results. Small companies have shown a high level of efficiency and competence in the innovation sector so several industrial groups have started to specialize in the development of new projects; either founding them directly or acquiring participation. These groups have also acquired minority participations in small enterprises that are technologically qualified. This form of financing allows small or medium firms to collaborate in a positive way with the big industrial groups (they will be explored more in detail in Chapter 9).

The private and venture capital system is a financial tool with potential to accomplish the competitiveness, innovation, and growth objectives implemented by the Lisbon protocol. The venture capitalist is motivated by the potential quality and long-term growth of industrial leverages operating in innovative industries as well as the ability to improve management skills.

Private equity operations realized during seed and start-up financing have to focus their attention on:

- Supporting the development of an entrepreneurial environment. Knowledge-based firms are still not widespread in Europe because there are no structured and uniform legal regulations. The prevalence of innovative businesses is possible due to the acquisition of financial, strategic, and corporate knowledge, which can be offered by a professional financial investor with international experience.
- Implementing research and development and the ability to spread the innovation through centers of excellence by firms focused on research. A key factor toward this evolution is a structured relationship between firms and universities.

## 4.5    SELECTION OF THE TARGET COMPANY

The first aspect the venture capitalist has to consider, to guarantee the optimal composition of his investment portfolios, is the effectiveness of the deal flow. In American markets, where risk capital is widespread and well established, deal flow is represented by a relevant number of well-structured business proposals formalized with business plans. These are sent by start-ups to specific groups of venture capitalists selected based on their previous investments and their industry and/or geographical areas of interests. In financial markets where risk capital is not so widespread, the venture capitalist needs specific ways to promote this form of financing; for example, his network of relationships is an effective and useful tool to create financial business opportunities.

An element that always catalysts a venture capitalist' attention is the opportunity to analyze the largest number of business projects, which allows a better range of choices, and proposals that include the optimal and ideal requirements needed by investors. For example, in the developed and complex risk capital markets, competition among venture capitalists to finance the best projects led the specialization for many operators concentrating their investments in different clusters of activity such as the specific stage of a company's life cycle, the average size of the funds required, and the industry.

Each venture capitalist decides the minimum and maximum investment entry size. The minimum investment has to cover fixed costs during the screening of all business projects such as due diligence and monitoring and managerial advisory costs. The setting for the maximum investment considers the size of the financial funds owned by the venture capitalist and the need to keep an equilibrium among the portfolio of investments realized in terms of risk and return profiles. Minimum entrance level investors operate in the seed or start-up financing phase. Early growth operations, such as those in the high-tech industry, are always strongly supported by extra financial services that require special and advanced preparation to guarantee the success of the target company, especially during the screening phase.

## 4.6    SUPPORTING INNOVATION DEVELOPMENT

The venture capitalist is a financial intermediary whose mainstay is the financial and managerial support of firms in the start-up phase. These firms operate in markets with huge information asymmetry regarding their valuation and guarantee of financial support from traditional lenders such as banks. The first example of information asymmetry is represented by what is known by the entrepreneur or management team and what is known by the investor. To understand better this situation, high-tech industries must be identified:

1. Software applications
2. Pharmaceutical technologies
3. Biotechnology

These industries need to concentrate their resources in research and development to reach their performance potential. Because of this, it is impossible to represent a valid guarantee for traditional banks.

The high level of uncertainty, typical for a company with a high level of innovative development, makes it difficult to use traditional financing for two reasons: it is impossible to forecast, with a high degree of certainty, the success of a highly innovative business project and the very real possibility of negative economic results for a long period of time. These conditions introduce a high level of complexity into the firm's valuation. The chances to select business projects with a positive net present value and a long-term view are low. This makes it possible for the venture capitalist to invest financial resources in highly innovative projects that are very risky, but may generate high economic return if the supported firms are successful.

The venture capitalist, because of a highly specialized knowledge in multiple investment areas, is able to collect and analyze all available financial information and to undertake the most conscious and optimal investment decision. The successful venture capitalist must be a highly specialized investor with topnotch managerial skills to work successfully with entrepreneurs and managers. He must also know the most important changes financed firms need:

- Easy improvement of the organization including planning and development of the company's informative flows and processes. This allows for wider contractual power and a better company image. These improvements make it easier for the shareholders to exit without damaging or taking resources away from the company.
- Introduction of advanced systems for management and budgeting to increase the rationalization of the target company due to joint ventures, acquisitions, and mergers that represent important solutions for the company's development.

## 4.7    PRIVATE INVESTOR MOTIVATION AND CRITERIA

Private investors are motivated by:

1. Return on investment—Venture capitalists have building operations that allow a minimum ROI of 30%.
2. Improved self-image, self-esteem, and recognition—Private investors desire satisfactory economic returns from their investments as well as the opportunity to increase the value of their brand to guarantee a successful investment, which will in fact be of help when they have to launch another fundraising.
3. Alleviating concerns and helping others—This is especially seen in Business Angels. Because early stage financing seems like charity, Business Angels very often decide to invest money in business ideas connected with an emotional past experience (if a relative of the investor dies due to a cancer, the investor might finance projects that can help find a cure).
4. Getting the "first crack" at the next high rise stock, prior to IPO; they realize this is the way to acquire higher economic return without dealing with public securities.
5. Having an aptitude for high risk; critical element distinguishes this type of investor from all others. Without it, this aptitude they would not consider such high-risk business ideas.
6. Having fun and leading challenging projects to economic success.

When studying how private equity investors operate in early stage firms, it is important to understand not only their motivation, but also the criteria they apply during their investment activity. Usually, venture capitalists want to know all about the businesses in which they invest, particularly the technology and the market, to execute due diligence with higher awareness of the people and the business idea. They especially search for investments that allow proprietary advantages for unique technology and leaps in innovation leading to growth opportunities to pass the competition.

Private investors have important criteria for selecting business ideas and start-up firms. These include a solid financial forecast leading to a return of 5–10 times their original investment with a minimum ROI of 30%. To ensure these requirements, private investors evaluate the existence of possible future profitability, because it demonstrates the ability of the Business Angel to select a good idea and improve their image in the financial market. According to these criteria, venture capitalists decide and select the investment opportunity based on a business plan, even if they must face the difficulties of analyzing just an idea and not an operating business. This makes forecasting the future performance of an investment formidable and a wrong evaluation plausible.

During the fundraising phase, the quality of the management team and the equity investor's track record, personal financial commitment, and the desire to achieve success are important to collect financial and economic data. It is easy to understand the value of managers who work hard and collaborate constructively and enthusiastically with the investors to build a trustworthy relationship between the funds provider and the team of promoters or researchers.

The level of commitment from Business Angels changes depending on how they wish to invest. We can identify, in terms of active and direct participation in the business project, four main types of Business Angels:

1. Angels who sit on a working Board of Directors—They are passive and not looking for operating management responsibility, but usually require periodic financial reports.
2. Angels who act as informal consultants—They are investors who provide consulting help when needed and requested.
3. Angels who are full- or part-time manager investors—They are investors who create value from the support provided, market knowledge, and contacts offered to the entrepreneur or to the research team.
4. Angels who are investor-owners—They assist founders by bringing other financing after presenting and promoting the business initiative to new investors and establishing strategic alliances with other companies that represent future clients or potential providers of technologies and manufacturing enhancement.

In early stage deals, private equity investors use these criteria to choose an investment:

- Possibility of entry in new markets
- Cost advantages
- Proprietary advantages or unique technology
- Business idea easily understood by investors
- Opportunity to have fun from the investment
- High level of ROI linked with solid financial indicators
- Business idea that is both innovative and profitable
- Management teams with competences, good track records, ability to financially commitment, and the desire to succeed
- Geographically close
- Clear exit strategy

# CHAPTER 5

# Investments in Mature Companies: Expansion Financing

## 5.1 GENERAL OVERVIEW OF FINANCING GROWTH

This chapter is the first one of the three chapters dedicated to private equity that deals with target companies that are not in their fast-pace growth stage anymore. On the contrary, the company finds itself in a very mature stage of the life cycle or it is facing a distressed situation. As such, these are "pure" private equity deals. In the following chapters, the following deals will be presented and described:

- Expansion financing—this chapter
- Replacement financing—Chapter 6
- Vulture financing—Chapter 7

Fig. 5.1 illustrates that expansion, maturity, and crisis are all phases of life that a target company goes through. The financial goal at this time is to support the growth or the survival in terms of revenues realized, products developed, and markets and customers serviced.

The demand of financial resources made by the target company at this stage depends on:

1. its competitive capacity, measured in terms of turnover trend,
2. the quantity of capital invested, which is connected with changes in the firm's industry,
3. cash flows generated, which rely on the efficient structure of the costs and revenues and the industry in which the firm competes.

These three elements help defining the financial resources needed to sustain the development and growth of the existing business.

From the company standpoint, financing growth through private equity is an alternative to corporate lending with the same high-risk profile in terms of the large amount of money invested and uncertainty about future performance. However, financing growth guarantees the direct involvement of the private

**51**

Private Equity and Venture Capital in Europe. https://doi.org/10.1016/B978-0-12-812254-9.00005-X

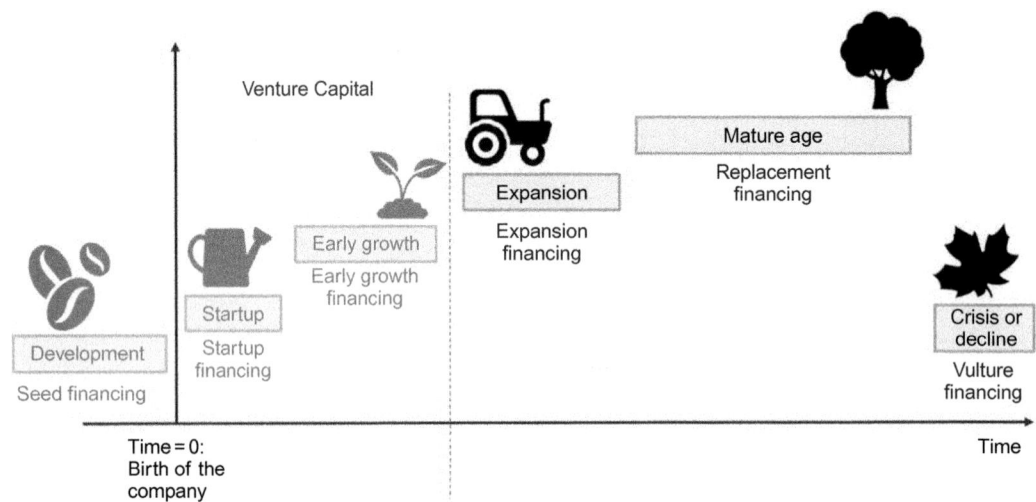

**FIG. 5.1** The second part of the company life cycle.

equity in the management of the company, which means the company will be managed skillfully and competently.

## 5.2   EXPANSION FINANCING

The fourth cluster of private equity deals (Fig. 5.2) made in this second part of the life cycle mainly:

- covers manufacturing tool-up and marketing commitment costs,
- builds or improves the necessary facilities,
- supports the working capital needs, and
- provides capital to finance a Mergers and Acquisition (M&A) strategy or campaign.

REMEMBER: What are the first three clusters of private equity investments?

The expansion financing takes place in the fastest pace of growth of a firm to consolidate its position in the market.

The money injection made by the private equity (PE) investor is used to fill in the (reducing) gap existing between the cash flow and money needed. In this phase, the level of risk is moderate, if compared with the previous stages of private equity clusters and the risk profile level in expansion financing depends on the industry in which the company operates. For this reason, in this cluster the stake held by the private equity investor is not usually very high.

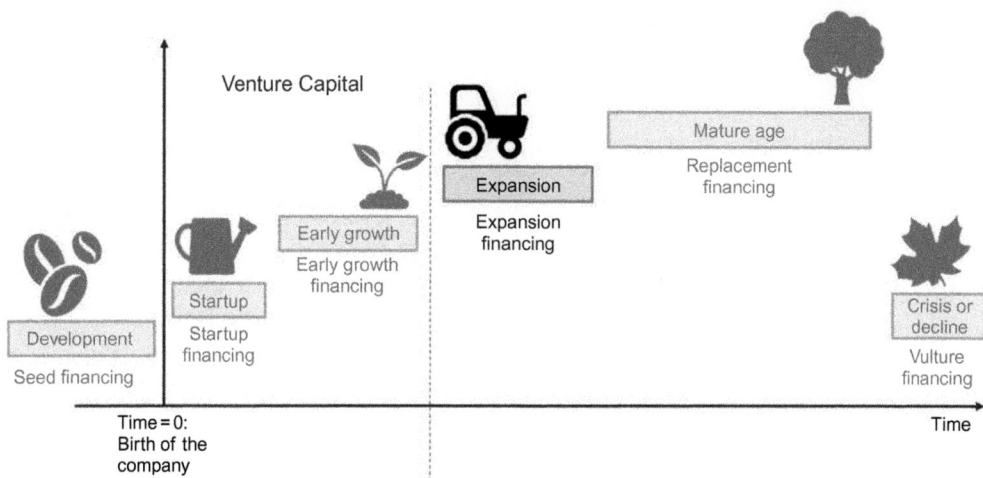

**FIG. 5.2** Expansion financing.

Investments in companies at this stage of life can usually finance two types of growth:

Internal growth:

1. entry by rights issue, subscribing usually a minority stake of the target company,
2. increase in production capacity by building new production plants and acquiring new equipment,
3. internationalization or domestic market enlargement to cover profitable groups of customers,
4. implementation of more aggressive commercial strategies and marketing activities; usually done in a very competitive industry, and
5. exit by listing or a trade sale of the target company.

External growth (i.e., acquisition of a target company):

1. growth opportunity in a fragmented sector by unifying different firms and
2. concrete opportunity for acquisitions of nonexploited products and/or technologies,

## 5.3  THE CLUSTER OF EXPANSION GROWTH DEALS

Expansion financing includes all risk capital invested in already existing and established companies used to incentivize development, dimensional growth, and potential quotation in a public financial market. This type of participation is less risky than those in the initial and start-up phase of a company, because there is already a tested and well-functioning company with a good base of customers. There is less difficulty in the valuation of these investments because the private equity is able to consider the company's historical data and economic information; conditions that are impossible to satisfy in venture capital operations. In Europe, investing in expansions is the most important private equity activity. They are usually realized by large closed funds and financial intermediaries with expertise and knowledge about the domestic and international financial markets. Sizable investors with expertise can better support entrepreneurs during the preinitial public offering (IPO) phase. The stage of growth of the company's life cycle can be divided into two subparts, development (second-stage financing) and consolidation (third-stage financing):

1. Second-stage financing—Financing at this stage supports the company's development (accelerated growth). After commercial validation of the product or service offered by the target company, the private equity intervenes and increases production and the selling and marketing capacity. The company is still medium or small, but the growth capacity of the business idea has improved. It is important to emphasize that the financial resources invested are reduced because the company has already acquired a good part of the market, and selling guarantees the resources needed for the production process.

2. Third-stage financing—The second-stage financing supports the consolidation of the development reached by the venture-backed company. At this point, the company has passed the initial development phase and wants to consolidate and enlarge its market position and consolidate the market share. The investor contributes with a large amount of money to protect the target company's market position and to support the management during the design of new growth plans. These types of plans involve the launch of new products, enlargement or diversification of manufacturing and distribution activities, or the acquisition of a competitor. Consequently, it becomes necessary to collect new funds dedicated to research and development, marketing, and production. As for previous deals, the company turns itself to a private equity deal not only for the financial needs but also for the network the private equity has in the industry in which the company operates.

## 5.4   CHARACTERISTICS OF GROWTH

Expansion financing deals work best with small- or medium-sized companies that want to grow quickly. As such, they have flexible production systems that adapt quickly to the changes that typically occur in expansion financing. At the same time, it is much more likely that a small company finds itself in this kind of cluster as the growth rates can be much higher than those experienced by a huge company. Companies seek expansion financing, to reach another element for their success—dimension. Increasing dimension allows the small and medium companies to exploit business opportunities that they otherwise would lose due to the lack or the low availability of effective and alternative tools to catch big strategic opportunities, such as internationalization.

During this strategic process, soft support given by private equity investors is critical. Their ability to provide financial resources as well as a set of advisory services helps the small and medium company to improve its competitive skills. The extensive support provided to these types of companies is also demonstrated in the average duration of the holding period, which is around 4 years or more, hence typically much longer if compared with the holding period of buy out operations.

The support given for the dimensional growth of the firm can be classified in two ways: quantitative and qualitative. Company performance can be quantitatively compared in terms of revenue and improvement in the margin and number of employees between venture-backed companies and companies that have never needed professional investors. Research demonstrates the high impact of the private equity operation by analyzing the increase in the employment level and turnovers. An expansion deal can lead to qualitative development facilitating the collaboration and joint venture with foreign partners that can result in export business.

As anticipated earlier on in this chapter, growth can occur in two ways in this kind of deals: internally and externally.

## 5.5 INTERNAL GROWTH

In the internal growth deals, the private equity investors compete with banks and other financial institution. A company seeking this kind of financing wants to pursue growth organically, which is to say by enlarging itself by getting new fixed assets or by increasing its working capital.

The investor needs to provide money to the venture-backed company in order to buy and/or sustain the procurement of working capital and to purchase new assets. At the same time, the private equity investor may support the company in the potential negotiation with banks for further needs of money.

Because this kind of deal is not characterized by a high level of difficulty and at the same time, it does require the private equity to have a strong network, the offer is very wide and there is a very high number of investors providing this financing, making this kind of deals less rewarding than other ones.

## 5.6 EXTERNAL GROWTH

External growth, from the standpoint of the bidder company, occurs through the acquisition of a target company. Acquisitions represent part of the merger and acquisition (M&A) operation. To be more precise, acquisitions are composed of all the services that support the closing of operations that produce structural and definitive modification on the corporate aspects of the involved company. M&A represent one of the technical solutions developed and supported by private equity investors during turnaround and replacement financing. M&A operations include a set of heterogeneous deals such as mergers, the acquisition of a business unit of a company, the acquisition of quotes that represent a minor participation of the capital risk of a company, and all deals that allow the transfer of the proprietary control.

In this situation, the role of the private equity investor is not only the soft support realized through advisory services but also the direct investment in companies with turnaround needs. When they act as advisory providers, economic returns are realized in the fees charged for this soft activity. When they invest directly, the economic return is higher and consists of gains they can realize on exit of the deal through an IPO or trade sale. Advisory support of the investor is critical, because the M&A deal is composed of acquisition search and deal origination, due diligence, valuation of the company and deal design, financial advisory and funding, and postclosing advisory needed in the integration process after the deal is finalized. This type of deal has a high rate of selection so there is little relation between deals closed and the cases analyzed. This makes the presence of professionals who improve the efficiency of the information and operative processes critical.

### 5.6.1 M&A Motivations

The main reason for M&A operation is to realize a higher total value with the merger of two or more business units or companies than can be obtained if they stand alone as single units or companies (i.e., synergies). After the merger, production costs are reduced, and there is the possibility of increasing debt capacity and reducing the cost of debt because of the company's improved rating. Finally, the company has a better market position that affects the estimated rate of the earnings growth. There are five main macro categories that determine if an M&A deal is feasible:

- Strategic motivation—An M&A can impact a company's competitive position; for example, it is possible to enlarge the market share if a dangerous competitor is acquired, activity on the core business can be refocused, entry into a new market or industry, internationalization, and expansion of activity downstream or upstream. It is also an opportunity to enter networks of specific companies.

- Economic motivation—One of the most important reasons for an M&A deal is the cost reduction obtained with the exploitation of the scale and scope of economies. It is widely accepted that the increase in company dimension in terms of production capacity is translated in the reduction of the average cost per unit of product. It is also well known, studied, and verified, that these deals improve the scope of economies by exploiting complementary skills and resources. Mergers and acquisitions create a new composition of the corporate governance and management team of the target company, which is another way to improve economic performance.
- Financial motivation—Acquisitions allow the realization of a future investment that was previously impossible to the acquisition company, because of different ways to collect financial resources.
- Fiscal motivation—This type of operation creates values with newly available fiscal opportunities; for example, possible future deductions of losses realized by the target company during the period previous to the acquisition.
- Speculative motivation—This trend in the M&A relates to economic and market cycles. For example, deals fall apart when the seller's expectations of future performance are vastly different from the buyer's expectations, as often happens with technologically innovative companies.

## 5.6.2 M&A Characteristics

Mergers and acquisitions can be realized in different ways: merger, equity carve out, breaking down, and joint venture. The merger solution is the natural conclusion of the buy operation formalized with a union between the target company and the new company.

The merger macro category is subdivided into a merger with consolidation and corporate merger. Merger with consolidation is less widespread because the entities involved do not buy each other but are consolidated into a unique entity without the desire to take over. The balance sheet of the new company is exactly the sum of the asset, liability, and equity of the original companies and they have different net worth value but the same equity value. The corporate merger is the most common merger solution. It involves an acquiring investor who does not have any share of the target company, an acquiring investor with participation in the risk capital of the target company, and an acquiring investor who owns the total property of the target. The latter is the case of a corporate merger after a leveraged buy out or successful and total takeover bid.

These types of operations are realized with cash or shares. Cash can completely change the corporate governance of the acquired company, but is really expensive. Payment by exchanging shares does not use cash funds, but it does not allow total renewal of the corporate governance structure in the target company, especially when some shareholders do not accept the agreements.

### 5.6.3 M&A in the Private Equity Business

As for the private equity business, there are three main reasons for financing through private equity an external growth:

1. Reinforcing the competitive advantages of the company to strengthen its distinctive skills in the existing activities and businesses—Acquisitions usually involve firms operating in the same markets with similar products and services.
2. Expanding competitive advantages to improve and extend the company's distinctive skills to neighboring sectors—Companies targeted for acquisition usually offer products and services with technological and marketing elements.
3. Exploring the competitive advantages of the company when entering a new sector that requires new skills—This type of target firm operates upstream or downstream or in sectors without any correlation.

The financing with private equity of external growth may occur for several different objectives; some need a long period of time to be reached, while others are realizable more quickly.

Long-period objectives are classified in three different clusters. The first type desires to increase the company's value and satisfy the interests of the different stakeholders. The second type is connected with a manager who wants to reinforce his personal visibility, and the last type looks for opportunities to collect earnings in a capital account.

Short-term objectives, that can be included among the strategic motivations, refer to:

- Researching and exploiting the scale and scope economies—These companies want to use their experience in marketing or production to improve production capacity through the skills and technologies of the acquired firm.
- Managing interdependence with stakeholders by accelerating growth in the industry where the acquired firm already successfully operates to improve their own skills.

- Improving the proposed system and markets served by acquiring a higher market share and entry into new markets by using the marketing skills of the acquired company and increasing the client base.
- Entering into new businesses to obtain critical resources from the acquired company or to reduce the risk related to the expansion in new industries.
- Exploiting and optimizing financial resources through the leverage capacity of the acquired company, stabilization of the cash flow, or the acquisition of an underestimated company that can be sold with a good economic return.

All the goals and reasons described in this paragraph have in common a fact: they cannot be pursued with the intervention of the banking system as they need an active financial player having a fundamental and active role in the operation.

As for the mere private equity deal, it can occur in two ways:

– through a direct investment and
– through the setting of a special purpose vehicle (SPV).

(i) Direct investment

Like in any other private equity transaction, the private equity investor invests in the equity of a venture-backed company in exchange for shares (Fig. 5.3). Thanks to the money injection, the company has liquidity enough and can afford to carry on the M&A and buy the target company. If the process is successful, the venture-backed company and the target will merge. This kind of deal is pursued when the merger of the two companies can generate a huge amount of synergies. On the other hand, the venture-backed company will be forced to share with the private

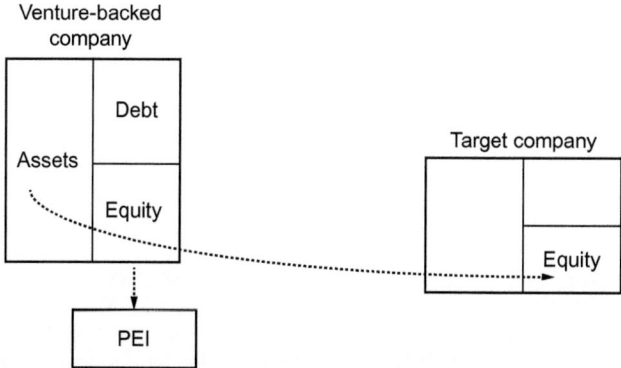

**FIG. 5.3** Direct investment in expansion financing with external growth.

equity a portion of such synergies. In order to avoid the division of the synergies, the deal can be carried on through the setting of an SPV.

(ii) Investment through an SPV

The second way in which this M&A can be done is through the setting of an *ad hoc* vehicle (that will lead the acquisition of the target company). The process develops over the following steps:

- The private equity investor sets up a SPV. The SPV is an "empty box" built with the only purpose of a specific extraordinary operation. This company does not have any assets nor liabilities and equity before the operation takes place (STEP 1 in Fig. 5.4)
- Once the SPV is set, the venture-backed company, with the help of the private equity investor, collects money from the banking system and transfers the funds collected in the assets of the SPV (STEP 2 in Fig. 5.4)
- The SPV can benefit of the funds given by the investor and by the banking system, through the bidder company and can buy the target company (STEP 3 in Fig. 5.4), which will not merge with the bidder company.

This option can be used in two cases:

a. When the venture-backed company has got a huge financial need and it does not want to further increase the amount of debt for accounting or reporting reasons.

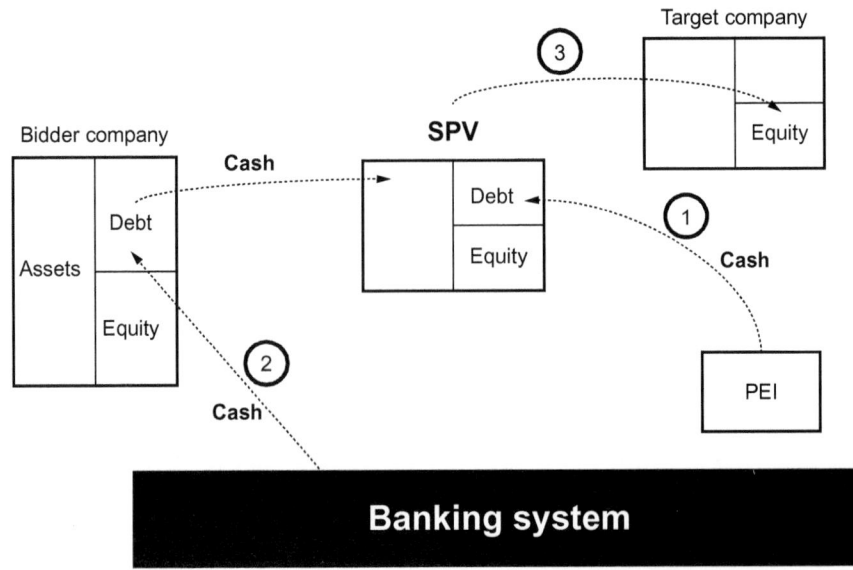

**FIG. 5.4** Investment through SPV in expansion financing with external growth.

   b. The company wants to keep the SPV as a separate entity as it does not want the private equity investor to share the gain deriving from the M&A process.

At the same time, this second option is more expensive than the first one, as it is not easy to collect a huge amount of debt from the banking system. Additionally, since the Private equity does not enjoy part of the synergies created, the investor has a lower incentive in generating value through the deal.

## 5.7 ADVANTAGES FOR VENTURE-BACKED COMPANIES

Venture-backed companies with private equity financed company growth have several advantages:

1. Screen and Scout of the market—the private equity helps the bidder/venture-backed companies in the research of the optimal target to buy
2. Money injection—Private equity investors provide the funds necessary to support key business activities.
3. Higher overall return—The support of private equity firms allows the original shareholders to obtain a higher return from their investments in the target company, especially when exiting through an IPO.
4. Sponsor in going public—Experienced investors are key assets in reassuring IPO investors, so their involvement increases the possibility of success in going public. Usually, IPOs realized with private equity investors create higher returns.
5. Spin-off support—Investors with a wide range of relationships can help when the target company wants to sell its subsidiaries.
6. Private equity improves the target company's ability to satisfy market demands—Today markets change quickly due to customer needs or technological revolutions, so it is critical to a company's success to be able to quickly exploit market opportunities.
7. Advisory support—Private equity can support the target company upon entry into new markets or industries because they are able to share their management skills and business know-how.
8. Private equity investment is a clear signal a business idea has potential. On the other hand, the lack of interest is a good indicator of an existing problem not easily recognized by the management team or the original shareholders.
9. Original shareholders receive critical support from the private equity investor—The bottom line of the balance sheet will be diligently watched and every possible action placed to maximize the potential return on the investment
10. Integration in the post M&A process—in case there is one.

## 5.8    DISADVANTAGES FOR VENTURE-BACKED COMPANIES

To have a clear picture of how private equity investments impact the expansion of a target company, a recurring group of potential disadvantages should be considered:

1. Culture changes—The target company's managers and employees have to work with a new partner who has a high-profit-oriented culture combined with an intense pressure to continue to develop the business.
2. After investing in the target company, private equity firms have greater control of the agendas and activities of the original shareholders and managers.
3. Timing of exit strategies may not be consistent with the plan of the original shareholders and management. Many conflicts can arise while managing the right time to exit.
4. Buyback options are usually limited. This means that original shareholders may not be allowed to repurchase the participation from the investor if the deal was unsuccessful. Private equity firms are usually reluctant to include a buyback option, because it can affect the real potential of the investment return.
5. Private equity investors require a high return from the investment. This means a high level of the value transfers from original to new shareholders. The high return expectations include the value of the money invested as well as the soft support consisting of invested time, networks, experience, and expertise. The original shareholders, before closing the deal with equity investors, have to understand that if the value of their business will be higher after the deal, then this justifies the high percentage of value that they must give to the investor.
6. Closing a transaction with private equity firms is complex and time consuming, because this type of deal includes agreements on liabilities and obligations that can take up a year to close.
7. A typical private equity approach comes with fast decision making. If there are bureaucratic delays, due to the timetables and procedure of the previous shareholders, the investors can decide to abandon a partnership.
8. The willingness of a private equity firm to commit additional financial resources in a specific investment already part of its portfolio is limited by the continuous focus on its expected returns. This situation can force original shareholders into adding new funds to the venture-backed company to avoid losing new business initiatives or opportunities due to lack of funds.

# CHAPTER 6

# Investments in Mature Companies: Replacement Financing

## 6.1 INTRODUCTION

This chapter is the second one of the three chapters dedicated to the deals of private equity aiming at financing the growth of the company and it describes the deals targeting companies in their mature stage. These deals are called of replacement financing.

These operations account for more than 50% of the private equity market, which includes deals realized when the target company is in bad condition or in a crisis. These deals are discussed because they both concern companies facing management, economic, and financial problems that have a direct impact on their growth, if not for their survival.

## 6.2 REPLACEMENT FINANCING

Fig. 6.1 illustrates the maturity stage of a company's life cycle and the private equity involvement in it. At this moment of the life cycle, the venture-backed company has grown considerably by enlarging the markets reached and the range of products or services offered. Financing may be a means toward listing or for a planned sale with another institutional investor to support the next steps. The private equity investor can also bridge financial difficulties and the quotation of the company.

In the financial environment, technology, competitiveness, and the expectation of demand change quickly. This makes it necessary for companies to modify and adapt their strategies and organizational structures to survive and remain competitive. Underperforming companies have to fight to exist and deliver a service or product able to generate a return that exceeds the connected cost of capital.

63

Private Equity and Venture Capital in Europe. https://doi.org/10.1016/B978-0-12-812254-9.00006-1

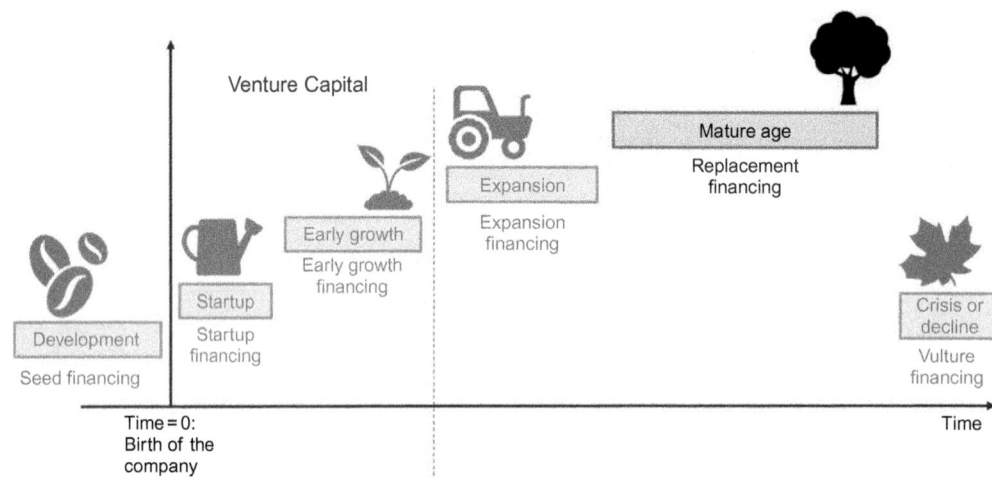

**FIG. 6.1** Replacement financing.

These rearranged strategies include a clear sense of purpose, direction, and realistic long-term rules that are viable because companies want to perform better and maintain a competitive edge.

A company that is targeted for replacement financing has already passed its embryonic stage and finds itself into a mature, sometimes stagnating, phase. Within this next stage there are problems connected with organizational structure (management) that make it difficult to move through this stage. Consequently, when a private equity decides to invest in a turnaround operation, he must know that a lot of energy will be spent solving issues related to management activity. Once these are solved, successful modification of the competitive strategy and structure can begin.

In this phase, the level of risk varies according to the deal. The deal characterizing this phase is named:

- PIPE (private investment in public equity) deals
- Corporate governance deals/turnaround
- LBO (leveraged buyout)

The three deals have a specific feature in common that allows them to be clustered under the same levels of replacement financing. They all have the goal to replace one or many existing shareholder or shareholders. In all three cases, after the exit of the private equity investor, the ownership structure will necessarily be different. To pursue successfully such goal, the nature and the role of the private equity investor adapt and change according to the deal they are carrying on (see Table 6.1).

**Table 6.1** Change in the Nature of the Private Equity Investor in Replacement Financing

| Replacement Financing Deal | Change in the Nature of the Investor |
| --- | --- |
| PIPE | Investment in a listed company |
| CG deals/turnaround | The company does not need financing |
| LBO | It is the investor that looks for the venture-backed company and not the other way around |

## 6.3   PIPE DEALS

PIPE is an investment made in a company listed in the stock exchange. Even though the investment is made in a public entity, it still belongs to the private equity world as the profit mechanism is not related to the stock exchange. The private equity aims at reaching capital gains and return using the usual private equity market, and not the stock exchange.

The purpose of the operation is not to speculate, but to buy a minority stake and to sell it to another potential shareholder at a price not based on stock exchange benchmarks (this price is usually three-four times bigger).

This stake has to be big enough to make the final buyer become the largest shareholder. To make this deal work the private equity investor has to understand the minimum amount of ownership necessary to be the owner of the company. For this reason, these deals can be hostile, which is to say, they can occur without the consent of the original ownership.

## 6.4   CORPORATE GOVERNANCE DEALS/ TURNAROUND DEALS

### 6.4.1   Characteristics of Turnaround Deals

During this type of deal, management skill and exceptional leadership profiles are the two most important elements for a successful outcome, as managing the replacement for a distressed company is fraught with difficulties. For that reason, turnaround financing risk is related to target company downsizing, but the central concept that must be considered is connected to leadership. First, the turnaround executive has to persuade the key stakeholders that this type of intervention is the best solution for the recovery of their company. Then a change of management is usually necessary, but it is not always easily realizable, because the financial intermediary has to negotiate with the previous chairperson. Another consideration is the financial and economic condition of a company that needs this type of financing. If it wants to avoid bankruptcy, there must be a sense of urgency in the process. Usually, the turnaround practitioner decides to implement an efficient and well-organized management and financial controls to develop and communicate a new vision for the business. When this is done, he will obtain the support and collaboration of the entire group of employees.

There are two types of turnaround executives: those who specialize in crisis stabilization and those who undertake the complete turnaround process and stay and work for the target company to manage growth and organizational transformation. In general, the first group of executives stays in the company from 6 to 12 months, whereas the second group is likely to stay in a leadership role from 12 to 24 months.

### 6.4.2   Reasons Behind Turnaround Deals

Strategic changes realized by companies are meant to move toward a future desired condition such as reinforcing competitive advantages. This process is very complex and only a few successfully manage it by launching new strategies and new structures to obtain an effective and renewed value proposition. It is important to recognize the sharp difference between strategic and organizational change. Strategic change refers to the realization of new strategies that lead to a substantial modification of the normal business activity of the firm, whereas organizational change is the normal consequence of redefining the business strategy. In conclusion, a strategic change always includes an organizational change, especially when it is suddenly implemented without relevant resistance.

As previously outlined, the typical company targeted for a turnaround deal is going through its mature phase and needs a renewal of the value proposition for its economic survival. Turnaround operations are part of strategic changes that includes the reengineering, reorganization, and innovation processes:

1. Reengineering—Sweeping change in the company's costs, production cycle, services, and quality with the implementation of different techniques and tools that consider the firm as a complex system of customer-oriented processes instead of just a cluster of organizational functions. The emergence of aggressive new competitors in the market can force the company to find new strategies to recover their loss of competitiveness. The company's management team has to focus its attention first on critical business processes such as product design, inventory, and order management and then on customer needs, constantly monitoring how to improve the quality of the value proposition with a lower price. Implementing quality methodologies such as total quality management to improve process efficiency should also be a focus of management.

2. Reorganization—This is the second way management can launch a change, and it is composed of two main phases. In the first phase the company reduces, in terms of number and dimension, business units, divisions, departments, and the levels of hierarchy. The second phase begins downsizing to reduce the number of employees to decrease the operational costs. A company decides to implement a reorganization because of the external environment; for example, a technology revolution that makes their product obsolete, a recession that depresses demand, or a law deregulation that changes the rules.
A firm usually reorganizes because it has not renewed its strategies and management to align with the environmental changes. Reorganization represents the only way to survive and regain the lost competitiveness.

3. Innovation—A strategic change promoted by new technologies that impact the production process and lead to a new configuration of the company service and product. To anticipate competitors, a company has to introduce a new production process or technology with a redefinition of its strategy and follow the innovation wave of the industry.

## 6.4.3 Valuation and Risk Management in Turnaround

The company targeted for a turnaround deal generally suffers from cash flow problems, insufficient future funding, or the inability to service their debt. It can also have an excessive debt-to-equity ratio and inappropriate debt structure, unbalanced between short- and long-term debt, and balance sheet insolvency.

The objectives of a turnaround is to change the leadership of the company in order to restore its solvency, in terms of cash flow and balance sheet, align the capital structure with the planned cash flow, and ensure that enough funds will be collected to implement the turnaround plan. These objectives are reached by modifying the existing capital structure; for example, raising additional funds, renegotiating the debt, or raising new equity capital from existing shareholders or outside investors (such as private equity investors).

The private equity investor has to consider four fundamental risks when structuring a turnaround deal:

1. Social risk—When a firm is in crisis, it strongly impacts both society in general and the firm's stakeholders. During this time the firm has problems with creditors, suppliers, employees, and customers. The community is affected by the loss of taxes paid by the firm and the costs to support employees who have lost their jobs.

2. Economic risk—The economic crisis of a company is analyzed by their return on investment (ROI); if it is lower than the average industrial ROI, the company is underperforming. This analysis can be problematic, and a

better indicator of economic problems is the decline of the entire industry. A company is in crisis when its financial performance is continually decreasing in terms of ROI and return on sales and when the net incomes are negative.
3. Legal risk—The bankruptcy of a company raises many legal issues.
4. Management risk—From a management point of view, a company is in crisis when the ROI starts to decrease. Managers are the first to understand the situation and know if the crisis can be averted.

There are five different types of turnaround strategies in terms of operation impact, operations changes, and exiting the crisis:

1. Management—The key factor is management change. The objective of this type of deal is to turnaround the weakness of the management and general culture of the company. This is the most frequent type of turnaround.
2. Economic cycle—Turnaround is provoked by the economic cycle of the sector. Management must maintain the stability of the company while exploiting the potential revival of the cycle.
3. Product—The company is able to exit the crisis by launching a new product because of a new technological innovation.
4. Competitive background—Firms come out of a crisis because general elements in the competitive background change positively, such as decreasing the costs of raw materials.
5. State and government—When the crisis is provoked by market conditions out of the firm's control, the government provides help to solve their financial problems; for example, the automotive industry.

## 6.5   LBO

Replacement financing deals involve not only equity capital but also debt financing when a leveraged buy out (LBO) is realized. As mentioned above, these deals change the share capital composition of the target company.

### 6.5.1   General Overview of Buy Outs

A buy out is a structured financial operation that, through merger, division, or acquisition of control participation, allows the transfer of the property from the old shareholders to a new entrepreneur with economic and technical support of a financial intermediary (usually a private equity fund). In a LBO, a major part of the capital is supplied by debt securities subscribed by a pool of banks and financial intermediaries. It is possible to define leveraged acquisitions as a particular type of M&A activity that leaves the acquired firm with a debt ratio higher than before the acquisition.

LBOs have a special structure, which consists of a holding company that founds a new company responsible for the collection of funds (with the financial solution of the debt) necessary for the acquisition of the assets or the shares of a target company. After the acquisition, the new company (named NewCo) is merged with the target company. This is realized with a forward merger where NewCo absorbs the target or a reverse merger where the target company absorbs NewCo. Financial and tax needs influence which option is used. The financiers of the NewCo are usually bankers and the purchasers. As collateral, for the debt repayment, they offer assets owned by the target company and its ability to create cash flow.

The LBO was initiated and developed in the United States in the beginning of 1970. There are two main differences when compared with venture capital operations: they acquire the majority or totality of the target company's shares and the buyer completely changes the shareholder structure. In the mid-1980s LBOs were used by banks to realize acquisitions through debt financing. They began to consider the economic value and profitability of companies and analyzed the potential development of business plans shared between the company's management and the private equity fund involved in the deal.

Based on these financial operations and the groups involved, several types of buy outs can be identified:

1. Management buy out (MBO)—This type of buy out is promoted by the management of the target company who usually acquires complete control of the firm.
2. Management buy in (MBI)—External managers plan, the deal and become shareholders with a considerable quota of participation to obtain control of the company.
3. Buy in management buy out (BIMBO)—External and internal managers of the company promote this type of deal.
4. Buy in growth opportunity (BINGO)—The value invested by the financial intermediaries exceeds the value of the company to finance its growth.
5. Worker buy out (WBO)—Employees enter into the shareholder structure of the target company so the property is enlarged to allow them to take part in the firm's management.
6. Family buy out (FBO)—Occurs when the company's proprietary structure is controlled by the family promoter. This type of company is the target of a buy out upon transfer of title between generations. Very often the newest generation of owners is unable to manage the company because they fight or they do not have the necessary entrepreneurial skills to make the firm profitable. The FBO is the solution to this type of situation, because it allows a family member to acquire total control of the company by paying off the other shareholders.

7. Investor buy out (IBO)—This type of operation is realized by a financial investor, such as a private equity fund, who decides to buy the entire equity of the target company. This decision is made because the company has good growth potential, a high probability of positive return from the investment, and to ability change and select a new team of managers chosen on the basis of their capability, previous experience, track record, and reliability.

8. Public to private (PTP)—A way to conclude a buy out by delisting the target company from the public financial market. This company had probably been the focus of an earlier buy out, but it represents a small part of the total transaction. The vast majority of buy outs are acquisitions of private firms and corporate divisions.

9. Reverse buy out (RBO)—The target company has already been subjected to a PTP and the buy out is concluded with a new quotation of the firm in the public financial market.

The most important ways to realize a buy out deal are the asset sale and merge sale; the main difference between them is the object of the acquisition. The asset sale uses a large amount of debt to acquire a defined part of the assets and liabilities owned by the target company. The merge sale modality buys the entire equity of the firm. With an asset sale it is necessary to have a friendly agreement between the parties involved in the transaction, whereas a merge sale can be concluded under hostile conditions.

Significant elements in buy out deals that guarantee improvements in the economic and financial performance of the target company can be identified:

1. Professional competences and managerial efficiency provided by the private equity funds.

2. An opportunity to realize an international growth because of the contacts and relationships of the institutional investor.

3. Creation, development, and expansion of a new entrepreneurship that allows managers to become entrepreneurs to reduce the expense and value destroyed by agency costs; this condition is particularly true during a management buy in or buy out and buy in management buy out.

4. External growth supported through new financial resources provided to the target company after acquisition.

5. Increase and development of the employment level necessary to maintain a well-balanced ratio between the structure and the fast growing nature of the target company. To guarantee a successful buy out highly qualified and trained human resources must be available to realize the corporate strategy. Involving highly qualified people is reflected in the pursuit of economically important innovations measured in terms of patents obtained after private equity investments.

To execute an accurate evaluation of a buy out, the duration of the holding period—a period of time included between the conclusion of the leveraged acquisition and the participation divestment—must be considered. The possible presence of foreign and international financial resources or investors and the debt and equity ratio should also be examined before a buy out is started.

The longevity of leveraged buy outs or how long firms stay in LBO ownership can be summarized by two disparate views. Academics argue that the buy out organizational firm is a long-term superior governance structure with strong investor discipline and strict behaviors because of the propriety and heavy leverage structure. An LBO is also seen as a short-term "shock therapy" that gives inefficient, badly performing firms an intense process of corporate governance restructuring before the company goes public. Between these two extreme point of views, there is the common opinion that an LBO is a temporary governance structure specializing in the improvement of a public company. This solves the problem of unused excess free cash flow.

## 6.5.2 Characteristics of a Buy Out Deal

### 6.5.2.1 Financial Structure

A buy out operation can be defined as an LBO if there is a change in the property composition and a complete restructuring of the leveraged dimension of the firm acquired. The elements that compose the financial structure of an LBO are senior debt, junior debt, equity, and all operations that create cash flow such as asset stripping and securitization. The distinction between junior and senior debt is based on the time estimated for repayment of the financial obligation and the presence of rights and specific options for the fund providers such as the covenants.

There are also differences between shareholders, including their involvement in daily operations of the target company, investment duration, and willingness to maintain their economic resources in the firm. To guarantee the success of an acquisition it is absolutely necessary for investors to have a deep interest in management along with an industrial vision of the deal, because it may be a long-term investment focused on improving and growing the target company. Another category of shareholder is the financial investor whose job it is to conclude the acquisition and collect the value created from their participation in a short-term investment.

The presence of these two types of investors helps realize a successful buy out, but it is important to manage their different goals without compromising the target company. The ratchet technique is one tool used to manage and monitor shareholder behavior and interest. This technique consists of a contractual agreement between the shareholders that makes the dimension of their participation variable due to a predefined and shared financial and economic performance goal.

If a target company is acquired through the debt, it is useful to undertake steps to collect the money needed for the heavy debt repayment. One step is asset stripping—selling assets owned by the target company that are not classified as an operating resource. These assets are easily liquidated and a sure source of cash. The presence of this type of asset on the firm's balance sheet is one of the reasons a company should be considered for a buy out acquisition. A second way to collect cash is the securitization of positive entries on the balance sheet unsuitable for asset stripping due to their operational nature such as unexpired commercial credits and financing inside firms controlled by the holding company.

### 6.5.2.2 Corporate Governance

Leveraged acquisitions strongly impact shareholder structure, so it is important to understand the role, function, and characteristics of boards. Their function in a public company is to provide management supervision. In private equity acquisitions boards seem useless as the private equity partner can easily directly monitor and support the firm in an advisory capacity. Therefore, it is important to identify the real role of board directors in companies acquired by one or more private equity groups, since it seems that a successful deal concentrates the ownership of the company into the hands of a few shareholders. Private equity investors are deeply involved in running the acquired company with extensive restructuring experience, so they have a strong incentive to maximize the value of the firm.

In private equity deals tough control is exercised by the general partner over the executive managers when defining and planning the implementation of the portfolio strategy. In many cases the venture capitalist sits on the board of companies in which they have invested and their participation increases during significant decisions such as changing the CEO. What happens in an LBO when the private equity sponsors are not actively involved in the management of the company? Research that analyzes the board structure observed these findings:

1. Size and composition—After a buy out, the number of board members decreases significantly while external directors are drastically reduced. There is no significant difference in board size of the MBO and the LBO, but existing differences in the dimension of the company must be considered. In private equity deals outside directors are substituted by individuals appointed by the private equity sponsor, but when there is an MBO the external board member disappears because this type of deal requires heavy involvement of the mangers.

2. Director engagement—With complex, hard, and challenging deals there is more active participation and cooperation of the private equity board members. This type of investor usually takes part when the company acquired has to realize critical investments or turnaround. Investors create a board ensuring that their power is absolute by changing the CEO and the key directors, except when there is a management buy out and buy in that excludes the external board members

3. Private equity policy—Structure and composition of the target company board depend on the attitude of each investor; the venture capitalist relies less on his own partners or employees and more on outside directors. If a group of private equity investors sponsor the deal, the proportion of LBO sponsors is larger, because they want a specific delegate on the board of directors.

4. Permanence—Private equity investors are always present on the target company board and are active up to the exit from the investment.

5. Turnover—CEO and director turnover is high compared with the turnover prior to the LBO or becoming private through an MBO.

In summary, extra management support or monitoring is needed in difficult deals resulting in a larger board with the likely presence of LBO sponsors on it. This explains the central role of the board in the restructuring process and the relation between management and shareholders. It is useful to have these sponsors on the board during the restructuring process just because they bring management experience and are able to conduct successful business practices. High turnover rates of CEOs and board composition does not support the opinion that private equity deals have a long-term view that creates less sensibility to the short-term changes and a higher interest in long-term investments, growth, and return.

## 6.5.3  LBO as a Private Equity Deal

As anticipated above, the role of the investors changes in every deal in replacement financing. In LBO, it is the investor that is looking for a company to acquire through a huge amount of financing. In addition to that, the target company, unlike in all other private equity deals is not looking for money.

When a private equity plans an LBO deal, as a first step, it has to identify the target company that the venture-backed company (which in this case is the SPV) has to buy at 100%. This operation takes place in the following steps.

After the target company has been identified, the investor sets up an SPV (see Fig. 6.2) and it becomes its sole owner. In that moment, the investor collects financial debt in order to carry on the deal. Through this cash injection, the

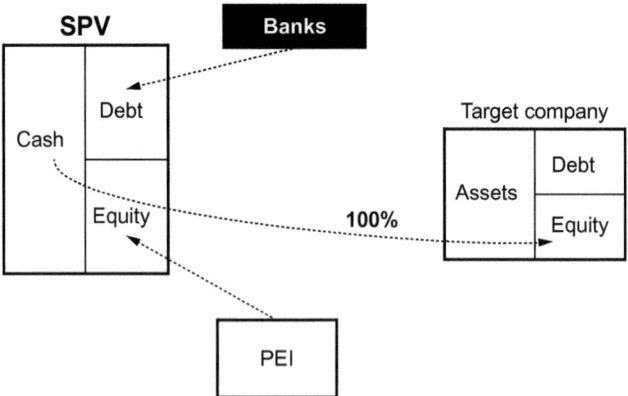

**FIG. 6.2** LBO operation.

SPV (hence, the private equity investor) is able to buy out the target company and will settle the payment of the loans through the cash of the target company.

After the deal is finalized, the investor may easily exit from the investment as it owns the whole company.

Due to the large amount of funds necessary to undertake these operations, data of 2015 show that they covered 76.6% of the funds raised in the private equity market in Europe, even if they involved only 12.8% companies of the total companies engaged in Europe in private equity operations.[1]

### 6.5.3.1   Valuation

The price of the LBO includes the funds necessary to buy the target company, which are calculated as the difference between the enterprise value (EV) and the net financial position of the firm to be acquired. The definition of the EV is very important because it represents the first step in a successful buy out. Considering the erratic state of the buy out financial structure, the calculation of the EV is very complex and creates problems when computing the rate used to discount future cash flows.

As it will be explained in Chapter 17 (see Section 17.2.3), to obtain a sure and precise EV, cross-validation of the results is realized through the simultaneous use of different approaches for the definitions of the deal price. This widespread practice applies both the comparable method and the discounted cash flows approach.

The use of comparable requires the availability of special economic and financial performance indicators such as the EBITDA, EBIT, and the sales or the book value of similar and listed companies, which have to be multiplied to

---

[1]Source: Invest Europe, 2016.

determine the EV of the target company. The discounted cash flow (DCF) method implies that the value of the firm is defined as the sum of the future and expected cash flows, then discounted at the year of the acquisition using as discount rate of a similar and comparable company operating in the same industry. The DCF approach includes both the net present value method and the adjusted present value method. This approach is perfectly suitable for the special and heavy leveraged structure used in a buy out operation.

### 6.5.3.2 Managed Risk

In a buy out transaction, the main elements are the private equity investor who decides to buy a significant participation in a target firm, and their key role in the management of the company in terms of control and the decision to take a private company public. Financial fundaments can predict a default of the buy out company. The deal also can be unsuccessful if it concerns a champion firm and the private equity managers have highly reputed deal expertise.

It is critical to understand how and if a change in the debt equity ratio can impact the value creation of a company. Discussing debt definition, the benefit and cost of the debt, tools used for assessing the leveraged level can help understand how debt equity ratio can impact a company's value.

Debt definition—There are three criteria used to classify debt.

1. Debt imposes contractual obligations that have to be respected both in good and bad times, whereas equity returns are only paid after good financial performances.
2. Contractual payment for the debt is positively affected by taxes, whereas the cash flow from equity shares does not profit from this benefit.
3. Any breach of these contractual agreements causes loss of control of the firm.

According to these criteria, debt includes all financing resources raised (long and short term) that provide interest but excludes any type of account receivable and supplier credit. Lease commitments should also be considered as debt, because interest is usually tax deductible. If the company does not meet the specific requirements it will suffer negative consequences.

The use of debt directly impacts the value of the venture-backed company in terms of costs and benefits, and the final value of the company will increase or decrease whether or not costs exceed the benefits.

Benefit and cost of debt—One benefit is that interest is tax deductible. Compared with equity, debt financing makes managers more selective about projects. Because the company has to repay the interest to investors, if a poorly performing project is selected, the firm could go into default or bankruptcy and managers could lose their jobs.

Debt has three disadvantages:

1. Increasing leverage increase the possibility of default. The direct costs of bankruptcy include legal fees and court costs as well as indirect costs. High levels of debt signal a company is in financial trouble. If this feeling is widespread among stakeholders, employees, customers, and suppliers, it can easily lead to default and bankruptcy. For example, suppliers may decide to reduce their credit or employees, worried for their jobs, leave the company looking for more reliable firms.
2. The necessity of debt limits future debt capacity, which can mean future and profitable business opportunities are out of reach for the firm.
3. Agency costs represented by the divergence of interest between equity investors and fund providers are ever present. This type of conflict causes parties to protect their respective rights by adding covenants, reducing financing, and modifying dividend policies. The natural consequence of this situation is increasing costs to monitor and service the debt.

Debt assessing tools identify a company's optimum level of debt. The first tool is the cost of a capital approach, which helps understand the debt to equity ratio that minimizes the company's cost of capital and maximizes its value. This approach is easy to use but does not include agency and bankruptcy costs. These are included when the optimal leveraged structure generates a combination between cash flow and cost of capital to maximize the firm's value.

The last tool is the adjusted present value method, which evaluates the costs and the benefits of debt separately without including any indirect costs.

### 6.5.3.3    Condition for a Good and Bad Buy Out

To realize a successful LBO, it is absolutely necessary that the feasibility conditions are satisfied. Investors will only conclude the acquisition if they are sure the target company will satisfy all of its financial obligations. These conditions can be classified into two groups: generic conditions connected with the target company and specific conditions linked to the financial structure of both the target and the new company.

There are three generic conditions:

1. The company should mature enough to guarantee, with a high degree of certainty, the availability of abundant cash flow necessary for debt repayment.
2. Target company balance sheets should be full of assets easily used as debt collateral or as a source of cash through asset stripping or securitization operations.

3. Previous shareholders should be willing to sell their participations in the target company to reduce costs and the time needed for negotiation and transaction activities.

There are three specific conditions:

1. Annual free cash flow unlevered from the target company that is higher than the yearly reimbursement of the debt.
2. Earnings before interest and tax (EBIT) of the target company is higher than the annual financial interests.
3. Company operations should guarantee the improvement of the post buy out rating of the company as a result of reducing debt cost.

It is important to emphasize that the firms operating in markets with intense levels of growth and offering high-tech products are unsuitable for a buy out because of the huge funds needed to support the increase in commercial credits, stocks, and marketing expenses as well as the resources necessary to enlarge the production structure. There is always a risk of high-tech products becoming obsolete, which not only causes enormous costs from a research and development aspect, but it is impossible for these products to be used as collateral for fund providers.

In conclusion, the ideal target company has to operate as a leader in a mature market, offer nonsophisticated products, and have a solid balance sheet containing mostly material assets, especially liquid assets, such as cash and cash equivalents, as it will have to pay off the loans that have been used to buy it out.

# CHAPTER 7

# Investing in Mature Companies: Vulture Financing

## 7.1 INTRODUCTION

This chapter is the last one of the three chapters devoted to private equity deals that target mature companies. This chapter explores the financing by a private equity of those companies finding themselves in a crisis or in a distressed situation. These kinds of deals are included in the umbrella label of "vulture financing."

## 7.2 GENERAL OVERVIEW OF VULTURE FINANCING

A vulture financing deal (Fig. 7.1) is an investment realized in a company that is facing a financial and economic crisis or is close to declaring bankruptcy. When a private equity decides to invest in a distressed financing deal it has to consider the pros and cons of bankruptcy, because it is negotiated with public authorities, under specific laws and rules, and without the freedom to act that characterize the business rules of financial markets.

The cash injected by the investor is used by the company to sustain the financial gap generated from the negative sign of the growth rate. The financial and business support provided by the private equity investor is used to launch a survival plan if the company is in a crisis, or to re-sell the valuable assets of the defaulted company.

Due to the life stage in which such deal occurs, this activity is very risky, even though the level of risk also depends on the business of the venture-backed company. For this reason, it is fundamental for a private equity that wants to operate in this cluster, to be business oriented, as the investor has to value all the assets and, potentially, scout the market to find buyers.

In the light of what explained above, it can be gathered that distressed financing is a hybrid form of investment halfway between expansion and

**79**

Private Equity and Venture Capital in Europe. https://doi.org/10.1016/B978-0-12-812254-9.00007-3

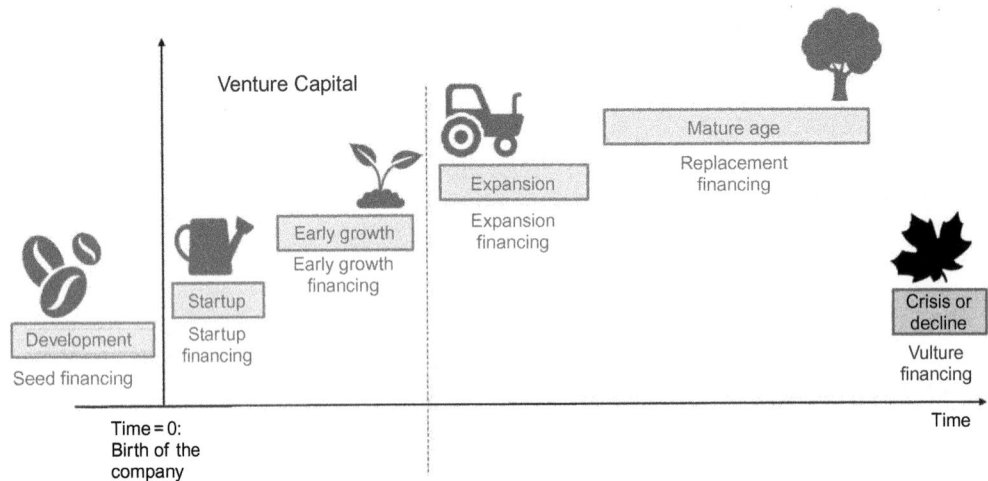

**FIG. 7.1** Vulture financing.

replacement financing. However, it makes one wonder why a private investor would decide to acquire a distressed firm. The answer is found in the valuation and comparison between the total value of specific assets included in the balance sheet of the target company, such as licenses and patents, and the negotiated acquisition price. The only way to manage the risk and return of this type of deal is to buy a company at a very low price, and this is easily done when a private equity investor purchases a company that is facing a crisis through the courts.

There are two main strategies applied by the private equity after it took control over the company: to immediately resell the company or gamble on its restructuring after considering the potential of its intangible assets.

The strategy applied by the investor depends on the kind of deal undertaken, as "vulture financing" includes two types of operations:

- restructuring financing and
- distressed financing,

Where the first one targets companies facing a crisis and that have not filed for bankruptcy yet. The second one targets the companies that have filed for bankruptcy.

In both deals, the approach of the investor is hands on and the stake owned by the investor is a majority (if not a 100% one).

## 7.3  CHARACTERISTICS OF RESTRUCTURING FINANCING

Restructuring financing deals with companies that find themselves in a crisis that is putting at stake their survival on the market.

The need of financing (hence, the need of the private equity investor) derives from the settlements of debts with banks and with suppliers. At the same time, the cash injected by the investor may be used to relaunch the business. This means that the funds are addressed to the purchase of further assets or to the redesign of the business plan.

These activities are carried together by the private equity investor and the venture-backed company as the distressed company needs the intervention of the private equity investor not only for financing purposes, but also for advisory purposes.

In addition to the restructuring and redesign of the asset side, restructuring deals can be identified on the liability side, as well. The main difference between this option and the asset side restructuring is that the group of financial creditors of the target company must agree on the deal. The agreement is usually composed of these elements:

1. Debt restructuring—Debt can be redefined in different ways: consolidation that reschedules for a longer term and debt maturities as well as reduction of the debt cost.
   - Debt settlement that closes the debt in front of the payment of only a part of the total debt.
   - Debt to equity swap is an accountability movement that converts all the existing debt, or a part of it, into risk capital.
   - Convertible bonds or with warrant—The financial creditor receives bonds with options to convert them into shares. This is a common tool that makes it possible to realize capital gain or take over the company.
2. Cost of financial resources.
3. Guarantees and covenants—Agreements that include rules protecting the creditors' interests. Guarantees usually concern real estate properties of the company, while covenants constrain the management of the firm such as limiting the investments or prohibiting asset dispositions.

Due to the high level of risk that characterize these deals, it is not frequent to find a private equity investor in this kind of deals that can be more easily found in the investment banking business. Nonetheless, the role private equity investors play in such deals is fundamental as they can change the future of the company. For this reason, an example is provided in Box 7.1. The case

> ## BOX 7.1 VALTUR. A PRIVATE EQUITY DEAL IN RESTRUCTURING FINANCING IN ITALY
>
> Valtur is an Italian tour operator founded in 1964. The company targets families belonging to the middle-income class, for whom it offers "all-inclusive" holiday packs. Valtur owns at the moment 14 structures in Italy and 1 in Croatia that can be enjoyed either in wintertime or in summertime.
>
> Valtur, headquartered in Milan, created the all-inclusive model "holiday village" in Italy. Its main distribution channels include a network of travel agencies and tour operators, and direct online channel through the company website. As one of the first-mover in this business of "organized travels," Valtur experienced a fast-pace growth until the late 1990s. In those years, people started to think of different ways of planning holidays and this trend was neither helped nor smoothed by the financial crisis that hit Europe in the late 2000s.
>
> In May 2016, Invest Industrial invested in the Group with the goal to generate value in the long run by helping Valtur grow and improve operational efficiency letting the founding family keep a minority holding.
>
> The investor, Invest Industrial, is a player specialized in mature companies in their mid-size (Valtur grosses around €75 million in 2015).

presented is a typical example of when the private equity is the right investor for a company finding itself in a temporary downturn.

## 7.4   CHARACTERISTICS OF DISTRESSED FINANCING

Distressed financing target companies that filed for bankruptcy.

Distressed financing can be executed by reorganizing the target company on the asset or liabilities side. As for the liability side, one should make reference to what has been presented in the previous paragraph. If asset restructuring is chosen, the private equity investor (or, the vulture investor) has to decide which assets are kept and which are divested to recover some value out of the target company. Asset redefinition is the starting point for the restructuring plan.

Contrarily to replacement financing, distressed financing is a very common deal for private equity investors, despite the high risk of the deal.

Why it is convenient to recover a distressed firm? This question can be answered after reviewing the three levels of distressed financing activity:

1. The opportunity to rationalize the existing structure of the target company—Focuses on the elements that generate economic results and reduce items of the net working capital. Operations on the working capital improve the company's capacity to create cash flows (especially unlevered).

2. Asset divestment—Selling assets, such as real estate properties, that can be sold directly or through extraordinary financial operations. Sometimes, assets are bought before a court, and the negotiation process can be tough between the court and the investor. As the court wants to maximize the liquidity of a company, so that it can pay off its debts. Other times, the court implements the "poison pill." This means that the private equity investor is going to buy a valuable asset mandatorily together with another less valuable assets or together with a debt of the company.

3. Extraordinary financial operations focused on specific strategic business units—To reorganize, the decision to sell out specific divisions, controlled companies, and branches has to be made. The vulture investor decides which area has to be divested after considering the strategic business served by the company and the valuation of the linkages and synergies (productive, commercial, and technological) existing between the business units. These areas are classified as no core business; core, no strategic business; and core strategic business. The first divisions to be sold are in the no core area. It can be difficult to sell the core and no strategic businesses because they should be maintained if possible.

Asset reorganization can be typically realized through:

1. Breaking down operations, which consist of an asset exchange between the operating and the financial management. External growth strategies without investing cash resources can be realized with this option.

2. Tracking stocks are special shares issued by a company and directly linked to the performance of a specific branch or division.

3. Carve outs and spin-offs are realized by dividing two or more branches or divisions to allow shareholders to reorganize the composition of their investments portfolio and, at the same time, to take out parties of the company still profitable.

# Legal and Fiscal Framework in the Private Equity Business

# CHAPTER 8

# Legal Framework in Europe for Equity Investors

## 8.1 INTRODUCTION

In the European Union (EU), private equity is considered as a financial service and, as such, it is supervised by the appropriate authority. Because it is supervised private equity financing is perceived as safer, more stable, and easier to control than unsupervised financing. Unfortunately, safety and regulations are put in place in exchange for higher costs and more specific constraints.

The second section in this chapter introduces options available for private equity finance throughout Europe, while the following section underlines differences and common rules of the EU. The most remarkable aspects of the fund-asset management company system are outlined in Sections 8.4 and 8.5.

Section 8.6 explains the relationship between closed-end funds and asset management companies (AMCs) and defines management fees and carried interest. The last section describes the vehicles available for private equity finance in the EU.

## 8.2 DIFFERENT FINANCIAL INSTITUTIONS THAT INVEST IN EQUITY: AN INTRODUCTION TO THE EU SYSTEM

According to the EU rules, private equity is considered as a financial activity and must be supervised. Private equity firms must comply with rules that regulate the entire European financial system. For example, in the Italian market and, more in general in the European Union, the organizational structure of investments in equity is regulated by

- Banking Act (1988–93)
- Financial Services Act (1998)
- AIFM Directive (Alternative Investment Fund Managers) (2011)
- MiFID (Markets in Financial Instruments Directive—2014, amending AIFMD)

Private Equity and Venture Capital in Europe. https://doi.org/10.1016/B978-0-12-812254-9.00008-5

As a Union of Member States, the EU issues directives that must be implemented on a local level with *ad hoc* laws. In Europe, these are the players allowed to carry on private equity operations:

- Banks
- Investment firms
- Closed-end funds (based on the UK or US models)

Banks and investment firms deal in credit intermediation, so investment in equity is only one of the activities they can undertake, and it will be explained later why they rarely undertake it. On the other hand, investment in equity is the core activity of closed-end fund.

## 8.3 BANKS AND INVESTMENT FIRMS: COMMON RULES AND DIFFERENCES IN THE EU

### 8.3.1 Banks

According to the EU legislation, banks can develop any kind of financial business except:

- Asset management activity
- Insurance activity
- Nonfinancial activities unrelated to financial activities

Nevertheless, banks are allowed to hold equities of AMCs, insurance companies, and nonfinancial firms. As such, they can invest in private companies, either directly or through an AMC.

Some countries have fixed rules due to the specific relationship between banks and nonfinancial firms. According to EU rules, if a bank invests in equity, it must cap the investment because equity investments, as well as other banking assets, affect regulatory capital. This means that the bank has to set aside some regulatory capital as a buffer in case of a collapse of the participated company.

The caps applied are similar throughout Europe, with an exception of Germany where there are no caps. This comes from the tradition of the German "Hausbank" relationship between firms and banks.

There are two groups of constraints applied to private equity investment:

- Capital adequacy
- Cap rules

Ordinary banks have regulatory capital under €1 billion, banks with permission have regulatory capital over €1 billion and manage equity, and specialized banks have regulatory capital over €1 billion and manage long-term equity and liabilities.

Caps applied to each category of bank have these distinctions:

- Concentration cap is related to every private equity investment and is calculated on the bank's equity.
- Global cap also refers to the bank's equity; however, it is related to the portfolio of investments held by the bank and includes the sum of all equity investments the bank holds in its portfolio. The cap is calculated using the equity of the bank.
- Division cap (or specific cap) refers to the owned company's equity. It is a specific investment using the equity of the company being invested as the variable instead of the bank's equity (see Table 8.1).

We should emphasize that there are further divergences because, in the Banking Act, there are no fixed parameters and the decision to apply caps is left to the regulator of each country. So we find two groups of countries:

1. Germany and France apply constraints. Banks can hold as much as 100% of a company's equity;
2. The rest of Europe allows a maximum investment of 15% of a company's equity.

Table 8.2 illustrates the calculation formulas related to the above mentioned caps.

**Table 8.1** Constraints Applied to Banks When Investing in Private Equity

|  | Concentration Cap (Computed for Each Investment) | Global Cap (Computed for the Whole Equity Portfolio) | Division Cap (Computed for Each Investment) |
|---|---|---|---|
| Ordinary banks | 3% of regulatory capital | 15% of regulatory capital | 15% of the owned company's equity |
| Banks with permission | 6% of regulatory capital | 50% of regulatory capital | 15% of the owned company's equity |
| Specialized banks | 15% of regulatory capital | 60% of regulatory capital (only for qualified equities) | 15% of the owned company's equity |

**Table 8.2** Calculation Formulas for Caps

$$\text{Concentration cap} = \frac{\text{Each investment}}{\text{Regulatory capital}}$$

$$\text{Global cap} = \frac{\sum \text{Investments}}{\text{Regulatory capital}}$$

$$\text{Division cap} = \frac{\text{Investments}}{\text{Company's equity}}$$

### 8.3.1.1    The Role of Basel Frameworks on Private Equity Investments for Banks and Investments Firms

The Basel III Accord updates the contents and constraints introduced by the two previous edition of the Framework (when referring to the Basel Framework, it is made reference to Basel I, released in 1988 and implemented in 1992, Basel II released in 2004 and Basel III, issued in 2013 and that was supposed to be adopted by 2017, but which will become effective in 2019). It updates the comprehensive measure and minimum standard for capital adequacy that national supervisory authorities are asked to implement through domestic rule-making and adoption procedures.

It is not the purpose of this book to explain the effects of the Basel Framework, but it must be emphasized that, according to the European directive on the capital adequacy of investment firms and credit institutions adopted in each country by *ad hoc* rules, private equity finance does not represent a profitable business for either investment firms or banks.

Among all assets, private equity (and venture capital) is declared as one of the most risky, and for this reason it requires a high level of capital to be set aside in the case a loss occurs. The Basel Committee suggests that national authorities use a risk weight of 150% or higher for investments made by banks directly in the equity of private companies.

At the same time and according to the same principles, participations in firms denominated as equity exposures follow similar rules. For regulatory and supervisory purposes, participations must be deducted from the capital base for the risk-weighted capital ratio calculation or must be risk-weighted at no lower than 100% independent of the approach used by financial institutions.

These rules do not ban direct and indirect investments in equity. Instead, they enormously reduce the opportunities, because banks and financial institutions find this type of deal very expensive compared with other transactions. In summary, the Basel Framework (and national authorities) assumes that banks and investment firms are not the right vehicles for promoting private equity and venture capital finance among countries.

According to the Banking Act, caps must always be respected. The Basel frameworks create new limitations for the capital ratio calculation for investments in insurance and financial companies. Participations in these firms, for regulatory and supervisory purposes, must be deducted from the capital base. For general equity exposures a special risk weight system is provided.

Private equity and venture capital deals are contemplated as "high risk" exposures so they must be risk-weighted at 100% (under the standard approach option). If the company the bank invests in shows negative net earnings for 2 years, the risk-weighted percentage is 200%.

If banks adopt the internal rating base (IRB) approach the treatment is the same and the high risk assumption remains. For equity participations different from those deducted from the capital base, there are three models. The simplest model, which is also the most wide-ranging, calculates the exposure at default (EAD) using these percentages:

- In all, 190% for private equity instruments only if diversification is adequate
- In all, 290% for listed equity instruments
- In all, 370% for all others equity instruments

Contrarily to the loss given default (LGD) factor of 45% that is a reference point for certain debt exposures, private, well-diversified equity instruments have an assumed LGD of 65% and 90% for all other cases.

## 8.3.2 Investment Firms

The second legal entity that can undertake a private equity investment is the investment firm. To start up an investment firm in Europe a firm must be regulated and supervised.

Investment firms cannot develop banking activity, but they can undertake the following financing acitivities:

- Equity investment
- Lending
- Payment services and money transfers
- Currency brokerage and dealing

According to EU legislation, all of the above listed activities are carried out with no limits and no caps. Investment firms in Europe are regulated by the Banking Directive and can undertake the same activity as banks with the exception of collecting money through deposits.

According to the regulation they comply to, there are two kinds of investment firms:

- Type 1 Investment firms
- Type 2 Investment firms

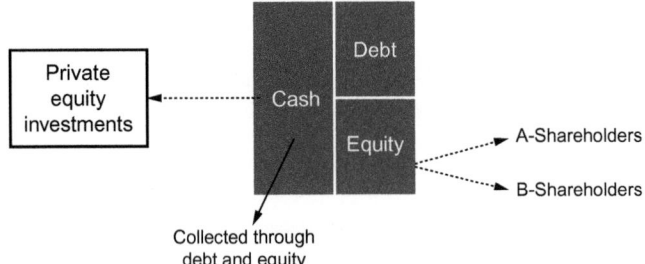

**FIG. 8.1** Investment firm shareholding structure.

Type 1-investment firms do not have any specific constraints to manage their activities and the supervision impact is quite soft and they do not undergo any regulatory capital rules. Type 2-investment firms face the same constraints set for banks and for them the supervision impact is hard. In this case, all investments undertaken by the firm entail a regulatory capital as if they were banks.

Regardless of the category of investment firms they belong to, they are owned by two typologies of shareholders. The two roles are necessary to replicate, in the investment firm, the relation existing between managers and investors within other forms of funds investing in private equity. The intent of the Authority is then to re-create a relation where one of the two parties manages the funds committed by the other party, where the latter does not have the power to decide the destinations of the funds (Fig. 8.1). More in detail:

- *A-shareholders* act as managers. They are remunerated with management fees and with a yearly carried interest.
- *B-shareholders* act purely as investors and cannot influence the management of the investment. They are remunerated with the difference between the profits and the carried interest given to A-shareholders.

There may be at least two main reasons to use investment firms to invest PE:

- Investors may want to leverage (it will be explored later how closed-end funds cannot leverage).
- A small group of investors may want to create a captive vehicle and they do not want to comply to very strict regulations. Such is the example of the so-called "family offices," a group of family members who wants to invest their own money.

## 8.4 CLOSED-END FUNDS

According to the definition of financial services proposed by the EU, there are some activities that cannot be offered by banks directly[1] but can be managed by specialized organizations such as funds, special investment firms, and other structures accepted by single country regulations.

## EQUITY INVESTMENTS THROUGH BANKS AND INVESTMENT FIRMS

"Golden rules" followed by banks and investment firms regarding equity investment:

- Equity investment is free for investment firms, while it is capped for banks
- Banks can operate on a wider basis than investment firms by giving deeper assistance and care to participated companies
- No caps for holding equity investment
- Both for banks and investment firms, the investment in equity generates a usage of regulatory capital
- Rules generated by the Basel Framework make private equity finance costly for banks and investment firms
- The usage of regulatory capital means the internal rate of return (IRR) of the investment must be compared and correlated to the cost of used regulatory capital.

In private equity business, the most relevant nonbanking activity is asset management, because it assumes a direct or indirect investment in firms. The following sections provide more detail about the most common structures used throughout Europe to invest in private equity.

There are two reference structures used to manage investment in private companies:

- Limited partnership
- Funds and AMCs

---

[1]According to the EU, there are six activities that banks cannot manage directly. They are also known as financial services and are regulated by the Financial Services Act:

- Dealing—buying and selling securities to obtain a profit
- Brokerage—buying and selling securities on a customer's behalf; in this case no risk is taken from the financial institution's side, therefore the profit derives from fees only
- Selling—selling the customer's securities in the primary market
- Underwriting—buying the securities in the primary market; the financial institution assumes the whole risk of the percentage of securities underwritten
- Individual (personal) asset management—managing the assets of private investors on an individual basis
- Nonindividual asset management—managing private individuals' wealth on a nonindividual basis; best used for its diversification advantages (since the wealth of a single investor might be not enough to appropriately diversify the portfolio of investments) and its related benefits

Limited partnerships are available in both the United Kingdom and the United States and will be presented in Chapter 9. The fund structures are presented in the following sections.

### 8.4.1   Funds

Funds are financial institutions where a separate manager or firm (AMC) manages a specific amount of money that does not necessarily belong to them. The operating structure of a fund is seen in Fig. 8.2. Funds are by far the most widespread vehicle in continental Europe to do private equity.

Because European legislation requires supervision of financial institutions, control of the responsible managers becomes inevitable. Managers created a separate entity, the so-called AMC, in countries where the fund system is adopted, the AMC is one of the financial institutions included and defined by acts providing for financial services management.

Generally speaking, there are three main groups of funds:

- Open-end funds
- Closed-end funds
- Hedge fund

An *open-end fund* is defined as a floating-sized fund; investors are able to enter and exit without specific time limits. The most relevant features of this fund are:

- Liquidity. It should be able to manage its liquidity at any time, which is the reason it invests mainly in listed securities.
- It is principally dedicated to the retail market.
- It cannot invest in private equity.
- It cannot leverage.

---

PAUSE: Can you think why an open-end fund can not invest in private equity?

---

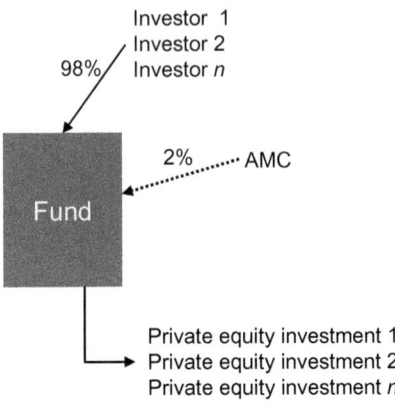

**FIG. 8.2** The organizational structure of funds.

A *closed-end fund* includes nonfloating size funds; investor are able to invest only at the initial phase of the fund (during the fundraising process described in Chapter 12) and exit only at the life-end of the fund. This fund can invest in private equity because private equity business needs resources and liquidity without any kind of exit pressure from the investor's side. Closed-end funds are a separate entity that invests money for a group of investors. The relationship between parties involved is mainly based on mutual trust. Investors invest their own money in a specific fund because they trust the manager's ability to successfully manage their money. Like the open-end fund, it cannot leverage. This means that the capital collected among the investors is the only (and maximum) monetary basis that can be used to undertake the investments.

A *hedge fund* is a fund that is allowed to leverage unlike the other two types of funds described above. It can be either an open- or closed-end fund depending on its purpose. The fund supervisor decides who invests in the fund (i.e., according to EU regulations, retail investors cannot invest in these funds due to the high risk).

The scheme used to invest in private equity is a double-level system made of the:

- AMC
- Closed-end fund

### 8.4.2  AMC

An AMC is a financial institution that hosts funds (both closed- and open-end) and manages financial services as defined by the Banking Acts (i.e., AMC may supply personal management of savings, dealing, brokerage, or advisory).

Rules concerning AMCs are the same throughout Europe. The set of rules for closed-end funds is very short with regulatory activity delegated to the country's supervisor and the internal code of activity of each fund created. This will be explained in more detail later in the following sections.

Generally speaking, AMCs can manage only one type of fund, either an open- or closed-end. This country-specific rule is in place to better regulate the typical relation between companies and the financial system.

Rules for AMCs:

- Minimum requisites to operate
- Governance
- Management

The application of these rules is verified from the supervisor of the country in which the AMC operates, and they can be partially modified from one country to another. Supervision is carried out for the life of the AMC.

### 8.4.2.1   The Minimum Requisites to Operate for AMC

The minimum requisites to operate for AMCs are similar in all EU countries:

1. Regulatory capital should exceed €1 million or should be over €0.12 million for the so-called "short capital asset management company" (junior asset management company)
   Should prepare a detailed business plan that clearly shows:
   a. Activities
   b. Services and products
   c. Organizational structure
   d. Future development of the company;
   e. Economic and financial forecasted statements
2. Shareholders must show requisites of capability to manage the company
3. AMC has to allow easy supervision

According to the law, junior capital AMC is very similar to standard AMC, but there are some fundamental differences:

- Junior capital AMCs should manage and promote closed-end funds only
- Majority shareholders should belong to universities, research centers, public institutions, public or private foundations, and chambers of commerce
- The amount of money managed at the start-up must be under €25 million
- Subscribers of the closed-end fund must be qualified and not retailers
- The minimum subscription must be €0.25 million

The mission must be venture capital financing and/or high-tech venture financing

Junior AMCs are usually set up by municipalities and regions encouraging investments in seed and start-up financing phases. In Europe no university owns a junior AMC.

Nevertheless, the disadvantage of a junior capital AMC is the elevated risk to investments. These investments require more invested equity to benefit from diversification. Therefore, considering their "short" capital determined by law, they are unable to diversify, so the risk borne by investors is quite high.

### 8.4.2.2  Governance Rules for AMC

All minimum requisites are actively controlled and monitored by a supervisor:

- Board of directors must show, at any time, requisites of "professional attitude, honor, and independence" (this is the only constraint applied by the Financial Services Act for the AMC, which is not used for any other financial institution regulated by the same act)
- Shareholders must grant fair management within the company
- No caps or limits is applied for any category of shareholders (i.e., the shareholding structure can be composed by banks, insurance companies, etc.)
- Management must be expressly stated and based on a strong organization

### 8.4.2.3  Management Rules for AMC

The supervisor also controls and monitors the following requirements that must be met by the AMC to perform the management activity:

- The AMC can develop a range of financial services as outlined in the Financial Services Act
- The AMC develops (and sells) consulting services in the field of corporate finance and strategies only for closed-end funds
- The AMC has to subscribe to at least 2% of every fund managed (closed- or open-end), creating a commitment to investors' interests
- Regulatory capital is driven only from operational and financial risks

## 8.4.3  Closed-End Funds

As previously mentioned, funds are a separate[2] pool of money given from the subscribers and managed by the AMC. This money is used to invest in financial assets or in other assets such as real estate, gold, etc. The funds can be open- or closed-end. As explained, the distinction is driven by two parameters:

- Maturity (fixed or not)
- Amount of money to invest (fixed or not)

Closed-end funds have a fixed maturity and a fixed amount of money to invest and thanks to these two features are allowed to invest in private equity. Because of the strong distinction between open and closed-end funds, it is typical to find that:

- Open-end funds are mostly retail oriented and their securities representative are listed on the stock exchange

---

[2]This amount of money, invested by the fund's investors, is separated from the asset management company.

- Closed-end funds are most often oriented toward institutional investors and their securities are rarely listed
- Investors in open-end funds take their profit or loss from selling the securities continuously and when they want
- Investors in closed-end funds get their profit or loss at the end of the fund's life, after the total disinvestment has taken place and after the fund has been closed, contrarily to what happens in investment firms, where the carried interest is distributed on a yearly basis, due to its indefinite lifetime.

Rules for closed-end funds include

1. General framework:
   - Maturity
   - Disinvestment process
   - Certificate
   - Loans
   - Amount of investments
2. Internal code of activity:
   - A clear pattern of rules
   - A complete set of rules
   - A synthetic approach
3. Investment policy:
   - Assets fund may invest in
   - Assets fund may not invest in
   - Limitation on asset allocation
   - Limitation on asset management
4. Relationships with the market:
   - Presence of public offering
   - Absence of public offering

In Europe the internal code of activity, according to the AMC funds system is not a contract but an act that must be submitted and approved by the supervisor defining the relationship between the AMC and the fund investors. It is a set of managerial rules supervised by authorities to be used during the life of the fund: it is a strong expression of the freedom of an AMC.

### 8.4.3.1  General Framework for Closed-End Funds

To create a structure for the development and use of closed-end funds, a number of general variables must be defined; for example, rules concerning maturity and amount of investment loans and securities grants to financial institutions and investors so they can evaluate the strategic consequences of their involvement.

The closed-end fund can have a maximum maturity of 30 years and the duration has to be strictly linked to the profile of investments. In Europe the average maturity is around 10–12 years. This typical time horizon is such that it allows to invest and exit twice from the investments over the life of the fund, considering a time necessary to raise the committed capital, a holding period of 3–4 years per investment, and the time necessary to find a potential buyer for the stake when the time to exit comes, considering that the latter can last several months.

> REMEMBER: PE is an illiquid investment. The whole business knows the private equity investor has a liquidity problem and this makes it very hard for the investor to find the right buyer without selling the stake for a lower value.

The total disinvestment cannot be realized all at once and, for this reason, general rules allow an extra-time to complete this phase. The EU disinvestment process can be extended for an extra 3-year time after the fixed maturity of the fund. The AMC can disinvest without investor approval, but investors should be notified at least 6 months before the fund closure. There are specific rules about the investment process. It must last for a maximum of 18 months and at the end it is possible to revise down the amount of money of the fund.

Specific regulations are also provided for securities issued by closed-end funds. The original securities have to be listed on the stock exchange if their value is under €25,000. However, the IPO and the listing in a stock exchange are very unusual for closed-end funds, because the portfolio of investments is mainly composed of private companies so the value of the securities cannot be fairly measured. The average value of each investment certificate size is of €1 million.

It must be underlined that the value of securities is set by the AMC. By law, there is a floor of €50,000 when investments are concentrated on unlisted assets.

The general framework is particularly severe about lending. Loans can be used by the AMC only when the AMC registers a lack of liquidity due to the transfer of disinvested amounts (the lack of liquidity is only a matter of days and occurs when the transfer of money requires a number of days; to respect the deadline date, this gap is covered by a loan). Through leveraging, the AMC gives the money back to fund subscribers before the end of the fund's maturity, but the amount of loans cannot exceed 10% of the overall investment.

Rules are also set for investments. The amount of investment is fixed and decided by the AMC (in Europe the average size of a fund is around €200 million to 400 million, while funds exceeding the amount of €1 billion are called mega-funds). No caps or floors are set by law, since this is mostly a matter of negotiation between the AMC and the supervising authority.

Finally, the general framework for a closed-end fund is characterized by the commitment plan: the investor commits himself to meet the percentage of the investment required by the AMC when investing. This is necessary because investments are not undertaken immediately after the fundraising phase, but during the first 2–3 years of the operating life of the fund. Investors must commit to pay the required amount during the investment period. This is mainly based on the mutual trust between parties.

### 8.4.3.2    Internal Code of Activities for Closed-End Funds

In the presence of a very detailed general framework, EU regulations still allow the AMCs independence and self-determination to define the closed-end funds they want to manage. According to the law, the AMC regulates each closed-end fund regarding certification size, maturity of the fund, geographical area of investments, etc.

These items represent the internal code of activities; the specific set of rules followed by a closed-end fund. Generally the internal code of activity can be divided into three parts:

1. Detailed scheme for each of the managed funds
2. Technical and legal profiles of the managed funds
3. The way of the fund works

The internal code lists critical traits that distinguish vehicles:

- Typologies of investment (typologies of shares, liquidity percentage, geographic areas)
- Use or no use of loans (percentage, goals, maturity)
- Governance rules within the venture-backed firms
- Amount of fees given to the AMC
- Criteria of subscribing the certificates
- Criteria of divesting
- Criteria of payback for subscribers
- Criteria of calculation (at least every 6 months) of the current value of certificates

### 8.4.3.3    The Investment Policy for Closed-End Funds

The closed-end fund internal code is the most important document for closed-end fund strategy and management. It is not only related to the general characteristics of the fund, but it also defines internal policies.

The internal code defines instruments, securities, and deals in which the fund can or cannot invest. Closed-end funds *can* invest in

- Financial instruments
- Real estate
- Commercial credits
- Other goods that have a market where quotations are available at least every 6 months
- Banking deposits
- Cash

Closed-end funds *cannot* invest in

- Forwards
- Securities issued by the AMC
- Securities issued by (or goods sold by) AMC shareholders

The investment policy is also related to asset allocation and use of voting rights. For closed-end funds there are several limitations:

- A total of 20% cap to invest within the same issuer for unlisted securities
- A total of 5% cap to invest within the same issuer for listed securities (up to 35% if securities are granted from a EU government or from an international institution)
- A total of 20% cap to invest in the same bank's deposit
- A total of 10% cap to invest in OTC derivatives
- In all, 30% cap to invest in financial assets issued by subjects belonging to the same group

At the same time, AMCs have to consider their limits:

- A total of 10% cap of voting rights within a listed company
- No possibility of full ownership on a listed company (except for LBO deals, where the maturity of the investment is short)

### 8.4.3.4 Definition of Public and "Reserved" Offer

For AMCs or closed-end funds, the relation with potential investors is key in order to distinguish when a public offer occurs.

Here the law is very simple: a public offer can never occur when the closed-end fund is "reserved." A closed-end fund is considered reserved if:

1. It is dedicated to less than 100 investors
2. The value of the certificates is higher than €50,000
3. Investors are all professional ones

When there is a public offer it is necessary to set up a circular offer and an information memorandum, applying local country rules.

Securities can be listed on the stock exchange, if the internal dealing code anticipates this possibility. However, the minimum amount to go public and trade on the stock exchange is €25 million for each fund. It is then necessary to follow domestic procedures to enter the stock exchange, which are the same as for an IPO (in Europe, a specialist is required).

## 8.5   REASONS FOR CHOOSING A CLOSED-END FUND RATHER THAN BANKS OR INVESTMENT FIRMS

The "golden rules" for equity investment in closed-end funds are different when compared with banks and investment firms:

- Equity investment is not capped for closed-end funds
- Closed-end funds can operate on a basis as wide as banks can only if they are related or joined with a banking group
- There is a cap to the holding period for the equity investment related to the maturity of the closed-end fund
- The investment in equity does not generate a usage of regulatory capital
- The IRR of the investment must be compared and correlated to the cumulated IRR of the portfolio and to the target IRR of the closed-end fund.

## 8.6   THE RELATIONSHIP BETWEEN CLOSED-END FUNDS AND AMCs: ECONOMIC AND FINANCIAL LINKS

The relationship between the AMC and the closed-end fund is quite complex both economically and financially (see Fig. 8.3). Groups with a significant role in this relationship include

- AMCs
- AMC's board of directors
- Closed-end fund(s)

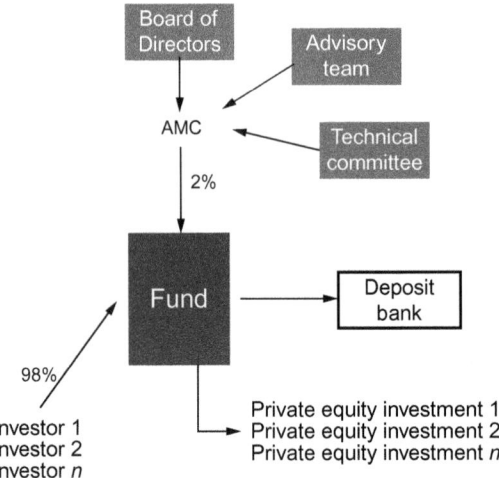

**FIG. 8.3** The relation among the AMC, closed-end fund, and the main groups involved.

- Investors
- Custodian or deposit bank
- Advisory team (or company)
- Technical committee
- Anchor investor

The AMC is composed of

1. Board of Directors—Oftentimes agrees with its shareholders who decide to launch the AMC
2. Advisory Company—External company that by law must be completely separate from the AMC
3. Technical Committee

Tasks and duties for all groups involved are quite clear and stated:

- AMC has the responsibility to manage the closed-end fund, even though the assets coming from investors are separate from AMC assets. AMC is responsible within the investors.
- AMC's Board of Directors is responsible for managing the AMC.
- Closed-end fund(s) are owned and managed by the AMC.
- Investors purchase certificates issued from the closed-end fund.
- Custodian bank receives the money raised by the fundraising process from the fund.
- Advisory team (or company). If it exists, it is a company chosen from the AMC to analyze potential investment, develop due diligence, and evaluate exit strategy.
- Technical committee is a team of technicians operating inside the AMC. It supports the Board of Directors to define strategies, to monitor the market, and to share the recommendations coming from the advisory company
- Anchor investor, if any, is the investor holding a stake particularly relevant in the fund (minimum at 20%). As the main investor, he has a very active role in attracting other investors to the fund. For this reason, he finds himself in a very strong position with respect to the private equity investor that launched the fund: he is aware of the fact that the fund would not be launched without his name or brand dragging other investors' capital. This is why, the private equity launching the investment usually agrees on some benefits; for instance, he gives the anchor investor the right of co-investing.

---

**Right of Co-Investing:** The right of co-investment is granted by an AMC to an investor when the latter played the role of "anchor investor" in a previous launch of a fund. When the AMC grants this right, it means that, if in the future it launches another fund, it will be forced to get the Anchor Investor on board before other potential investors.

---

### 8.6.1    General Overview of Costs and Revenues

The closed-end fund is the origin of costs and revenues for all groups. Its revenues include:

- Capital gain from investments
- Dividends and interests from investments
- Interest from deposit bank

Its costs include:

- Losses from investment
- Interest due for loans
- Management fee to AMC
- Carried interest to AMC

The AMC distributes costs and revenues created from the closed-end fund and receives as revenues:

- Entrance fee from investors
- Management fee from the closed-end fund
- Carried interest from the closed-end fund

The costs it bears are

- Operating costs
- Deposit bank fee
- Percentage of management fee for the advisor
- Percentage of carried interest to advisory company for its efforts with helping to identify the best-possible opportunities in the market

### 8.6.2    Management Fee

The management fee[3] is due annually[4] and is calculated as a percentage of the net asset value (NAV)[5] of the closed-end fund. However, the higher the management fee, the lower the amount of money left for investment activity. Defining the percentage of the management fee is negotiated between the AMC and investors, since it is in the best interest of the investor to pay a lower percentage of fixed costs, while the opposite holds true for the AMC.

This fee cannot be too low, because it is meant to cover all operating costs incurred by the AMC. The management fee is a gross fee, since it covers

---

[3]The average amount could range between 2% and 3.5%.

[4]It can be computed at the initial phase at time 0.

[5]Net asset value is the total value of the portfolio of investments less any liabilities. But, as mentioned previously, closed-end funds cannot leverage.

operating expenses, pays the Advisory company and the Technical committee and fixed costs, and in the end the remuneration[6] for the AMC director.

### 8.6.3 Carried Interest

Carried interest is due only at the end of the closed-end fund and it is a percentage[7] of the difference between the global IRR of the closed-end fund and a fixed interest rate ("hurdle rate" or "floor IRR") as defined at the starting date of the closed-end fund. It is computed as follows:

Carried interest $= \%$ [Final IRR $-$ Hurdle rate]

It is the percentage of profits the AMC receives from investors in the form of capital gain and it goes to the directors/managers of the fund itself.

Carried interest and the floor rate are fixed at the beginning of the fund's life and they appear at the internal code of activity of each fund. They are determined through long negotiations between investors and the AMC.

Sometimes, by using a private agreement, a predetermined percentage of both the management fee and the carried interest are transferred by the AMC to the advisory company. There is a strong link between the reputation of the Advisory company and the percentage it can obtain by the end of the disinvestment phase as capital gain.

More details about the remuneration of the fund will be given in Chapter 17.

## 8.7 VEHICLES FOR PRIVATE EQUITY FINANCE IN THE EU

Despite all attempts to standardize the regulatory approach in the EU, several financial institutions may be used as vehicles for the realization of private equity finance in each country. For example, in Italy, a closed-end fund is the best way to manage private equity finance, despite banks or investment firms that may also realize these deals.

The same conclusions may be reached for every European country. Throughout Europe, a double system is evident:

- Limited partnership model (similar to the United Kingdom and United States)
- AMC funds scheme

---

[6]Salaries but not the capital gain.

[7]Typically ranging between 15% and 40%.

Across Europe, the legal and tax environment is not homogeneous. Here are shortly presented some cases.

### 8.7.1 The Legal Framework for Private Equity Finance in France

France provides several structure typologies for private equity finance such as

- "Fonds commun de placement à risques" (FCPR)
- "Fonds commun de placement dans l'innovation" (FCPI)
- "Fonds d'investissement de proximité" (FIP)
- "Société de capital-risque" (SCR)

The first three are organized as funds in a collective investment scheme, while the SCR are commercial companies that have opted for special tax treatment with specific requirements. Among these options, the FCPR is the most common.

FCPR is a closed-end fund, but it is not a separate entity, therefore, it has no legal capacity to enter into agreements. Any agreement must be executed by the management company on the FCPR's behalf.

Management companies have to be approved by the Autorité des Marchés de France (AMF) and comply with organizational and conduct of business rules intended to ensure investor protection and the legality of transactions. The equity capital must be at least €125,000 and once authorized, it must be at any time equal or higher than

- €125,000 + 0.02%* asset under management in excess of €250,000
- A total of 25% of general expenses of the preceding financial year

Moreover, the FCPR and SCR must meet several quotas and ratios regarding their invested assets.

### 8.7.2 The Legal Framework for Private Equity Finance in Germany

In Germany there are no specific laws regarding private equity, but there are laws regarding promotion of venture capital and equity investment companies. Thus, under German law, there is no specific vehicle for private equity.

Theoretically, all legal corporate forms are available for private equity finance development. The most common and suitable form is the limited partnership where a limited liability company (GmbH) is a general partner (so-called GmbH & Co. KG). There are no restrictions on foreign entities who want to invest in Germany or want to market themselves to German investors.

German corporate law establishes that the minimum share capital depends on the legal form of entity: €25,000 for a limited liability company and €50,000 for

AG. Also, companies qualifying as either a venture capital company or equity investment company need a capital of €1 million.

### 8.7.3 The Legal Framework for Private Equity Finance in the Netherlands

There are no Dutch laws solely concerning private equity finance. The Financial Service Authority (AFS) interprets private equity operators as investment institutions that must be licensed and regulated under the existing financial laws.

Private equity deals may be realized using the available forms for nonfinancial companies. The options include public company (NV, Naamloze Vennootschap), mutual funds (FGR, Fonds voor Gemene Rekening), private company (BV, Besloten Vennootschap), or limited partnership (CV, Commanditaire Vennootschap). Limited partnership is the most common.

AFS regulated investment managers must have an equity capital of at least €225,000 if assets under management are above €250 million, €125,000 if below.

### 8.7.4 The Legal Framework for Private Equity Finance in Spain

In Spain nonregulated private equity vehicles (NRV) follow rules provided for commercial companies and regulated private equity vehicles (RV). RVs enjoy favorable tax treatment but have to comply with a number of regulatory requirements such as investment and concentration limits, reporting, and all regulatory rules issued by the market authority (CNMV).

Within RVs, the two structures most suitable for private equity finance are:

- Regulated private equity entities under corporate form or SCR
- Regulated private equity entities under contractual form (i.e., funds) or FCR

RVs have their own law and regulations, and they can be run by:

- Regulated private equity management companies (SGECR), which are regulated by specific private equity regulation and must have an initial capital of at least €300,000
- Investment collective scheme management companies (SGIIC), which are regulated and must have an initial capital not lower than the highest of the following amounts:
  1. €300,000 + specific amount depending on the executed activities
  2. In all, 25% of the structure costs of the previous fiscal year

There are no specific capital requirements or regulation rules for NRVs.

# CHAPTER 9

# Legal Framework in the United States and United Kingdom for Equity Investors

## 9.1 INTRODUCTION

In the Anglo-Saxon world (to the extent of this book by the expression "Anglo-Saxon" world, it is meant for the US and the UK environment unless otherwise specified) investments in equity are not regulated by financial system laws because of the common law framework. The general idea is that a market discipline is more powerful and important than regulating financial players. Hence, it can be inferred that private equity investment is not recognized as a financial service, rather as an entrepreneurial activity. These are reasons why UK and US legislators do not supervise private equity investors.

---

PAUSE: How is a private equity investment perceived in the Continental European Area?

---

When approaching this chapter, one should bear in mind the following:

- The private equity market in the United States is the largest one in the world, therefore it is able to identify the proper rules governing its activities
- The United Kingdom is the most important market in Europe with rules very similar to the US market

This chapter describes the regulating frameworks of the US and UK financial markets.

The second section introduces the topic and underlines different options available for private equity investments and causes that lead to the different financial environments of continental Europe and the United Kingdom. Sections 9.3 and 9.4 illustrate which financial vehicles are used in the United States and the United Kingdom, respectively. Section 9.5 presents some preliminary definition and calculation modalities of carried interest and management fees in the Anglo-Saxon environment. The last section analyzes the most important legal clauses signed in a limited partnership agreement (LPA).

**109**

Private Equity and Venture Capital in Europe. https://doi.org/10.1016/B978-0-12-812254-9.00009-7

## 9.2   WHY THE UNITED STATES AND UNITED KINGDOM DIFFER FROM THE EU: THE COMMON LAW VERSUS CIVIL LAW SYSTEM AND THE IMPACT OF SUPERVISION AND REGULATION

There are different vehicles/investors used to set up equity investments:

- Banks (and investment firms)
- Private firms
- Business Angels
- Specialized vehicles to invest

In each country's framework these vehicles/investors have different organizational structures and different involvement profiles as direct investors in equity investments.

The analysis of the private equity business cannot be generalized, as the most important features depend on how the policymakers create the legislative environment for the development of the whole industry, and how financial institutions interpret the industry and its capacity to create concrete opportunities for growth.

In both the United States and the United Kingdom, as mentioned, no special discipline for equity investment exists. However, it is possible to summarize some general rule about equity investments in the United Kingdom that differ from the European framework:

- No limits on holding shares for shareholders
- No distinction in investment based on the European "banking system" and "financial services system"
- Usage of rules for
  - Market discipline (corporate governance)
  - Investors duties and rights

## 9.3   RULES FOR US EQUITY INVESTORS

The US financial market is common law driven and great importance is given to laws from both local as well as federal courts. Federal laws have created a general framework for a financial system based on relevant financial activities, and not financial institutions.

The pillars are

- Discipline for stock exchange and securities—The stock exchange represents the financial market and there are no financial market laws in place.

- Corporate governance rules—Rules concerning the governance of each company issuing securities.
- Discipline for insurance and pension funds—These are the most important players in the US market; pension funds are the largest investors followed by insurance companies.
- General rules for banks—In the US banks do not collaborate with investment firms, so rules concern only banks; in the EU there are no equity holding constraints.[1]

In US fiscal history there are three main Acts that drive trends in equity investment development.

- Small Business Investment Act (1958)—Created small business investment companies (SBICs). These investment vehicles were set up as public-private partnerships to invest in private equity. The federal government backed the SBICs by giving them the financial support needed to invest in private equity and therefore enhance the development of the country.
- Revenue Act (1978)—Introduced the mark down for capital gain taxation. The federal government decided that private individuals investing in private equity are exempt from paying tax on capital gains when they are reinvested in private equity.
- Employee Retirement Income Security Act (1979)—This act wrote off the "prudent man rule"[2] facilitating investment in private equity for pension funds.

Despite these laws it is still impossible to find a specific discipline for equity investment, and a specific discipline for equity investment for the bank sector does not exist. However, from a legal point of view, equity investors in the United States could be

- Venture capital funds
- SBICs
- Corporate ventures
- Banks
- Business Angels

---

[1]This decision was made in 1999 after The Glass-Steagall Act was dismantled. This Act, was passed by Congress in 1933, prohibited commercial banks from collaborating with full-service brokerage firms or participating in investment banking activities.

[2]The Prudent Man Rule is based on common law stemming from an 1830 Massachusetts court decision, which adopted a standard to guide those responsible for investing other people's money. Per the standard, such fiduciaries (executors of wills, trustees, bank trust departments, and administrators of estates) must act as a prudent man or woman would be expected to act, with discretion and intelligence, to seek reasonable income, preserve capital, and, in general, avoid speculative investments.

Today, venture capital funds along with SBICs account for approximately 60% of the US private equity market, while the other investment vehicles (corporate ventures, banks, and Business Angels) account for the remaining 40%. In 2016, 1562 venture capital funds were managing $333 billion.

## 9.3.1 Venture Capital Funds

Venture capital funds (VCF) are not based on the European system of closed-end funds, it was in fact the European legislator that tried to implememt a successful way of investing in private equity in Europe after the good experience in the United States. The first thing that should be remarked is that VCF are the vehicle investing in the private company, but the legal entity beneath such vehicle is the limited partnerships (LP). The name refers to the limited liability of the providers (limited partners) of capital that is limited only to the extent of the investment made. A venture capital funds is a typical way to create a company in the United States and its common forms include:

- Sole proprietorship (SP)
- Partnership (P)
- Limited-liability partnership (LLP)
- Limited partnership (LP)
- S corporation (S-Corp)
- C corporation (C-Corp)

This means that equity investment is considered simply as a business and not a financial activity, unlike the European framework.

Despite there is no such indication in the US law, most VCF have a maturity of 10 years as the maximum maturity and is one of the condition to benefit of tax exemption (other conditions will be stated in Chapter 10).

The shareholding structure of LPs (see Fig. 9.1) is made up of two different categories of partners (shareholders):

- Limited
- General

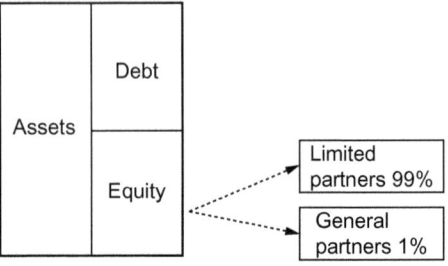

**FIG. 9.1** Shareholding structure of an LP.

In an LP the investment manager is the general partner, while providers of capital (i.e., investors) are the limited partners. The partnership is governed by an LPA negotiated and signed by the parties involved. This agreement is similar to the EU internal code of activity introduced in Chapter 4.

When drafting an LPA the following shall be kept into account:

- The state[3] where the fund is established, since it is crucial that the environment understands the business. The level of expertise on private equity differs depending on the state, for instance the court of California is specialized in venture capital disputes.
- The contract must include everything because this type of business is unsupervised. This means that in the unfortunate event of a lawsuit, the only rules that will be considered as valid are the ones included in the LPA.

Limited partners are investors of funds, they do not manage the company and their liability is limited to the extent of their investment. However, their participation in the company's equity is consistent (99% of the stake). In American private equity funds, each limited partner must be an "accredited investor"[4]: a person or legal entity, such as a company or trust fund, that meets certain net worth and income qualifications and is considered to be sufficiently sophisticated to make investment decisions about complex securities and businesses. If there is no accredited investor, then it is necessary to use the protection of Securities Act for common investors.

General partners are managers of the company and they are fully liable for business debt. General partners control the company and manage investments. The investment of general partners is about 1% of invested funds. Due to the high risk exposure of general partners, these partners operate as limited partners of an advisory company that is set up as a LLP to reduce their risk. In the LLP, the liability of partners is limited to the extent of their investments; nevertheless, the partnership is fully liable for business debt. For this reason, the assets of the LLP are used as a collateral of the LP. General partners cover their risk exposure by signing insurance contracts with insurance companies. These rarely used contracts considerably reduce risk but they are very expensive[5] and negatively impact the final IRR of the overall investment portfolio (see Fig. 9.2).

---

[3]California, Delaware, the Brooklyn region and Massachusetts are the states that best understand the environment.

[4]Regulation D of the Securities Act of 1933 permits accredited investors to invest in a private partnership company without the protection of a registered public offering under the Securities Act. Qualifications for a person are $1 million net worth or annual income exceeding $200,000 individually or $300,000 with a spouse.

[5]Generally the total cost is around 2% of the overall fund managed.

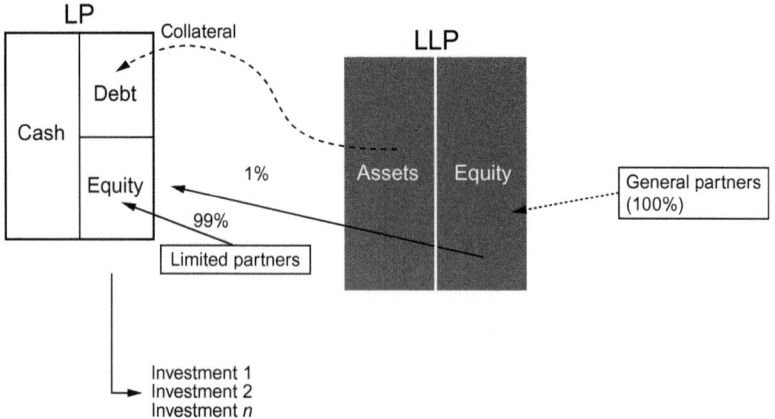

**FIG. 9.2** Organizational structure of venture capital funds.

The great success of limited partnerships is due to two main reasons: they are simple to manage and they can benefit from tax exemption on the proceeds of the investment provided that some conditions are met. There is full flexibility regarding earnings distributed and the allocation of capital gains and losses to the limited partners. Therefore, each limited partner keeps it specific to fiscal profile with no exemption applied.

LPs typically attract investors such as banks, insurance companies, pensions funds, private investors, etc.

VCF, unlike closed-end funds, are allowed to leverage. Because of this, they combine equity and debt that can lead them to reach a higher IRR, as they have a larger investment capacity.

> REMEMBER: What is the name for a fund that can leverage?

General partners should be able to manage fundraising with the limited partners and financial institutions that provide debt to the fund. American LP also allows extra time for the disinvestment phase. As established by law, a maximum extra time is allowed after the end of life of the fund.

### 9.3.2 Small Business Investment Companies

The Small Business Investment Act (SBIC), enacted by the US Congress in 1958, created a partnership between the federal government and private capital to finance the country's small business community.

SBICs are financial institutions that provide equity capital to small businesses. They are licensed by the US Small Business Administration but are privately managed. In return for pledging to finance businesses, SBICs qualify for long-term financing from the public authority. Therefore, SBICs are partnerships between private and public investors in an equal percentage. The federal

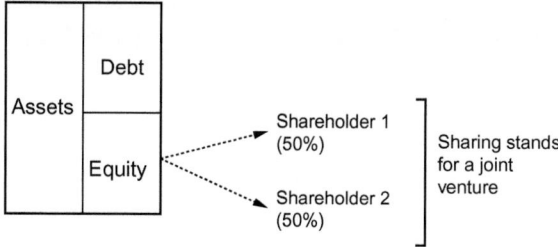

**FIG. 9.3** Shareholding structure of a SBIC.

government gives loans with a fixed low interest rate with a cap of one-third of the total debt and capital gains and other revenues are not taxed. Taxation starts with the distribution of earnings. Features of these companies include

- Two different categories of shareholders each with 50% of the stake: public authority and private investors (see Fig. 9.3)
- Only private investors can manage the SBICs
- SBICs can raise money through debt; a maximum of 33% of the debt is lent by the public authority with a very low interest rate[6]

In the fiscal year 2016, the financing through SBIC amounted for $5991 million. As SBICs too are allowed to leverage, it is worth mentioning that out of the total amount financed, less than 20% ($1042 million) was financed with pure equity. The remaining part was either debt or debt with equity features. This stream of financing created or sustained 122,381 jobs in 2016.

### 9.3.3 Corporate Ventures

Even though no specific laws are dedicated to corporate ventures (CV), direct investment in equity made by corporations is quite developed in the United States. This vehicle is not a separate legal entity, but it is a division or a department of a corporation which wants to invest in venture capital. The only aim of the CV is to run seed and start-up financing.

Corporations invest in teams, ideas, and projects that could be launched successfully. The investment is done to promote R&D, outputs, patents and unlike in VCFs, the aim is not to generate IRR but to enhance the value for the corporation.

They invest in this the type of vehicle to create new businesses and new companies that could prove useful for market positioning and competitiveness. In most cases corporate ventures are business related and represent a tool to sustain seed and start-up financing to increase their presence in the market.

---

[6]As of April 2017, interest rates applied are around 1.25%. https://www.federalreserve.gov/monetarypolicy/discountrate.htm.

## THE COCA-COLA COMPANY: AN "OLD" COMPANY INVESTING IN SEED AND START-UP VENTURES

Marius Swart, has been the head of Coca-Cola Founders and he defined in this way the Coca Cola corporate venture unit: "Coca-Cola Founders operates like a traditional early-stage venture capital fund. But we aren't exactly like a Venture Capital fund for two reasons: we invest off the balance sheet and we are primarily focused on co-creating companies together with repeat founders."*

Coca-Cola Founders has been a rib of "The Coca-Cola Company" and has been active since 2013 through 2017 and it was a very good representation of the Corporate Venture idea.

The American company "big" by definition founded an entrepreneurship hub after more than a century of life, through which it has incentivised ideas from experienced entrepreneurs.

For this reason, Coca-Cola has financed every year experienced, though independent, entrepreneurs around the world in a win-win combination. Coca-Cola got to have access to new, fast-growing markets and growth opportunities for the business, and the financed entrepreneurs got access to the resources of a multinational company in becoming part of the Coca-Cola family (in this relation of collaboration the US company used to get a minority participation after a validation of the business plan).

The model by which Coca-Cola Founders has operated was one-of-a-kind as they did not accept spontaneous applications, but they hand-picked the entrepreneurs by screening the start-uppers community all over the world.

The "only" two requirements a startup should have had to be selected were quite straightforward: the startup must have a strategic fit within Coca-Cola and the business it must be scalable. After all, it is of a one of the biggest companies in the world that we are talking about.

*The interview is dated September 16, 2016.

### 9.3.4    Banks

It is rare to find banks involved in direct investments in equity, instead they invest through LP. The banking system is involved in the equity market through dealing and brokerage rather than advisory and placement.

### 9.3.5    Business Angels

Business Angels are private investors that directly invest in private equity. They do not represent a legal cluster, instead they are equity investors devoted to sustaining seed and start-up financing but do not seek profit. In the United States these investors are exempted from taxation on capital gains generated by their private equity investment (transparency principle).

Examples of Business Angels are high net worth individuals, foundations, research centers, nonprofit societies, corporations acting as donors, etc. They usually invest in a start-up, early-stage, or developing firm. They are significantly sustained by private equity investors, because they generally enhance investment possibilities and bear most of the risk. They often have managerial and/or technical experience to offer the management team as well as equity and debt finance. Furthermore, their investment view is medium- to long-term oriented and principally concentrated in high-risk situations.

## 9.4 RULES FOR UK EQUITY INVESTORS

The financial market in the United Kingdom is common law driven like the United States, and great importance is given to laws from both local and federal courts. These laws have created a general framework in the UK financial systems; however, laws designed by the EU Banking and Financial Services Act are also available. This means that there is a great variety of legal solutions/typologies for equity investors. In the UK social and political attention is given to the "equity gap."[7]

These laws are considered crucial for equity investment development in the United Kingdom.

- Industrial and Financial Corporation Act (1945)—Created public funds to sustain small medium entities (SMEs) and start-ups.
- Business Start-Up Scheme (1981) and Business Expansion Scheme (1983)—Gave fiscal incentive for both corporations and private individuals to invest in equity. The intent of these schemes is to support and promote new, small businesses as well as expanding businesses to bring vacant retail units back into the investment stage.
- Enterprise Investment Scheme (1994) and Venture Capital Trusts Act (1997)—The Enterprise Investment Scheme (EIS) was designed to help small, higher risk trading companies to raise financing by offering a range of tax reliefs to investors who purchase new shares in those companies. The Venture Capital Trusts Act was designed to encourage individuals to invest indirectly in a range of small, higher risk trading companies whose shares and securities are listed on a stock exchange by investing through venture capital trusts (VCTs).

Today, these Acts still work for companies as well as for private individuals. It is impossible to find a specific discipline for equity investment, and a specific discipline for equity investment and banks does not yet exist.

Equity investors in the United Kingdom use these vehicles:

- Venture capital funds
- Venture capital trust
- Merchant banks

---

[7]See MacMillan Committee, Report of the Committee in Finance and Industry, London, 1931.

- Business Angels
- Dedicated public institutions

As in the US private equity market, venture capital funds along with the VCTs constitute over 50% of the UK private equity market, while the other investment vehicles (merchant banks, Business Angels, and dedicated public institutions) constitute the rest of the market.

### 9.4.1    Venture Capital Funds

This investment vehicle is structured as an LP, exactly like it is in the United States. In the United Kingdom these vehicles have a long operating history. The first venture capital fund operating in the United Kingdom started in 1907, and these early LPs are still operating even today. Like the US framework, they enjoy tax transparency in capital gains and dividends if they have a maturity of 10 years plus 2 years.

As in the United States, limited partners include:

Banks
Insurance companies
Pensions funds
Private investors
Corporate investors

### 9.4.2    Venture Capital Trusts

First introduced in 1995, VCTs were created by the Venture Capital Trust Act and have met since then a great success in the UK market. Their relationship is defined through the mutual trust agreement between the parties involved (Fig. 9.4).

The organizational structure of VCTs (see Fig. 9.5) is based on a Trust defined as an amount of money separate (or separate amount of wealth) from the owner managed by professionals indicated as Trustee (see Box 9.1 for further information).

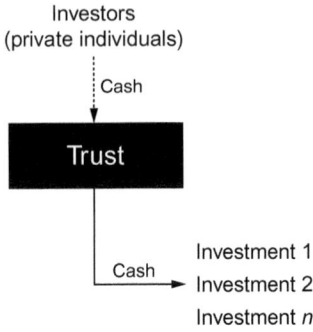

**FIG. 9.4** Investing process structure of trusts in the United Kingdom.

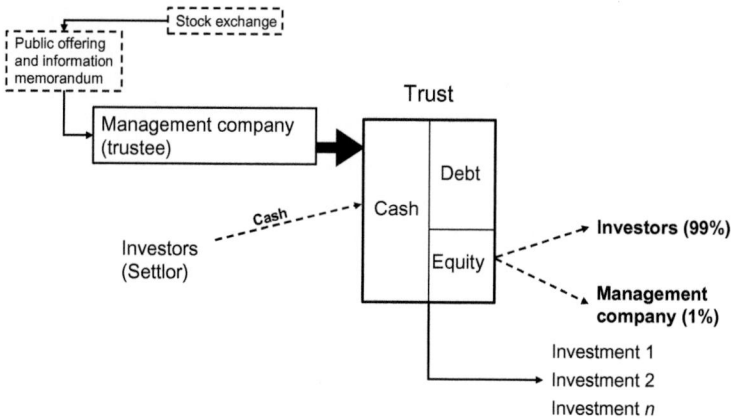

**FIG. 9.5** Organizational structure of VCTs.

## BOX 9.1  WHAT IS A TRUST?

A trust is a way used of managing assets (money, investments, land, or buildings) for people. The Trust scheme dates back in the Middle Ages and it basically involves three parties:

o  the "settlor"—the person who puts assets into a trust
o  the "trustee"—the person who manages the trust
o  the "beneficiary"—the person who benefits from the trust (which is not necessarily the settlor)

Generally speaking, trusts are (mainly) set:

o  to control and protect family assets (even in case someone is too young to manage their assets or when they are incapacitated)
o  to pass on assets while the settlor is still alive
o  to manage successions

In the very moment in which the assets are put in the trust, the owner (i.e., the settlor) loses any kind of right on the assets and the trustee is in charge of the management of the assets, which he has to do by the contract, called the "trust deed." After the assets are put in the trust, the trustees become the legal owners of the assets held in a trust.

In particular cases (such as in VCTs), the settlor can also benefit from the assets in a trust.

The trustees can change, and the trust can still continue, but there always has to be at least one trustee in charge of the management of the assets.

There might be more than one beneficiary. They may benefit from:

o  the income of a trust only or the gains deriving from the investments made with the assets of the trust,
o  the capital only,
o  both the income and capital of the trust.

1. Trust—Group of investors (private individuals) investing their personal wealth
2. Trustee—Group of individuals managing the wealth of the trust.

VCTs are companies listed on the stock exchange.[8] They are based on the concept of UK Trust, where the Trustee[9] has the same function as general partners in LPs. Because they are listed companies, VCTs have no fixed maturity, hence they are considered as perpetual investments.

Only private individuals can subscribe to or buy shares in VCTs, which invest in trading companies by providing them with funds to promote development and growth. VCTs realize their investments and make new ones periodically; however, at least 70% of their investment portfolio is composed of unlisted companies. Fiscal incentive such as participation exemption and reduction on earnings tax operate strongly affect the choice of investing in a Trust as VCTs are exempt from corporation tax on any gains arising from the disposal of their investments.

The main difference between the VCT and the European closed-end is their transparency level. After investors have transferred their personal wealth into a VCT, they are unable to influence decisions made by the trust or trustee managers.

Closed-end funds are completely transparent as defined by the EU regulating framework, whereas the VCT is completely blind because investors are uninformed about the composition of the investment portfolio. Therefore, there is no disclosure of the trust's investment activities. That is the reason why the Trust is listed on the Stock Exchange: in this way liquidity is granted to the investors. A VCT's trend cycle shows no correlation with the London Stock Exchange.

VCT are certainly a very popular scheme to invest in private equity, even if their popularity decreased progressively after reaching a peak in the period 2005–06 in which they raised £780 million (in the period 2015–16 the funds raised amounted for £435 million, the same amount as in 2014–15). In tendency with the amounts of funds raised, the number of funds decreased in 2015–16 in which the number of VCTs managing funds were 80 (in the period 2005–06 they were 108). Since their introduction of VCTs, they have raised nearly £6.4 billion as funds.

### 9.4.3   Merchant Banks

Direct investment in equity is developed, even though they it is declining in volume, within banks dedicated to merchant banking business.[10] Like the United States, the UK banking system is much more involved in the equity market through dealing and brokerage rather than advisory and placement.

---

[8]In the London Stock Exchange.

[9]They are fund managers that run the VCTs, and are usually members of larger investment groups.

[10]Financial institution that engages in investment banking, counseling, negotiating mergers and acquisitions, and a variety of other services including securities portfolio management for customers, insurance, the acceptance of foreign bills of exchange, dealing in bullion, and participating in commercial ventures.

However, private equity investments through merchant banking are common during seed, start-up, and early stage financing.

### 9.4.4  Business Angels

As in the US market, Business Angels do not represent a legal cluster but are identified as equity investors devoted to sustaining seed and start-up financing without a profit goal. Since these investors do not generate profit, they are represented by

- High net worth individuals
- Foundations
- Research centers
- Nonprofit societies
- Corporations acting as donors

### 9.4.5  Dedicated Public Institutions

These are joint ventures between private investors (corporations or financial institutions) and public partners supported by a special act dedicated just for them. Management rules are totally private, but some legal/fiscal ad hoc incentives are still in place. Unlike the SBICs operating in the US market, this type of investment vehicle operates at local levels under local laws with direct involvement by municipalities. Even though there is a profit goal, social valuations are considered during investment decisions.

## 9.5  CARRIED INTEREST AND MANAGEMENT FEE SCHEME: US AND UK SYSTEMS

The only complete integration of UK countries with the EU framework occurs during the origin of costs and revenues. As it will be described in Chapter 17, vehicles through which investments generate revenue include

- Capital gains from investments
- Dividends and interests from investments
- Interest from a deposit bank

While costs include

- Losses from investment
- Interest due for loans
- Management fee to managers[11]
- Carried interest to managers

---

[11]When considering LPs, the management fee goes to general partners who manage the company.

Considering the case of venture capital funds, revenues to general partners are the

- Entrance fee from investors
- Management fee
- Carried interest

While the costs general partners bear are the

- Operating costs
- Deposit bank fee
- Percentage of management fee for the advisor
- Percentage of carried interest to the advisory company for identifying the best opportunities in the market

### 9.5.1    Management Fee

This is a fee charged by the general partners to the limited partners. Management fees in a private equity fund are annual and calculated as a percentage of the NAV[12] of the fund. Typically the fee ranges between 2% and 3.5% of the NAV, depending on the type and size of the fund.

The general partners' management fee may vary over the life of the fund; it might decrease over time as the limited partners' original committed capital is paid back from investment returns. However, the higher the management fee, the lower the amount of money left for investment activity.

The percentage of the NAV is a matter of negotiation between the general partners and limed partners, since it is in the investors interest to pay a lower percentage of fixed costs, which is just the opposite for general partners. Since the percentage is meant to cover all operating costs, it should not be too low. The management fee is a gross fee covering the operating expenses as well as paying the Advisory Company, the Technical Committee, fixed costs, and the managers' remuneration.[13]

### 9.5.2    Carried Interest

Carried interest is the general partner's share in the profits of a private equity fund. Typically, a fund must return the capital received from the LPs before the general partner can share in the fund's profits. The general partners then receive a percentage ranging from 15% to 40% of the net profits as "carried interest."

---

[12]NAV is the total value of the investment portfolio less any liabilities.

[13]Salaries but not the capital gain.

Like in the EU framework, it is due when the fund matures. Carried interest is a percentage of the difference between the global IRR of the closed-end fund and a fixed interest rate (hurdle rate or floor IRR) as defined at the starting date of the closed-end fund and can be expressed with the following formula:

Carried interest $= \%[$Final IRR $-$ Hurdle rate$]$

Carried interest and the floor rate are fixed by the parties involved before the LP agreement is signed. They are determined after long negotiations between limited partners and general partners.

By using a private agreement, a predetermined percentage of both the management fee and the carried interest can be transferred by general partners to the advisory company. There is a strong link between the reputation of the advisory company and the percentage obtained at the end of the disinvestment phase as capital gain.

## 9.6 CLAUSES SIGNED IN AN LP AGREEMENT

Contrary to the EU countries, in United Kingdom and United States there are no legal requirements dictating private equity investment agreements. However, for the United States and the United Kingdom, the national association of venture capitalists and private equity operators have proposed some "models" of legal documents and agreements that can be used for private equity deals. The most common vehicle for private equity investment is the LP. Clauses typically signed in an LPA include[14]:

- Parties—Identifies each person or institution who takes part in the initiative
- Introduction (or recitals)—Explains why the LPA is signed
- Definitions and interpretation—A list of references and terms used throughout the LPA
- Name and place of business—These self-explanatory statements are required by law, because an LP must have a name; the name and the principal place of business, together with other details, must be reported in the LPA
- Establishment—Information in this section is related to the most important features of the LP organization and key people proposing the deal
- Purpose of the partnership—Fund description and the way general partners will carry on the fund's investment activities; description of investment strategy constraints and limitations

---

[14]See the British Venture Capital Association Web site (https://www.bvca.co.uk/) and the American Venture Capital Association Web site (https://nvca.org/).

- Duration of partnership—Termination of partnership—Life period of the partnership and rules or conditions for its termination
- Capital and loan contributions—Specifies the role and financial commitment of LPs
- Allocations, sharing, and distributions of partnership profits—Governs the order in which partners are repaid, partnership profits are allocated, the ratio in which the partners share profits between themselves, and how the profits are to be distributed to the limited partners and general partner
- Carried interest—How the manager calculates the general partner's share of a private equity fund
- Appointment and removal of the general partner—Specifies under what conditions a general partner is appointed and/or removed from his position
- Powers, rights, and duties of the general partner—Rights and duties of the general partner; the general partner is authorized to do everything necessary to operate the partnership
- Powers of limited partner—Limited partners are excluded from managing the partnership to ensure their limited liability against creditors; other powers cannot be generalized and are specified in every agreement
- Withdrawal of partners—Rules for when a partner wants to leave the partnership or the partnership wants to expel the investor from the partnership
- Borrowing and bridge financing—Rules for the LP financial management
- Fees and expenses—Rules concerning the calculation of the management fee, establishment costs, transaction costs, fee income
- Accounts and reports—Documents and information prepared by the manager for the limited partners and investors
- Consents, meetings, and votes—Constraints on the general partner's powers or topics requiring the limited partners' consent before the execution
- Representations and warranties
- Deed of adherence—An extra form (not compulsory) is attached to the back of the LPA; it is the formal means by which most investors become limited partners specifying the number of commitment units and how these commitments are divided between capital contribution and loans
- Miscellaneous legal issues—Governs law and jurisdiction, power of attorneys, confidentiality, notices, etc.

# CHAPTER 10

# Taxation Framework for Private Equity and Fiscal Impact for Equity Investors

## 10.1 INTRODUCTION

This chapter presents the role of taxation in private equity and venture capital throughout Europe and the United States. A deep theoretical and analytical analysis country by country will be demonstrated in the following sections. The second section shows how private equity and venture capital industry is tax sensitive, underlining the role of policymakers, and that the taxation technique and its application must always be considered together. Sections 10.3 and 10.4 will analyze taxation models and define areas of taxation for investors, vehicles, and companies requiring funds who conduct private equity and venture capital deals. Section 10.5 proposes a comparative analysis of the tax system for European countries and the United States underlining the differences between corporation taxes, withholding taxes, and personal taxes applicable to financial incomes. Focusing attention on the private equity and venture capital industry, the Invest Europe position is analyzed and reviewed. Finally, the last section analyzes taxation on vehicles used to implement private equity and venture capital deals the interrelation of taxation on vehicles, investors, and companies in the European Union (EU).

## 10.2 FUNDAMENTAL ROLE OF TAXATION IN PRIVATE EQUITY AND VENTURE CAPITAL

Policymakers play a fundamental role in private equity and venture capital development. They must address regulatory and administrative barriers and ensure coherent policies. This enables investors to provide a continuous financing cycle for start-up, spin off, company development, transition, and buyout investments to create taxable value or returns (see Fig. 10.1). Investors should be considered in the valuation framework of investment strategies used to allocate financial sources, taxation, and the entire country taxation system.

**125**

Private Equity and Venture Capital in Europe. https://doi.org/10.1016/B978-0-12-812254-9.00010-3

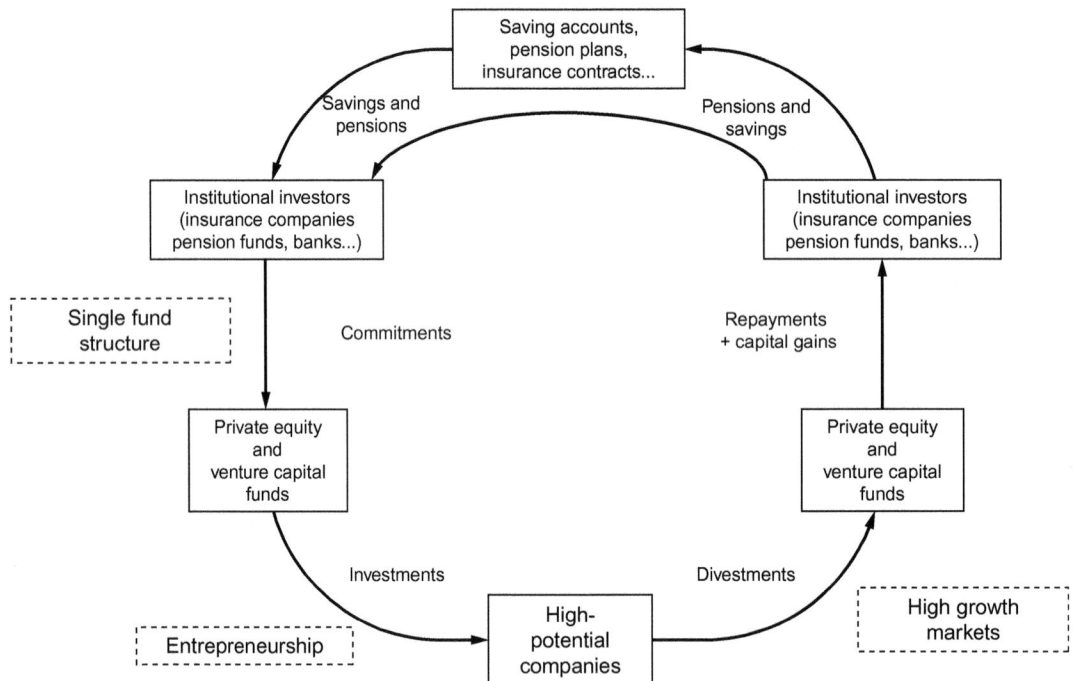

**FIG. 10.1** Financing cycle of private equity and venture capital. *From Invest Europe.*

Private equity and venture capital portfolios are structured to trade off the risk and return from diversified combinations of assets, and are influenced by institutional and regulatory factors where taxation is essential.

As noted in previous chapters, the private equity industry is regulated on a national basis in most EU member states: there is no cohesive framework for private equity at the EU level, and a number of EU legislative measures indirectly affect the industry, such as the AIFM Directive, the MiFID, UCITS, the Pension Funds Directive, and the Basel III Principles or Capital Requirements Directive. The entire fiscal policy is local, so every government and every country legislates autonomously.

In this environment, it is very difficult to find a strictly defined tax system for investments of private equity operators and venture capitalists, because the fiscal systems are wider than the regulations of this industry. In a general structure, government policies supporting the development of private equity and venture capital industry may be direct or indirect and related to the supply side rather than the demand side.[1]

---

[1]See Caselli, S., Gatti, S., "Venture Capital. A Euro-System Approach." Springer-Verlag, Berlin, London, 2004.

**Table 10.1** Government Options to Improve the Private Equity and Venture Capital Industry

|  | Demand Side | Supply Side |
|---|---|---|
| Direct intervention | Public incubators | Public private equity or venture capital funds |
| Indirect intervention | Tax policy<br>Promotion of enterprise, management, technology park, incubators | Tax policy<br>Upside leverage schemes<br>Promotion of financiers' network<br>Exit or fund's operating scheme<br>Downside protection scheme |

Table 10.1 illustrates how important the fiscal environment is and how governments can make investing easier for both firms and financial institutions. Tax policies shape incentives for private equity and venture capital to approve particular types of financing. Whatever these firms decide, that is, capital gains taxes or investment subsidies, it has to solve a double moral hazard resulting from a joint effort.

Entrepreneurs tend to focus on technological aspects such as product development, whereas financial institutions draw on their commercial experience and industry knowledge to provide managerial support and to promote the development of the firm. To reduce all potential risks and biases, an equity contract becomes necessary. However, it is inefficient when both parties equally invest in a deal, but must share the total results and each party is taxed differently. The effects of taxation are hence interesting to evaluate; for example, the introduction of a uniform capital gains tax on both entrepreneurs and financiers delays entrepreneurship, while increasing incentives for the financier. On the other hand, an investment subsidy boosts entrepreneurship but depresses total returns thereby diminishing incentives for private equity support.

Taxation for private equity and venture capital is analyzed considering the:

- Taxation technique
- Application area

Section 10.3 analyzes the taxation technique and taxation, while Section 10.4 defines areas of taxation for investors, vehicles, and companies requiring funds who conduct private equity and venture capital deals.

## 10.3   TAXATION AND EQUITY INVESTORS: LESSONS FROM THEORY AND RELEVANT MODELS

There is a strong relation between taxation rules and private equity market development; evidence demonstrates a strong, worldwide correlation between specific tax benefits and the increase of private equity volumes. Examples include

- Taxation on capital gains
- Taxation on earnings and dividends
- Fiscal incentive to start-up
- Fiscal incentive to R&D investment
- Fiscal incentive to increase the leverage ratio or to increase the equity

### 10.3.1   Taxation on Dividends, Earnings, and Capital Gain

Capital gain is a value greater than zero defined as the difference between the final and the initial value of the equity participation bought by private equity operators. A capital gain is distributed among the investors (either managers or pure investors) only if the vehicle that invested in private equity has got a definite life.

Earnings are usually defined as the gross difference between revenues and all monetary and nonmonetary costs. However, the definition of earning is not always the same and sometimes it considers some of the types of revenues and costs. For example, the EBITDA is a type of earning—more precisely, it is the earning before interests, taxes, depreciations, and amortizations—and EBIT as well is a type of earning, but it is the earning before interests and taxes.

Taxation on capital gains, earnings, and dividends may be different, so there are various modalities of realization:

- Participation exemption (PEX) schemes
- Flat tax approach
- Transparency taxation approach

*Participation exemption* schemes provide shareholders an exemption from taxation on dividends received and potential capital gains arising on the sale of shares. A *flat tax* is a tax system with a constant tax rate, usually lower than the ordinary standard one. Flat taxes are used for specific cases such as household income or particular corporate profits that are taxed at one marginal rate. This is different from progressive taxes, which varies according to income levels or brackets. In *transparency taxation* systems, generated income is not taxed becoming "transparent" from the tax system's perspective. This system is put in place in order to avoid double taxation. These incomes are only relevant for people (or organizations or entities) who receive them, and not for the vehicle that generates them (e.g., VCF or closed-end fund) and they are taxed by different rules.

### 10.3.2  Fiscal Incentive to Start-Up and to Incentivize R&D Expenses

There are various modalities of fiscal incentives to start-up a business or to incentivize R&D expenses:

- Carryback and carryforward
- Temporary taxation rate mark down
- Shadow costs usage
- Tax credit

*Carryback and/or carryforward* are tax benefits that allow business losses to be used to reduce tax liability in previous and/or following years. Under most jurisdictions, there are a maximum number of years to recover losses and use the relative tax benefits. Another incentive for entrepreneurs is the temporary reduction of the whole tax rate, the so-called *mark down*, where the tax relief is often linked to the amount of invested sources. A third way to spur entrepreneurship is the creation of a *shadow cost* system. In this system, the fiscal provision supports the indirect cost, which is often concealed and linked to investments. Examples of shadow costs are downtime, administrative costs, learning costs, etc. Finally, *tax credit* is a tax voucher granted to the company under special conditions that the company can use over the following fiscal years in order to decrease the tax liabilities. It usually has an expiry date and it usually can be deemed under specific conditions.

### 10.3.3  Fiscal Incentive to Increase Leverage and/or Equity

There are two fiscal mechanisms that can influence the way in which a company recurs either to equity or to debt capital, namely:

- Thin capitalization (or, thin cap)
- Dual income taxation (DIT) schemes

In the presence of a *thin cap* regime, a limit for the company to use interest rate paid on debt to reduce the fiscal burden. This is done to avoid that a company is thinly capitalized. *Dual income tax* schemes consider two types of income to tax. For every fraction of the whole income a particular percentage of taxation is applied, so the taxation rate depends on the variation in the equity of the company. Usually, dual income tax schemes are applied to reduce the firm's leverage and spur equity financing.

## 10.4  TAXATION PLAYERS: INVESTMENT VEHICLES, INVESTORS, AND COMPANIES DEMANDING CAPITAL

Taxation and incentive rules may be applied to all companies, vehicles, and investors participating in a private equity or venture capital deal. Usually, there is a distinction between rules for companies and rules for vehicles and investors. A different set of rules is applied if one or both of the deal participants are domestic or foreign.

Out of companies, investors, and vehicles, companies are the easiest subwhole to identify from a fiscal point of view. Companies are the demand side of private equity business, and from the government's perspective, they develop deals with the intention of improving the private equity and venture capital industry. So fiscal policies increasing the entrepreneurship trend are specific and implemented as fiscal incentives for start-up, investments in R&D, or investments in general assets.

Fiscal policies for companies may be planned not only from the investment and asset side of the balance sheet, but also to provide incentives or disincentives to use a particular source of funding, that is, debt rather than equity.

Taxation rules for investors and vehicles are primarily defined by earnings and incomes related to private equity or venture capital investments and capital gain or loss, potential or effective, coming from the purchase and the sale of a company. The study of these two categories is more difficult as both investors and the vehicle can be either domestic or international with respect to the VBC. In Fig. 10.2 the links between domestic and foreign groups are outlined.

For these three categories of players involved in a private equity deal, relevant fiscal areas can be identified:

- Vehicles used to invest in private equity (closed-end funds, limited partnerships, etc.)
- Private and corporate investors
- Corporations demanding private equity capital

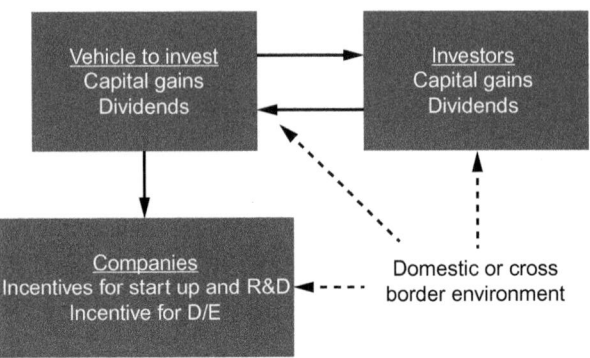

**FIG. 10.2** The link between taxation and private equity players.

**Table 10.2** Link Between Tools of Taxation and Private Equity Players

|  | **Vehicles** | **Investors** | **Venture-Backed Company** |
|---|---|---|---|
| Taxation on capital gains | Relevant to increase NAV and IRR | Relevant for personal taxation profile (final net IRR) | Not relevant |
| Taxation on dividends | Relevant to increase NAV and IRR | Relevant only for gains given trough earnings | Not relevant |
| Incentive to startup | Not relevant | Not relevant | Relevant to reduce company tax rate |
| Incentive to R&D investment | Not relevant | Not relevant | Relevant to reduce company tax rate |
| Comparative incentive D vs E | Not relevant | Not relevant | Relevant to compose capital structure within net WACC |

In the Table 10.2 the players involved in the fiscal private equity business and the areas relevant for taxation purposes are correlated together.

Generally, measures implemented as incentives to start-up or R&D investments or those affect the leverage ratio are not relevant for investors and vehicles. They are only relevant for companies because they reduce the entire company tax rate and enhance the potential demand for private equity intervention. If these measures are meant as incentives for companies to use equity, then they must face a disincentive to use debt often realized by a rise in the tax rate. Along with these measures vehicles also have to deal with an artificial environment; for example, if the vehicle is an equity pooled investment these incentives may make the deal easier.

A company's choices are not affected directly if taxation concerns capital gain and earning, but investors and vehicles are. Taxation on dividends and capital gains may reduce the IRR of vehicles, and they may diminish the final profit for investors.

## 10.5 TAXATION FEATURES AROUND THE WORLD: A BRIEF COMPARATIVE ANALYSIS

The most important characteristics of European and American fiscal schemes are reported in this chapter.[2] The focus is not on the private equity industry, but the entire economic system; however, only financial taxable incomes (i.e., interests, capital gains) are considered.

---

[2]https://ec.europa.eu/taxation_customs/home_en, and publications about taxation of EY, Deloitte and PWC (updated in April 2017).

For each country, three types of taxes are analyzed:

1. Corporate tax
2. Withholding tax
3. Personal tax

Corporate tax (or corporation tax) is a tax levied by each jurisdiction on profits made by companies or associations. It taxes the value of the corporation's profits. This analysis examines the taxes levied on dividends and capital gains paid to firms, rather than the fiscal and R&D incentives provided for companies.

Withholding tax is an amount withheld by the party making payment to another and paid to the taxation authorities. The purpose of withholding tax is to facilitate or accelerate collection by collecting tax from a small number of payers rather than a much greater number of payees, and by collecting tax from payers within the jurisdiction rather than payees who may be outside the jurisdiction. This section analyzes taxes withheld by dividends, interests, and royalties. Because of it is importance for the domestic and international development of private equity and venture capital, the analysis will focus on the presence/absence of any branch remittance tax.

Personal tax is the last tax scheme to be analyzed. The items compared are the tax rate, the concept of taxable income, the taxation of capital gains, and the presence or the lack of any net wealth or net worth tax.

## 10.5.1   Taxation in Italy

The Italian tax system is one of the most difficult to analyze, so a general overview is necessary to define corporate, withholding, and personal taxes. For corporations, the aggregate standard tax rate is 27.9%; the sum between the IRES (24%) and the IRAP (3.90%). However, some local authorities (i.e., regions or municipal authorities) may increase the total amount with a spread.

In Italy, principles of participation exemption applies, so dividends are 95% exempt, except when the subsidiary distributing dividends is directly or indirectly a resident of a country on the Italian black list. Capital gain also benefits from the 95% exemption only if the participation is held for at least 12 months and is recorded as a financial asset, the company is not resident in a country on the Italian black list, and the company is run effectively. Otherwise, capital gains are taxed at the standard rate.

A number of incentives are available for firms in Italy, but there are requirements to satisfy regarding location, size, and type of business. The Italian fiscal system offers companies the chance to carryforward losses under special requirements, however losses incurred in the first 3 years of activity of a company may be carried forward to offset the tax liability, but only if the losses relate to a new business activity. Carryback is not permitted.

The Italian withholding tax system is detailed and intricate because of the presence of tax treaties and the application of an EC parent-subsidiary directive.

Under the Parent-Subsidiary EU directive, dividend payments may be fully exempt from withholding tax if all of the following conditions are met:

a. the parent company takes one of the forms listed in the directive;
b. the parent company is resident of a EU country for tax purposes and, under the terms of an income tax treaty concluded with a third state, is not considered to be resident for tax purposes outside the EU;
c. the parent company is subject to one of the taxes listed in the directive without the possibility of an option or of being exempt;
d. the parent company has a 12-month holding period of, at least, a 10% direct interest in the capital of the subsidiary.

In general, dividends paid to nonresident companies are taxed at 26%, but tax treaties or EC parent-subsidiary directive may reduce the amount. Interest may be taxed at 26% or 12.5%, the latter is applied to all government bonds and similar financial instruments. Management fees are exempt from withholding tax, royalties paid to a nonresident company are subject to a 30% withholding tax usually calculated on 75% of the gross royalty (resulting in a net tax burden of 22.5%).

In Italy there is neither net wealth tax nor net worth tax, but the personal taxation system is progressive and rates range from 23% to 43%. Nevertheless, it must be underlined that private investment incomes are subject to a rate of 26%, after it has been reduced in 2012 and increased again in 2014 while capital gains may see a reduction in the standard rate in many cases.

## 10.5.2 Taxation in France

Even though the standard tax rate for companies is 33.33%, lower rates apply to SMEs and new businesses. Social surcharge of 3.3% apply to corporate income tax liability exceeding €763,000.

French domestic law does not allow credit for foreign taxes.

The principles of participation exemption are applied to capital gain to an 88% of exemption. The participation exemption applies if the participation is at least 5% of equity capital and the holding period is at least 2 years. Losses from French companies may be carried forward indefinitely, and carried back for

1 year and in certain cases, up to €1 Million. The most important incentives concern R&D investments, which are usually allowed as tax credits. If participation exemption is not applied, capital gains follow different rules and, if they derive from the sale of securities, the applied rate is 19% plus a special social security surcharge.

Thin capitalization is applied in France in a sense that the deduction of interest expenses on related party-debt is deferred if the interest exceeds the highest of the following parameters:

1. The interest expense on a debt is equal to 1.5 times the equity
2. About 25% of the borrower's adjusted EBITDA
3. The amount of interest income received from related parties

The withholding tax system depends on the presence of tax treaties or the provisions of the EC directive that may reduce the amount, rather than applying the participation exemptions. It must be emphasized that after-tax income of branch also to be distributed to nonresidents is subject to a 30% branch tax. Dividends paid by a French company to a nonresident shareholder are taxed at 30%, unless a tax treaty can be applied, while interests paid by a French company to a nonresident lender are not subject to withholding tax and royalties paid to a nonresident entity are subject to a 33.33% withholding tax. Regarding personal taxes, all incomes, including investment incomes, are considered taxable and the applied tax rate is progressive from 0% to 45%., unless a tax relief can be applied.

## 10.5.3   Taxation in Germany[3]

German corporate taxation is based on a national rate of 15% (15.285% including the solidarity surcharge) and on a local rate from 14% to 17%, leading to an effective corporate tax rate ranging between 30% and 33%. The participation exemption system leads to a tax exclusion of 95% of dividends and capital gains received by German resident companies. Many aid programs are available for German companies, and, in case of losses, the fiscal system provides an unlimited carryforward and a 1-year carryback. Losses may be offset against profits up to €1 million without restriction, but only 60% of income exceeding €1 million may be offset against loss carryforwards. In specific cases of intragroup restructurings loss carryforward forfeiture is not allowed.

There is not a withholding tax on interest except for interest on publicly traded debt, interest received through a German payment agent, convertible bonds and certain profit participating loans.

---

[3]In late 2008 an important tax reform, with substantial consequences on private equity and venture capital was discussed in Germany.

Branch remittance tax is not found in Germany.

As for dividends, if the application of the parent-subsidiary directive does not reduce the amount, a statutory rate of 25% (26.375%, including the solidarity surcharge) applies, with a possible 40% refund for nonresident corporations, giving rise to an effective rate of 15.825%, unless the rate is reduced under a tax treaty. For royalties the rate applied is 15% (15.825% including the solidarity surcharge).

German personal tax rates are progressive (up to 45%) and consider only incomes because net wealth or net worth is not taxed. The normal tax rate applies for capital gains, as well even though different scenarios are provided by law to reduce the total amount.

## 10.5.4 Taxation in Spain

The standard corporate tax rate in Spain is 25% (even if special rates applies to different kind of entities, for instance for banks it is 30%). Dividend and capital gains are subject to this rate (i.e., 25%), even though the participation exemption rules or tax treaties may reduce the effective amount of tax. When applicable, tax exemption is equal to 100% and, to exploit all benefits, Spanish companies must hold a participation of at least 5% and for at least 12 months. Incentives are available for investments and export activities, and the tax system allows companies to carryforward losses indefinitely, but it does not allow carryback.

The withholding tax system is particularly complicated because of the presence of domestic rules, tax treaties, and EC directives that may reduce the applied rate. Generally, unless a more favorable tax treatment applies, dividends and interest paid to nonresidents are taxed at 19%, while royalties are taxed at a rate of 24% by law (19% if the recipient is resident in the EU or if the country of residence exchanges tax information with Spain). There is also a branch remittance tax equal to 19%. The personal progressive rate ranges between 19% and 48%, with the maximum rate varying according to the region of the Spanish resident. Capital gains are generally included in the investment taxable base. Taxation concerns only income and no net wealth or net worth tax is applied.

## 10.5.5 Taxation in Luxembourg

Companies in Luxembourg exceeding a taxable income of €30,000 are required to pay a standard corporate tax rate of 19% (from 2018, it will be 18%), a surtax of 7%, and municipal authorities may request a further spread. Dividends and capital gains are exempt from tax if the shareholder holds at least 10% of the share capital or there is an acquisition value of at least €1.2 million, and the holding period lasts at least 1 year uninterrupted and if the acquisition price is not lower than €1.2 million for dividends (or €6 million for capital gains). Otherwise, dividends and capital gains are included in the taxable income.

In Luxembourg tax credit and other measures for venture capital and tangible and intangible investments are available, and for losses, laws provide for unlimited carryforward, for losses incurred up to December 31, 2016. Losses incurred as from 2017 are allowed to be carried forward for 17 years. Losses carryback is not permitted.

The withholding tax system is extremely clear: there is neither a remittance branch tax nor taxation on interest and royalties, while dividends paid to non-resident companies are taxed at 15% or less in the presence of tax treaties or an EC parent-subsidiary directive. The benefits of the EC directive may also be exploited for companies in countries where tax rules are similar to those in Luxembourg.

Personal incomes are subject to a progressive rate up to 42% with no net wealth or net worth tax. Income tax is further increased by a contribution of 7% for the employment fund.

## 10.5.6 Taxation in Netherlands

The Dutch fiscal system regarding withholding taxes is easy to understand, while it is a little more difficult when companies or people are considered. The withholding system is clear: no remittance branch tax or taxation on interest and royalties is applied. A normal taxation applies on capital gains, unless participation exemption is applied.

The corporate tax rate is 20% on the first €200,000 of taxable profit and 25% on the rest.

Participation exemption applies provided that the stake represents at least 5% of the share capital and if the following criteria are met: (1) the subsidiary is not held as a mere portfolio investment, (2) the subsidiary is subject to a reasonable effective tax rate on the basis of the Dutch principles (the so-called "tax test"), or (3) less than 50% of the assets of the subsidiary is made of "passive" assets (i.e., their value is determined on the basis if the fair market value—the so-called "asset test"). If the participation exemption is not applicable, a credit for the underlying tax can be granted.

There are various incentives for investments and financing in different cases. For losses, rules provide a carryforward for 9 years and a carryback for 1 year, apart from some special restrictions for financial firms or holding companies.

The Netherlands taxes its residents on their worldwide income, whereas non-residents are subject to tax only on income derived from specific sources in the Netherlands (mainly income from employment). The worldwide income is classified in three types of income, each corresponding to a "Box." Box 1 refers to taxable income from work and home ownership, Box 2 refers to taxable income from a substantial interest, and Box 3 applies to taxable income from savings and investment.

## 10.5.7  Taxation in the United Kingdom

The British main tax rate is 19% as from April 1, 2017. This main rate does not apply to profits coming from some specific business. No surtax is demanded.

From a corporate point of view, the benefit of a full exemption on dividends is only available to resident companies that receive these sources from a resident company. Dividends received from a foreign company are taxed, but a tax credit is available for the amount already paid abroad.

Generally, capital gains are taxed, but an exemption exists for companies disposing substantial shareholdings (i.e., higher than 10%). Incentives are available for certain R&D expenditures. For losses the carryforward is unlimited and the carryback is admitted for 1 year.

The British fiscal system states that there is neither withholding tax on dividends nor a branch remittance tax. Interests and royalties paid to nonresidents are taxed at 20%, but tax treaties or EC interest and a royalties directive may reduce the amount.

For personal tax purposes, all income, including capital gains and interest, must be considered. In the United Kingdom the personal tax rate is progressive up to 45%, as from April 2016 an annual divided tax allowance of £5000 has been introduced, the rates on dividends exceeding the allowance range between 7.5% and 38.1%. Capital gains are taxed at 20%.

## 10.5.8  Taxation in the United States

In the United States, the federal corporate income tax applies at rates ranging between 15% and 35%. An additional 5% tax (subject to caps) may be imposed.

The total maximum effective tax rate is 39.5%. Branch income that is effectively connected with a US trade or business is taxed at the corporate rate. The United States also imposes a remittance branch tax under which branches of foreign corporations are generally subject to a 30% tax on their profits (their "dividend equivalent amount") sourced in the United States.

Dividends, interests and royalties paid to a nonresident are subject to a 30% withholding tax unless the rate is reduced under an applicable tax treaty.

The participation exemption scheme is not available in the United States, so gains derived by companies on assets held for investment are taxed at the same rate as ordinary income. A deduction is available for dividends paid and received between US corporate shareholders.

Laws provide a number of tax credits related to R&D investments. A corporation's gains are taxed at the same rates as ordinary income. In general, capital losses may offset only capital gains, not ordinary income. Subject to certain restrictions, a corporation's excess capital loss may be carried back and forward.

The general withholding tax according to whether it refers to dividends, interests or royalties, and branch remittance paid to foreign subjects are taxed at a rate of 30%. It must be emphasized that in certain circumstances, linked to the export profile of firms, dividends are tax exempt or that certain interest (mainly paid by government bonds) are exempt from withholding tax.

Personal taxes encompass all forms of remuneration that are not specifically exempted, while net wealth is not taxed. The rate is progressive up to 39.6%.

## 10.6   FISCAL FRAMEWORK FOR EQUITY INVESTORS AND VEHICLES: THE EU CONDITION

This chapter demonstrated that many differences among EU countries persist despite efforts to create a standardized legal environment for the private equity industry. Tax procedures are different because of dissimilar legal systems and the level of country development.

Previous chapters showed that EVCA proposed a way to appraise the ability of a country's fiscal system to spur the private equity and venture capital industry: calculate a comprehensive score from 1 (the best) to 3 (the worst) by rating these items:

- Tax environment for most usable fund structure
- Presence of fiscal or incentive schemes for private equity and venture capital investment
- Tax environment for companies requiring sources
- Tax environment for fund managers and private individuals

Items considered regarding aspects related to vehicles and investors include the

- Availability or the accessibility to any tax transparency option
- VAT environment for the private equity and venture capital industry
- Necessity of permanent establishment
- Presence of any fiscal incentive meant to encourage investments in private equity and venture capital
- Capital gains and income tax for private individuals and entities
- Taxation of carried interest

Table 10.3 illustrates that the European fiscal system is still far from being standardized. The fiscal policy does not develop the private equity and venture capital industry, instead it is the result of variables linked to each country's fiscal approach that are satisfying a greater number of objectives.

There is negative relation between taxation for private individuals and entities and taxation of carried interest. When the taxation of carried interest is profitable, the negative relation between taxation for private individuals and entities appears to be expensive. Taxation of carried interest is also negatively related to the presence of fiscal incentives for the private equity and venture capital industry: it seems that governments tend to separate the encouragement of investments in private equity and venture capital from tax rules for investors. A negative relation is also evident between the availability of a transparency rule and the VAT environment as well as the permanent establishment restriction. This confirms that vehicles and investors are considered separately by governments.

There is a positive correlation between the VAT environment and the presence of incentives for private equity and venture capital investments; that is, the relation between the VAT environment and the permanent establishment restriction. These items run together and are available just for businesses operating with a domestic and enduring headquarters in the country of choice, where the choice of the country may also depend on the TTR (total tax rate) of a country (Box 10.1).

## 10.6.1 Taxation of the Most Important Private Equity and Venture Capital Vehicles

The fiscal framework for private equity and venture capital vehicles depends on the legal framework and the organization of the fiscal system. In each fiscal system private equity deals may be realized in a different way.

Table 10.4 illustrates the tax profile for the vehicles used most often in private equity investments.

## 10.6.2 Vehicle Taxation: Italy[4]

Italy's fiscal framework is highly volatile due to the political cycle and the use of taxation as a short-term tool of political economy. However, taxation related to financial investments and its vehicles is not so volatile (see Fig. 10.3).

Investment vehicles, investors, and companies demanding capital round out the fiscal picture. Private equity and venture capital investment can be done

---

[4]Sources: Deloitte and PwC 2017 publications—see references for further details.

**Table 10.3** Invest Europe Comparative Analysis of European Fiscal Systems

| Country | Tax Transparency Option | VAT Environment | Permanent Establishment Request | Fiscal Incentive to the Industry | Taxation for Private and Entities | Taxation of Carried Interest |
|---|---|---|---|---|---|---|
| Italy | 3 | 1 | 1 | 2 | 2 | 2 |
| Austria | 3 | 1 | 1 | 1 | 3 | 2 |
| Belgium | 1 | 1 | 1 | 1 | 3 | 2 |
| Czech Republic | 3 | 1 | 1 | 3 | 1 | 2 |
| Denmark | 1 | 1 | 2 | 3 | 3 | 1 |
| Finland | 1 | 1 | 1 | 3 | 3 | 1 |
| France | 1 | 1 | 1 | 1 | 3 | 1 |
| Germany | 1 | 3 | 1 | 3 | 3 | 2 |
| Ireland | 1 | 1 | 1 | 1 | 3 | 1 |
| Luxembourg | 2 | 1 | 1 | 1 | 1 | 2 |
| Netherlands | 1 | 1 | 3 | 1 | 2 | 3 |
| Norway | 1 | 1 | 2 | 3 | 3 | 2 |
| Poland | 3 | 1 | 1 | 3 | 3 | 2 |
| Portugal | 1 | 1 | 1 | 1 | 2 | 3 |
| Spain | 3 | 1 | 1 | 1 | 3 | 2 |
| Sweden | 1 | 3 | 3 | 3 | 3 | 1 |
| Switzerland | 1 | 1 | 2 | 1 | 2 | 3 |
| United Kingdom | 1 | 1 | 1 | 1 | 3 | 1 |

## BOX 10.1 EFFECTIVE CORPORATION TAXATION AROUND EUROPE

World Bank proposes an annual study measuring the ease of paying taxes for small- to medium-sized domestic companies in countries around the world. There are three indicators:

- Firms expected to give gifts in meetings with tax officials (% of firms)
- Labor tax and contributions (% of commercial profits)
- Number of visits or required meetings with tax officials
- Other taxes payable by businesses (% of commercial profits)
- Profit tax (% of commercial profits)
- Time to prepare and pay taxes (hours)
- Total tax rate, TTR (% of commercial profits)

Considering the theme of this book, the TTR is the most interesting if the corporate taxation system is attractive for domestic or foreign entrepreneurs. According the World Bank definition "Total tax rate measures the amount of taxes and mandatory contributions payable by businesses after accounting for allowable deductions and exemptions as a share of commercial profits. Taxes withheld (such as personal income tax) or collected and remitted to tax authorities (such as value added taxes, sales taxes or goods and service taxes) are excluded." In general, the data below presented confirms that corporate income tax is only one of many taxes that businesses have to bear. Any reform needs to look beyond corporate income tax: companies make important tax contributions as employers, and they are also influenced by taxes on consumption (VAT).

| Country Name | TTR (% as of 2016) |
| --- | --- |
| Luxembourg | 20.80% |
| United Kingdom | 30.90% |
| Netherlands | 40.40% |
| United States | 44% |
| Germany | 48.90% |
| Spain | 49% |
| Italy | 62% |
| France | 62.80% |

through have different vehicles (i.e., closed-end funds or investment firms) in the presence of two fiscal frames:

- Flat tax system for closed-end funds
- Participation exemption on capital gains and earnings for investment firms

Closed-end funds do not pay ordinary Italian tax (i.e., IRES and IRAP) but pay a flat tax fixed at 20% instead. Italian fiscal law considers capital gains, interest, and others earnings on both the revenue and cost side in the calculation framework as well as other types of costs and revenues.

**Table 10.4** Tax Profile of the Most Important Vehicles in Europe

| Country | Preferable Vehicle | Tax Profile |
|---|---|---|
| Italy | Fondo chiuso | Italian closed-end funds follow a particular treatment. A flat tax rate of 12.5% is applied on the fund results |
| France | Fonds Commun de Placement à Risques | FCPR itself is not subject to any taxation.<br>In particular:<br>- No corporate income tax is payable by an FCPR on any dividend income remitted by a target company in which the FCPR has a participating interest;<br>- No capital gains tax is payable by the FCPR on any profitable sales of its shareholding in a target company |
| United Kingdom | Limited partnership | Capital gains are de-taxed, while other revenues and costs are tax sensitive |
| United States | Limited partnership | Capital gains are de-taxed, while other revenues and costs are tax sensitive |
| Spain | Sociedad de Capital de Riesgo (SCR) and Fondo de Capital de Riesgo (FCR) | SCR and FCR are taxable according to the 30% corporation tax. Nevertheless, there are special tax arrangements established in the Corporation Tax legislation and their principal characteristics and requirements are as follows:<br>- Participation exemption of 99% of revenue obtained from the sale of securities representing equity of companies in which they have invested;<br>- The application of the deduction for internal and international double taxation of dividends on 100% of the tax base relating to dividends |
| Germany | Limited partnership (GMbH & Co KG) | Corporation and solidarity tax is payable on profits and another trade tax on trade earnings<br>Business expenses, interest, trade tax, and amortization are deductible |
| Luxembourg | Société d'Investissement en Capital à Risque (SICAR) | Profits realized by a SICAR are subject to corporate income tax and municipal business tax. However, income derived from portfolio items consisting of securities, capital gains derived from the sale of such securities, and income from temporary investment in liquid assets held for a maximum period of 12 months before investment in risk capital are excluded from the tax base |

If private equity and venture capital deals are made by investment firms, they are forced to pay Italian corporation tax (i.e., IRES and IRAP) as well as other legal entities. However, in the case they can benefit of the participation exemption, for IRES purposes, capital gains (difference between sale consideration and tax basis of the shares) on sales of shares are 95% exempt, provided all the following conditions are met:

    i. the shareholding was held uninterruptedly for at least 12 months prior to the sale;

| | Vehicles | Investors | Venture-Backed Company |
|---|---|---|---|
| Taxation on capital gains | **Closed-end funds:** flat tax at 20%<br><br>**Investment firms:** they can benefit of the mechanism of PEX with a discount of 95%. Main requirements are:<br>• Holding period larger than 1 year<br>• Losses can not be deducted as costs<br>• No real estate investments | **Private individual — Domestic:** Closed-end funds: 0%<br>Investment firms:<br>(a) for Qualified Investors: 49.72% * personal level of taxation<br>(b) for Non-Qualified Investors: 26%<br>**Private individual — Foreign:** Closed-end funds: 0%<br><br>**Legal entity — Domestic:** Closed-end funds: 27.9% + tax credit equals to 15% of the capital gain that expires in 5 years<br>Investment firms: PEX applies<br>**Legal entity — Foreign:** Closed-end funds: 27.9% + tax credit equals to 15% of the capital gain that expires in 5 years (it must be used in Italy)<br>Investment firms: 27.9% | |
| Taxation on dividends | | | |
| Incentive to startup | | | **Carry forward:** Losses of the first 3 years of activity can be carried forward |
| Incentive to R&D investment | | | **R&D tax credit scheme** was introduced for FY2015 through FY2019 that offers a 25% or 50% credit of the annual R&D incremental expenditure exceeding the average expenditure incurred during FYs 2012, 2013 and 2014 |
| Comparative incentive D vs E | | | **Thin cap:** interest expenses are fully tax deductible up to the amount of proceeds, the exceeding part is deductible up to 30% of the gross margin<br>**Allowance for corporate equity:** deduction from the taxable basis of a rate multiplied by the net increase of equity |

**FIG. 10.3** The fiscal framework in Italy.

ii. the investment was classified as a financial fixed asset in the Statutory Financial Statements relating to the first tax period ownership;

iii. the majority of the subsidiary's income is not generated in a "tax haven country" or in a country with a privileged tax regime;

iv. the subsidiary is currently carrying out a commercial activity (e.g., investments in companies mainly operating in the management of their own Real Estate are not entitled to the PEX benefits).

Conditions (iii) and (iv) must be valid at the moment of the sale of the investment as well as for the last 3 years before the sale. If these conditions are not met, the capital gain realized by the investment firm is ordinarily taxed (IRES only). Capital losses arising from the sale or the write-down of shareholdings meeting PEX conditions are not tax deductible, management fees are deductible for tax purposes. Finally, the capital losses realized on sales of "non-PEX" investments are deductible.

There are two ways to compare investment vehicles in Italy to decide which one to use. Investment firms have higher revenues coming from capital gains and earnings, whereas closed-end funds have a higher increase in market value of shares during the holding period. This is related to the behavior and strategic plan of investors: if there is a short-term strategy, the better choice is an investment firm, but if the strategic view is long-term, closed-end funds are more appropriate. A different amount of tax is paid if income comes from closed-end funds rather than investment firms, and if investors are private or legal entities.

If income originates from closed-end funds, private investors (domestic or foreign) do not pay taxes on capital gains, whereas domestic legal entities pay taxes using a tax credit of 15% on the capital gain. Foreign legal entities do not pay taxes in Italy, only in their domestic country. If incomes originate from investment firms, private investors (domestic or foreign) pay a flat tax of 12.5% on the earnings, whereas legal entity investors use the participation exemption scheme for earnings.

If the income is originated from an investment firm, resident and nonresident individuals are asked to pay 49.72% tax rate on dividends if they are qualified shareholders. One shareholder is considered as qualified if the participation represents more than 5% of the share capital or represented more than 2% of the voting rights in a listed company; in an unlisted company the participation is considered as qualified if it represents at least 25% of the share capital or at least 20% of the voting rights. If the participation is not qualified, the tax rate is 26%.

Companies in Italy are asked to pay IRES and IRAP. There are many ways to calculate this taxable income. Private equity and venture capital deals may be realized with debt instruments so there is a rule defining the maximum amount of interest that may be deducted. Generally, interest expenses are fully tax deductible up to the amount of interest proceeds. Interest expenses exceeding interest proceeds are tax deductible up to 30% of the gross operating margin (interest deduction capacity). The Law defines "gross operating margin" as earnings before interest, taxes, depreciation, amortization, and finance leasing fees (it can be inferred that this is the definition of EBITDA). Starting from Fiscal Year (FY) 2016, dividends received from foreign subsidiaries are included in the computation of the gross operating margin. Net interest expenses in excess of the yearly limitation can be carried forward without any time limitation and can be deductible in any future tax period, as long as the net interest expenses in that tax year do not exceed 30% of the gross operating margin for the same period. In addition, if the yearly interest deduction capacity (i.e., 30% of the gross operating margin) exceeds the net interest deduction taken in that year, the excess of the interest deduction capacity may also be carried over to following periods to increase the future interest deduction capacity.

As for the incentives in the equity increase since 2011 a rule has been introduced on newly adjusted equity. This deduction is known as Allowance for Corporate Equity (ACE) or, in other words, Notional Interest Deduction (NID). The ACE is a deduction from corporate tax (IRES) basis an amount that corresponds to the net increase in the equity employed in the entity, multiplied by a rate yearly determined by the Italian Ministry of Finance. This rate is 4.5% for FY 2015 and 4.75% for FY 2016. The ACE not used in one fiscal year can be:

- carried forward in future fiscal years;
- transferred to the fiscal unit if the company is part of a tax group in a taxable income position;
- transformed into tax credit to be offset against IRAP payments made in five installments of the same amount.

An incremental R&D tax credit scheme was introduced for FY2015 through FY2019 that offers a 25% or 50% credit of the annual R&D incremental expenditure exceeding the average expenditure incurred during the three previous years depending on the nature of the expenses incurred. Italy also introduced a patent box that provides a 50% tax exemption phased-in over a 3-year period: (i) a 30% exemption for FY2015, (ii) a 40% exemption for FY2016, and (iii) a 50% exemption for FY2017.

### 10.6.3  Vehicle Taxation: United States

Principles for taxation in the United States include

- Transparency, that is, taxation on investment vehicles is simple: excluded or partially excluded

- Investors sustain, that is, provisions from specific schemes dedicated to private investors or to Business Angels
- R&D support, that is, provisions of rules that reduce the actual expenses for a start-up company, rather than for investing in R&D

In the United States different ways to invest in private equity and venture capital can be found. Deals can be run by

- Venture capital funds
- SBICs (small business investment companies)
- Business Angels

Venture capital funds refer to a pooled investment vehicle, very often a limited partnership (LP) that primarily invests the financial capital of third-party investors in enterprises that are too risky for the standard capital markets or a bank loan. To gain benefits provided by law, venture capital funds must be structured as a 10-year LP, extra-time must be 1 year as a maximum and the fundraising must last 1 year as a maximum.

In 1958, the Small Business Investment Act officially allowed the licensing of private SBICs to help the financing and management of small entrepreneurial businesses in the United States. It was believed that fostering entrepreneurial companies would spur technological business to compete. This federal program used public funds to develop the economic system by supporting SMEs. Today, rigid regulatory limitations minimize the role of SBICs. For SBICs as well, capital gains and dividend benefit of tax transparency.

Business Angels are private entrepreneurs who provide capital for a business start-up. The tax profile of Business Angels is more complicated and can be summarized by the following:

- Capital gains are de-taxed in case of reinvestment of money in 60 days in qualified small business stocks (QSBS) or SBIC shares
- Capital gains are de-taxed for 50% if the holding period of QSBS is higher than 5 years

Taxes are paid differently if the investor is a private individual or a legal entity.

Net capital gain and dividends received by individuals from domestic corporations and "qualified foreign corporations" are taxed at the same special rates as those applicable to net capital gains, for both the regular tax and the alternative minimum tax. Consequently, dividends and capital gains are taxed at the following rates:

- with 0% for individuals in the 10% or 15% progressive tax rate range
- with 20% for individuals in the 39.6% progressive tax rate range
- with 15% for individuals in all other progressive tax rate ranges

As for the dividends, to qualify for the 15% (or 0% or 20%) tax rate, the share-holder must hold a share of stock for more than 60 days during the 120-day period beginning 60 days before the exdividend date. Other dividends are taxed at ordinary rates. As for the capital gain benefit, the holding period must be larger than 12 months.

Capital gains received by a legal entity are always taxed (in the United States the participation exemption principle is not applied). A corporation's gains are taxed at the same rates as ordinary income (ranging from 15% to 39.5%). In general, capital losses may offset only capital gains, not ordinary income. Subject to certain restrictions, a corporation's excess capital loss may be carried back 3 years and forward 5 years to offset capital gains in such years.

Start-ups are provided as a mark down of the company tax rate between 0% and 19% related to the amount of revenues.

For R&D costs and investments, the "traditional credit" is equal to 20% of the amount of the qualified research expenses (QREs) exceeding a "base amount." The base amount is computed by: (i) first determining the ratio of QREs to gross receipts for the period of 1984–88. This ratio is called the fixed base percentage and reflects the amount of gross receipts a company has historically committed to R&D. There is a special start-up company rule that applies in determining the fixed base percentage if the company was not around during the base period (1984–88). The fixed base percentage is then multiplied by the average gross receipts of the taxpayer for the 4 years preceding the credit year. The product of this calculation is the base amount, that is, reflecting the amount of gross receipts a company would expect to commit to qualified research. The base amount must be adjusted for acquisitions and dispositions. This can be challenging considering that records dating back to the early 1980s are often not readily available Qualifying activities must be performed within the United States and the related qualifying costs must be incurred by a US taxpayer (although such costs may be reimbursed by a foreign affiliate). The alternative simplified credit (ASC) is equal to 14% of the excess of the QREs over 50% of the average of the previous 3 years' QREs. The ASC base amount is therefore much easier to determine than under the traditional method and most tax-payers elect the ASC.

Although the United States has no fixed rules for determining whether a thin-capitalization situation exists, a facts and circumstances test may be applied based on US case law. The United States has in fact some sort of thin-capitalization principle to limit the deduction for interest expense if a US cor-poration is thinly capitalized. In such case, funds loaned to the company by a related party may be recharacterized as equity in order not to be perceived as thinly capitalized. As a result, the corporation's deduction for interest expense may be disallowed, and principal and interest payments may be considered distributions to the related party and be subject to withholding tax as distributions.

### 10.6.4   Vehicle Taxation: United Kingdom

The principles for taxation in the United Kingdom are similar to those in the United States, but the actual tax systems are different; the British scheme for private equity and venture capital deals is more complicated. In the United Kingdom, private equity and venture capital deals are run by

- Venture capital funds
- Venture capital trusts
- Business Angels

A venture capital trust (VCT) is a highly tax efficient closed-end collective investment scheme designed to provide capital finance for small expanding companies and capital gains for investors. First introduced by the Conservative government in the Finance Act in 1995, VCTs have proved to be much less risky than originally anticipated. The Finance Act created VCTs to encourage investment in new UK businesses. VCTs are companies listed on the London Stock Exchange that invest in other companies who are not listed.

VCT enjoy tax transparency both for capital gains and for dividends, provided that:

- At least 70% of their investments must be in qualifying investments— small companies (maximum size £15 million) that are unquoted or traded on the AIM rather than the main stock market.
- They invest in the companies within 3 years of raising new money. They may invest elsewhere while making these decisions, so the risks can be different.

The remaining 30% of a VCT's money can be invested in basically any investment. These are often stable investments like cash, listed equities and large company debt instruments. Some VCTs use higher risk options, which increase the overall risk of your investment.

As for the trust investors, the VCT shares which qualify for the special VCT tax reliefs are ordinary shares in an approved VCT. Investors disposing his VCT share may not have to pay Capital Gain taxes and enjoy the so-called "Disposal Relief" if the following is met:

- relief is limited to acquisitions not exceeding £200,000 worth of VCT shares in any one tax year (£100,000 for the year 2003–04 and earlier years)

- the investor is an individual (not a trustee)
- the investor is 18 or over at the date of disposal
- the company was an approved VCT both when the shares were acquired and when they are being disposed
- the shares have been acquired for commercial reasons and not as part of a tax avoidance scheme.

Business angels in the United Kingdom, must act as individuals, so they can only be investors. There are different tax structures for investors considered as Business Angels, legal entities, or private or corporate investors. Business Angels in the United Kingdom can only be private investors, and their investment generates a tax credit of 20% if the holding period is longer than 3 years and the amount of the investment is lower than £150,000. Capital gains are de-taxed (and losses are deductible) if the holding period is longer than 3 years.

In both the United Kingdom and United States venture capital funds organized as 10-year LPs can deduct capital gains, while other revenues and costs are tax sensitive. Venture capital funds are pooled investments in companies believed to be too risky by banks or other financial institutions. In the United Kingdom the most common vehicle used to create a venture capital fund is the LP. To obtain benefits provided by law, the LP must run for 10 years, exceed with an extra time of 1 year as a maximum and raise the funds necessary in 1 year.

If the investor is a corporate venture there are general restrictions: they are only allowed to be unlisted companies and however under 30%. Corporate ventures generate a tax credit of 20% and capital gains are de-taxed if money is invested in the same investments within 3 years.

For private individuals the system is less intricate, because capital gains are taxed depending on the amount of income (an annual exemption of £11,100 is available to reduce capital gains). Legal entities are unsuitable vehicles for private equity and venture capital deals, because costs can be higher than other vehicles: capital gains are always taxed (in the United Kingdom the participation exemption principle is not applied) and earnings are always taxed.

Like the United States, there are many incentive schemes for start-ups and R&D expenditures. Fiscal rules allow a mark down of the company tax rate within a range of 0%–19% of the amount of revenues for a start-up.

The United Kingdom offers "super" deductions and credits that vary depending on the size of the taxpayer: a super deduction scheme for companies that fall within the definition of a SME and all other companies (large companies) can have an R&D credit or a super deduction. Generally, the criteria for qualification as a small and medium-sized company (SME) follows the EU definition except that the criteria are all doubled. The company must have fewer than 500 employees and either gross revenues of less than €100 million or gross assets of less than €86 million. Affiliated companies generally are considered in determining if a company qualifies as an SME.

SMEs that qualify for the following expenditure-based tax incentives enjoy:

- In all, 230% super deduction
- Cash credits in a loss position, up to 33.35% of the expenditure

However, there is a cap that restricts the amount of tax benefit available to SMEs, over and above the benefit that would have been available had the company not been an SME, to €7.5 million per R&D project.

In the United Kingdom there is a strict thin cap scheme and interest rate costs are not deductible.

PART

# Managing a Private Equity

# Investment

# CHAPTER 11

# The Managerial Process

## 11.1  INTRODUCTION

The fourth part of the book is dedicated to the best practices that a manager has to implement over the managerial process to make sure they select the right investment, they monitor it in the most adequate way and that they realize the internal rate of return (IRR) they granted to the investors.

This chapter is dedicated to providing an overview of the whole process, whereas following chapters will deal each with one the four pillars of the managerial process.

## 11.2  THE NEED OF A STRUCTURED MANAGERIAL PROCESS FOR THE PRIVATE EQUITY BUSINESS

Empirical evidence clearly shows that private equity and venture capital deals cannot be considered "traditional" financial deals for two reasons: the different evaluation system and the above average risk profile. As Benveniste et al. underlined, this industry develops where a greater informative opacity exists, because of sectors considered (i.e., venture capitalists tend to specialize in high-tech and high-growth sectors), the agreement characteristics (i.e., private equity operators and venture capitalists usually define the exit strategy before the deal), and the traits of issued securities (i.e., warrant rather than preferred shares), apart from the expectations of the entrepreneurs and financial institutions.

Gompers and Lerner stated that all difficulties found in the private equity industry analysis may be attributed to informational problems and to the different incentives of the subjects involved in these deals. Private equity operations are concentrated in sectors with a high degree of uncertainty and where informative gaps are common among investors, entrepreneurs, and financiers. Moreover, Gompers and Lerner believed firms requiring private equity interventions had problems connected to intangible valuations whereas investors care about how to fund the firm and how the funds are used.

**153**

Private Equity and Venture Capital in Europe. https://doi.org/10.1016/B978-0-12-812254-9.00011-5

Gompers and Lerner wrote about the "venture capital cycle" and further expanded the idea: from a financial standpoint, private equity financing or venture capital financing may be described as a process that starts with funding, followed by investment and monitoring phases, and concluded with the exit. They further stressed the venture capital cycle can be applied to private equity deals, even though the typical information concerns are more prevalent in venture capital.

Gompers and Lerner are not the only ones analyzing the private equity and venture capital process. Reid and Smith have also analyzed the relationship between financiers and entrepreneurs in a "principal-agent framework" where the entrepreneur is the agent and the financier is the principal. They underlined the different typologies of risk faced in the private equity industry, and explained agency and nonagency reasons that lead to the signing rather than to the abandonment of initiatives.

Nevertheless, the analysis proposed by Gompers and Lerner represents a clear reference point for the analysis of the entire sector because of its simplicity and ability to subdivide the venture capital (and private equity) cycle into standard phases: fundraising, investing, and exit.

This is the right way to analyze private equity and venture capital because it does not depend on the characteristics of investors, deals, and the level of involvement.

Analysis of the private equity cycle considers at least three different types of subjects: suppliers of financial sources, private equity operators, and beneficiaries of financial sources. The first group supplies funds to financial institutions because they are not skilled enough to analyze deals or they cannot bear the risk. The second group is made up of financial institutions whose tasks are to define, select, control, and monitor investments. Finally, beneficiaries are companies that receive financial sources, implement expansion projects or turnaround or change of ownership, and accept all conditions and clauses provided by financial institutions (see Fig. 11.1).

Furthermore, the analysis should focus on the characteristics of each step to evaluate the activities emerging in the typical relationships created during deal evolution. In this sense, fundraising, which involves suppliers and investors in venture capital and private equity, presents issues intended to respond to specific needs of the subjects involved. Thus the comprehension of which players are involved, their needs, their fears, and the characteristics of agreements they sign is the first step in understanding how to improve the first phase of the private equity process and the first step to develop a successful private equity deal.

The investment activity (and subsequent management and monitoring) is based on the results of the previous phase and must also provide solutions

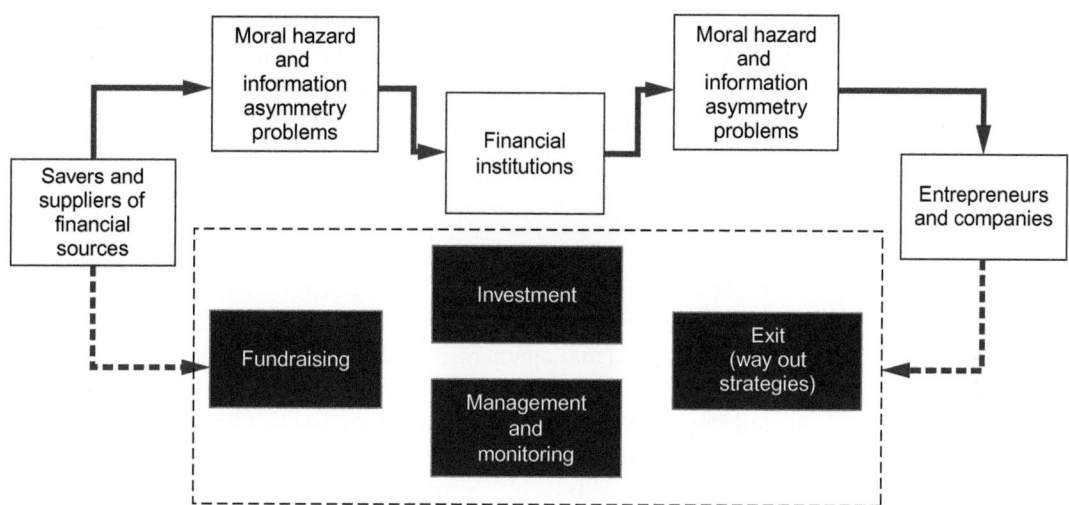

**FIG. 11.1** The private equity cycle.

to the typical problems incurred in this step. It must be emphasized that most of the potential troubles of this phase present the same structure as those addressed during the fundraising phase but, at the same time, they present internal variables that make them difficult to standardize and are more complicated. All issues regarding the evaluation of the counterparty must be resolved as well as the quantification of nonfinancial involvement of financial institutions or the definition of characteristics of individual securities that must be issued. In addition to the characteristics of the subjects involved, the most important items to be analyzed include the vehicle, the characteristics of each contract, and the relationships among investors involved.

The last phase of the private equity cycle is the exit of investors from companies. Here the analysis focuses on modalities used for the way out, the time of exit, and on the role played by operators. Relationships between entrepreneurs and venture capitalists or private equity operators, and between providers of financial sources and financial institutions, are very important for the process of liquidation and exit from the investments.

## 11.3 EQUITY INVESTMENT AS A PROCESS: ORGANIZATION AND MANAGEMENT

Equity investment satisfies two different needs: (1) companies collect funds because their entrepreneurs do not have sufficient financial resources to support and increase the development of their businesses and (2) these financial resources are held by investors that finance high-risk high-reward projects.

Equity investments can be developed through vehicles that allow institutional private equity and venture capital activity. Such pools of money are distributed among different companies representing potential sources of high economic returns for investors.

As mentioned in the previous chapters, different vehicles for investment activity include

1. Partnership. Shareholders are responsible for the management of the private equity fund and they respond directly with their personal assets; in some cases, the management of the fund can be delegated to external professionals (management company), but the total funds reserved for shareholders and the fund are equal, and the fund does not represent an autonomous legal entity. This partnership has a life of about 10 years that can be extended for 2 more years depending on the shareholders.

2. Limited partnership (LP). Similar to the partnership presented in the first bullet point, this vehicle presents two clearly defined categories of shareholders: limited partners and general partners. Limited partners are institutional and individual investors who provide capital. They have limited responsibility in the fund's management and investment decisions, which only extends to the capital they contribute. The general partners, in addition to their contribution of capital, are responsible for organizing the fundraising, managing the funds raised, and the reimbursement of the quotas to the subscribers at the expiry of the fund. Their responsibility is extended to their personal assets. Almost all partnerships allow a single partner to close the partnership in case of a death or withdrawal of the general partners and/or fund bankruptcy. Usually the LPs include some private agreement allowing the limited partners to dissolve the partnership and replace the general partner if the limited partners represent more than 50% of the fund and the general partners are damaging the fund. This vehicle is the one used in the United States and in the United Kingdom to invest in venture capital.

3. Corporation. A company where the shareholders are the investors, that is, the venture-backed company. The main disadvantage, compared with the previous organizational forms, is that the corporation is subject to taxation on capital gains realized (and not distributed), whereas the partnership and the LP have full "fiscal transparency." The law does not allow specific parties to operate through partnership or LP in a corporation.

4. Closed-end fund. An autonomous legal entity independent from both the subscribers and the company that manages the resources. The subscribers, however, cannot interfere in the management or investment activities of the management company. The management of the fund can also be supported by one or more advisory companies.

Depending on the format the investors want to use, which is to say European or Anglo-Saxon, the closed-end fund is allowed to leverage.

Regardless of the legal structure, a set of common characteristics distinguish venture capital funds from other types of financial intermediaries:

1. Limited life. This fund has a predefined expiry date at which the stakes of different investors are redeemed on a pro rata basis. This minimizes the risks to venture capitalists and investors during the time and methods of redistributing the invested funds. Returning the subscribed quotas to investors is a powerful incentive to optimize the efficiency of management company investment policies. If the results are worse than expected, it will seriously compromise the fund's ability to raise money in the future.

2. Flexibility. A management company can launch several funds simultaneously, each one characterized by a distinctive duration, capital, and investment philosophy; therefore, it is possible to satisfy a variety of investor categories, each with a specific risk/return/liquidity profile, widening the depth of the risk capital market. This flexibility allows the manager to delegate (to advisor companies) some of their institutional activity (fundraising, identification of the target companies, investment selection and/or monitoring, analysis of the exit opportunities). Therefore the company is always able to supply the clientele with highly specialized and sophisticated products without possessing wide and specialized expertise.

3. Remuneration mechanisms. Parties appointed to the fund management receive a fixed management fee, generally between 2% and 3% of the total capital raised. The management company also participates in the final result of the fund, through the carried interest mechanism, allowing it to receive a certain percentage of the total capital gains realized in the exit phase. Hence, private equity investors are more responsible in the investment selection and management activities because this affects an important part of their own remuneration and ultimately their track record and reputation.

Venture capital funds constituted through LPs provide two distinct investment categories, general partners and limited partners, with a different level of involvement and responsibility in the management of the capital raised. This separation is typical in closed-end funds, but it does not occur between the reserves of the venture capital fund and the fund managers; the general partners allow the management team to act autonomously in the selection of the best investment opportunities, accelerating the decision-making process relative to the preparation and conclusion of the investments.

To avoid the risk of opportunistic general partners, they are explicitly prohibited from trading operations on their own behalf (self-dealing), which could allow them to receive benefits unavailable to the limited partners.

In contrast to the closed-end funds, subscribers can exit the investment before the end of the fund's life, that is, the limited partners can ask at any time for reimbursement of the subscribed quota. It is thus possible that liquidity risks might arise within the LP jeopardizing the stability of the financial resources given to the companies financed.

LP is not a company with share capital so it is not eligible, in the countries whose legal regulations provide for such a company structure, to be admitted for quotation on official stock markets. The quotas of a closed-fund, on the other hand, can be traded on a regulatory market, and in case of quotation, it is possible to subdivide the quotas to permit greater marketability of their certificates and increase the liquidity profile.

In the countries where it is possible to constitute an LP, the largest part of its success is related to favorable fiscal schemes. This is different from the schemes applicable to other intermediaries operating in the venture capital market, for example, the closed-end fund.

## 11.4   THE FOUR PILLARS OF EQUITY INVESTMENT

Vehicles dedicated to equity investment have a specific value chain with phases and organizational functions that can be classified worldwide. For each phase there is a different contribution from the management, the advisory board, and the board of directors. The typical phases of the managerial process are fundraising, investing, managing, monitoring, and exit.

### 11.4.1   Fundraising

Fundraising is the promotion of a new equity investment vehicle within the business community; the purpose is to find money and create a commitment. The main motivation, considered by investors during the selection of the funds, is based on obtaining higher returns than those offered by the financial market. Private equity investors normally want a premium of about 5% compared with the gain. This extra performance covers the extra risk connected with the minor liquidity of the fund and the higher risk connected with private companies. Track record of the investment managers based on their competencies, their reputation, and their previous performance are also factors that can make a difference in the fundraising phase. Investment managers should demonstrate that past deals have been successful on a series of good capital allocations not just one successful deal. The success of a private equity investor is measured through IRR. The money multiple (the number of how many times the fund has been able to multiply the initial endowment of capital) is also used because it is influenced less by distortions over the duration of the investment. Investors also evaluate the terms and rules included in the corporate governance structure of the fund.

The fund subscribers do not just consider the IRR realized by the investment, but also the performance of the fund netted by the costs, the fees, and carried interests paid. It is important to define the carried interest: it is a part of the earnings generated by the fund and given back to the management team at the end of the fund. It is around 30% of the fund performance and can be calculated in two different ways:

1. The fund as a whole—The carried interest is based on the total performance and result of the fund and is paid only when the investors receive their total capital before subscribers.
2. Deal by deal—The investment manager receives a part of the profit obtained from the investment, but they have to avoid the eventual losses provoked by management activity.

Mixed solutions are also frequently applied allowing the investment managers to receive the carried interest deal by deal but only at the end of the fund after reimbursing the risk capital to subscribers.

Fundraising is a tough step for all funds, especially for those ones without a track record, because many investors are reluctant to invest in an unproven team even if the partners have successful individual track records. There are many ways in which new private equity funds can solve this problem. The first solution is to identify and involve investors who are not focused only on financial returns but look for some strategic benefit from the fund. In this case the investors are willing to accept a lower return in the light of the indirect benefit provided by the investment. The second strategy is to arrange a partnership with an existing institution such as an investment bank or another private equity fund providing a joint management of the funds raised.

---

PAUSE: How is named an investor that is called to invest with the primary purpose of attracting other investors?

---

The main benefit of this strategy is improved credibility but, at the same time, there are some real costs; for example, investors should suspect that the institutional partner will affect the quality of the investment strategy. Another solution is to hire an anchor investor. This is an institutional investor who leads the investment strategy. His is often called a special limited partner because he subscribes a relevant amount of capital and usually provides the financial resources needed by the fund to cover the costs of marketing (seed funding).

Fundraising activity is directly influenced and determined both by the supply of private equity (the relative desire of institutional investors to allocate capital in the sector), and the demand for private equity (the number of entrepreneurs with a good idea who want to be financed). Many analyses of fundraising activity have been performed and one theory suggests that this activity is impacted, in inverse proportion, by the change in tax rates that should foment or lower fund demand. Other theories argue that fundraising activity depends on the public equity market status: during robust phases the market allows new firms to issue shares and entrepreneurs to achieve liquidity and monetize the value of their companies.

There are many sources of capital and the following are six of the most common investor types:

1. Family and friends are the most common source of seed money and probably the easiest way to raise funds, but are also the most likely to cause problems. If the business fails, the financial troubles of the parties involved may be dwarfed by the emotional consequences. Nonetheless, many of America's successful companies have been created from this type of financing.
2. Private placement funds are subscribed by private "amateur" investors instead of professional investors. There are big risks when playing such an important role in the development of major innovative firms.
3. Private pool of funds are partnerships between different shareholders who decide to invest part of their own assets.
4. Corporate funds are funds and financial resources managed by venture capital with the intention of financing companies in the development stage.
5. Mutual investment funds are financial vehicles that provide capital by issuing and placing participation quota with investors.
6. Bank financial intermediaries, in particular merchant banks, are entities most oriented to long-term investments and are prepared to sustain risk levels.

REMEMBER: Do you remember how each of this financier is associated to each private equity cluster?

## 11.4.2  Investing

To reach financial and competitive goals, a private equity investor creates value through the scouting and screening of available investments. The type of investment is chosen through the use of debt, because the private equity management team is involved in the governance of the venture-backed companies financed.

There are different practical types of investment: investment in a private equity fund, in a private equity fund of funds, or the direct investment in equity or the construction of a private equity fund and the involvement of the private equity fund in the firm-financed shareholders under the control of a single entrepreneur. The first two types of equity investment follow a logical financial strategy, whereas the last two follow an industrial strategy and the third one (direct investment in equity) has both a financial and industrial logic.

The investments, depending on the specific phases of the life cycle of the target firm, can be classified into six clusters presented in the first and second part of the book.

Investors of risk capital must focus on the origination activity, which consists of a steady flow of investment opportunity. This is the key factor in starting the investment process. The origination phase includes selection of an investment opportunity realized through appropriate professional resources and information. This phase requires a lot of time due to the extremely selective nature of the investment decision through risk capital, especially if early stage expansion or the buy out of a small-to-medium family firm with a high level of innovation is selected. The selection is based on the industry and the position inside the industry of the target firm, the validity and reliability of the business plan, the entry price, the quality and skills of the entrepreneur and/or management of the target firm, and the exit strategy.

Scouting activity should create good proprietary deal flow and its strategy must be consistent with investment policies, the type of investor, and their cultural and industrial characteristics.

The scouting, screening, and eventual choice of the investment are realized using different tools:

- SWOT analysis
- Industry analysis
- Future financials analysis
- Valuation of the company by different techniques, that is, comparables, fundamentals, net present value, adjusted present value, and discounted cash flow
- Industrial and human resources skills valuation
- Valuation of management skills and track record
- Due diligence (market, environmental, accounting, financial, legal, and tax).

During investment activity, it is important to have a clear entry and exit strategy as well as rules established between investors and the entrepreneur regarding transparency, involvement in the board of directors, and the general overview of the company management. It is critical to define the timing and the privacy of the investment deal, to be fully engaged in the negotiation process, and to ignore the rumors and deal inside the financial market and with other equity investors.

As the mere goal of the private equity is to generate IRR, when in this phase, managers should define covenants, the timing of divestment, contractual IRR expected, and identification of subscribers.

### 11.4.3   Managing and Monitoring

The third phase of the managerial process, managing and monitoring increase the likelihood to create value and ease the activity to control opportunistic behaviors of the venture-backed companies. The two activities aim at creating, measuring, and establishing rules, the first one requires the availability of deep expertise and advisory skills, the second one requires a valuable network of relationship of financial investors.

The private equity investors supports the financed company by participating in all activities concerning the Board of Directors and other committee meetings, with professional expertise, and the ability to impose severe discipline. Investors also help hiring some of the management team of the venture-backed company because they have a great depth of knowledge about specific companies and their sectors. Another source of value is the investors' network of customers, suppliers, governmental lobbying, and the ability to arrange additional financing.

According to the survey from MacMillan, Kulow, and Khoylian (1988), there were three different types of investors directly involved in the management of target companies. The first cluster is represented by the "laissez faire" investor who participates little in the firm's daily activity. This investor provides funds and advice which is used to improve the financial structure of the target company and the relationship with other financial supporters. These are the investors adopting the so-called "hands off approach."

> REMEMBER: Do you remember how the hands on/off approach is related to each of the private equity clusters?

The second group is composed of shareholder investors with a higher level of involvement. Not only do they contribute money, but they also support management and operation choices. The third and last type of investor is fully involved in the daily activity of the target company. These investors take part in marketing and operation strategies as well as monitoring the strategies during the implementation phase. These are the investors adopting the so-called "hands on approach."

## 11.4.4 Exiting

When exiting, the decision to sell equity owned in the portfolio to gain the value added created during the managing of the investment is considered. It is a decision that has to be planned with broad vision, because it directly impacts the portfolio performance. This phase of the venture investment is critical and a good time and the best way to exit must be identified. The investment manager should have a clear idea about the potential disinvestment from the beginning, especially with minority participation where the team has to avoid any arbitral constraints connected with the financial partner's exit.

Exit decisions are not only based on the economic return created. Every investment implies the arrangement of specific rules and covenants regulating their relationship. This prevents and mitigates any agency problems and opportunistic behavior. Exiting is also directly influenced by external or internal factors related to the status of the company and its industry as well as the financial market.

Every exit strategy must have a concrete way out that transcends the logic and the legal structure of the investments. There are a number of common and widespread exiting strategies:

- Trade sale happens when the private equity investor sells its participation to a corporation or an industrial shareholder
- Buy back strategy sells its stake to already existing shareholders or other people they choose
- Sale to other private equity investors
- Write off is the devaluation, partially or totally, of the participation value as a consequence of the loss of money unrelated to a transfer of property
- IPO, or sale post IPO, allows the private equity investor to exit by selling its stake through the stock exchange market

It is important to plan the exit in advance is because the timing of the exit strategy depends on when the economic return is monetized for both the subscribers of the private equity fund and the investment manager. Private equity investors are compensated by the potential revaluation of the participation in the venture-backed company, but the investor manager and his team are compensated in other ways:

Structuring fees are the costs directly connected with the creation and organization of funds. They are also related to the fiscal and legal advisory activity; these costs are directly deducted from the total funds available for the investment activities that will be undertaken.
Management fee is a commission between 1.5% and 2.5% of the total capital subscribed.

Transaction fee is a commission for each single operation charged to the single venture-backed company where the investment has been realized; this commission can also include the aborted costs (costs connected to an uncompleted deal).

Carried interest is a part of the total gain realized by the fund, usually 30%, paid to the investment manager only if the rate of return of the fund is larger than the hurdle rate agreed between the parties. This mechanism plays a double role: an incentive for the private equity manager to work hard and a signal that attracts potential subscribers fascinated by the explicit trust in the investment manager's dealing skills.

## 11.5   THE RELEVANCE OF EXPERTISE AND SKILLS WITHIN THE PROCESS

The expertise and attitude needed in the investment process (see Fig. 11.2) is different depending on the specific step of the managerial process. The specific skills necessary during the venture capital activity (Table 11.1) include:

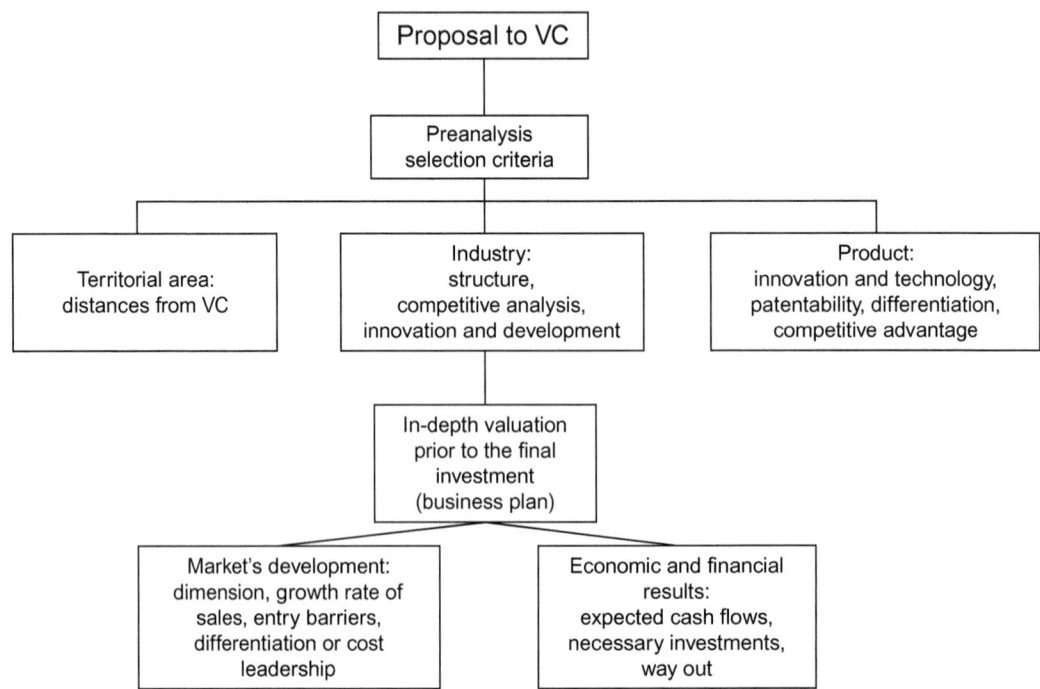

**FIG. 11.2** The process of equity investment analyzed in the preinvestment phase.

**Table 11.1** Skills Necessary in the Private Equity Managerial Process

| | Company Valuation | Legal and Fiscal | Governance | Reporting | Promoting and Selling | Recruiting | People Management |
|---|---|---|---|---|---|---|---|
| Fundraising | | ♦ | ♦ | | ♦ | | |
| Investing | ♦ | ♦ | ♦ | ♦ | | | |
| Managing and monitoring | | | ♦ | ♦ | | ♦ | ♦ |
| Exit | ♦ | ♦ | ♦ | | ♦ | | |

- Company valuation skills are relevant during the investing and exiting phases. If the investment activity is to hit its economic returns target, then it is critical to wisely select the investment target and choose the right time and way to exit.
- Legal and fiscal skills are important during the deal structuring, closing, and exiting because they are the stages when the private equity fund has to define and respect specific legal and tax requirements balanced with the needs and desires of the investors.
- Governance skills are relevant during all the processes because they allow the investment manager to structure and lead critical relationships early in the investment, during the phase of management and monitoring, and within the entrepreneur and/or the management team of the financed firm.
- Reporting activities are concentrated during the core phases of investing and managing funds owned by private equity. They are important for solving or reducing agency problems between subscribers and managers of the fund and also to guarantee a higher level of transparency.
- Promoting and selling skills are critical at the founding and at the closing of the fund, because they help realize the desired economic return at the exit.
- Recruiting and people management skills are part of the soft support that a private equity gives to the venture-backed company during the managing and monitoring phase. These skills try to satisfy the needs of a team that works well together while researching the success of an entrepreneurial initiative.

# CHAPTER 12

# Fundraising

## 12.1 INTRODUCTION

The financing of entrepreneurial projects cannot be separated from collecting the necessary funds to realize investments. This activity is fundamental within the managerial process regardless the legal status of the deal, the organizational structure of subjects involved, and the characteristics of firms or projects selected later.

Unfortunately, this issue has never attracted any academic interest so there has been little research done to understand the phenomena that drive the business and the success of fundraising.

The elements of fundraising are classified by the

- Players involved
- Problems and risks
- Objectives

In this phase, the most important players have the financial sources to invest in risky projects. Typically, there are two broad categories of investors: individuals and institutional.

Individuals are ordinary savers who have a significant amount of resources available for investments, the propensity and the preference for high-risk investments, the desire for portfolio diversification, and who search for high returns. However, the individual investor typically invests less than the institutional investors who typically are in the financial industry. They know the market environment and they are able to accurately understand the risk and expected return of an investment or financing. These investors are known as professional investors. Typically, the professional investors have more resources to invest and operate in a medium/long term, because they can ensure private equity operators or venture capitalist a substantial flow of resources and are able to wait a reasonable period of time to achieve their performance targets.

Private Equity and Venture Capital in Europe. https://doi.org/10.1016/B978-0-12-812254-9.00012-7

Investors and venture capitalists (financiers and money collectors) deal with different types of risk. Business risk is borne by venture capitalists or private equity operators, because they identify opportunities and exploit economies of scale. The components related to agency risk are similar with different nuances. The resource providers face information asymmetry and the risk of opportunistic behavior by financial institutions. Financial institutions, at least in theory, are at risk for opportunistic behavior by suppliers of funds that cannot make the agreed payments, change the terms, alter expectations, etc. An appropriate contract structure can overcome these difficulties, but they cannot be totally eliminated.

Problems related to the nature of risks and potential troubles that arise in the relationship between groups involved in the fundraising phase are attributed to the different objectives they are each trying to achieve. Unfortunately, no empirical tests have been done on specific objectives of financiers and private equity operators during fundraising limiting the conclusions drawn on this vital topic.

Balboa and Martí (2003) concluded that investments made the year before the fundraising and fundraising activity from the following year are strongly connected as well as the divestment of assets, the earnings history of transactions, and the amount of sources available for these deals. Kanniainen and Keuschnigg (2004) stated that the size of a private equity investor is directly connected to its capacity to collect money. Based on these assumptions, Cumming (2008) postulated that the size of the portfolios held by institutional investors in risky deals was a function of the market conditions, organizational structure of financial institutions, types of investments, level of development, and sector of funded companies. Fundraising sells a proposal or business idea to a particular market. The funds raised are used to create and invest in an equity vehicle that produces value shared between the promoters–managers and the investors. Funds may be raised over a period of 1–2 years. This can create information asymmetry and moral hazard problems between the venture capitalist and the individual investors that are typical for a principal-agent relationship.

The information asymmetry occurs because the investors have trouble monitoring the venture capitalist. Investments are generally made during the start-up stage so it is difficult to compare the investments with the market activity until the conclusion of this stage. Moral hazard is generated from the venture capitalists. They generally subscribe up to 1% of the capital with the aim of maximizing their gain and at the same time to diversify the risk.

To reduce moral hazard and information asymmetry and to ensure a high rate of success, fundraising has to be studied and structured as a selling game where reputation, mutual trust, and "love for gambling" are the pillars of a risky job dedicated to the raising of large amounts of money.

The only way to solve the information asymmetry is to impose regular and smooth communication about the investment's performance. Moral hazard can be avoided through

- Fixed deadlines for the return of the funds to the investors
- Exiting revenues distributed to the subscribers
- Gradually collecting equity subscribed

There are certain steps in the fundraising process that lead to a successful result:

- Creation of the business idea
- Venture capital organizations
- Job selling
- Debt raising (only for funds in the United States and in the United Kingdom)
- Calling plan
- Types of investment

## 12.2 CREATION OF THE BUSINESS IDEA

The creation of a business idea starts by explaining the idea to the business community and catch the attention of potential investors.

Business idea creation is aimed at producing an information memorandum to be promoted in the market.

Before an information memorandum is produced a preparatory phase named "testing the waters" occurs. This phase is carried on in a very informal way among the professional network of the private equity firm to assess, for instance, whether it makes sense for the private equity investors to invest in a specific cluster of private equity or not.

After the managers have received an informal consensus about their activity, a more formal part begins and the information memorandum is produced.

The information memorandum has to explain the rationale of the business idea to the business community (and to the supervisors, in case the fundraising occurs in Europe) and has to appeal to the potential audience of investors.

The success of the involvement of an investor into the business idea is strictly linked to the reputation and to the track record of the promoter.

The information memorandum includes at least the following elements:

- Choice of the vehicle
- Target to invest (countries, sectors, life cycle stages)
- Size of the vehicle and minimum for closing

- Corporate governance[1] rules (i.e., relationship between promoters–managers and investors)
- Size and policy of investments
- Internal code of activity if the fund is set in Europe; LPA if the fund is set in the United States/United Kingdom
- Track record of the promoters–managers
- Usage and size of leverage
- Costs

In the United Kingdom and the United States, private equity investors are generally structured as a single company that simultaneously manages different funds that are legally separated in a limited partnership (LP). There are fiscal advantages for this type of structure: the venture capitalist has unlimited responsibility by subscribing only 1% of the fund and investor responsibility is limited to the amount of capital subscribed.

The typical Italian structure for private equity activity is the closed-end fund.[2] Like in the case of the LPs, it is impossible to commit further capital after the fund has been launched (i.e., when all shares have been subscribed) and the investor exit is possible only when the fund expires or by agreement. The normal duration of the fund is 10 years divided into two periods (investment and disinvestment period).

---

PAUSE: how is a fund called when the investor can enter and exit any time?

---

Topics considered when analyzing the valuation of the target company:

- Country where the target is based
- Industry
- Status of quoted company
- Availability and reliability of data used for valuation
- Life cycle stage

Each fund applies its own strategy when choosing the investment target. It is common to mix the previously listed elements, but valuation of the company can also be based on cash flow methods, market-based methods, or income-based and balance sheet methods. Different approaches to valuation of the target company depend on dissimilar industries (old vs new economy), different weight of the intangible assets, and the opportunity for the target company to

---

[1]Instrument governing the rules for the nomination and function of supervisory boards, function of the business control, and greater control of particular acts.

[2]This term refers to the legal structures operating in the United States that are similar to closed-end funds; in Great Britain, the venture capital trusts; in France, the *fonds communs de placement à risque*; in Germany the *unternehmensbeteiligungsgesellschaft*; and in Spain, the *fondos de capital-riesgo*.

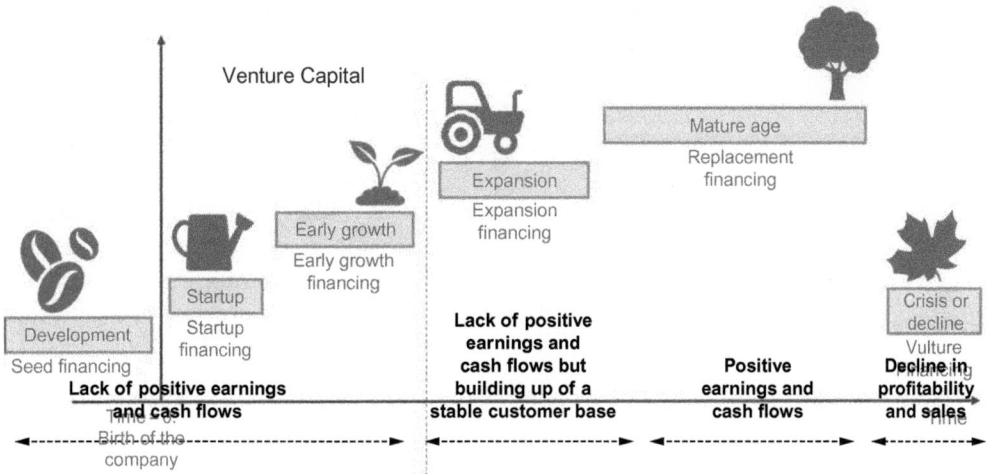

**FIG. 12.1** Life cycle of a company.

compare its value with the average value of similar public companies. In general,[3] income-based methods are often used in

Italy,[4] France, and Germany, whereas the other methods are more prevalent in the United Kingdom and the United States.

During valuation of possible targets, regardless of the method, it is necessary to consider the position of the company along its life cycle curve (Fig. 12.1); this affects both the value and the duration of the investment.

Creating or absorbing cash flow is strictly connected with a company's life cycle stage. A company early in its life cycle will not create cash flow for a long time so it will take a while to obtain the desired return on the high-risk investment. A mature firm, on the other hand, may ensure a steady cash flow and lower risk thanks to a shorter payback period.

Each investment fund has its own investment policy, which is a consequence of the

1. Amount of capital collected
2. Strategy of the promoter

---

[3] Americans use the concept of enterprise value added (EVA), which is very close to the "goodwill" tradition of Europe. European venture capitalists and investment companies increasingly use free cash flow or multiples for valuing not only high tech firms but also old economy ones. This is not a surprise considering the globalization of financial markets and relative practices.

[4] In Italy, the use of net worth based methods or earning methods has been ratified at a statutory level by the Bank of Italy, which recommends these metrics for the valuation of companies included in closed funds portfolios. Cash flow methods are not openly recommended.

3. Composition of the total fund's portfolio managed
    1. The amount of capital collected affects the flexibility of the fund's management. This allows fund promoters to choose between megadeals, which are pooled investments focused on very big, highly visible target companies on the market, and low risk investment with a diversified group of small- to middle-sized firms
    2. The strategy of the promoter is related to the financial market in which the fund operates and that influences its size; in Italy for a fund to be considered large it must have €500 million while in the United Kingdom and in the United States it is necessary to collect at least $1 billion.
    3. Fundraising is not a mere money collecting. It also involves a strict and constant relationship between the promoters-managers and the investors that can improve investor retention when it is conducted with transparency. This phase also indirectly involves all aspects of the business reducing the risk of moral hazard and agency costs.

Structured, well-planned, and exhaustive communication helps the temporary marriage among investors. It is executed through the investors plenum summoned at least annually and within 6 months after the end of the fiscal year and through the quarterly performance report, which includes:

1. Fund summary describing structure, strategy, and relevant news
2. Executive summary detailing funds raised, investments, and changes related to fund managers
3. The trend of a monthly IRR and the actual value of the sum invested
4. Important news about target companies

Many funds have an advisory board and an investors' committee. The advisory board solves potential conflicts of interest and supports the managers, whereas the investors committee takes care of the relationship with the key investors. It is advantageous to avoid an excess of involvement in the daily operation without delegation of audit and planning authority.

The value of the investment is strictly influenced by a tax shield; the value created from financing through the debt allows the deduction of interest paid from the companies' incomes. This fiscal benefit allows companies to increase leverage up to the optimum value of the debt equity ratio, which permits the tax shield benefit without creating financial distress or reducing the value created.

> REMEMBER: what are the fiscal mechanisms that can be used to affect the *D/E* ratio?

It is impossible to conclude the analysis of the first step of fundraising without considering the costs connected with the creation of the deal in terms of time spent and economic resources and the due diligence that has to be executed. Preparation of the business idea involves an audit of the legality of the fund structure and the predisposition of the marketing presentation. The most expensive part of building a new private equity fund driven by the costs of legal and fiscal advisors.

In addition, costs incurred by promotion fees from the placement agent have to be taken into account. The placement agent is a specialized operator with a big network of potential capital-raising clients whose experience contributes to the definition of the fund and the marketing strategy. It is necessary to hire a placement agent from the beginning because his expertise is important from the initial stages. Therefore, the general partner or manager of the fund hires the placement agent to facilitate a quick end of the fundraising and attract a more effective segment of target investors. Another advantage of employing a placement agents is his ability to dedicate all of his time to investment selection. The placement agent is paid a significant commission, about 2% of capital raised, applied only in case of success. In Europe it is common to form a sponsorship with banks and consulting companies with well-known and widespread reputations. Sponsors of the fund are selected because of their professional track record and success with previously closed financial operations. The expertise and the high standing of the investment managers guarantees the interest of potential investors. It is also possible that sponsors can participate in investment decisions by selecting and evaluating investments and possible conflicts of interest. The purpose of sponsorship is to reassure investors the venture-backed company, often small and little known, is a reliable and trust worthy one. Moreover, if the sponsor is a bank or a financial intermediary, they are likely to take part in investment decisions. Sponsors are used especially in Europe.

It is important to underline the importance of investment managers who manage and maintain the relationship with the potential underwriter of the fund. They organize several meetings (in general four or five) to inform potential investors about the fund. Fund managers must also manage and develop a relationship with financial markets. This is a fundamental element for the entrance and maintenance of the fund's position inside the financial market and for future successful fundraising.

The due diligence process allows investors to acquire all necessary information to make the investment and guarantee close quicker. When due diligence is done properly, it focuses on the market, environment, financial structure, and legal and tax position of the company financed.

## 12.3 VENTURE CAPITAL ORGANIZATIONS

According to the outcome of the business idea creation, there may be different option to set up a venture capital organization:

1. Business Angels—Private investors, with a large amount of available personal finance and a detailed knowledge of the sector in which they wish to invest, who finance new entrepreneurial initiatives. They take on high-risk, high-reward projects that have higher potential than the institutional venture capital companies. The principal limit of this type of investor is related to the limited dimensions of the assets invested.

---

PAUSE: where do they most operate?

---

2. Private pools of funds—Partnerships in which several shareholders (limited partners) have decided to invest a part of their own assets. Typically these funds originate from entrepreneurs or holders with substantial assets who are interested in jointly investing part of their wealth in new enterprises with potentially high returns. Historically, these entrepreneurs consolidated the success of their own company and decided to invest their own know-how and financial resources in new initiatives with excellent development prospects. Their solid financial background and expertise sustained high-risk projects in familiar or different sectors to diversify the portfolio. Transfers made between shareholders can range from $25,000 to $10 million individually. These are typically small deals.

3. Corporate funds—Funds and financial resources belonging to companies managed by venture capitalists that finance developing companies. Some companies also finance the start-up phase, but in certain cases the culture and interests of the developing company can block the development of new initiatives because they lack defined objectives and are incapable of managing rapidly evolving situations.

4. Mutual investment funds—Very important financial channels for venture capital because of the amount of capital raised publicly and the diversification requirements. They are financial vehicles that provide capital by issuing and placing a participation quota on investors (institutional and/or private). Closed-end funds meet the requirements of start-up companies, because the capital is stable for a medium- to long-term horizon and there is high-risk. In the UK and US markets fundraising for closed-end funds comes from pension funds, both public and private, whereas in Europe the largest investment comes from the banking system and other institutional investors. Closed-end fundraising occurs during the initial formation phase through financial intermediaries until the capital requirement is reached. Therefore the fund is managed by a specialized intermediary who will invest in development projects whose returns will be distributed to investors on exit.

5. Public private equity firms—They go public in order to obtain greater financial resources than those obtained from private investors. The greater inflow of capital is a consequence of the greater notoriety and transparency as well as the possibility for investors to exit from the operation due to a secondary market. In Europe the largest part of the capital in venture capital companies is held by founders and families belonging to the general partner.

6. Financial intermediaries (insurance companies, finance companies, investment banks)—Normally they have the necessary expertise to value industrial projects and raise funds for their realization. Merchant banks are entities most oriented to long-term investments and are prepared to sustain risk levels.

7. Public funds—Promote and satisfy objectives through the development of new company innovations such as research, creation of new employment, and growth of specific geographical areas. Some states have jointly accumulated wide-ranging funds from between $5 and $10 million reaching hundreds of millions of dollars. At the same time the size of the fund remains contained compared to the largest venture capital private companies with average investments from $100,000 to $500,000.

Academic foundations and institutions may invest in venture capital through the acquisition of holdings in closed-end funds, but their contributions are limited because of risk levels.

## 12.4 JOB SELLING

It is critical to identify the category of investors potentially interested in a fund, because the main channel for venture capital fundraising is the direct contact between company and investor. The fundraising strategy is profoundly influenced if the fund is new or it represents the continuation of a previous initiative; the absence of a track record and the necessity to develop a network of contacts makes the fundraising complex and burdensome.

The involvement of a placement agent increases the probability of success.

After deciding the channel and the parties to be employed to raise funds, the following step is to identify the target market and develop the fundraising strategy (Fig. 12.2).

To raise funds potential clients must firstly be identified. Domestic investors should be consulted and brought on board first as their confidence in a fund attracts foreign capital who take into account the economic prospects of the

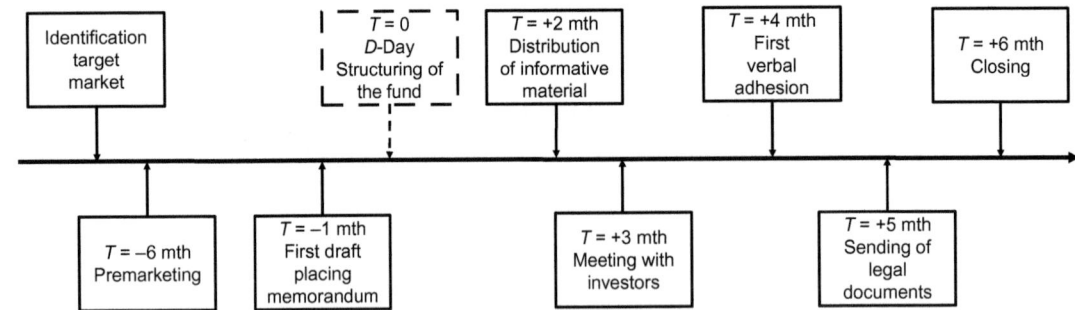

**FIG. 12.2** The fundraising process for venture capital.

country's fund, its capital markets, the presence of interesting entrepreneurial initiatives, etc.

The size of the fund becomes significant if large institutional investors are involved. When selecting potential clients it is also necessary to note the increasing role played by gatekeepers, that is, institutional investors offering consulting management or services. Originating in the United States, but now diffused also in Europe, gatekeepers raise funds from small- or medium-sized institutions, large institutions without experts in the private equity sector, or high net worth individuals who wish to invest in private equity initiatives. The presence of a gatekeeper in a venture capital fund attracts further potential clients.

The premarketing phase focuses on understanding the potential market in order to evaluate interest and gather useful information for the investment proposal. This usually occurs through meetings to update existing investors about new possible initiatives. A purely informative meeting such as an international road show will be organized with new potential investors. Managers must be prepared to give precise information relating to the track record of past initiatives specifying details relative to the structure of the operation, cash flow, the growth of the investments, and the values and timing of exit. At the same time managers should offer a list of potential investors.

Once the fund has market approval, its structure must be defined in cooperation with legal and fiscal advisors. The project must remove any legal, fiscal, and technical factors that could discourage investors. In Europe, this could cost a fund between €300,000 and €500,000.

Next is the preparation and sending of legal documentation to the probable adhering investors (partnership agreements, copy of contract, fiscal and legal matters, etc.); the operation will be closed once the final adherents are notified.

## 12.5  DEBT RAISING

As previously mentioned, the profitability of an investment is strictly connected to the value created by debt leverage. The financial structure of a venture capital deal is generally a mix of debt and equity (capital structure) used to acquire the target company.

Defining optimal capital structure is a topic that has always interested academics and market insiders. The most relevant and well-known theory about leverage use is formalized by the first Modigliani and Miller proposition through three statements, that have been named M+M I, M+M II, and M+M III, respectively.

The first statement states that the mix of debt and equity does not create any impact on the company value in a world:

- Without tax
- Without any type of financial distressed costs
- Without any form of information asymmetry
- With flat investments
- Without cost for the transaction

If one of the listed conditions is not present, it is very likely M + M I will not be supported. If the debt increases free cash flow raises proportionally with the tax rate applied to the interest paid $(T \times i \times D)$, and as a consequence the debt creates a tax shield that increments the company value (M + M II).

Even if the second statement maximizes the weight of debt, the presence of financial distressed costs leads to the disruption of the company value due to the legal expenditures and the daily pressure on management to service the debt (M + M III).

In conclusion, if we visualize these three statements we have Fig. 12.3:

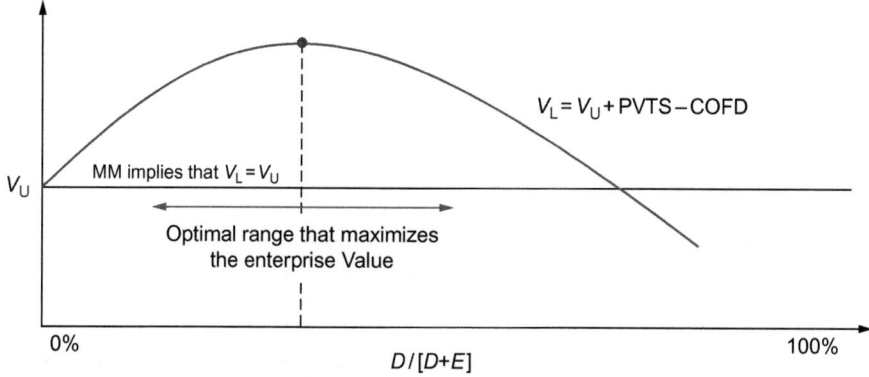

**FIG. 12.3**  Optimal capital structure ($V_U$ is unlevered value; the value of a company without any debt. $V_L$ is the value of a company with debt, PVTS is the present value of tax shield; and COFD is the cost of finance distress.).

The optimal capital structure is a range of $D/E$ that ensures tax shield benefits and avoids any risk connected with distressed financial structure.

Assuming a target company is acquired with a mix of equity and debt, it is important to choose the appropriate type of debt and equity.

1. Equity is represented by the risk capital subscribed by investors as full power of corporate governance and the right to receive a fixed yield or priority in the dividend paying out.
2. The shareholder loan has the same risk profile as capital share, but it allows investors to receive a piece of their return without or before the selling of the share.
3. The increase of equity is an incentive to motivate management especially if it is used with a stock option plan that provides a premium related to company performance.

The other financing tool is debt. It can be divided into different categories depending on two main elements:

1. Seniority or the level of guarantee and protection ensured to the investors in case of default
2. Operational issue financed (acquisition finance, working capital facility, CAPEX facility)

Senior debt is the main part of the debt in a private equity deal that ensures the investor will be repaid before any other creditor. There are three different typologies:

1. Acquisition financing is generally covered by specific rights placed on the company's assets or facilities. It can be also granted by the expected future cash flow of the target company. Assuming the earnings before interest, tax, depreciation, and amortization (EBITDA) is a good predictor of cash flow, investors apply a multiple to define the company's capacity to repay debt. This capacity is predicted by comparing the EBITDA to the total debt and/or the cash interest.
2. The refinancing facility is a turnover of the capital structure to reduce the number of creditors (banks).
3. Working capital facility is a tool that, along with a revolving structure, finances the daily company operations.
4. CAPEX facility is dedicated to the acquisition or improvement of the assets used by the company to develop their productivity.

If the senior debt does not cover the entire acquisition price or the promoter wants to reduce the level of equity, it is possible to be financed with the junior debt, which has a lower level of guarantee but a higher level of interest and duration of 6 and 10 years. If these debts are traded on a public market, without collateral, they are called high yield bonds. This category of debt will be settled only after the total repayment of the senior facilities.

Halfway between equity and debt is mezzanine debt. This is a sophisticated and complex financing instrument developed in the United Kingdom and United States. It is covered by the same senior collateral, and its reimbursement always happens between the senior and the junior debts. The servicing of mezzanine debt is broken down into three different types: interest paid yearly, structured with a capitalization system with payment at the end of the loan, and represented by equity linked to company performance. This type of debt is used in competitive situations, because it allows the increase of the debt equity ratio while protecting the company from financial distress. This topic will be explained with more details later on in this book.

## 12.6 CALLING PLAN

The calling plan is a technique used to increase the IRR for investors without reducing revenues for the managers at the same time. The IRR is a measure of the net present value on the outgoings (purchases of quotas) and proceeds (dividends, exits) of one or more operation. This method can be considered the most accurate because it is the only one capable of taking into account the time variable while calculating a single investment or a number of operations.

The calling plan illustrates the time period investors have to wire the subscribed funds; at start up subscribers contribute only a percentage of their investment (commitment) and then complete the investment following the calling agenda. The investor carefully prepares the commitment agenda, because it is the only way to balance the short-term view of the investment, typical for the investors of the fund, and the medium long-term view of the investment that the deal needs.

## 12.7 TYPES OF INVESTMENT

Intervention in risk capital has different sizes, prospective, and requirements and is defined as the combination of capital and know-how. Intervention in risk capital is classified according to the target company's life cycle phase by operators, associations and research centers, and even for statistical purposes.

The types of venture capital intervention are based on the participation in the initial life cycle phase, which consists of

- Seed financing (experimentation phase). The risk capital investor takes part in the experimentation phase when the technical validity of the product/service still has to be demonstrated. He provides limited financial contributions to the development of the business idea and to the evaluation of feasibility. The failure risk is very high.

- Start-up financing (beginning of activity phase). In this stage the investor finances the production activity even if the commercial success or flop of the product/service is not yet known. The level of financial contributions and risk is high.
- Early stage financing (first development phase). The beginning of the production activity has already been completed, but the commercial validity of the product/service must still be fully evaluated. This intervention consists of high financial contributions and lower risks.

The increasing complexity of financing and the problems in each of these stages means that the level of company development and the financial needs do not fit to the pattern. Additionally, investors of risk capital have developed advanced financial engineering tools that are more complex and sophisticated.

It would be useful to define a more analytical classification relating to the possible strategic requirements of a company considering the threats and opportunities faced by the sector and the final investors' objectives. We can group and classify the transfer of risk capital by the institutional investors in three principal types of the mere private equity business (following the types previously listed; Fig. 12.4):

- Expansion financing
- Turnaround and leveraged buy out (LBO) financing
- Vulture and distressed financing

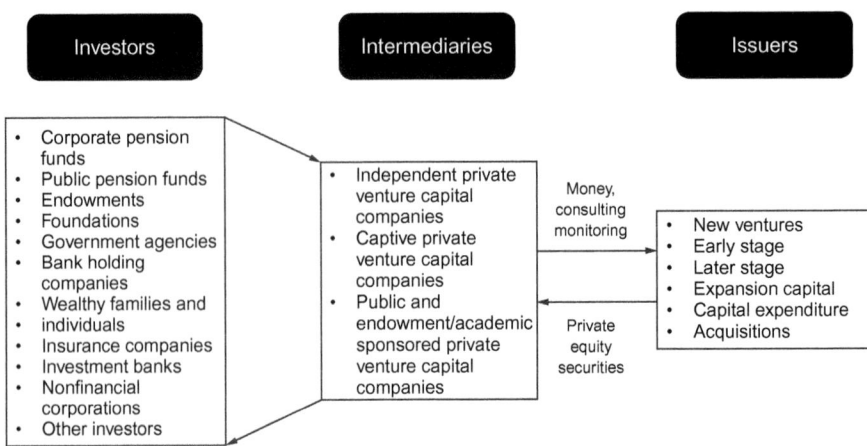

**FIG. 12.4** Participants in the venture capital market. *From Fenn et al., "Board of Governors of the Federal Reserve System Staff Studies," p. 168, 1995.*

# CHAPTER 13

# Investing

## 13.1 INTRODUCTION

When fundraising is complete, the next objective is how to use the accumulated resources. This objective kicks off another phase of the private equity cycle: investment.

The investment phase can also be analyzed according to:

- Groups involved—that will be further explored below
- Problems and risks
- Objectives

### 13.1.1 Groups Involved

Groups involved in the investment phase include venture capitalists (or private equity operators) and entrepreneurs (companies). The venture capitalists focus on techniques and activities carried out by firms asking for money, while the latter group is considered for projects to be financed.

Contrarily to the fundraising phase, the relation between the reception of funds from private equity operators (or venture capitalists) and the level of performance of the funded company has attracted greater interest, although attention is often limited to the business of venture capital.

In the fundraising phase, different interests, information, behavior, and purposes converge in the second step of the private equity cycle. Gompers and Lerner proposed an interesting analysis of the risks and problems during this step. They stated that the problem of risk should be interpreted as a "limited capacity" of companies to raise capital. At the same time, they recognized four factors that affect whether financial institutions are interested in investing: uncertainty, information asymmetry, the nature of the assets of the company, the state of target markets and/or financial markets.

181

Private Equity and Venture Capital in Europe. https://doi.org/10.1016/B978-0-12-812254-9.00013-9

Problems related to the nature of risk and problems arising in relationships between groups involved in this phase are attributed to the different objectives that these groups are trying to achieve. In an interesting study of the UK market, Reid and Smith showed that financial institutions and entrepreneurs are able to assess the risk level of a private equity deal. Consequently, the broad division between venture capital and private equity, as well as the more specific early stage financing and expansion, management by objectives (MBO), turnaround, replacement, and vulture financing are adequately shared by the world of financial practitioners. From a purely economic point of view, this means that companies and financial institutions similarly interpret the same investment opportunities.

From the same study, financial institutions are shown to be particularly sensitive to the organization of funded companies and to the concrete chances of project realization. As such, they are subject to agency risk. Entrepreneurs demonstrate their primary interest is solving the business risk, even in a venture capital or private equity deal.

These results are consistent with the findings reported by MacMillan et al., but do not match the results of Fried and Hisrich, where the expected return on investment seems to play an important role (if not even higher) as the capacity of management.

Manigart et al. studied the investment process put in place by British venture capitalists for transactions with companies operating in the biotechnology sector. The study found that management and its capabilities are important only when the projects are already started. If the investment still has to be defined (i.e., seed or start-up financing), the financial variables, market, and technology come first. However, the structure of contracts and initial requirements asked by financial institutions for such transactions are no different from sectors with a high degree of risk (i.e., the high-tech or Internet projects).

## 13.2 THE INVESTING PHASE

Investing is the core of private equity business and the way to develop a business idea for the investor. When investing the private equity investor:

1. Acts within established time limits
2. Acquires only the stake that is necessary to control the entrepreneurial risk, either a major or a minor share
3. Place emphasis on investment returns in terms of capital gain and goodwill; the participation in risk capital is only partially remunerated during the period of ownership from dividends or compensation for consulting
4. May supply some services that the closed-end funds cannot due to statute clauses

There are two main relevant moments in the investing phase:

> Decision making—Valuation and selection of opportunities and matching them with the appropriate investment vehicle. Target company valuation, the "core competence" of a private equity fund, is a proper blend of strategic analysis (about the business, the market, and the competitive advantage), business planning, financial forecasting, human resources, and entrepreneur and management team assessment.
>
> Deal making—Activity of negotiation of the contracts by which the private equity firm can invest and actively participate in the company. These contracts include, for instance, the calculation of the shares the investor has to buy, the corporate governance rules.

Through acquisitions and participations, the private equity investor finances new entrepreneurial initiatives or small nonquoted companies with the objective of sustaining growth to realize an adequate gain at exit. Venture capital operations are thus distinguished by returns expected, time horizon, and minimum size of the investment.

Returns expected are normally very high, and only the perspective and expectation of attractive gains justifies the considerable risk of financing a start-up or a private company. The duration of the investment is usually between 4 and 7 years, and even if the venture capitalist qualifies as a medium long-term investor, they will not be a permanent partner of the company financed. Instead, the venture capitalist expects to easily exit from the investment. The selection of projects to finance and the monitoring of the project requires significant resources, which can only be justified for investments of a certain amount. At this point, it is necessary for the entrepreneur to seek financing. Significant variables that influence this choice include the:

- Sector of the new initiative
- Strategy followed
- Level of preparation of the potential entrepreneur

The type of activity and strategy chosen affect the financial needs and potential growth of a new company, whereas the level of preparation of the potential entrepreneur affects the ability to attract external financing. When the launch of a new initiative occurs in traditional sectors by investors without a reputation, financial needs must be covered by the entrepreneur's personal resources. But the scarcity of financial resources can represent an opportunity rather than a restraint by motivating innovative behavioral strategies.

For new initiatives the involvement of institutional investors is unlikely because the financial requirements are too large and the involvement of a venture capitalist would not provide any real advantage. Value added by the institutional investor is very limited in terms of knowledge and competitive dynamics as well as rapid growth. The intervention of an external financier would complicate the management of the new company undermining the flexibility that is essential during the start-up phase.

It is now necessary to distinguish between entrepreneurial commitments for seed financing and start-up financing. Involvement is possible and convenient during seed financing and only necessary in the process of venture creation (start-up financing). The development of the business idea requires research and development, analysis of the market, identification of potential collaborators and employees, etc. Financial requirements needed to select the appropriate investment are not large, and the risk of failure of the initiative is remarkable with an uncertain rate of success. Financial needs come from the promoter's personal resources as well as financing from state agencies. When financing new entrepreneurial initiatives, it seems that the start-up phase is better managed and financed by state agencies.

## 13.3　DECISION MAKING

Investments' selection as made by the investor is a complex process, because there is information asymmetry based on the interaction between impartial components, analyses with strong methodological rigor, and subjective experience and intuition. The first valuation step is the preinvestment phase where a series of critical factors are defined to see if and how they affect the investor. The decision making in the investing step can be summarized in Fig. 13.1 in the following steps. These steps are listed from the one with lowest level of commitment to the one with the highest level of commitment (and consequent costs).

| Origination | The equity fund is able to generate opportunities from its network |
|---|---|
| Screening | The preliminary analysis of opportunities made by the management and supported by the technical committee<br>The golden rule is that, starting with 100 investment proposals, only 10 will live through screening |
| Valuation and due diligence | Three different activities take place: meeting with the entrepreneur and the management; use of financial and strategic techniques; due diligence activities |
| Rating assignment | It consists of the transformation of the previous valuation and due diligence activities into a rating within the process chosen by the equity investor as per Basel rules |
| Negotiation | Equity fund has "to sell" the valuation to the entrepreneur in competition (or in cooperation) with other investors |
| Decision to invest | The negotiation leads to a final price |

**FIG. 13.1** The decision-making process in the investment phase.

### 13.3.1 Deal Flow (Origination)

In this phase, the investor has to decide the destination of the money is collected.

The decision that will be taken is based on two different forces:

- A part of the origination is spontaneous. In fact, the whole financial business community is aware of the fact that the investor has just started the research for a target company in which to invest. The financial community, at the same time, knows that the investor is looking for a target company with a high liquidity availability. This generates for the private equity investor a huge selection of potential projects in which to invest.
- On the other hand, origination is based on a proactive activity. The fund managers have to scout the market and find the most suitable solution for their investment portfolio. This task can be carried on together with the other players involved in the fund (i.e., the technical committee and the advisory board) who can also help and scout the market.

### 13.3.2 Screening

Once a panel of project is created as in the previous stage, the screening is strongly influenced by the strategic orientation of the investor; for example, the geographic location, the sector, and the type of product (technology used, trademarks, leadership in differentiation or of cost, etc.). Fifty percent of proposals received by the venture capitalist in this phase are refused. The remaining proposals are examined in greater detail by analyzing the depth of the chosen market and its development, economic-financial results expected, and amount of financing required. In this case, many projects will be dismissed, especially if the investment is addressed to a venture capital cluster.

REMEMBER: Do you remember the golden rules in Start-up Financing?

Also in this role, the task is driven by the managers together with the technical committee. After the screening phase only a very small number of dossiers are left for the investor to study and investigate further.

### 13.3.3 Valuation and Due Diligence

The core of the decision-making process is concentrated on several key steps where the investor has to study and assess the business plan of the target company.

At the company level, the project plan is defined as business plan; it is the first way to establish the relation between entrepreneur and institutional investor to create a virtuous circle of trust as well as a request for risk capital. For these reasons, the management of a target company prepares the business plan very carefully, communicating any relevant information that makes the project unique and interesting. An exhaustive business plan includes an executive summary that examines the basic elements of the project: opportunities, risks, expertise of the management team, and timing. The entrepreneur must communicate the concept of a feasible business idea that is missing only enough capital to start.

The first key aspect the private equity wants to understand is if the business idea is related to a product or a service, a combination of the two, or the creation of an original and more complex model. The description of the product or service provided must be focused on the principal attributes that make it unique, because the investor is interested in knowing the limits of the product and the service offered. The investor also considers the target market in terms of boundaries, foreseeable market share, and total market value.

The investor must trust the management team of the target company. He will need information about the team expertise, experience, cohesion and motivation focusing on capabilities, limits, interest, and commitment to the project.

A successful project can maintain its status over time defending its competitive advantages. It is useful to conduct a project analysis through the "five forces" as represented in Porter's model (Fig. 13.2 and Table 13.1).

Strategy analysis is the most important part of the business plan, because it sets the company's targets, how they will be reached, and if the business is coherently defined and consistent with the economic-financial forecasts. Financial

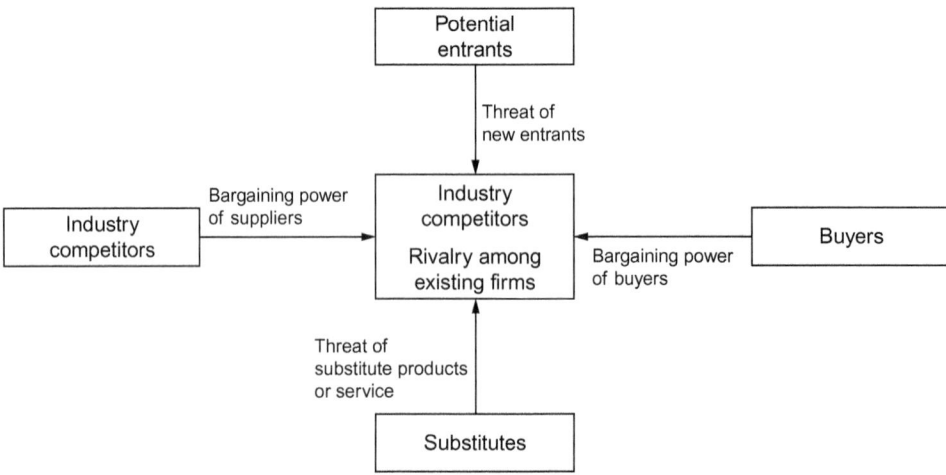

**FIG. 13.2** Porter's "five forces" model (Porter M.E., "Competitive Strategy. Technique for Analysing Industries and Competitors," New York, The Free Press, 1980).

**Table 13.1** Elements to be Considered in Porter's Model

| Supplier Power | Barrier Entry | Buyer's Power | Substitute Product or Services |
|---|---|---|---|
| Supplier concentration | Absolute cost advantages | Bargaining leverage | Switching costs |
| Importance of volume to supplier | Proprietary learning curve | Buyer volume | Buyer inclination to substitutes |
| Differentiation of inputs | Access to inputs | Buyer information | Price-performance trade off of substitutes |
| Impact of inputs on cost or differentiation | Government policy | Brand identity | |
| Switching costs of firms in the industry | Economies of scale | Price sensitivity | |
| Presence of forward integration | Capital requirements | Threat of backward integration | |
| Cost relative to total purchase in industry | Brand identity | Product differentiation | |
| | Switching costs | Buyer concentration vs industry | |
| | Access to distribution | Substitutes available | |
| | Expected retaliation | Buyers' incentives | |
| | Proprietary products | | |

forecasts explain costs and revenues, investments, and cash flow. They are the basis for the evaluation of the business idea because they help identify economic and financial equilibrium.

Business plan time span depends on the project or on the company. The time period of the plan covers the life of the project or it covers between 3 and 5 years with a very detailed degree of analysis in the first year and a more generalized approach for the following years.

The next step within this phase, that is, the due diligence, refers to the investor's actions that are necessary to reach a final valuation. It also contributes to the protection of the institutional investors' capital. A good management of the due diligence phase guarantees a quicker closing of the deal and allows the investor to acquire all the necessary information for a professional investment.

There are five ways to classify due diligence:

1. Market—The way investors understand the positioning, the potentiality, and risks of the specific market in which the company operates. To check the consistency of the company data presented and market due diligence must be connected with financial due diligence.

2. Environmental—Comparison among company profitability, legislation and regulations, and the internal organization of environmental control and pollution. Identifies and verifies the impact on the environment and the pollution problems not yet resolved.
3. Financial—Final evaluation of the economic-financial aspects (cash flow and working capital) and definition of the necessity of funds (budget and business plan for 3–5 years) of the company financed with the historical economic trend of sales, margins, production costs, and fixed costs highlighting liabilities and risks connected.
4. Legal—Examines any legal problem such as lawsuits, commitments with third parties and relative risks, contractual guarantees, employee labor agreements, or stock option plans.
5. Tax—Analyzes fiscal aspects related to liabilities, structure of the acquisition operation, future fiscal benefits, and to the fiscal effects of the potential exit.

### 13.3.4 Rating Assignment

In this phase the investor rates and grades the dossiers of the different companies. This is fundamental to assess the level of risk and is important to understand if (and how) the private equity firm has to collect funds through debt.

In addition to the ordinary case in the Anglo-Saxon world where funds are allowed to leverage, this step is particularly important in LBO deals. In these deals, the assessment of the level of riskiness and of indebtedness can change the decision of the investor and change the strategy of investment. If the level of risk is too high after the rating assessment, the deal cannot be taken further.

### 13.3.5 Negotiation

Investment decisions are made based on several factors: the current and potential market shares of the company, its technology, and the creation of value during the exit phase. The negotiation step lasts 3 or 6 months after the preparation of the business plan, depending on the clarity and completeness of the information supplied by the entrepreneur. This information also defines the price and the timing and method of payment.

If there is an agreement on the key points of the deal, the parties sign a letter of intent in which the economic and legal aspects of the operation are defined (the value of the company, the presence of the investor on the Board of Directors, the informative obligations, etc.) and that will be refined in the investment contract.

### 13.3.6 Decision to Invest

Once the negotiation step has been carried out, then the managers of the fund have to convince the whole Board of the private equity firm that it is worth investing in that specific company. The decision of investing does not mean to invest immediately in the company; rather it sets the beginning of the second part of the investing phase: deal-making or contract designing.

## 13.4 DEAL MAKING

Signing the contract deals with the terms of the agreement regarding pricing, quota of participation, and administrative aspects, between the company, its shareholders, and the investor. Once the final agreement is achieved, then operation is formalized with the

- Transfer of the shares
- Payment of the price
- Issue of the guarantees
- Reorganization of the Board of Directors and the management team

All these aspects are presented in this section dedicated to the "deal making" phase.

The deal making or the "contractual package" defines the commitment of the equity investor with respect to the venture-backed company. It impacts and sustains value creation and allocates duties and rights between the equity fund and the venture-backed company.

The contract facilitates management and control and identifies the proper combination between risk and return. Contract design is developed through three different approaches:

- Targeting
- Liability profile
- Engagement

Each approach is broken down as presented in Fig. 13.3.

### 13.4.1 Targeting

The first task to be carried out is the targeting of the right vehicle; the valuation of the alternative investment or company or a special purpose vehicle (SPV) set up just for the deal. A direct investment is recommended when the investor is interested in the business, there is total control of the project, and there is a commitment between the investor and the company. An SPV is recommended when the investor wants only relevant assets or a branch, the investment is

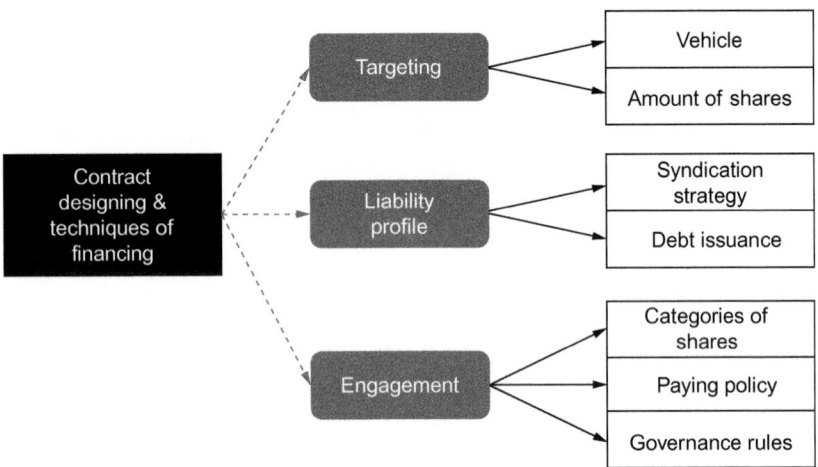

**FIG. 13.3** Deal making.

tailor-made on the business plan, there are no inefficiencies, and the SPV supports collateral schemes.

Another way to choose an investment vehicle is based on the amount of shares or the percentage of shares to buy and the role of the venture capitalist within the shareholders. This decision is driven by

- Majority versus minority participation in the risk capital
- Relative and absolute size of investment
- Capital requirement impact
- Voting rights and effective influence within the Board of Directors

### 13.4.2 Liability Profile

The liability profile of an investment vehicle should also be considered in the deal making. Debt issuing can be realized through banking loans or bonds placement, and the most common scheme is an investment in an SPV through a leveraged buy out (LBO) to acquire a target company.

There are two financing tools available for this scheme:

1. Syndication strategy—The promoter finds other equity investors and builds a syndicate.[1] This tool is recommended because it increases investment power while sharing risk as pros and cons are blended. The pros are the
   a. Reduction of credit risk for each member

---

[1]This tool started in the United States during the 1960s to satisfy the huge financial needs of big firms that could not be handled by a single bank.

b. Opportunity to diversify the portfolio of the investments in terms of industry, geographical area, etc.
c. Opportunity to take part in a deal with international relevance
d. Opportunity to increase services
e. Huge amount of capital collected
f. Cost reduction
g. Timing and certainty of funds
h. Flexibility
i. The cons are the
j. Hierarchy inside the syndicate
k. Agreement between the investors
l. Risk of losing market control and knowledge
m. Duration is shorter then corporate bond

The bank that organizes the syndication is named arranger and is selected according to its relationship status, speciality, queue, and open bidding.

The financial structure can be fully underwritten, partially underwritten, or best effort. The syndicate can be a "direct loan syndicate," when the agreement is signed off by a group of banks or "participation syndicate" when only one bank signs and then looks for other bank investors. Banks participating in the syndicate gain through management fees, commitment fees, agency fees, and interest charged.

After the syndication is organized, communication about the financial market and operation details and structure begins.

2. Debt issuance—The decision is to combine equity investment (with or without SPV, syndicated or not) with leverage. The decision of using leverage allows multiplying the impact of equity investment, in terms of value, provided that the higher financial risk is sustainable.

Placement can be public or private. Public placement debt servicing has an overall lower cost with a higher cost for marketing, legal representation, and management. Private placement has higher costs for the debt servicing, but it allows the issuer to be aware of the price that is fixed on a priori notice with the institutional investors. Bond placement can be done through a syndication between different banks where the banks involved is named as lead manager of the syndicated bonds and is responsible for the preparation of the offering circular. Within this document, the bond characteristics are explained and sent to other banks suitable to be the management group, underwriter, or seller.

With public placement, the issuer understands and realizes the cost of the operation only at the closing time.

Among the advantages there is the huge amount of capital provided and the long duration of the financing. On the contrary, the high level of structure standardization is considered a disadvantage.

### 13.4.3 Engagement

The last aspect to be considered in the deal making is the engagement.

It begins by choosing categories of shares or share classes that can guarantee the best way to support the investment and follow managing and monitoring phase.

Typically, the private equity investor chooses between a range of shares with different rights and duties:

- Common shares are securities representing equity ownership in a corporation, providing voting rights, and entitling the holder to share the company's success through dividends or capital gain. The holders receive one vote per share to elect the company's Board of Directors and to decide on company matters such as stock splits and company objectives.
- Preferred stock usually does not include voting rights, or at least limited rights in extraordinary matters. This is compensated by priority over common stock in the payment of dividends and upon liquidation. Their dividend is paid out prior to any other dividends. Preferred stocks may be converted into common stock.
- Shares with embedded option provide different rights entitling the holder to buy company stocks issued at a predefined price due to an attached option. It is not traded by itself and it affects the value of the share of which it is a part.
- Tracking stock is a security issued by a parent company related to the results of one of its subsidiaries or line of business. Financial results of the subsidiary or line of business are attributed to the tracking stock. Often, the reason for issuing this type of stock is to separate the high-growth division from a larger parent company. The parent company and its shareholders remain in control of the subsidiary or unit's operations.

Another investment choice during the engagement step is connected with the paying policy; the technique of issuing shares and the relationship of management within the company corporate governance.

To ensure a useful and satisfactory paying policy, three basic questions need to be answered.

1. What is the nature of the shares held by the investor? The investment can be obtained through new shares issued by the company or old shares sold to the private equity by the entrepreneur.
2. What is the expectation of the entrepreneur? The entrepreneur can choose these types of financial operations for two reasons: just because he wants to earn money by selling company shares or because he needs financial or strategic support to sustain activity and its growth.

**Table 13.2** Corporate Governance Rules

| | |
|---|---|
| Shareholders duties and rights | • Discipline of activities shared between shareholder assembly and Board of Directors;<br>• Connection shareholders' assembly—Board of Directors;<br>• Directors, executive directors, president and vice-president nomination;<br>• Special quorum policy. |
| Board of Directors activity | • Power of executive director(s);<br>• Inner rules of Board of Directors activity;<br>• Nonexecutive directors presence and specific role. |
| Information flow | • Content of information flow;<br>• Scheduling of information flow;<br>• Auditing activity rules to control information flow. |

3. What is the relationship among the existing shareholders? The private equity could invest in the company and maintain total control of the risk capital, or maintain all or part of the existing shareholders and negotiate the exit of those fired.

The last aspect included in the engagement process are governance rules; the general agreement on shareholders duties and rights, Board of Directors activity, and information flow (see Table 13.2). Governance rules can be formally written in the Limited Partnership Agreement, in the internal code of activity, or in a formal autonomous agreement designed to discipline the power of the shareholders.

The logic and the structure of the governance rules affect the:

• Percentage of shares owned
• Effective power of shareholders

Corporate governance rules regulate the activity of the shareholders' assembly and the Board of Directors as well as their relation. These rules also define who has the power to appoint the executive director, the president, and the vice presidents along with their duties and rights, generally fixing a special quorum.

Good governance structure should provide a group of policies and processes that ensure smooth management from the Board of Directors, while settling key controls to minimize abuse of the power connected with the executive role. When the size or a particular industry where the firm operates suggests in doing so, a good rule is to give nonexecutive directors on the Board of Directors the ability to exercise control on executive members.

The last matter covered by corporate governance includes the auditing staff, its activities, and the information flow provided by the directors. These rules define the structure of the auditing staff in terms of number of people and their competencies and the power to look into company activities, as well as a planned list of controls to be executed.

## 13.5   PROBLEMS AND CRITICAL AREAS OF VENTURE CAPITAL OPERATIONS

Venture capital operations involve three key figures: the financier of the venture capital operations (pension funds, other types of institutional, or private investors), the venture capitalist for managerial and financial support to the entrepreneur, and the entrepreneur who developed the highly innovative idea.

The typical structure of venture capital contracts, focusing on the relationship between institutional investor and the company financed, may suffer from asymmetric information or moral hazard, especially when the investment decision has been made because of the behavior of the entrepreneur or the venture capitalist. The entrepreneur is directly responsible for the success of the company's project. If a valid mechanism of control it missing, the possible and predictable consequence is opportunistic behavior; the entrepreneur follows personal interests. For example, if the entrepreneur is incapable of financing the idea with his own capital, he could motivate the risk capital investor to continue financing a project even when the conditions for its valid and effective development no longer exist. The opportunistic behavior of the venture capitalist exploits the entrepreneur's ideas by financing competitive companies similar to the initiative already financed.

Because of this opportunistic behavior, binding contracts are important. They solve and control possible interest conflicts between the entrepreneur who wishes to limit the possible leakage of information concerning competitive advantages, and the institutional investor who is interested in maximizing the motivation of the company's management for the most efficient development of the plan. The form of the financing selected solves these problems because it influences the incentives of both the entrepreneur and the venture capitalist.

Venture capitalists support high-risk initiatives with potentially high remuneration. It is necessary to identify the mechanism of fundraising and employment of the necessary financial resources for their initiatives. To raise funds, large institutional investors frequently agree to a significant quota of the capital gains obtained (approximately 80%) from the potential positive outcome of the IPOs or merger operations. Pension funds are also used as a source of funds. From an employment perspective, the venture capital companies provide financing for a portfolio of companies, granting technical and managerial support and financial resources to the entrepreneur in exchange for becoming a minority shareholder (equity between 5% and 15%). The primary objective is to achieve high profit (capital gains equal to at least 20%), which results from the difference between the cost price of the participation at the moment of acquisition (subscription) and the sales price to third parties during the exit phase (with operations of IPO, LBO, or mergers).

Venture capitalists influence the development of investments in these three areas:

1. Closed ownership model of companies
2. Growth process of family companies
3. Innovative processes

Entrepreneurs do not always appreciate the participation of third-party shareholders as they dread there might be interference during the decision-making process, the definition of the strategic lines, and the selection of the managerial direction of the company. In the second area venture capitalists choose small companies with high competitive potential and adopt adequate operating strategies connected with the business choices of accelerated growth. Innovative processes are represented by the little cooperation and collaboration among universities with scientific and technological centers and companies, which can delay the development of new companies with high technological content.

Venture capitalists affect investments by

1. Providing high technical qualification, level of experience, managerial expertise, and professionalism
2. Developing intermediation for risk capital inside the market

## 13.6   THE ROLE OF MANAGERIAL RESOURCES IN VENTURE CAPITAL

The realization of a venture capital operation is a demanding task. To ensure success there must be a high degree of consulting, awareness of the high potential risk, and a high level of participation in all aspects of definition and organization of the final objectives of the operation starting with the set up of a Board of Directors.

Venture capitalists deals succeed in reaching a high capital gain thanks to the professional quality of the human resources dedicated to performing managerial activity. The value of knowledge and expertise brought to a project by venture capitalists is one of the principal requisites that guarantee the feasibility of a project. Venture capitalists also bring confidentiality, business intuition, flexibility, a critical mind, and a decision capacity based on a precise calculation and estimation of the risks to a project. It is also important that the resources utilized by venture capitalists to support entrepreneurial initiatives have proven experience evaluating companies. This guarantees a business analysis not limited to economic-financial aspects, but widened to include the strategic analysis of the sector (opportunities and threats of the possible product-market combinations), and to the study of the strengths and weaknesses, at competitive level, of the future development programs of the company.

The role of venture capitalists during the transfer of risk capital is more complex than just supporting and assisting activities. They provide a specific professional contribution that includes human resources that guarantee a service with a proven image of "active neutrality." The participation in the shareholding of small- and medium-sized companies by the institutional investors of risk capital must therefore be based on a responsible entry in the best entrepreneurial initiatives.

With a venture capitalist it is possible to combine the expansion of the company while maintaining its family character. Choosing venture capital allows the entrepreneur to place shares outside the family that are under his control, to issue preference shares, to trade on or outside the quota of minority shares in companies controlled by the holding company, and to create real and proper groups of companies capable of carrying out autonomous recourse to the capital markets.

Venture capitalists support and participate in companies that have:

1. An undisputed entrepreneurial expertise and experience
2. Analytical business plans and innovative market strategies capable of guaranteeing a potential level of development compatible with the dynamics of the market and with the situation of the company
3. New shareholders breaking down psychological and cultural barriers
4. High performance (or at least, an expected one) aligned with a level of risk-return, with a good economic-financial equilibrium guaranteeing a "secure" return of the investment
5. Absolute transparency

By choosing venture capital, the real and potential advantages for the company include

- Providing new financial resources to develop the company's initiatives
- Access to new financing funds for family operated companies
- Entry of a prestigious shareholder, which permits greater contractual power between suppliers and competitors and greater guarantees for customers
- Enhancement of the company public image due to the presence of partners that assure the solidity of the company and its programs
- Strong distinction between corporate and personal interests for greater weight toward market policy and the business strategies adopted by management
- Possible synergies between the expertise of the company's management and the minority partner

The greatest advantage is the change in mentality that grants the small- and medium-sized entrepreneur to expand his financial horizons.

## 13.7   POSSIBLE UNSUCCESSFUL FINANCIAL PARTICIPATION

The main reason of an unsuccessful financial participation is related to management. Because management is responsible for finance, marketing, distribution, and production, they are considered the "dynamic element and the source of life of any business." If management makes the wrong strategic choices related to the business in which it operates, financial participation could be unsuccessful.

## 13.8   INVOLVEMENT OF THE PRIVATE EQUITY IN THE BOARD OF DIRECTORS

It is difficult to control a venture capital operation because of information asymmetry between the entrepreneur and management. The best way to safeguard the transferred capital is to involve the venture capitalist in the management of the company. With their own people exercising control over the Board of Directors, it permits the institutional investors to participate in key decisions connected with suppliers, market policies, extraordinary financial operations, and ordinary management of the company. The theory of the financial intermediary labels this type of monitoring as "soft facet" and "hard facet." Soft facet merely monitoring and supports management regarding principal operating choices and decisions. "Hard facet" monitoring is that controls the entrepreneur with the purpose of limiting possible conflicts of interest between the objectives of the entrepreneur and the venture capitalists. The foundation of a positive outcome to an investment initiative with risk capital is based on the irreplaceable role of the venture capitalist in the support, assistance, and participation in the development of an entrepreneurial project.

# CHAPTER 14

# Managing and Monitoring

## 14.1  INTRODUCTION

This chapter illustrates the second phase of the managerial process. As such, it will describe the managing and monitoring of a private equity deal after highlighting its importance from a practical point of view.

## 14.2  WHY IS THERE A NEED FOR A MANAGEMENT AND MONITORING PHASE?

After closing the deal, both the investor and the venture-backed company need to organize, plan, and manage the relation with their respective partner, as they are about to live a "temporary but important marriage." First, they have to define and share various details and agree upon both medium-long term and daily rules. Second, they must commit to working together and under total transparency and information sharing as they will be managing typical agency problems.

The goal shared between the investor and the venture-backed company (or the entrepreneur) is always the same: the creation of value will entail a high level of remuneration for both parties. This condition divides successful operations from failures allowing the investor and the company to reach the expected returns. Although they may have this common goal, this is unfortunately the only one they have in common as many other aspects, operations, and views are completely different.

Critical topics that provoke debates and problems include:

- Duration of investor involvement
- Strategies used to increase company value
- Financial and industrial alliances
- New opportunities that modify the preinvestment situation

Private Equity and Venture Capital in Europe. https://doi.org/10.1016/B978-0-12-812254-9.00014-0

Both the investor and the entrepreneur try to solve all potential disagreements prior to this phase, during fundraising; however, it is impossible to forecast the future and regulate everything. Conflicts also arise because the investor has his own portfolio to manage with constraints coming from the internal rate of return (IRR) objective, the residual maturity, the regulatory capital, and covenants settled between the fund's originators. On the other side, the venture-backed company (or entrepreneur) has its own industrial, financial, and personal goals that may differ from the investor's ones.

## 14.3    PERFORMANCE DETERMINATION

Before analyzing specific monitoring and controlling activities, it is critical to define how funds evaluate the success of their investment activity. This is done by performance determinations consisting of a set of guidelines defined by industry associations and specific government regulations that are generally different in each country where the "directives" are acknowledged by the financial sector regulatory organizations. For instance, in Italy in the private equity business, professionals and private equity firms follow the guidelines proposed in March 2001 by the then European Venture Capital Association. These guidelines are a reference for all investors.

The huge increase of investments in risk capital has made other types of performance determinations inadequate. The model proposed by Invest Europe is not mandatory for operators, but in a business where reputation plays a fundamental role in the success of the initiative, not using such framework may lead to damage of the private equity investors' reputation and make fundraising much more difficult than it already is anyway.

Problems determining an investment's performance arise when no efficient market exists or when trading is carried out in a nontransparent context. In these cases it is difficult to determine the final value of a company because not all operators are using the same calculation rules.

Invest Europe suggests calculating the investment's performance with the IRR, which compares cash outflows (purchases of stakes) with cash proceeds/inflows (dividends, exit gains) for one or more operations. This choice, even if from a mathematical point of view the most difficult to perform, is considered the most correct because it takes into account simultaneously the time variable and number of operations.

Performance is calculated to provide an indicator of the manager's ability to select target companies and deliver success as well as to obtain an indicator of effective costs faced by subscribers. Because the starting data are not the same for all investments, we identify three different IRR:

- Gross return on the realized investments—Net present value of the entries and exits of the investments made; for example, any pending write-offs or bankruptcies are not estimated or included.
- Gross return on all investments—Includes the value of the operations still to be realized; for example, a quota yet to be invested or a write-down yet to be made excluding the liquidity reserve.
- Net return to the investor—The most interesting measure for the subscriber because it clearly shows the final result and net of costs and commissions applied by the fund manager. The liquidity reserve is also taken into account during the calculation of the return.

Each closed-end fund manager decides whether or not to include "external" data in the IRR calculation; for example, when participating in foreign companies, the return calculation could use the exchange rates. The information of the net return, even if it includes all of the previous aspects, considers a series of information that does not allow the comparison among several managers; if the weight of the liquidity is different or the commissions and estimates are unequal, the comparison loses its usefulness. For these reasons, the indicator most frequently used is gross return on the realized investments, because it offers a balanced vision of the operation analyzed.

Another critical aspect to the private equity business at every level is the liquidity problem. The liquidity management process is a source of value for the investor, so it is relevant and critical, especially for the acquisition of a nonquoted company when realized in several stages. The financial deal promoter limits the importance of the liquidity by allowing fund subscribers to give their funds in different stages. This reduces the "mass" of liquidity initially held. If this option is not considered, the problem becomes urgent only for the short period necessary to make the investments.

---

PAUSE: What is this phase called (i.e., when the committed capital is put in the fund?)

---

The liquidity strategy is different between the open- and closed-end funds. Closed-end funds, not investing in nonquoted companies, usually place the liquidity in nonrisk tools that are easily convertible to legal tender. Once the investments are realized, liquidity management problems decrease and become almost negligible because the quota subscribed cannot be turned into cash. With open funds, the problem of liquidity management is more important and difficult to manage because of the unpredictability of investors' requests. Over time these strategies have established a special trend in the liquid reserves. In the closed-end funds, for example, the trend is similar to a parabola. In the early period of activity researching opportunities and the technical timing cause the "supply of liquidity" to be high; whereas in the short and medium term, liquidity assumes secondary importance as the participations must be left to mature slowly. Problems managing the liquid reserves arise toward the end of the fund's activity when the previous investments made by the fund are transferred into cash for the redistribution of final returns to investors.

It is possible to draw a similar trend for open-end funds. First, the research for activities to invest in is much easier when a reference market exists because the amount of initial liquidity does not stay still for an excessive period. The same phenomenon happens at the end because the exit process of the quota is simplified by the same variables. However, throughout the process the manager of an open-end fund must pay attention to its liquidity, which is normally used to meet the subscribers' quotas and the commitments of the fund.

## 14.4    THE MANAGING AND MONITORING PHASE

The managing and monitoring of investors must ensure the creation of value and the control of any opportunistic behavior of the financed venture firm. There are two completely different areas of interest in the managerial phase that are relevant both to create and protect value (see Fig. 14.1):

- Area of actions to create and measure value
- Area of actions to protect value

### 14.4.1    Actions to Create and Measure Value

Typically, the actions involved qualify the presence and nature of the investor within the managerial process of the venture-backed company. These actions depend on

1. Stage of the investment—Depending on the phase of financing (seed, start-up, early stage, expansion, turnaround, buyout, vulture, and distressed) the deal faces different types of risk such as development, production, marketing, and growth risk (see Fig. 14.2). The high amount

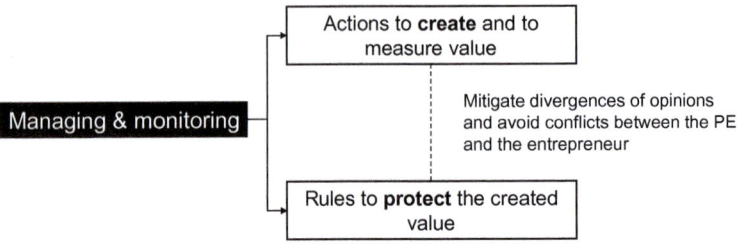

**FIG. 14.1** Activities of managing and monitoring.

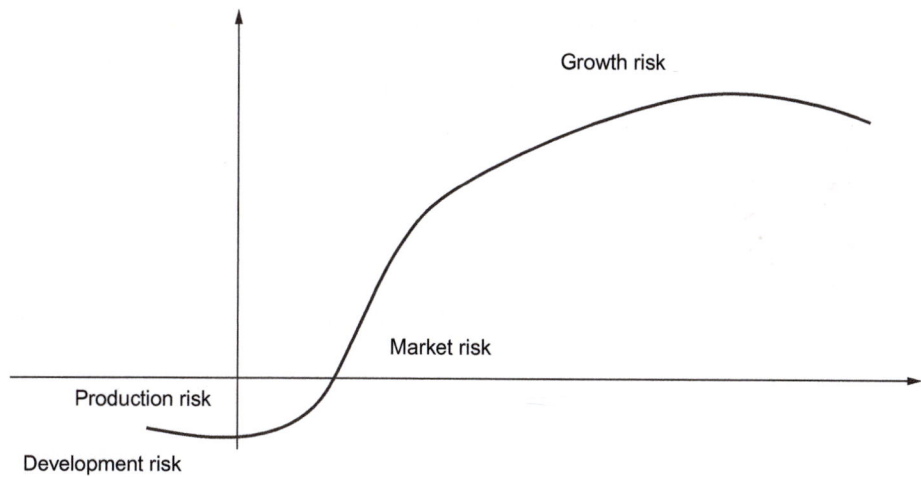

**FIG. 14.2** Risk during investment stages.

of resources invested warrants a seat on the Board of Directors, even if the amount is not enough to ensure a real commitment.

Throughout the stages of investment the investor's involvement gradually decreases and changes. In both seed and start up, investor involvement could be of industrial and strategic nature, while in expansion and replacement phases investor support could be reduced to an advisory capacity about financial and legal issues.

The quantity and the intensity of monitoring activities are linked to the duration of the participation in the target company. Because the investor and company management spend time together, there is a basis for a fair and trusting relationship with a decreasing need for control.

2. Style of the investor and the nature of the investment agreement (mentioned in previous chapters, briefly reprised below)—Generally these have different profiles:
   a. Hands-on approach—A deep involvement both in corporate governance and financial and/or strategic decisions
   b. Hands-off approach—A presence in the corporate governance and involvement only in financial decisions
3. Geographical distance and the expertise of the investor—The number of meetings between the investor and financed firm decrease over long distances. It is difficult to assess whether the impact of the investor's expertise is higher or lower with the frequency of contact between the directors and the other board members.

Regardless of the stage and style of investment, the key activities to manage and monitor are

1. Board services consisting of all activities concerning Board of Directors and meetings of other committees meetings—Creation of value happens

with decision-making support, with the introduction of professional expertise, and with the imposition of severe discipline.

2. Performance evaluation and review—The investor fixes and plans a set of required processes used to monitor and measure the value inside the company and between the company and the investor.

3. Recruit management—Investor support is critical when hiring the right people for the management team. The management team coming from the ventured-back company is often inadequate in terms of skills and/or numbers for the development of the investment. The investor involves new people knowledgeable about specific companies and sectors or who have a professional background compatible with the project's entrepreneur.

4. Assistance with the external relationship—The investor usually has a network of customers, suppliers, and governmental lobbying that supports both current and strategic activities. The importance of the venture capitalist network is demonstrated by the direct correlation between the industries they invest in and the number of industries acquired. Consequently, there is usually a relationship between acquisition, dimensional growth, globalization, and internationalization when a venture capitalist takes part of a firm.

5. Arrange additional financing—When more financing is needed, the investor plays a critical role in finding the financer, arranging the deal, and negotiating its terms and conditions. The investor's reputation can enhance his ability to secure financing.

6. Mentoring—The investor has to be completely and fully available for the entrepreneur 24/7. The entrepreneur expects the investor's support to help him take decisions in any moment. This is considered "soft assistance" with technical and human support to both the management and the entrepreneur (or shareholders).

The usual structure of management control is based on a set of rules and procedures that must be observed to in order to obtain the desired results. Assigning tasks and objectives needed to accomplish the company's goals and a structure of rewards and punishment are critical to motivate employees during their daily activities.

- Goal setting—Goals can change over time so the traditional 5-year plans are not long enough. The first rule is to attach the company's goals to its operations and to identify measurable goals.
- Setting standards—Once goals have been identified they have to be translated into standards to become effective.
- Using motivators for the venture backed companies—The main tools to motivate employees are money, status, and recognition.

## 14.4.2   Actions to Protect Value

The participation of the investor, within the governance and management of the venture-backed company requires rules to reduce conflicts and mitigate agency problems between the investor and management. The investment period may be defined as a "temporary marriage"; a time when both the investor and the venture-backed company have very specific risks to avoid, different for each of the two parties.

The investor must avoid the following risks:

- Wrong industrial decisions from the management team of the venture-backed company that affects the firm's performance and thus its value in the medium-long term.
- Lack of commitment within the management can reduce the effectiveness of the target company strategy.
- Divergence in timing to create value can directly impact the IRR created by the investment.
- Entrance of new shareholders can create new conflicts between parties.

The venture-backed company must avoid these risks:

- Exiting at the wrong time, as it can impact the overall result of the investment in terms of less financial resources than expected (if the investor exits too soon) or excessive meddling from the financial partner (if the investor adopts a late exit strategy).
- Lack of commitment from the investor can reduce financial resources or the advantages connected to his network or expertise and knowledge.
- New shareholders entering the investment impact the balance reached between the entrepreneur and investor as well as the company strategy planned.
- Exiting surprises interrupt the investment cycle and negate the realization of value for management and the entrepreneur.
- Psychological constraints on management decrease its effectiveness due to external factors.

Private equity operations are implemented in different industries, companies, countries, and at different stages of the life cycle of a firm. Because of this, they are realized by different investors, in terms of participants, deal structure, and fund amount, the objectives are numerous. Consequently, the number and the nature of risks make it impossible to forecast and solve all the possible conflicts. During the contractual design process there is a set of rules used to help reduce these risks.

First, mutual trust and patience is the best way to avoid risks combined with a new integrated company culture created by a talented management team.

Secondly, with intelligence and wisdom the venture capitalist uses particular contractual rules that help sustain the mutual trust and patience.

These rules are usually created to fit the deal, but they are also used worldwide by financial investors and entrepreneurs often combined and blended.

The key element for a successful private equity deal is the trust the financial investor has in the expertise and management skills of the company's founder and the members of the Board of Directors. Thus it is reasonable at this stage to adopt a mechanism to ensure the stability of the property and the ongoing commitment and involvement of the management and the entrepreneur. This strategy is realized by using the best practice rules adopted by the firms through contractual schemes such as covenants and ratchets.

Covenants are rules settled and defined in order to regulate the relationship among investors and managers. These rules underline duties and rights while minimizing opportunism, moral hazard, and conflict of interest. The covenants are presented in the Internal Code of Activity or in the LPA.

The covenant setting has three different classifications:

1. Overall fund management—These covenants regulate the general aspects of the investment activity in order to realize the expected return. Because significant financial and managerial resources are invested in innovative projects with high potential and high risk, it is critical to define the maximum dimension of the investment in a single firm to diversify resources into a sufficiently high number of initiatives (portfolio approach). At the same time capital gain should be realized within 3–5 years. Different types of debt are available so covenants need to define a suitable financial structure in terms of maturity, amount, collateral usage, and seniority. This is necessary to balance between the leverage benefit, the cost of the debt, and the risk of finance distress. The covenants clearly state that if the profits can be reinvested these criteria are to be applied.
2. The general partner must follow a policy that defines and limits the possibility of personal investing in portfolio companies to control conflict of interest and ensure the minimum standard of professional care. Specific restrictions on the investment powers of the general partner include:
    a. Diversification—No more than a specified percentage of total commitments (25%) are to be invested in a single or linked investment
    b. Bridge financing—When the general partner intends to sell part of an investment within a specified period after its acquisition, the 25% limit is often raised to 35% of total commitments
    c. Hedging—Not permitted except for efficient portfolio management

    d. **Publicly traded securities**—Since investors are unwilling to pay private equity fees for the management of publicly traded securities, there are often strict limits placed on the circumstances in which these may be held by the fund

    e. **Fund documents**—Regulate the terms and circumstances in which co-investment opportunities may be offered to investors

    f. **General partners' investment**—Usually limited to a very low percentage of the investment

3. The rules are needed to set the type of investment in terms of restriction on asset classes, defining the amount and type of equity to be subscribed, and restriction due to conflict of interest with debt financers.

> REMEMBER: What is the percentage held by a GP? And by an AMC?

Covenants can be positive or negative.

*Positive covenants* are the list of things the company agrees to do including producing audited reports, holding regular board meetings, and paying taxes on time. *Negative covenants* are included to forbid an action. They are used in the private equity agreement and they serve to limit detrimental behavior by the entrepreneur and, as a consequence, certain actions are expressly forbidden or require the approval of a super majority of investors. The ratchets are contractual agreements that provide the ability to change duties or rights in case those specific conditions occur.

These rules include:

1. Lock up—An agreement between the investor, existing shareholders, and/or the management that prohibits them to exit by selling their quotas to third parties. It is good to adopt a series of agreements connected with the transfer of the shares that start at the end of the lock-up period. The most important and frequent rule is the preemption clause, which gives the exiting partner the right to buy shares from an existing party. To ensure this rule is recognized, all parties assign their shares to an escrow agent, usually a trustee company, who will act according to the agreement signed by the parties so any opportunistic behavior is avoided.

2. Permitted transfer clause—A provision between the investor and existing shareholders that prohibits both existing shareholders and private equity investors from selling their shares without the approval of the other party. This rule protects the stability of the parties' commitments.

3. Staging technique—This makes sure that financial resources are invested in the firm with multiple installments. Investment of these installments is done after specific business targets are hit. This provision

ensures that the money is not squandered on unprofitable prospects; it is also known as a "tranched" investment. This covenant is used to ensure that money is used according to the business approved by the private equity. Sometimes, due to the needs and to the nature of the business of the venture-backed company, this is not possible.

4. Earn out agreement—A payment system consisting of a postponed payment of a part of the original acquisition price. This is done at the realization of defined performance indicators fixed a priori by a common agreement between the seller and the venture capitalist. This check is made within a year or two after acquisition of the shares. This tool reduces the financial investor's economic risk.

5. Stock options—The holder of the venture-back company's stock has the right to buy or sell it at a predetermined price and a specific date. These stock options can be assigned both to the management and to the entrepreneur to motivate and increase their desire to maximize the company's value. This is easily accomplished with a public company where the parameter of the objectives reached is exposed by the stock's price, while in nonpublic companies they can be used after specific adjustments. It is common to fix operation and managerial goals for each function, but the parameters to which they are linked are easily manipulated. The solution is to use stock options linked to the final value of the company at the exit moment, utilizing the IRR realized through the investment as the parameter.

6. Callable and puttable securities—These are part of the financial agreement in which the private equity investor has the right to sell the stocks to the existing shareholders (puttable) and the existing shareholders have the right to buy the stocks from the private equity investor (callable). In both cases, the option agreement can be executed with or without a specific date on which to exercise these dates. These securities can be single or combined; that is, only callable or puttable or callable and puttable together. In underwriting a puttable security, the investors assume that the entrepreneur will have liquidity enough to buy back the stake. As this is not always the case, the private equity investor can arrange either an agreement by which the liquidity of the entrepreneur is held in an escrow account at which the entrepreneur does not have access. In this way the private equity is sure that the entrepreneur will have liquidity enough to buy back the stake of the share capital. Alternatively, a Payment in Kind (PIK) may be linked to such option. This means that in case the private equity does not have liquidity enough to buy back the shares, it will be mandated to give to the investors his stake of the share capital. In this way it will be easier for the private equity to exit the investment in that he will be holding the whole company (or at least the majority of it). For a focus on this covenant see Section 14.4.2.1.

7. Tag along right—An agreement that states when the private equity investor has a minority participation in the financed firm. If the majority shareholders sell their participations, the private equity investor has the right to join (pro quota) the deal so he can sell his minority stake in the venture-backed company at the same terms and conditions to the same buyer.

8. Drag along rights or antidilution clause—If the venture capitalist wants to sell his stocks, this mechanism provides the right to ask to all other shareholders to sell their stake at the same conditions and to the same buyer. This rule was created so that the venture capitalist could maximize the sell pricing by selling to all the participants included in the selling. This allows the buyer to take the entire company all at once.

9. Right of first refusal—If other shareholders want to sell their stakes, this provision allows the private equity investor to avoid including undesired new shareholders in the company. The investor has the right to refuse the new shareholders' entrance, but he must acquire the stake of the selling shareholders at the same conditions offered by the potential buyer.

10. Exit ratchet—This is a motivation method for the entrepreneur (and manager). It provides an exit when the company's shares are reallocated between the entrepreneur (and manager) and the investor to allow the entrepreneur to obtain a part of the capital gain realized by the private equity investor at the exit. This ratchet is based on the periodic evaluation of the increasing value reached by the ventured-back company. It is a technique frequently adopted in leveraged buyout operations (especially in case of management buyout and management buy in) combined with management objectives.

11. Asset sales covenants—Restrictions placed on selling assets above a certain value or assets representing a certain percentage of the firm's book value. This prevents the entrepreneur from increasing the risk profile of the company and changing the firm's activity from its intended focus and also from making "sweetheart" [1] deals with friends.

12. Merger or sale covenants—Limitations preventing a merger or sale of the company without the approval of the investor. Transfer of control restrictions are important because venture capitalists invest in people and, if the management team decides to remove its human capital from the deal, venture capitalists would want to approve the terms of the transfer. Controlling transfers may hurt the position of the private equity investor if the terms are unfavorable to earlier investors.

13. Asset purchase covenant—Restrictions placed on the purchase of major assets above a certain sized threshold that may also be forbidden

---

[1]The term sweetheart deal, or sweetheart contract, is used to describe an abnormally favorable contractual agreement.

without the approval of the venture capitalist. These restrictions may be expressed in absolute terms of value or as a percentage of the book value of the firm. These covenants may help prevent unwanted changes in strategy or wasteful expenditure by the entrepreneur.

14. New securities restrictions—Limit the issuance of senior securities without the approval of previous investors and prevent the transfer of value from current shareholders to new security holders. Approval for this must be obtained by the super majority consensus of the shareholders.

In addition to the previously listed rules, corporate governance rules also provide a set of dispositions that discipline the structure and operation of the main company's functions. Usually the investor has his own representatives on the Board of Directors proportional to the dimension of the capital subscribed. In addition, rules for the Board of Directors may grant veto power to the investor representatives on the most important matters.

It is a good idea to support the Board of Directors with committees that have at least one member appointed by the venture capitalist; these committees are dedicated to specific matters that can affect, directly or indirectly, the investor's interests, such as the executive committee, the remuneration committee, the nomination committee, and the audit committee. For the Board of Directors to function effectively, it is advisable to allow at least one independent member who does not have

- Any type of personal relationship, such as affinity or family relationship, with the other members of the board or with the shareholders
- Directly or indirectly, any participation in the risk capital of the company
- Any power to influence the autonomy of the other members; for example, by his own economic resources.

The Board of Directors should meet at least quarterly if not monthly once the executive committee is in place. The quorum provided should be higher for all topics relevant to the company's existence such as dividends and reserves distributions, changes of the articles of association, and for all extraordinary operations; for example, a merger and acquisition or an initial public offering.

The previously mentioned veto power should cover annual budget approval, appointment and firing of the Chief Executive Officer and Chief Operations Officer, stock option plans approval, restructuring and turnaround plans, delegations of authority and remunerations of the directors, financing operations (debt issuing), capital expenditures operations, and putting up collateral.

To ensure ongoing dialog between management, the entrepreneur, and the venture capitalist, the company should produce monthly communication that allows the venture capitalist to verify the management team's skills and to exercise his deliberation power during the shareholders' assembly.

The company should communicate all information regarding

- Potential risks that can affect the investment performance
- Shareholders, directors, and employees
- Financial and operation data such as balance sheet reclassified, monthly financial plan, yearly budget, and capital expenditures
- Company objectives.

In Table 14.1 are presented the covenants and it is specified for which of the two party they are applied. In addition, the conflict they are trying to address is indicated.

### 14.4.2.1 Liquidity Management in the Presence of a Put Option

The underlying condition for generating a high IRR in the presence of a put option is a solid business plan, as the strike price of the put option can be set in the following ways:

- Fixed strike price
- Floating strike price
- Floating strike price with a floor

**Table 14.1** Representation of the Main Covenants

| Covenant | Private Equity Investor | Entrepreneur | Main Conflict Addressed Through This Covenant |
|---|---|---|---|
| Lock up | X | X | Divergence in time |
| Permitted transfer | X | X (sometimes) | Divergence in time |
| Staging technique | X | | Wrong decisions |
| Stock option plan | | X | Wrong decisions |
| Callable option | X | X | Wrong decisions/divergence in time |
| Puttable option | X | | Wrong decisions/divergence in time |
| Tag along | X | | New shareholders |
| Drag along | X | | Divergence in time |
| Right of first refusal | X | | New shareholders |
| Exit ratchet | X | X | Divergence in time/exiting surprising |
| Asset sales covenants | | X | Wrong decisions |
| Merger or sale covenants | | X | Wrong decisions/new Shareholders |
| Asset purchase covenant | | X | Wrong decisions |
| New securities restrictions | | X | Wrong decisions/new shareholders |

In the first case, like the name itself suggests, the fixed strike price is set in advance and it is agreed by the entrepreneur and the investor. The advantage in adopting this solution is that the entrepreneur is ensuring to receive a given strike price. On the other hand, if the set strike price is low, the investor may be losing a portion of the upside, and the price could have been higher in case the price has not been fixed in advance. Clearly, the higher the amount of the price, the higher the risk the entrepreneur may not have enough liquidity.

In the second and third case, the strike price is set basing on some multiples starting from the values of the business plan. This is usually calculated as

$$(\text{EBITDA multiple} \times \text{EBITDA} - \text{Net financial position}) \times \text{Shares held}$$

In this option, there may be two scenarios: one without a floor (hence where a minimum is not granted) and a second scenario where a minimum threshold is granted, that is usually lower than the fixed strike price.

As mentioned above, in case there is a put option, the biggest risk for the private equity is that the entrepreneur may not have enough liquidity to pay the stake of the entrepreneur. Hence some analytical model is required to be used in these cases to assess the feasibility of the conditions agreed.

Here follows an example illustrating how liquidity can be managed and how IRR can be calculated on the basis of the strike price that the investor will receive if the put option will be used.

## Example

Assume an investor invested €25 M to buy 25% of a private company, presenting a business plan up to year 5 (Table 14.2).

The fixed strike price, as anticipated in advance, is set at the beginning of the investment, hence there is no need to compute such value. The IRR can be hence calculated as

$$\text{IRR} = \frac{\text{Fixed strike price}^{1/n}}{\text{Investment}} - 1$$

where $n$ represents the end of the holding period.

The following IRR can hence be calculated as shown in Table 14.3.

As for the floating price, the floating price will be calculated as

$$(\text{EBITDA multiple} \times \text{EBITDA} - \text{NFP}) \times \text{Shares held}$$

**Table 14.2** Data 1

| YEARS | 0 | 1 | 2 | 3 | 4 | 5 |
|---|---|---|---|---|---|---|
| investment (€) | 25.000.000 | | | | | |
| % held by the investor | 25% | | | | | |
| | | | | | | |
| EBITDA | 45.000.000 | | 50.000.000 | 55.000.000 | 55.000.000 | 60.000.000 |
| EDITDA multiple | 5 | | 6 | 6 | 6 | 6 |
| NFP | 125.000.000 | | 110.000.000 | 100.000.000 | 90.000.000 | 85.000.000 |
| | | | | | | |
| fix strike | | | 32.500.000 | 37.500.000 | | |
| floating strike | | | ? | ? | ? | ? |
| | | | | | | |
| IRR +2 fix | ? | | | | | |
| IRR +2 float | ? | | | | | |
| IRR +3 fix | ? | | | | | |
| IRR +3 float | ? | | | | | |
| IRR +4 fix | | | | | | |
| IRR +4 float | ? | | | | | |
| IRR +5 fix | | | | | | |
| IRR +5 float | ? | | | | | |

**Table 14.3** IRR With Fixed Strike Price

| YEARS | 0 | 1 | 2 | 3 | 4 | 5 |
|---|---|---|---|---|---|---|
| investment € | 25.000.000 | | | | | |
| % held by the investor | 25% | | | | | |
| | | | | | | |
| EBITDA | 45.000.000 | | 50.000.000 | 55.000.000 | 55.000.000 | 60.000.000 |
| EDITDA multiple | 5 | | 6 | 6 | 6 | 6 |
| NFP | 125.000.000 | | 110.000.000 | 100.000.000 | 90.000.000 | 85.000.000 |
| | | | | | | |
| fix strike | | | 32.500.000 | 37.500.000 | | |
| floating strike | | | ? | ? | ? | ? |
| | | | | | | |
| IRR +2 fix | | 14,02% | | | | |
| IRR +2 float | ? | | | | | |
| IRR +3 fix | | 14,47% | | | | |
| IRR +3 float | ? | | | | | |
| IRR +4 fix | | | | | | |
| IRR +4 float | ? | | | | | |
| IRR +5 fix | | | | | | |
| IRR +5 float | ? | | | | | |

Entailing the following results.

In this case, the IRR will be computed as shown in Table 14.4 with the following formula:

$$IRR = \frac{\text{Floating strike price}^{1/n}}{\text{Investment}} - 1$$

**Table 14.4** Data 2

| YEARS | 0 | 1 | 2 | 3 | 4 | 5 |
|---|---|---|---|---|---|---|
| investment € | 25.000.000 | | | | | |
| % held by the investor | 25% | | | | | |
| | | | | | | |
| EBITDA | 45.000.000 | | 50.000.000 | 55.000.000 | 55.000.000 | 60.000.000 |
| EDITDA multiple | 5 | | 6 | 6 | 6 | 6 |
| NFP | 125.000.000 | | 110.000.000 | 100.000.000 | 90.000.000 | 85.000.000 |
| | | | | | | |
| fix strike | | | 32.500.000 | 37.500.000 | | |
| floating strike | | | 47.500.000 | 57.500.000 | 60.000.000 | 68.750.000 |
| | | | | | | |
| IRR +2 fix | 14,02% | | | | | |
| IRR +2 float | ? | | | | | |
| IRR +3 fix | 14,47% | | | | | |
| IRR +3 float | ? | | | | | |
| IRR +4 fix | | | | | | |
| IRR +4 float | ? | | | | | |
| IRR +5 fix | | | | | | |
| IRR +5 float | ? | | | | | |

Giving the following results as shown in Table 14.5.

The IRR is certainly much higher in the case of a floating strike price, however the amount required with the formula are very high and the entrepreneur may not have such liquidity, making it necessary to use some further cautions such as an escrow account or the payment in kind clause. In this last case, the IRR will further increase, as the percentage of shares held will be even higher.

**Table 14.5** IRR With Floating Strike Price

| YEARS | 0 | 1 | 2 | 3 | 4 | 5 |
|---|---|---|---|---|---|---|
| investment € | 25.000.000 | | | | | |
| % held by the investor | 25% | | | | | |
| | | | | | | |
| EBITDA | 45.000.000 | | 50.000.000 | 55.000.000 | 55.000.000 | 60.000.000 |
| EDITDA multiple | 5 | | 6 | 6 | 6 | 6 |
| NFP | 125.000.000 | | 110.000.000 | 100.000.000 | 90.000.000 | 85.000.000 |
| | | | | | | |
| fix strike | | | 32.500.000 | 37.500.000 | | |
| floating strike | | | 47.500.000 | 57.500.000 | 60.000.000 | 68.750.000 |
| | | | | | | |
| IRR +2 fix | 14,02% | | | | | |
| IRR +2 float | 37,84% | | | | | |
| IRR +3 fix | 14,47% | | | | | |
| IRR +3 float | 32,00% | | | | | |
| IRR +4 fix | | | | | | |
| IRR +4 float | 24,47% | | | | | |
| IRR +5 fix | | | | | | |
| IRR +5 float | 22,42% | | | | | |

# CHAPTER 15

# Exiting

## 15.1 INTRODUCTION

Exiting is the final step in the investment process made by the venture capitalist. This step is very important because the venture capitalist sells the stake to gain the value added created by the investment and the managing and monitoring activities of the venture. The moment in which the investor will exit cannot be determined ex ante as it depends on each individual deal as every private equity has specific goals of internal rate of return (IRR) and has to meet investors' requirements. In addition, it is related to external factors such the financial market trend in that moment with reference to the industry or cluster in which the investor is investing.

For these reasons, for private equity, exiting is an extremely important and delicate step. It requires two fundamental aspects: determination of the channel to be used and identification of the best time for divestment.

Schwienbacher, Hege, and Palomino (2003) have attempted to rationalize the issue of exit strategies considering the sector, the investment length, the external economic environment, the stage of development, etc. The final results are quite interesting: the sector is a very important variable in the definition of both timing and kind of exit. Cumming (2008), in contrast, linked the issue of exit strategies to the characteristics of individual agreements and found that the governance, the dividend policy, and the existing financial leverage have a significant effect on exit strategies. Gordon Smith (2005) discussed the question of the agreement terms and forms in private equity transactions. He concluded that the prediction of an exit strategy in the initial agreement is an incentive for the financial institutions, and that private equity operators tend to sign agreements in which there are clauses that give them the opportunity to increase their power when the time for exit is near.

Schwienbacher (2002) compared the exit strategies of both American and European private equity operators to test if a "common strategy" exists. Results showed that the most used exit strategy in both markets is the trade sale, even

**215**

if all players consider the initial public offering (IPO) more profitable and a better solution for developing a solid reputation for future deals. It also showed that the length of the investment is almost equal in both markets, and the involvement of financial institutions is similar in operations based on the same assumptions. The main difference is that the Europeans showed a lack of liquidity in all of the deals; in particular, the length of divestment is higher, the financial instruments used are less modern, and the syndicated deals are poorer with fewer participants.

Private equity investors usually maintain the participation in the venture-backed company between 5 and 7 years, for that they are considered temporary partners whose final objective is an economic return within a medium–long term. As such, the moment of exit has to be coordinated together and in accordance with the entrepreneur. This type of investment is very risky so the private equity will never be able to plan in advance with absolutely certainty the best moment to sell the participation. The investor's amount of return depends on successful fund allocations and the quality of the work done by the private equity operator. From the beginning of the investment, it is critical to have a clear idea about potential disinvestment and way-outs, as this is the biggest driver of IRR for the investor and the element the private equity business will use to assess his job. It is fundamental to avoid any type of arbitral constraints connected with the financial partner's exit.

## 15.2    THE EXIT VADEMECUM

The following aspect should be taken into consideration during the exiting strategy plan:

- The specific rules and covenants of the investment—Every deal has specific agreements that regulate the relation between the parties. This is done to prevent and mitigate any agency problem and opportunistic behavior. These agreements are meant to directly affect the reasons for exiting as well as its timing to protect the needs and the rights of the firm and the investors.
- Timing opportunity driven by the company's business—The moment of exit is directly influenced by the position of the company along its life cycle, which is due to external or internal factors. For example, global recession can decrease the capacity of revenue generation or new regulatory rules changing the competition dynamics.
- Timing opportunity driven by the financial and merger and acquisition markets—Economic and financial situations impact the demand or offer of money, the potential opportunity to place the shares on the market at a good price, the possible reduction of value, etc.

- Capital requirement—Regulatory rules, such as "Basel 2," place specific value on capital ratios required by financial companies. Consequently, the specific needs of recapitalization may cause an early exit in order to use the cash realized to satisfy the required ratios.
- Constraints from the residual maturity of the investment vehicle and from the final IRR goal—Because the IRR is determined by the duration of the investment, the venture capitalist has to balance the duration with the IRR desired.
- Exiting track record of the portfolio—Selecting the best way to exit depends on the strategy followed by each private equity fund; for example, there are some funds that prefer an IPO as an exit strategy rather than a trade sale.

Investors should also consider these causes of failure connected with an exit:

- A lower level of appreciation of the target company by the financial market
- Lack of interest demonstrated by the public or institutional investors toward the IPO operation
- Lack of interest demonstrated by potential industrial acquirers during trade sale operations
- Short collaboration from the management or the co-investors
- Unsatisfactory performance of the target company
- Negative outcomes and feedback from due diligence.

There are two exit strategies followed by the investors: path sketcher and opportunistic behavior. The path sketcher strategy is realized without any exit planning. The opportunistic behavior strategy is based on management skills and the development of the company, and is usually realized through an IPO.

Finally, according to PwC, there are two types of investors, each with their own exit plan. The first type is defined as a proactive investor who acquires majority quotes with a stock option plan to motivate the target company management. These investors plan from the outset to target an IRR reachable by the allocated funds. The second type is the passive investor who acquires minority quotes without a clear exit strategy. This strategy is usually realized through the buy-back of the participation by the management and/or original shareholder of the company with attention to IRR maximization.

## 15.3 EXIT ALTERNATIVES

Although equity investment has different profiles (i.e., seed, start-up, expansion, replacement, and vulture), theory and market trends show no correlation between the stage of investment, the holding period, and the exit strategy. Every deal has a specific strategy with rules driven by the needs of both the investor and the entrepreneur. These are typical exiting strategies relevant to today's market:

- Trade sale
- Buyback
- Sale to other private equity investors
- Write-off
- IPO or sale post-IPO.

### 15.3.1   Trade Sale

A trade sale exit occurs when the private equity investor sells the stake to a corporation or, for example, to an industrial shareholder. This exiting strategy it is often used in European markets. It is based on industrial relationships among the private equity investor, the buyer, and the venture-backed company. The trade sale can be realized through public tender or private negotiations between the parties.

A trade sale is generally motivated by the buyer's strategic business plan and because a trade sale can be executed in different ways; it avoids specific financial market conditions and the lack of interest toward investment stakes.

Several types of trade sale can be identified:

- The buyer enters the company through a minority participation to develop an alliance with the target company or to launch an offer to buy the company from the majority shareholders.
- The buyer becomes a majority shareholder to consolidate this participation or merge.

The strengths of a trade sale exit are the chance to realize a higher premium price and the possibility for the venture capitalist to divest the whole participation through an operation cheaper and faster than an IPO. It is also easier to negotiate with fewer potential participants than with the entire financial market. This is the only exit option for investments realized in small medium firms.

There are also disadvantages to this type of exit: lack of trade buyers in some countries, management opposition, and investors not wanting to provide the required collateral.

There are several condition for realizing a profitable trade sale:

- Private equity investors have a strong network of relationships in which to find a potential buyer

- If the existing shareholders exit at the same time as the private equity investor the buyer can acquire a majority and have total control of the company
- Existing shareholders agree to integrate with another industrial corporation
- Negotiations with potential buyers can be developed at the same level of reputation and power

### 15.3.2 Buyback

A buyback exit occurs when the private equity investor sells its stake to existing shareholders in the corporation or their representatives. The buyback alternative is an opportunity to support and develop a business when shareholders do not want to leave the company.

The exit through a buyback most likely will occur when:

- Shareholders have initiated a venture capital operation to collect funds for development of the business idea (seed financing), the business development (start-up financing), or the company's growth (development financing).
- Shareholders manage a governance turnaround.
- Shareholders transfer ownership to other people.

A profitable buyback can be accomplished when shareholders want to own the business, have the money to buyback the shares, and have a clear problem of turnaround or inheritance. This option of exit assumes that the entrepreneur has the liquidity necessary to buy the stake, which is not always the case.

### 15.3.3 Sale to Other Private Equity Investors

This type of exit consists in selling the stakes to another private equity or venture capital fund. It is an exit strategy frequently used in the US market and is based on the strong relationships among private equity investors. In the past, this strategy was more widespread and used as a secondary buy out. The strategy was also used when the investor, specialized in a specific stage of the target firm's life cycle, sold the participation to a partner specialized in a different life cycle stage (i.e., from seed to start-up, from start-up to expansion, etc.).

Typical sales between private equity investors include:

- Seed financer sells the stake to a start-up financer to "start the engine"
- Start-up financer sells its stake to an expansion financer to sustain growth
- Expansion financer sells its stake to a replacement financer to develop acquisition, turnaround, or IPO

- Vulture financer (rarer) sells its stake to a replacement financer to end the work of restructuring

Conditions that must be satisfied to develop a profitable sale to other private equity investors:

- A strong network of relationships in which to find potential private equity buyers
- A market where there are vehicles dedicated to investment in the different life cycle stages
- Existing shareholders agree to a continuous presence of equity investors
- Existing shareholders have a clear plan to develop the firm from a small to medium size business

This type of deal can be motivated also by fund duration or the status of the relationship between the investors, the entrepreneur, and the management team of the target company. This type of exit allows the ongoing development or growth of the firm. If there is a bad relationship between the shareholders and the venture capitalist is unable to realize the desired and expected return, he should accelerate the exit by accepting a lower price.

When this strategy is realized through a secondary buy out, total control of the company passes from one institutional investor to another. This type of divestment is similar to a trade sale; the only difference is that the buyer is a financial investor not an industrial partner. This strategy is utilized when there is no debt and the target company is mature.

The main drawback of this kind of exit is that the buyer (i.e., the private equity investor) aims at the inverse goal as the seller (i.e., another private equity investor). In this sense, the buyer will want the lowest possible price, in order to maximize the capital gain, and at the same time the seller will want to the highest possible price in order to maximize the capital gain.

### 15.3.4    Write-Off

A write-off is usually included during the disinvestment as well as devaluation, partially or totally, of the participation as a consequence of money loss unrelated to a transfer of property. This is included because it is a different from other exit strategies; it reduces or the removes specific assets on the balance sheet. Investors decide to write off a deal when the stake and the company are unable to produce value in the future.

The write-off process is used when no economic return is generated from the stake. Bankruptcy laws are followed and sometimes an investor can get back part of the face value of his shares if the cash resources of the company's assets exceed the total amount of the debt.

The typical write-off occurs when there are

- Private equity investor asks the court to declare that the company is in default
- Creditor asks the court to begin bankruptcy proceedings
- Equity investor negotiates the closing of the company with shareholders and they decide to see the company's assets; this is very common in seed and start-up ventures.

Before deciding to write off an investment, the venture capitalist must make sure the following conditions are satisfied to realize a profitable disinvestment:

- No possibility the company will produce profit in the future
- Assets of the venture-backed company can be sold with satisfactory results through the market
- Costs of write-off are insignificant with short-term management
- Social impact of the write-off is irrelevant and does not generate negative consequences for the investor.

## 15.3.5   IPO or Sale Post-IPO

When the private equity investor sells the stake through the stock exchange, the exit strategy is called an IPO. This type of divestment is attractive in terms of reputation and economic return even if the realization is very difficult and rare.[1] The exit is complex, especially for small or medium companies, and is considered in a long-term strategy after the target firm has reached an adequate level of development and seniority.

The private equity investor is strongly involved in the IPO process, acting as a global advisor or manager. Here are reported the typical categories of IPO sales:

- Private equity investor drives the IPO and the selling of its stake is written into the info memorandum. This is a bad signal but it helps to control the exiting price.
- Private equity investor drives the IPO and sells its stake at the start of negotiations (using the underpricing effect). This option probably maximizes the exit price through the underpricing.
- Private equity investor drives the IPO and sells after, with or without lock up, a certain period of time. The lock up is an agreement between the parties that prohibits them from exiting by selling their quotas to third parties just before the IPO. This is a good signal for the market, but the private equity investor faces the risk of floating the exiting value.

---

[1] Real data show that the IPO occurs one in a hundred.

A profitable IPO can be realized during a favorable stock market if the company satisfies the required criteria for the listing. It becomes a successful solution when the venture-backed company heightens its profile in the financial community and due diligence produces satisfactory results. For an IPO to be successful it is necessary that corporate governance, management, and the company's entire organization show a positive attitude to face post-IPO life with the existing shareholders.

There are advantages and disadvantages to the IPO exit strategy. Advantages include the opportunity to sell the participation at a higher price, satisfying management, and further potential gain by the institutional investor.

In an IPO exit strategy disadvantages to the investor include higher costs related to the exit and risk connected to the lack of liquidity in European markets. This type of exit is not feasible for the small companies because lock-up contract conditions, which prevent investors from selling the stakes before quotation, need a large number of investors to obtain a successful IPO.

Due to its importance, the topic of a private company going public is analyzed thoroughly in the next chapter.

## 15.4  QUOTATION OF PRIVATE EQUITY COMPANIES

### 15.4.1  Potential Advantages and Disadvantages

When a venture capitalist decides to go public, the preliminary step is the selection of the most appropriate market and the best-possible structure in which to offer the participations. Private equity operators review the stock exchange quotation and the financial market before considering an investment opportunity and financial markets dedicated to innovative companies with an intense growth level offer venture capitalists the best opportunities.

In order to attract investors, the ability of the fund to create value must be assessed. This is done by considering elements such as the track record of the previous investments in the portfolio, the rate of investment failure, the professional profile of the management team, the quality of the founders, the company governance, the risk profile of the specific investment activities, and the level of transparency and clarity when reporting and communicating.

Today's international banking community reflects the presence of numerous private equity companies quoted on the financial markets. There are more private equity companies in the most developed financial markets with numerous venture capital companies quoted on the NASDAQ, the London stock exchange, and the Swiss market where there is a specific segment that regulates venture capital companies in terms of admission procedures and requisites for permanence. In the past, this type of quotation was possible because financial markets trended toward riskier investments.

For private equity companies, the decision to go public represents growth, recognized by the market, and allows advantages and benefits such as:

- An increase in fundraising at an international and national level due to the investor. This solves the problem of limited capital raised from other sources such as banks and debt financers.
- Access to public small investors interested in venture capital activity. This represents the opportunity to enhance visibility and increase the interaction with supplier and customer.
- International projects to view and invest in. Becoming a public company projects an image of stability.
- Easier partnerships with technological suppliers and operators connected to the high-tech sector.
- Managing a wider and more diversified portfolio of companies guaranteeing opportunities to support projects requiring large investments.
- Fulfilling private equity investors' desire to achieve liquidity.

However, going public involves high costs that can hence discourage many private equity firms from this option: legal, accounting, and investment banking fees are heavy. In addition, as a public company there is a higher degree of disclosure and transparency, which means a decrease of privacy. Managers may be afraid that the company could be tainted by market rumors, which can affect and influence their strategies with dramatic floating of the stock price not based on the real value of the company and the global level of IPO activity.

Unlike the quotation of an industrial or service company, the quotation of a venture capital or investment company reflects a high-risk profile with high-risk combined with industrial and financial risks typical of risk capital investment. The degree of risk varies according to the operator. It is higher when the investment is focused on the company's initial development phases (from start-up to early stage), which operates in technological and innovative sectors with a lower degree of diversification.

In summary, it can be said that industrial or service companies invest in companies with a lower economic risk profile, while investment companies prefer to invest in funds and quoted companies that are historically found in stock markets.

Limited liquidity of the portfolio assets represents a critical element in the quotation of a company. It reflects the uncertainty of the created value as well as the ability of investors to monitor it. The value of a company with a portfolio without listed participations depends on the ability to realize capital gains only when exiting from the investment. When the exit occurs through an IPO, the economic return can be dissolved over time due to lock-up conditions obliging the shareholders to maintain their shares for a specific period after the IPO (usually between 6 and 12 months). Part of the gain may be realized through the sale of the shares in an IPO at a fixed price defined at the moment of the closing; the other part can be obtained through a later trade sale or with a private arrangement at the expiry of the lock up.

Today a high-growth company has no partial exit because the presence of the institutional investor in the shareholding structure is an unconditional element when accepting a high degree of risk. The uncertainty on the value created is extended over time, as the effective time and value of the exit for the venture capitalist depend on the market conditions and the trend of the quoted security after the quotation as well as many other specific and market factors.

These factors may be the because there are many institutional investors, particularly those operating in the most advanced phases of a company's life cycle, to prefer an exit through a trade sale instead of an IPO. This exit strategy guarantees a sure and immediate value through the capital gain realized with a sale to third parties. Although a preferred solution, it is not always possible; a full sale of shares through an IPO is more feasible for companies subjected to an LBO or turnaround operation. Younger companies with a higher risk return profile and a lower level of fame and prestige normally receive new capital to finance growth so the sale of existing shares is not compatible with its quotation (at least not in the initial phase of the company life cycle).

In the absence of exiting, the value of participations in a portfolio must be periodically estimated to calculate the net asset value of the fund or the assets in the financial statements. This practice, based on techniques used by specialized operators, must deal with the uncertainty and structural difficulties in defining values for companies still immature and subject to market, technical, commercial, and operating forces.

The uncertainty and the possible decrease in the net asset value of a pool of investments are critical in the quotation of a venture company. Long-term duration of the investment and the difficulty in comparing it with other similar companies should also be considered. This is reflected in two different problems: the lack of alternative diversification and the difficulty in forecasting annual results for these private equity funds. It is difficult to forecast annual results of a private equity even when the quotation imposes quarterly reporting and analysis. Therefore, the quality and quantity of research available for operators in these sectors tend to be limited, particularly in smaller markets.

Considering the advantages and disadvantages of the issuer party and the market, private equity investors must review their exit strategy for each investment.

The issuer considers that the

1. Quotation increases the funds collected and reduces the time spent for fundraising, providing a channel normally used by institutional operators. In favorable market conditions such as during the high-tech boom in the United States, quotation allowed the quick raising of funds and a high diversification of the fundraising channels.
2. Moment of quotation provides liquidity to the fund's original subscriber from the buyer; however, effective liquidity depends on the negotiation of shares on the secondary market.
3. Quotation increases and enforces the reputation and visibility of the fund influencing the companies financed by the fund and taking advantage of new business opportunities.
4. The original holder of the fund is an industrial company or a diversified holding, so the quotation allows a better valuation of the total assets held by the original holder because it permits the separation of the investment activity from other businesses.

These operations can be attractive to the market because of the following reasons:

1. Private equity companies, with quotation, offer an investment opportunity that includes securities issued by several different companies. This type of investment allows retail investors to put their financial resources into shares that otherwise would be unavailable. During the high-tech boom in the United States, investors were looking for participations in new companies due to the expected high returns. They were able to realize these investments because these high-tech securities were included in venture capital quoted funds. The appeal of the investment in a fund, or in the investment company, is greater when the participated companies are closed to quotation because of the expectation that the exit value will be higher than the net asset value of the companies and the market will reflect it with a higher stake price. If the market is trending up, then investor behavior supports the investment company, but if the market is trending down, the sensibility to the risk is higher and can damage the operation. The mood of the market can lead to a higher level of expected default of the underlying portfolio penalizing the private equity companies more than the companies financed due to the greater liquidity costs and uncertainty of obtainable results.
2. Composition, size, and diversification of the portfolio strongly influence the placement of venture capital funds on the stock exchange. Industry specialization makes these investments more desirable for highly specialized institutional investors (industry related funds). Still, the preference is to quote funds with a significant amount of quoted

investments due to the higher level of transparency of net asset value and the higher liquidity of assets. The size is usually related to the company's diversification (or by companies and funds), therefore representing additional criteria for market opinion.

3. The required fund quoted in return is compared with its risks and other potential investments in equity to appraise its potential for increasing portfolio return.

4. The reputation and track record of the fund managers (past successful investment operations and the relative high IRR generated) should be evaluated during the investment decision. The qualities of possible co-investors, represented by strategic participations in other funds, are also important factors because funds with good reputations act as a guarantee. Co-investment with these funds provides an important message to the market about the quality of the relationship.

The previous list provides several elements that help explain the relatively recent and important phenomenon of venture capital quotation. The venture capital quotation trend, which started in the United States during the high-tech boom, moderately developed in Europe, and never took off in markets where private equity industry is historically more developed. High risk and lack of suitable European target companies (most of them based in industrial investment) made it difficult for a venture capital quotation boom to occur in European markets because industrial groups are rarely subject to spin-offs or quotations.

## 15.4.2   Segmentation of Private Equity Operators

Analysis of the advantages and risks of private equity operators in the stock market cannot be performed without considering the segmentation of the specific market in terms of risk and economic return correlated to the different phases of the company life cycle. For this purpose it is useful to organize private equity operators into three macro categories: incubators, venture capitalists, and investment companies. These categories are differentiated by the financial commitment and timeliness of the investment, type of risk faced, and the support needed.

Financial commitment and timeliness of the investment depends on the growth curve of a company over a period of time. The greatest investment made by an institutional investor occurs in the initial start-up phase with a limited financial commitment and greater correlated risks due to the high level of company mortality during this phase. The financial commitment in this phase is typically medium-long term (from 4 to 7 years) with limited liquidity of the participation. Investments made in a company during a more mature level of development are higher with a lower risk of company mortality. The length of these investments is shorter with greater liquidity. In summary, the rate of return requested is higher when the investment is related to the initial phases in the life cycle of a company and decreases over the time.

The type of risk faced by an investor is strictly connected with the life cycle phase of a company. During the start-up phase, the risk of failure is typically embodied in the fact that the company must still build a business model, develop a product/service, set up a business structure, source managerial expertise, acquire market share, etc. For more mature, consolidated companies the greatest risk is the financial risk related to the relationship between debt and equity and the optimization of financial leverage. Support requested by start-ups consists of a series of operating services offered by the investors who not only act exclusively as the financier of the initiative, but also contribute to the company's growth by providing value-added services.

Incubators take part in the initial phase of a start-up with a limited financial commitment and a greater risk of company mortality. This requires higher returns and offers financial and operative support such as rental of space, recruitment, accounting, consulting, etc.

Investment companies are involved during the maturity phases of a firm providing a high level of financial resources with a lower company mortality risk. During this life cycle phase economic return will be lower and the investor offers just financial support.

Venture capital companies intervene in the intermediary business life cycle arranging their portfolios to balance risks and returns. It is important to emphasize that venture capital activity is specialized in terms of a business model. Venture capital companies can be either incubators or investment companies.

Because there is no precise boundary between the different typologies of private equity operators, it is difficult to identify which type is necessary. The business model and the value creation of private equity companies change significantly depending on whether they are incubators, venture capitalists, or investment companies. The incubator's value creation is developed through five critical phases:

1. Identification of investment opportunities by analyzing the business plan and the management team
2. Investment of financial resources, typically consisting of seed capital, necessary to launch the entrepreneurial initiative
3. Supporting the company at an operations level so that business development can be realized by management
4. Sharing their network of contacts to support management activity
5. Divestment with a high level of return through the best-possible exit

Investment companies create portfolios of diversified participation to realize a diversification strategy in terms of value and risk. Their business model is structured to

1. Identify investment opportunities in nonpublic companies in development phases, companies already quoted, or companies in need of funds
2. Invest financial resources needed for expansion
3. Divest with a higher value and exit compatible with the diversification strategy

When incubators, venture capitalists, and investment companies go public they respond to the different requirements expressed by the market: higher risk and consequently higher returns for the incubator and greater risks and diversification for investment companies.

# CHAPTER 16

# Listing a Private Company

## 16.1 GENERAL OVERVIEW OF AN IPO

The listing of a private company can be considered from two different perspectives. First, it can be hidden inside a complex financial restructuring of the company. The initial public offering (IPO) is a tool that allows the rebalancing of the passive side of the balance sheet because it infuses new financial resources (risk capital) into a company. Second, the listing process of a company is key to supporting the firm's growth; since the funds raised on the public market can be used to realize new development opportunities.

The IPO is used to exploit a stable financial source, reach specific development entrepreneurial goals, and during the succession processes of family firms, protect the financial stability of the company and the improvement of its economic performance.

The reasons to take a company public have changed over the years. In the 1990s, the entrepreneurs exploited an upward trending market and placed their shares in advantageous positions. Listing a company also became an opportunity to rebalance the ratio between equity and debt, especially after a period of large investments. Until the mid-1990s, the quotation decision was led by entrepreneurs wanting to divest or diversify their portfolios. During the second half of 1990, the reasons to list a company completely changed. Many family-run small-to-medium firms decided to go public to exploit the tax benefit and the positive economic situation. Placing shares in a regulated stakes market represented a desirable exit strategy for institutional investors and private equity funds because it allows:

- The placement of minority shares of the risk capital, obtaining a capital gain and continuing to hold the control of the company
- A return higher than other exit solutions
- The satisfaction of management's preferences
- Potential capital gain to be obtained through the increase in the price or value of the shares over time

**229**

Private Equity and Venture Capital in Europe. https://doi.org/10.1016/B978-0-12-812254-9.00016-4

In this chapter, the characteristics of a target company that goes public will be addressed as will the disadvantages connected with this strategy and the relevant advantages analyzed from a management, company, and shareholder perspective. The main steps of the IPO process will be reviewed at the end of the chapter.

## 16.2    CHARACTERISTICS OF A COMPANY GOING PUBLIC

Several studies focused on the characteristics of companies eligible for a successful IPO strategy. The first group of studies shows the tendency of these firms to analyze their financial structure to determine if this strategy is applicable; for example, considering the optimal level of the debt leverage connected with the cost of the risk and debt capital. The second group of studies measures the tendency of the firm to list a company based on the position of the company in its life cycle and the related potential sources of financing. Finally, it was found that the main reason and motivation to list a company is the tensions that may rise between the majority and minority shareholders. These studies discovered the changes in target companies before and after going public.

There are several different potential types of companies interested in the listing process. We can identify four main groups related to the firm's life cycle:

1. Development companies—Firms that want to leave the status of family company and move toward a business structure that is more complex and articulated.
2. Replacement financing companies—Entities facing changes in the composition of the property related to a family succession. This category includes companies with private equity participation that want to use the quotation as an exit from their investment.
3. Growing companies—Firms that have reached the critical dimensional threshold and intend to continue growing by using a merger and acquisition strategy (external growth strategy) or to enlarge and reinforce their production capacity. The quotation decision is motivated by the intention to build and exploit a network of relationships that can help the company to grow its domestic dimensions by improving its position in the industry and collaborating with other firms that have complementary knowledge, skills, and resources.
4. Financially stressed companies—Companies developed from an internal or external growth strategy that need to rebalance their financial position by addressing the new funds to cover their previous investment plan. An IPO is a way to sustain development, rebalance the debt equity ratio, and diversify financial sources.

---

PAUSE: Can you list the private equity cluster for each of the above categories of stage life?

## 16.3 ADVANTAGES OF AN IPO FOR THE COMPANY

The advantages that an IPO offers to target companies have been the focus of many economic studies. One approach, based on the paradigm of the relationship between principal and agent, solves the agency cost problem by using the financial market. One benefit of quotation is higher visibility for the target company, which imposes more control by the investors and reduces agency costs in favor of improving performances from the target firm. Another approach focuses on the relation between the development level of the financial system and the growth of the company in a particular country. The stock exchange market solves several specific problems such as facilitating a match between demand and supply of capitals, simplifying the collection of the funds needed by the firm for its development, and control transfer.

Based on these approaches, the advantages created by the quotation in favor of the target company can be classified into two clusters:

1. Economic and financial advantages—All positive effects from reinforcing the financial structure are made possible by collecting new funds (risk capital resources). Direct access to new financial sources at a low price is done without the involvement of professional intermediaries. This should be considered both from a quantity and quality point of view, since the funds collected, as risk capital, do not include a contractual agreement for the periodic remuneration and repayment, while improving the debt-raising capacity. Several specific strengths of the quotation can be identified:
   a. Moving from financial problem-solving actions to a medium-long-term financial strategy
   b. Ability to decide how and when the investors are remunerated
   c. Expansion of available financing sources due to the improvement in the contractual power and transparency that IPOs offers to listed firms
   d. Improvement of the company's rating translated into the reduction of funding costs
   e. Diversification of collected funds in quantitative terms, which means less dependence on the bank system and the possibility of reducing the cost of funding supplied by the banks
   f. Different and specific structured categories of financial tools
   g. Reduction of collateral and other quantitative constraints
   h. Improved investment capacity due to fresh financial resources that reduce the debt servicing impact on the cash flows
2. Extra economic advantages include the positive effects caused by the quotation; being public generates a good reputation and increases visibility in the economic and financial community. These effects can be used as leverage in marketing and corporate strategies because they can

attract more qualified managerial resources. Public companies are more attractive than private ones, because they have highly skilled managers with a better prospective for growth. Reputation capital, which is gained by enhancing the company image, is very useful in the marketing strategy because it increases the firm's visibility if there is an internationalization campaign planned.

Very often, when a company goes public, the connection and the personality of the founder tend to disappear from the operative and strategic decision processes.

## 16.4    ADVANTAGES OF AN IPO FOR SHAREHOLDERS

If the IPO is a way to produce positive effects on the target company, then these advantages are reflected by the shareholders. In particular, it is possible to create liquidity from an investment realized in shares of a quoted company. Monetization of a firm's value allows the entrepreneur to diversify his portfolio, and guarantees a successful way out for the private equity investments realized in private companies.

The main advantages of an IPO for shareholders are

1. A solution to succession problems
2. Increased share value
3. Exploitation of tax benefits
4. Share liquidity that allows the realization of financial operations
5. Cancelation of personal and real guarantees offered by the entrepreneur in favor of the company
6. Recapitalization of the firm without using the founders' personal resources who maintain control because shares are now are issued with voting rights

## 16.5    ADVANTAGES OF AN IPO FOR MANAGEMENT

There are also benefits realized by managers when a company goes public including improved personal image, international visibility, and recognized expertise. These positive aspects are balanced by an increased monitoring of their daily performance because their work is constantly subjected to the judgement of the financial market expressed in terms of share price. The listing allows diversification of managers' salary so it can be divided into flat and variable remuneration linked to long-term incentives. The quotation for the employees is an opportunity to be involved in a stock options plan or subscribe to the increase of risk capital for free.

## 16.6 DISADVANTAGES OF AN IPO

An IPO for a target company also has its disadvantages. Every company going public suffers from one major disadvantage—the huge costs caused by this operation.

Ensuring an appropriate economic return to the new shareholders can be a problem particularly for the family-run company. If the net income of the firm before the IPO can be totally reinvested, after the listing it is important to define and follow a good dividend strategy. Going public leads to big changes for management. The global trend of the market directly affects management's decision process. A negative trend in the industry can push the company to move up investment opportunities because the risk capital operations would be unprofitable.

Once a private company is listed, it has to make several critical changes in the internal organization to work in the external financial and economic world. These changes are related to different aspects of the life of the firm such as

1. The need for transparency pushes the company to make its activities and processes more visible. The increase in decision constraints and the potential interference of third external parties decrease the control power of the entrepreneur. These problems are solved by the establishment of a shareholder agreement.
2. Implementing reporting and control requirements that usually imply investment and changes in the information and informatics system.
3. Huge costs; the IPO process imposes costs related to the fulfillments that target companies have to execute. After listing, public firms face several costs to adjust their organizational structure. The main sources of costs include the following:
   a. Advisory services supplied by the sponsor and the quotation syndicate
   b. Costs related to the certification and audit of the company's balance sheet
   c. Marketing costs related to the promotional activities of the IPO
   d. Fees for the public stock market manager
   e. Print and circulation of informative prospects
   f. Legal advice
   g. Printing shares certificates
4. The need to split the estates of the firm and the entrepreneur apart; this is solved with a special purpose vehicle and the estate that remains with the entrepreneur is concentrated.

## 16.7 THE IPO PROCESS

The process for publicly listing a company can be divided into two main subphases: the organization and the execution of the listing.

### 16.7.1  The Organization Phase

This phase consists mainly of a feasibility study of the quotation project, which analyzes all the elements that must be evaluated before going public such as the real will and desire of the majority shareholders, the market where the shares will be listed, the definition process for the price of the share, and checking the quotation requirements. The organization activities are usually executed with the involvement of one or more specialized financial intermediaries (named advisors who also participate in the quotation syndicate).

The main responsibility of the advisor is to check and verify the existence of both the formal and substantial requirements needed for the quotation. Formal requirements include all of the qualifications established by the law defined by the regulatory entities. Each country and public trade market has its own laws and regulatory rules. Substantial quotation requirements impose big changes in the structure of the company and, consequently, are more onerous than the formal ones. They can be classified into two categories:

1.  Organizational requirements:
    a.  Clear settlement of the relationship between the shareholders and the firm and, consequently, between the estate of the company and the estate of the entrepreneur.
    b.  Check the skill level of the management team and the real delegation of power and authorities assigned to people irrelevant to the entrepreneur.
    c.  Effectiveness of the organizational structure of the company is critical because it affects the ability of the firm to offer the necessary complete and accurate information to the financial market. The importance of the structure depends on the appreciation of the investors, which is directly linked to the company performances and the trust existing between it and the investors. An effective structure, which works with accurate control systems, ensures better control of the company performance so that faster changes can be made to the strategy in case of unsatisfactory results.
    d.  The involvement of a reliable and prestigious leader can guarantee optimal business execution of company activity.
2.  Economic and financial requirements—The first aspect to be evaluated and verified is the placement of the firm in its industry to define its potential in terms of future growth. Analysis focuses on the valuation of the firm's capacity to grow not only in terms of revenue increase, but also in terms of net income to be realized with a well-balanced financial strategy. The last critical aspect is the future ability of the company to generate dividends for the shareholders. This potential attracts investments from the market and improves the company's share value.

The organization phase is closed, after analyzing the formal and substantial requirements, with the selection of the market where the IPO will be realized. This implies the valuation of three elements: the country, the type, and the structure of the market.

### 16.7.1.1 The Country

The market country is not only the place where the shares will be negotiated, but there is also the problem of dual listing. Empirical evidence demonstrates a high correlation between the domestic country of the firm and the location of the market chosen for the launch of the IPO. Choosing the market where your firm is located is justified by many reasons such as the cost, cultural similarity, and the ability to manage the relevant financial community. Selecting a foreign market increases costs and imposes a cultural gap while representing a powerful marketing opportunity for the company. During the selection of the appropriate market, the company has to consider a dual listing strategy (simultaneous quotation in two public financial markets, domestic and international). A firm considers dual listing for the marketing potential and the opportunity to launch an acquisition campaign across foreign markets. Another critical factor is the importance of the country selected in terms of its position in the company's business.

### 16.7.1.2 The Market Type

The second main aspect to be evaluated is identifying the segment and type of market. In all countries, several different markets can be identified according to specific substantial and formal factors defined by the public authority as well as the dimensions of the listed companies. These specific characteristics have a direct impact on the visibility and the reputation of the company and the volatility of the share price.

### 16.7.1.3 The Market Structure

The last element considered is the structure of the market, and the choice is made by classifying the markets in three main categories: market with a "market-making" condition, specialist market, and stand-alone market. Market making occurs when financial intermediaries guarantee their assistance to the company after the quotation. They continue to offer the bid and ask price quotation without assuming direct position in the share trading. A specialist market implies a market maker that takes a position in the negotiations related to the shares quoted with specific obligations. When neither of the above two conditions are met, there is a stand-alone market.

### 16.7.2  The Execution Phase

The organization phase ends with the validation of the substantial requirement of the company. Once the quotation is validated, a critical and complex process starts to complete the listing of the company.

There are several activities to be executed with necessary steps to be followed:

1. Board of Directors resolution—this defines the decision to quote the company and the high level guidelines of the process and appoints the financial intermediaries that will act as sponsors of the listing.
2. Due diligence—this is the check of the legal, economic, and financial valuation of the company.
3. Meeting with market authorities to plan the activities required by the law.
4. Meeting and agreement with quotation syndicates (a group of financial intermediaries appointed to arrange the shares).
5. Company valuation.
6. Compilation of the comfort letters. These are certifications, signed by external audit companies, guaranteeing the existence of correct and effective planning and control systems in the target company.
7. Shareholders assembly resolution that allows the company to go public.
8. Preparation of the documentations for the financial analyst.
9. Premarketing, book building, and road show; these activities are critical to the success of the quotation because they prepare the financial market for the operation.
10. Shares price fixing and beginning of the negotiations.

Shares price definition is critical because the price assigned to the company's shares depends mainly on the financial needs of the company, the costs for collection, and the timing of the operation. In reality, the definition of the pricing is the result of the combination of five different forces. The first one is the desire of the old shareholders of the target company to maximize their economic return from the IPO. The second force is the need of the target company to get the highest possible price, even if it has a more long-term view compared with the old shareholders. The arrangement syndicate expects a price lower than the old shareholders and the company's price, because it wants to minimize the risks of the arrangement. The two forces that push for the reduction of the shares price are the sponsor market maker and all the investors; the first one is moved by the desire to minimize the speculation activities on the company's shares price, while investors want to pay the lowest possible price.

The interaction of these five forces is critical in how the shares are arranged. Two types of arrangements can be identified:

1. Initial selling public offer—This quotation happens through the selling offer launched by the old shareholders. This solution is not appreciated by the market because, even if it maximizes the economic return for the old shareholders, it does not create new financial resources for the company. It is simply a handing over of the property.
2. Initial subscription public offer—The sold stakes to the investors are issued ex novo through an increase of the company's risk capital. This solution is preferred by the investors because it allows the company to collect new financial resources that can be used to ensure the growth plan of the firm. This is not the best solution for the shareholders, because they do not receive the economic return from the IPO.

Usually, the interactions of the previously defined five forces lead to a mixed solution between the initial selling public offer and the initial subscription public offer.

During the execution phase of the quotation, the syndicate of financial inter-mediaries assumes a critical role in the process in terms of costs that the target company has to face and the final success of the operation. Depending on the specific roles attributed to the arrangement syndicate, the costs are related to the management fees, paid to the syndicate leader (global coordina-tor) to remunerate his advisory and organization activity, the selling fees, rec-ognition of the intermediaries that sell the shares to the single investors, and the underwriting fees that occur on the funds supplied in advance and the back clauses.

The characteristics and the roles of the arrangement syndicate depend on the type of risk it takes. There are four types of arrangement syndicates:

1. Selling group—Distributes shares to the public investors. Residual shares not sold are returned to the company. Receives selling and management fees.
2. Purchase group—Financial intermediaries involved in purchasing the shares quoted. Sells directly to the investors. The economic return for these intermediaries consists of the difference realized between the purchase price and the selling price of the shares.
3. Underwriting group—Purchases the shares not arranged to public investors. They require underwriting fees.
4. Arrangement and guarantee syndicate—Financial intermediaries involved in distributing shares to investors. They are obliged to purchase the unsold shares. Fees paid to this group include management, underwriting, and selling fees.

The job of financial intermediaries does not end with the quotation. There are three main post-IPO jobs they perform:

- Stabilization—Moral, or contractual, commitment of the global coordinator to support the price of the listed company.
- Investor relation activity—Managing the periodical information flow to the market, quarterly or monthly.
- Market maker or specialist.

# 4 PART

# Company Valuation, New Solutions, and Industry Trends

# CHAPTER 17

# Company Valuation in Private and Venture Capital

## 17.1 COMPANY VALUATION

As explained in the previous part of the book, the managerial process can be divided into four different phases. One of these is the investing phase, which includes, *inter alia*, choosing the target company to finance and closing the deal with the selected target company. During this phase, company valuation is critical since it is fundamental to the investor future economic return.

The types of financing available to private equity investors are completely different; for example, an entry strategy with a majority participation and a position of control (typical in a buyout) and minority participation that supports the quotation of a firm for a short time.

It is possible to identify standard phases common to all investments, which are necessary to fulfill the valuation process:

- Identification of the target company—This is executed differently in the United States and in the United Kingdom, with respect to the European market. In the United States and United Kingdom, investment opportunities offered to private equity are already defined and structured by the entrepreneur. In Europe, researching potential target companies is up to the institutional investor and done by direct marketing operations; therefore, European investors need a developed and efficient network or relationship to find potential and interesting deals (deal flow).
- Valuation of the entrepreneur profile and/or the management team—This phase follows the identification of the target company and consists in a complete analysis of the entrepreneur and/or the management team's profile, especially when they invest risk capital together with the private equity operator. It is important to check the reliability, knowledge, expertise, and reputation between the management team and the validity or coherence of the business idea.
- Deep valuation of the target company and the operation structure—This phase is critical because it focuses on researching the equilibrium between

**241**

Private Equity and Venture Capital in Europe. https://doi.org/10.1016/B978-0-12-812254-9.00017-6

the entrepreneur's needs, the investor's goals, and the real necessity of the target company. Analysis is carried over to verify the potential and the real market of the company, its technology potential, possible increase of company value, and the likelihood of an exiting strategy. If the results are satisfactory then the investor proceeds with the deal structuring and defining the company's value.

- Negotiation and setting of price—This is the direct outcome of the previous phases. It is focused on price setting as well as timing and payment execution.
- Monitoring and exiting—After closing the deal the investor monitors the venture-backed company's performance to identify any problems inside the target company. On exit the venture capitalist realizes the economic return from the deal.

## 17.2   FIVE PHASES OF COMPANY VALUATION

Company valuation calculates the fair value of the target company as well as supports value creation among investors so that they can reach their economic goals in terms of expected IRR. The process of company valuation is realized through these phases:

- Business plan analysis
- Financial needs assessment
- Enterprise value analysis
- Price setting
- Exiting

It is important to accomplish the previously listed valuation steps in the right sequence. Before this can be completed, it is necessary to know and use specific techniques and methods to approach the items in the correct order. First, the investor must have focused goals that support the whole valuation process to execute appropriate investing or exiting decisions. However, the process has to be coordinated within the constraints of the investment vehicle such as global portfolio IRR, residual maturity, capital requirements, and expected IRR on the specific investment and the entire portfolio.

Before analyzing each valuation phase, it is necessary to clarify critical aspects and key issues. This chapter identifies and discusses the content of each phase, the equity investor's role, and the goals and content of each stage.

### 17.2.1   Business Plan Analysis

To start the valuation process the business plan must be created and analyzed. This document explains and illustrates the strategic intention of the management team, competitive strategies, and concrete actions necessary to realize company objectives, key value drivers, and financial outcomes. It shows the management team's vision and allows investors to evaluate and understand the potential returns of the business. The business plan has a large target audience which includes not only the investors and the management team, but also other financial supporters such as banks or leasing companies and members of the Board of Directors.

A typical business plan that supports risky capital investment contains the status of past strategies (history of the firm) in terms of performance and analysis of strengths or weaknesses and opportunities or threats. Based on the analysis, the business plan describes the future of the company regarding the development of strategic goals, an action plan needed to realize the value proposition, assumptions about financial planning, and financial forecasts (see Fig. 17.1).

A business plan contains these elements.

- Global view on the company—Information about the past, actual, and future organizational structure, relevant industries including the analysis of the competitive factors, and all the critical elements for an in-depth knowledge of the company such as legal entity structure, revenues, mission, and dimension.
- Global view and explanation of the entrepreneurs and shareholders—This demonstrates the importance of the human factor in a business deal. A critical element is the clear disclosure of who controls the capital.
- Market competitive analysis—Includes the macroeconomics profile (definition of its global dimension). The business plan uses the Porter Model[1] to analyze the market at a lower level.
- Technological characteristics of the product and/or services of the firms—This section describes the product and/or the service of the company in the easiest possible way emphasizing the innovative content of the offer.
- Operation plans and financial data—It contains detailed information regarding the operative actions executed in terms of production and marketing plans and costs. This part of the business plan shows a series of

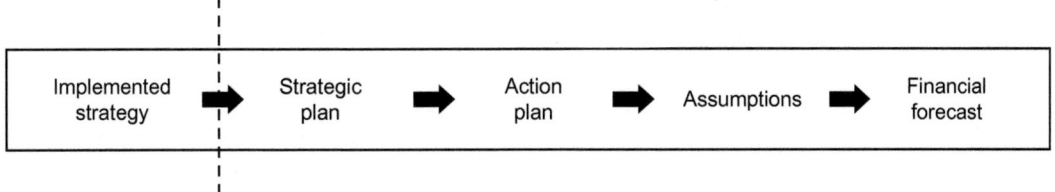

**FIG. 17.1** Business plan structure.

---

[1]See Part 2 of the book.

simulations about how the product and/or service would be realized considering different levels of bulk production.

- Financial structure—Based on the previous analysis and defined needs, this phase covers two main areas: financial requirements and the desired debt/equity ratio. Financial requirements, satisfied by equity and debt, include different types of investments such as working capital investments, capital expenditures, immaterial expenditures, merger and acquisitions investments, and repayment of debts incurred in the past. Equity contribution does not create any charged interest guaranteeing the company in case of default and the investor is directly interested in the performance of the firm. This structure limits the entrepreneur's decision power as well as the profit he must split with the new shareholders. Raising debt avoids the entrance of new shareholders, but interest has to be paid regardless of positive economic results. This form of financing requires collateral issuing, which is not well perceived by the entrepreneurs. The key aspect of debt is the tax benefit created by a significant contribution to the global value generated by the business idea.

The business plan is usually prepared by the company with the help of a consultant and it is the proposal sent to investors. It is common for the private equity investor to take part in the business planning process, even if it is risky and time consuming. In the cases in which this happens, it may be a consequence of an incubation strategy. Private equity investor assistance comes from the network of relationships in which the investor is involved.

Different stages of investment, from the seed to vulture financing, have specific capital requirements and assumed levels of risk. This is reflected in the business plan.

Seed financing—There are three key issues: assessment of the potential entrepreneur's curriculum vitae, creative understanding of the feasibility of the business idea, and identification of the product's potential market.
Start-up financing—It is necessary to verify both the market potential of the business idea, in terms of potential demand trend, and expected level of price and plan of investments is necessary.
Early growth and expansion financing—The business plan concentrates on the expansion trend of the demand and the sustainability of the required investment must be checked.
Replacement financing—Key issues of the business plan include the feasibility of the acquisition and restructuring of the deal.
Vulture financing—Focuses on verifying the new potential market with an accurate analysis of costs and the investment plan.

The validity of the business plan, decided by the private equity investor, depends on the financial sustainability of the industrial project. Sustainability is established based on the quality and quantity of the financial resources, coherence between the realized strategies, strategic intention, real conditions of the firm and its economic and financial hypothesis, and its reliability. The last condition is satisfied when the industrial plan is drawn based on a realistic and reasonable hypothesis and expected and acceptable results. When the business plan includes a comparison with the past performance, it also includes further analysis related to forecasting possible scenarios and statements consistent with the competitive dynamics of the relevant industry.

From the business plan the investor should trust the management about the business, the way capital will be used, the motivation of the management team, and the risk sharing.

## 17.2.2  Financial Needs Assessment

If the analysis of the business plan is favorable, the investor moves to the second step of the company valuation process: financial needs assessment. This step calculates the amount of money required to sustain company growth.

The financial assessment adds forecasting statements to the business plan, and its goal is to define external financial requirements and verify their use by the company.

This step further identifies the size of the potential demand for investment, percentage of the potential equity investment, and potential new debt to be raised in a medium-term run. The financial needs assessment is typically executed in house by the private equity investor, even if interaction with the company is necessary to discuss and/or to revise the business plan.

For an accurate financial assessment it is necessary to answer a series of key questions to help decide whether or not it is convenient to launch an investment. First, the capital investor must understand the size of the financial need and then have a clear idea of how much can be financed from the investor, the correct mix of debt and equity, and, at the end, if it is possible and/or necessary to recruit a new equity and/or debt investor.

It is impossible to predict a financial solution. It depends on the deal's level of risk, risk profile of the project, and trust in the entrepreneur's skills.

During the financial needs assessment these are key issues to be addressed:

- Seed financing—Financial requirement consists of sustaining the investment to study, develop, and test the business idea or the project. It is very hard to identify the correct mix of debt and equity. The resources needed are not usually considerable, but it is necessary to have a large amount of support for a high-tech initiative.

- Start-up financing—Financial needs evaluation is the key point of the deal. It is critical to verify how much of the deal is financed through equity capital. The resources required are designed to define and develop an already launched project. The outcome of start-up financing depends on the quality of the previous investment (seed financing). The investment requirement is not urgent because it is needed for the enhancement of existing corporate and business competences.
- Early growth financing—Represents the moment of launch for the initiative and the consolidation of previous research. This stage needs considerable financial support, because funds are necessary to hire suitable human resources and develop know-how. The level of risk is quite high, but if the business initiative is successful, remuneration is considerable.
- Expansion financing—Financial resources support corporate growth. The business idea and the combination of product and market have already been tested; consequently, financial resources support commercial and marketing activities. Funds will probably be absorbed by the working capital because warehouse goods increase and payment terms are postponed to satisfy customer demand.
- Replacement—Controlling how finances are used during the development of corporate finance deals is a key issue. Economic resources are provided to relaunch the company through restructuring and development operations. Since the relaunch is a new activity for the firm, an enormous amount of money and specific competences are necessary.
- Vulture financing—Similar to start-up financing, the financial needs evaluation is key in the decision to turnaround a business. This type of financing includes the relaunch and renewal of a mature company, and the available resources are used to maintain market position and sustain the development process, which can be realized with either existing or nonexisting technology (diversification strategy).

### 17.2.3    Enterprise Value Analysis

During the screening phase, the investor decides if the financial need, as defined and valuated, is sustainable. In doing so, he moves to the third step of this process—analysis of the company's value. This phase is based on the forecasting statements included in the business plan. The goal is to understand and quantify the real value of the company and the business plan to define the value of the investment.

The enterprise value analysis identifies the amount of money to be spent, the percentage of shares to be held by the investor, and the financial impact that these two have on the company. The private equity investor executes the enterprise value analysis in-house after hearing his advisors and the technical committee. The valuation of a private company, especially when it is in the early stages of the life cycle, is difficult and subjective because early-stage companies usually forecast a period of negative cash flow with uncertain future economic returns.

Enterprise value analysis finds a "right value" and an "adjusted value" of a company after comparing general trends in valuation within companies operating in the same business. Usually, the output of the analysis consists of values attributed to the equity of the company. The analysis further focuses on different valuations for different stages of investment.

- Seed financing—Equity valuation is impossible and can only be developed if the business plan is built on a realistic business idea.
- Start-up financing—Valuation is based on forecasting, but there is a high risk of uncertainty regarding the future sales trends and the terminal value. Comparison with similar deals is useful here.
- Early growth and expansion financing—Valuation analysis faces the same issues as start-up financing. At this point comparison with similar deals can be very useful. Evaluation is usually easier here than during start-up because the company is considered successful and there are similar firms with which to compare.
- Replacement financing—Equity valuation is connected to the profile of the deal and related to the replacement structure. Typical deals are LBOs or buy ins and family and management deals where the counterparties involved are critical and affect the definition of the company value (inheritance).
- Vulture financing—Typical target companies are mature and equity valuation is based on forecasting, but there is a high risk of uncertainty regarding sales trends. The terminal value of the deal and the amount and structure of costs carried are hardly quantifiable. It is also difficult to support the equity valuation through comparison with similar companies.

In the following chapters, the methods mostly used for company valuation will be analyzed more deeply. Next are highlights of the most widespread methods.

1. Comparables—This valuation method provides a quick and easy way to obtain a rough valuation for a company. This method is used when a company with similar values, operating in a similar industry, exists. Elements compared include risk, growth rate, capital structure, and the size and timing of cash flow. This method is quick, simple to understand, based on the market, and common in the industry. There are many potential problems when this method is used for private companies, such as the lack of public information on private companies and problems in

finding comparable firms. When it is used to compare public companies, it is necessary to adjust the outcomes due to the private company's lack of liquidity. Their shares are typically less marketable than public firms, so a discount for the lack of liquidity is applied (lack of marketability discount falls between 25% and 30%).

2. Net present value (NPV)—This is by far the most common method for cash flow valuation. NPV of a company is obtained by computing the expected value of one or more future cash flows discounting them at a rate reflecting the cost of capital. This method considers the potential tax benefit created by leverage. A problem with this method is the forecasting of the "last" cash flow, called Terminal Value. The terminal value is greatly affected by the interest rate used, so it is critical to identify the correct interest rate when discounting future cash flow. One solution is to use the weighted average cost of capital, which is quite easy to calculate based on the current debt equity ratio at the time. In reality, this ratio is always subject to change, especially in LBO operations.

3. Adjusted present value—A variant of the NPV approach used when a company's level of indebtedness is changing or it has past operation losses that can be used to offset tax obligations. This method attempts to solve the problems faced by the NPV by calculating cash flow without debt and discounting by using an unlevered (defined as the equity capital invested in the company) interest rate. It further requires the quantification of interest and the relevant tax benefits discounted at the pretax rate of return on debt. This method is appropriately used when the capital structure (highly leveraged transactions such as LBOs) and the tax rate are changing. It is more complicated than the NPV and presents difficulties when estimating future cash flow and selecting the correct discount rate.

4. Venture capital—It values the company at the end of a defined period of time using one of the methods previously discussed. Then it discounts this terminal value by a target rate of return that is the yield assumed by venture capitalists as remuneration for the risk and efforts of this specific investment. This TRR is usually between 40% and 70% and is the biggest source of criticism of this method. Venture capitalists use such a high level of discount because of the lack of liquidity of private firms, the provision of strategic advisors to the target company, and because the entrepreneur's forecasting, included in the business plan, is usually too optimistic.

5. Asset option—The methods previously explained are not usable when managers or investors are capable of making flexible decisions. This flexibility affects the value of the company and these changes are not accurately computed in the discounted cash flow methods. According to

the venture capitalist, the value of a company depends on the value assumed by independent predictor variables. The asset option method is not well known and the real-world opportunity for simple options and the exact pricing of these options is difficult to define.

## 17.2.4    Price Setting

Finance theory on company valuation states that value and price are two different measures, not always coincident and sometimes clashing, that depend on various factors. The theoretical concept of company value, which differs from market value, is connected with the idea of economic capital: the value of a company in normal market conditions compatible with company capital without the considerations of the parties, their contractual power, their specific interests, and potential negations. As per this definition, the economic capital, as a measure of the company value, is independent of the eventual deal between the parties, the possibility that a new buyer will interfere, the contingent demand and supply situation, and the status of the M&A market. Calculating the economic capital is necessary to have an objective value creation realized by management defined as fair value.

It is easy to understand that the market value of a firm is affected by the same external pressures as company value. These pressures are influenced by financial market efficiency and demand and supply. The price of a public company depends on the participation negotiated; should the participation entail a minority presence in the capital subscribed or a majority control of the firm. Market and company values are also measured by cash flow forecasting and the determination of risk and other stock variables computed through specific formulas, whereas the price is defined by market dynamics.

For private equity deals, the valuation of a firm is never theoretical; it is always linked to a real and concrete price so the final value defined is the result of the counterparty's negotiations. The estimate of the target company's value is usually executed using simple and proven methods and techniques such as the comparables approach to avoid complicated financial models.

Price setting while negotiating equity value with the entrepreneur moves from the value of the company to the price (value) of the deal. During this phase the entrepreneur has specific personal goals, over self-estimation, and personal and moral involvement while the investor reduces the amount of money requested by the single deal and aligns the capital requirement and IRR targets. It is impossible to identify any standard rules within this negotiation, because it is a complex struggle to agree on a final price and, consequently, many deals fall apart over price disagreement.

Price setting is typically developed by the management team with the support of the directors and advisors during the negotiation phase. The negotiation for pricing setting is more relevant than valuation with mature companies and corporate governance based deals. The way negotiations are conducted is influenced by both technical and structural variables from the operations side and psychological and cultural values related to the profile and knowledge of the counterparts and their advisors. It is critical to select appropriately skilled advisors and intermediaries during negotiation.

The final step in this phase is closing the deal. Investor need to understand how price setting is used during specific stages of the investment.

- Seed financing—Insignificant because it does not affect this phase.
- Start-up financing—Company valuation is more relevant than price setting because money is channeled to the development of the investment.
- Early growth and expansion financing—Investors balance company valuation with price setting, but firm valuation is more relevant.
- Replacement financing—The main point is the price setting.
- Vulture financing—Price setting is insignificant.

## 17.2.5   Exiting

During this phase, enterprise value and price are calculated based on the investor's exit. The same enterprise value analysis and price setting activities are carried out, but the investor has to calculate the "right value" of the firm and negotiate with the potential buyer of the stake.

Price setting is critical for the investor to get the effective IRR of the investment and to sustain global portfolio IRR. For that reason, price setting becomes more relevant than enterprise value analysis when choosing an exit strategy.

# CHAPTER 18

# Techniques of Equity Value Definition

## 18.1 ENTERPRISE VALUE ANALYSIS

Company valuation is a critical phase of investment policies put in place by private equity investors. It is important because the task of valuing the company creates an occasion for both the entrepreneur and the investor to bargain over the amount of money required by the entrepreneur and the number of shares that the former can give to the latter. After agreeing about the amount of the investment and to which portion of the share capital this corresponds, the deal will be closed eventually.

The importance of the enterprise value analysis is even more important when the object of valuation is a high-risk, high-tech company with little (if none) historical data and little economic and financial performance. In this situation, most of the financial need must be covered by equity capital supplied by investment companies. This makes the correct pricing of an equity stake one of the most important keys to success in the private equity industry.

Company valuation is based on the forecasted financial statement and balance sheet. An inaccurate business plan can lead to an incorrect equity value. To calculate the value of equity, it is necessary to use dedicated techniques to identify the real and underlying value of a firm.

Theoretically, the following techniques can be used to calculate the equity value of a potential venture-backed company:

1. Comparables
2. Net present value
3. Adjusted present value
4. Venture capital method

Private Equity and Venture Capital in Europe. https://doi.org/10.1016/B978-0-12-812254-9.00018-8

These techniques originate from the theory of corporate finance and each of them provides a different perspective and rationale for the equity value:

- Comparables—Equity value is calculated by comparing similar companies in terms of industry, dimension, and country during valuation.
- Net present value (NPV)—Equity value is calculated as the present value of future cash flows of the company and a defined period of time is used to calculate the terminal value.
- Adjusted present value (APV)—As for the case in which the NPV method is used, cash flows are discounted over time. The difference stands in the fact that with the APV, the financial structure of the firm is also taken into consideration.
- Venture capital method (VCM)—Equity value is calculated as the present value of the terminal value of the firm taking into account the expected return of the investment and a particular expected holding period.

These four theoretical approaches have each pros and cons, but in the real world and in practice it is widely recognized that comparables are surely a fundamental step in producing inputs that are necessary for the NPV and the VCM, as well as when comparing the outputs of the other approaches.

The most widely used approach is NPV or discounted cash flow (DCF), while the VCM is used primarily when price setting is more important than the enterprise value analysis per se.

## 18.2  CHOOSING A VALUATION METHOD

Before company valuation begins, an appropriate method of valuation has to be chosen. Factors that affect this choice include

1. Country where the company is based
2. Industry
3. Quality of data needed for the valuation
4. Status of the company—public or private

### 18.2.1  Country Where the Company Is Based

When a company has to be appraised, the business practices of the country in which the company plays must be taken into consideration. If an investor estimates the value of a company using a method that is unknown in the relevant country or unaccepted by the counterpart and the advisors, the probability of the deal closing is strongly reduced. The differences in valuation methods among countries, especially between Continental Europe, the United

Kingdom, and the United States, are less important today, but they still exist and as such shall be taken into account.

In Continental Europe, academics, and professionals prefer a valuation based on data retrieved from the balance sheets and income statements of a company. Income-based methods, balance-sheet-based methods, or a mix of the two are used in Italy, Germany, and France. More rarely used are the cash-flow-based method and the market-based (or multiple) method. The reason underlying a rare choice in these two methods is their lack of objectivity in the final estimation of the value. In addition to that, these methods are not as widespread as they are in the Anglo-Saxon world due to the smaller size and impact of stock exchanges and capital markets in Continental European countries that hence is reflected in the method chosen to assess the value of a company.

In the United Kingdom and in the United States, the chosen method is based on the idea that the value of a firm is in its ability to generate positive free cash flows to debt and equity holders. If a company is going public, then the value should be close to the price that the markets are ready to pay for similar companies.

## 18.2.2  Company Industry

Different industries have different value drivers that reveal where the value of a firm is created. In industries where tangible capital (fixed assets and working capital) is a large part of the capital invested—such as the manufacturing of metals, banking and insurance, chemistry, or the real estate business—the value of this capital should be included in the final valuation. Other industries such as fashion, consulting, biotechnology, or Internet-related firms do not report a large amount of tangible capital because their competitive strength is connected to intangible assets that are not included in the balance sheet. Brand equity, R&D, or marketing expenses are not counted as assets because it is not allowed in many countries, but these expenditures positively impact the future performance of a company. In these types of industries only cash flow-based or income-based methods can be used to estimate correctly the company's value.

## 18.2.3  Data Availability and Reliability

The choice of the valuation method is strongly affected by the availability and reliability of data on the firm, its markets, the future evolution of its sectors, and its competitors. These data should be representative of the past, present, and future value of all relevant variables regarding the firm's performance. If the conditions of availability and reliability are not satisfied, the valuation must be performed with cash flow and income-based methods making it strongly subjective and with the risk that the valuation results inaccurate.

The availability of reliable data on the company and its competitors, on the contrary, allows the valuation to be executed with forward-looking methods.

### 18.2.4   Public or Private Status of a Company

The fourth element used to choose the correct valuation method for a company is its availability of market prices and stocks. If a firm is listed on a public regulated stock market, the valuation can be based, as a control method for other estimates, on the market prices over an extended period of time. The use of market prices allows the analyst to calculate multiples derived from stock quotes of comparable firms. This approach can be used to value companies without historical information or with little or no available data. The main problem with this method is finding companies that are very similar to the one that is being valued. It can be then gathered that the valuation of a private company by the private equity investor can sometimes become very difficult due to the absence of industry or comparable references. This is particularly true in the case of start-ups offering a product or a service with a very high technological content. In such case, if the innovation and the level of technology offered is disruptive, the difficulty is even higher, not only are past data missing but also data on comparable companies cannot be found.

## 18.3   BASIC CONCEPTS OF COMPANY VALUATION

Before analyzing the three main techniques used to calculate equity value, it is necessary to define the basic financial and economic elements of a company:

- balance sheet,
- profit and loss statement (or income statement),
- cash flow statement,
- cost of capital.

### 18.3.1   The Balance Sheet

The first element is the balance sheet as seen in Fig. 18.1.

The left side of the balance sheet includes all of the company assets (what the company owns) and they can be divided into:

1. Current assets—Account receivables, inventory, and liquid assets.[1]
2. Fixed assets—Material investment realized during the life of the company used to implement operations. The following is included in this category: plants, equipment, land, and buildings.

---

[1]Sometimes, and according to the criterion under which a balance sheet is reclassified, liquid assets (such as cash and cash equivalents) are deducted from the financial debt reported on its left side.

**FIG. 18.1** Balance sheet.

3. Financial investments—Participation in equity of other companies and marketable security; an item can be classified as a financial investment if he rationale behind its acquisition of that stake is nonspeculative.
4. Intangible assets—Patents, trademarks, and goodwill.

On the right side are the company's liabilities (what a company owes) and they can be divided into:

1. Current liabilities—Accounts payable due to all the products and services provided by the suppliers (trade debts).
2. Debt—All financial debts raised by the company, both long-term debt (bonds and loans) and short-term liabilities.
3. Other liabilities—Allowances for retirement plans and deferred taxes.
4. Equity—The company reports the initial share capital subscribed by the shareholders, plus or minus all the increases and decreases related to the yearly profits and losses, and plus or minus every special operation realized on the stakes; for example, an increase in the equity capital value.

## 18.3.2 Profit and Loss Statement (or Income Statement)

Fig. 18.2 illustrates the profit and loss statement. The profit and loss represents how the company has performed netting the incomes realized with the costs borne to generate such incomes, starting from the revenues realized by the core activity of the company. All the costs created by the operations including research and development expenditures are first deducted. This "operating" difference gives rise to a gross operating margin, called "earnings before interest, tax, depreciations, and amortizations" (EBITDA). As anticipated above, this value is the gross margin realized by the company performing its core business. After the EBITDA, after deducting the company depreciation and amortization (D&A),[2] lies the operating profit (earnings

---

[2]D&A are a way in which the value of the assets reported on the left side of the balance sheet is diminished over time. It represents the decrease in value due to the fact that the asset is used over a period of time.

```
+ Sales and other operating revenues
- Operating costs (including R&D)
= EBITDA
- Depreciation & Amortization
= EBIT
+ Other income
- Interest expenses
= EBT
- Income taxes
= NET INCOME OR LOSS
```

**FIG. 18.2** Profit and loss statement.

before interest and taxes; EBIT). Then, netting the EBIT by the revenues not realized through ordinary operations (for instance, financial revenues) and by interests expenses paid, the earnings before taxes (EBT) can be found. In the end, netting the EBT with the taxes referred to that specific fiscal year for which the income statement is being drawn there is the net profit or loss of the company.

### 18.3.3    The Cash Flow Statement

Cash flow statements outline whether the business has created or absorbed cash flow. In case the company has generated positive cash flow, the cash flow statement is a useful tool to understand how this cash flow has been generated.

The starting point for the cash flow statement is the EBIT computed in the profit and loss statement. To calculate the cash flow, the EBIT is reduced by the taxes paid, decreased by the net working capital (WC), and capital expenditure (CAPEX). These last two items are calculated comparing the value of the WC and the CAPEX with the current and previous period. This value has a negative impact in that if it is greater than zero then the company has absorbed cash, for example, increasing the stock of inventory between the two comparison periods. If the company has reduced the inventory, it means the cash flow has increased, so the value of inventory reducing has a positive effect on the company's cash flow. The final cash flow includes the D&A realized during a specific period of time; it does not represent real cash movement as it is a non-monetary cost so it has to be added back to the EBIT. This method of calculating the cash flow (free cash flow unlevered) does not contain information about the capital structure. Instead it represents the cash flow available for the financers and shareholders calculated without considering raising new debt and the repayment of the old debt.

If obtaining a cash flow that includes the impact of the debt and the changes realized on the debt equity ratio is the goal, include the increase and decrease of the debt. To be more accurate, add all of the new debt raised to the free cash flow unlevered. This will show that the company has new cash to spend, and the repayments of old debt are deducted because they absorb liquidity. This value is called free cash flow levered (see Fig. 18.3).

## 18.3.4 The Cost of Capital

There are three categories of cost of capital:

- cost of debt capital,
- cost of equity capital,
- weighted average cost of capital (WACC).

The use of these three measures has to be perfectly consistent with the free cash flow discounted and the perspective of the valuation. The cost of equity capital has to be used to discount cash flow for the shareholders (levered cash flow), whereas the WACC has to discount the cash flow for the whole company (unlevered cash flow) because it contains information on the whole capital structure.

These three costs of capital are also calculated differently. The cost of debt capital is easily computed, because it is based on information reported on the balance sheet:

$$i_d^* = i_d(1 - t)$$

**EBIT**

- Income taxes

+ Depreciation & Amortization

- Increase in Net Working Capital

- CAPEX

= **FREE CASH FLOW UNLEVERED**

+ New Debt

- Debt Repayments

= **FREE CASH FLOW LEVERED**

**FIG. 18.3** Free cash flow statement.

where

- $i_d$ is the average weighted cost of debt capital obtained from the balance sheet and analytically computed by dividing the net interest expenses by financial debt;
- $t$ is the corporate tax ratio;
- $i_d^*$ is the cost of debt capital netted by the benefit of debt leverage.

The computation of the cost of equity capital is not as immediate as one of the cost of debt capital, as it is not reported on the balance sheet. The Capital Asset Pricing Model (CAPM)[3] suggests the following formula to compute the cost of equity capital for a specific equity investment:

$$i_e = r_f + \beta(r_m - r_f)$$

where

- $r_f$ is the risk-free rate of return (matched in terms of maturity with the investment);
- $r_m$ is the rate of return investors expect from the market (measured by historical series);
- $(r_m - r_f)$ is the so-called "market risk premium" and is the difference between the market rate of return and the risk-free rate of return;
- $\beta$ is the degree of correlation between the investment and the market;
- $i_e$ is the cost of the equity capital.

$\beta$ measures the volatility of an investment with respect to the whole market. As the total market is assumed to have a $\beta$ equal to 1, a stock whose return varies less than the ones of the market have a beta lower than 1. On the contrary, a stock whose return varies more than the returns of the market has a beta larger than 1.

To estimate the $\beta$ coefficient of a specific stock, the regression of the returns of the stock against returns on a market index is used. If the stock does not have a $\beta$ coefficient, and such is the case when a company is not listed, it is necessary to use the $\beta$ of the comparables. This requires identifying the $\beta$ of a comparable, then unlever (exclude the effect of capital structure) the $\beta$ with comparable data, and at the end re-lever (insert the capital structure of the company) the $\beta$ with the company's debt and equity structure.

The method to unlever the $\beta$ is represented by the following formula:

$$\beta_u = \beta / [1 + (1 - t) \times (D/E)]$$

---

[3]The CAPM is a model of financial market equilibrium, proposed by William Sharpe in 1964, that establishes a relationship between the return of a security and its risk level, measured by only one risk factor, $\beta$.

where $D$ and $E$ are the market value of debt and equity of the chosen comparable firm.

The formula used to re-lever the $\beta$ is

$$\beta = \beta_u \times [1 + (1-t) \times (D/E)]$$

The third measure of the cost of capital is the WACC. It is calculated when both the equity and debt cost of capital are available. It represents an effective measure of the cost of all the liabilities towards shareholder and financial institutions of the company that are being weighted for the company capital structure (i.e., using the debt-to-equity ratio). The formula is

$$i_{\text{WACC}} = \left[i_d^* \times (D/D+E)\right] + \left[i_e \times (E/D+E)\right]$$

## 18.4 THE FUNDAMENTAL OF COMPARABLES

Comparables are ratios calculated on performances realized by firms that are similar to those of the company being evaluated. Using comparables it is possible to calculate or estimate the value of a company. Comparables are widely used, especially in private equity business, because these ratios are a good combination of risk, plans, accounts, and valuations of similar companies. At the same time, comparables use common metrics and methods used worldwide to verify the effectiveness of other valuation methods. For this reason, comparables are mostly used to fine-tune the valuation process, create inputs for valuation, and compare across the market valuation.

To completely understand this approach, it must be emphasized that comparables become less important when companies are evaluated in the seeding and start-up phases; firms are usually unprofitable and experiencing rapid growth at this time.

The most common comparables include

- EV/EBITDA—The ratio between the enterprise value (EV) and the EBITDA illustrates the capability of the firm to produce value through gross margin. EBITDA is a good measure of the company's ability to create cash from its operational activities and avoid distortions from accounting policies that affect the net income. It is by far the most common ratio.
- EV/EBIT—The ratio expresses the ability of the firm to produce value from operating profit. It avoids distortion connected with debt structure and tax strategy, and it can represent both the actual value at the moment of valuation and the prospective value of the firm. With this ratio, the EBIT value is a prospective figure that can be discounted to present the

corresponding years considered in the estimation of future margins. The EBIT is useful to value a company because it only includes ordinary depreciations such as material depreciations, leasing fees, and immaterial amortizations including trademarks, patents, and computer software. Immaterial amortizations do not include the one referring to goodwill and transaction costs that may have arisen during buyouts and acquisition operations.

- EV/S—"How many times do I have to multiply the sales to buy the company?" is a question answered by the ratio of enterprise value/sales, which is based on the ability of the firm to produce sales. Sales are the easiest measure to determine, but the value must be computed considering only the revenues realized through the sale of goods and services offered by the firm excluding discounts and returned products.
- P/E—Price/earnings is a ratio used by listed companies to investigate the relationship between the current price of the stock and the ability to produce earnings. Since earnings (profit after tax) reflect the capital structure of the company, they are calculated after interest expenses and taxes, which can turn out to be misleading. It would be better to use EBIT to further investigate this relationship.
- P/BV—Price/book value of equity can be obtained for listed companies by identifying the relationship between the current price of the stock and the nominal value of equity.

Enterprise value is the sum of the equity (100%), shareholders value, and financial debt. It represents the total value of the company divided between the shareholders by the equity subscribed, and the debt holders by the debt subscribed.

## 18.5  DISCOUNTED CASH FLOW APPROACH

The discounted cash flow (DCF) approach includes the determination of future cash flow generated by the company for 5 or 10 years. This is then discounted with an appropriate discount rate and summed. The final value of the company is obtained from the actual value of this flow added the net financial position will be deducted if it is negative and added if it is positive.

There are two main steps in the valuation process:

- cash flow determination and
- identification of the discount rate to be used.

Results from DCF are verified with comparables to check if the results can be compared with similar companies.

DCF is used because the value of a company includes the future cash flow even if the different definitions of cash flow must be coordinated with appropriated discount rates. Depending on the type of cash flow (levered or unlevered) and the discount rate used (WACC or cost of equity capital), two different methods of DCF can be identified as: net present value and adjusted present value.

## 18.5.1 Net Present Value Method

The most common DCF approach is the NPV method where enterprise value is calculated using WACC and unlevered cash flow of the firm. WACC includes the effects of the capital structure in this rate and not in the cash flow. The enterprise value is equal to the present value of future unlevered cash flow added to the terminal value; however, it is necessary to reduce the enterprise value for the minorities and the net financial position and to increase the value for nonoperating assets if they exist.

The formula used to calculate equity value for a mature investment is

$$\text{Equity} = \underbrace{\sum_{t=1}^{n} \frac{CF_t}{(1 + WACC)^t} + TV_n}_{\text{Enterprise value}} + (SA - M - NFP) \tag{18.1}$$

where

- TV is the terminal value of the firm at time $n$,
- SA are surplus (not operating) assets,
- $M$ are minorities,
- NFP is net financial position, and
- SA, $M$, and NFP refer (if they exist) to the time of valuation.

The determination of the terminal value, which is an important element used to define enterprise value, is a critical item calculated by the following formula:

$$TV_n = \frac{\dfrac{CF_n \times (1+g)}{(WACC-g)}}{(1+WACC)^n} \tag{18.2}$$

where $g$ is the perpetual growth rate of the cash flow.

## 18.5.2 Adjusted Present Value Method

An alternative to the NPV is the APV, which is a DCF approach using the cost of equity capital and the cash flow levered for the shareholders in its calculations.

APV is more appropriate to use than NPV when the firm's capital structure is unsteady or when the company has realized net operating losses that can be used to offset taxable incomes. NPV is inappropriately used when the capital structure is initially highly leveraged but the level of debt is strongly reduced as repayments are made. Typical deals include leveraged buyouts where the target capital structure changes over time.

The APV method overcomes this drawback by dividing the analysis into two levels. First, it considers the cash flow created by the company's assets. Not taking into consideration its capital structure, these flows are discounted with a rate that expresses the capital cost of the company, including the leverage structure. (Refer to the cost of equity capital as explained in Section 18.3.4.) Using the cost of equity capital means that the capital structure effects are included in the cash flow and not in the discount rate. Secondly, APV calculates financial flow created by the capital structure of the company including the tax benefits of the deductible interest paid servicing the debt. These flows are discounted to the pretax rate of return on debt that is lower than the cost equity capital.

The equity value is equal to the present value of future cash flow and terminal value of both the NPV and APV. Analysis must consider the effects on the enterprise value created by the minorities, the net financial position, and the nonoperating assets.

The previously described DCF methods are particularly useful for

- The valuation of a private company where the shareholders are less interested in a stable and continuous flow of dividends. It is more important to know the amount of cash still available after investing in working capital and fixed assets, rather than the amount of dividends in the short run.
- The valuation of a firm performed by a controlling shareholder or a financial partner because the key point is the identification of the amount of cash needed to fund new investments. If free cash flow is negative, shareholders have to decide how to fill the gap. This is often a strategic choice for the future success of the company.
- For the valuation of highly leveraged firms, in the process of changing leverage over time, APV is important because high debt can affect the development strategy of a firm when cash available after the needed investments is not enough to repay the old debt.
- The valuation of turnaround plans. DCF helps identify if the turnaround that depends on generating sufficient unlevered free cash flow to repay the debt is feasible.

## 18.6 VENTURE CAPITAL METHOD

The VCM focuses on the relationship between the expected internal rate of return (IRR), the growth of the firm, and the percentage of shares to buy. Its use depends on the definition of the participation price and the return required for the single investment. This approach is typically used when the price setting is dominant and during seed or start-up deals where there are negative cash flows and earnings with high uncertainty but potentially substantial future rewards.

The VCM asks a very simple question: What amount of shares does the investor buy based on the amount of money needed to invest and the expected IRR? To answer this question valuation of cash flow is considered the final expected value of the investment at divestment. The value is usually defined using comparables.

In a second step, the terminal value is discounted back to the present using a very high rate between 40% and 75%. This high discount rate is a source of criticism of this method, but venture capitalists argue that a large discount rate is appropriate to compensate for the illiquidity of investments in private firms. Venture capitalists provide a very valuable service so the high discount rate compensates them for their efforts. Finally, because the entrepreneur's projections are often too optimistic, a large discount rate is used to mitigate these inflated forecasts. The discounted terminal value and the expected rate of return on the investment are necessary to calculate the desired ownership interest of an investor.

Major critics of the VCM feel that the venture capitalist has to presume there will be no dilution of his participation and that very often venture-backed companies go public or require other types of financing.

### 18.6.1 Key Steps to the Venture Capital Method

The key steps to the VCM are

Step 1: Terminal value calculation
Step 2: Future value of the investment
Step 3: Percentage of shares to subscribe
Step 4: Amount of shares to issue
Step 5: Value of newly issued shares

*Step 1: Terminal value calculation*—The expected holding period and the calculation of the terminal value are addressed. The terminal value is usually calculated with comparables, typically P/E and DCF approaches. *For example*: If the expected holding period is 4 years and the expected net income at $y - 4$ is €6 million, a terminal value calculated through a P/E comparable of 5 would be €30 million.

*Step 2: Future value of the investment*—Calculation of the future value of the investment taking into account the expected holding period and the expected IRR, which is defined from the constraints of the investor. *For example*: If the investment is €2 million, the holding period is 4 years, and the expected IRR is 55%, the future value is €11.54 million.

*Step 3: Percentage of shares to subscribe*—Calculation of the shares the investor has to buy to acquire the expected IRR. The number of shares is found by dividing the future value of the investment by the terminal value of the firm. *For example*: If the future value of the investment is €11.54 million and the terminal value is €30 million, the percentage of shares for the investor is 38.46%.

*Step 4: Amount of shares to issue*—Calculation of the number of new shares that the venture-backed company has to issue to ensure a particular percentage of capital to the investor. This calculation consists of a simple proportion:

$$\% \text{ Shares to be issued} = \frac{\text{New shares}}{\text{New shares} + \text{Old shares}} \tag{18.3}$$

$$\text{Number of shares} = \frac{\text{Existing shares} \times (\% \text{ of shares})}{(1 - \% \text{ shares})} \tag{18.4}$$

*For example*: If the percentage of shares the investor must have is 38.46% and existing shares are 300,000, the number of new shares available to issue is 187,488,

where $187,488 = (300,000 \times 38.46\%)/(1 - 38.46\%)$

*Step 5: Value newly issued shares*—Calculation of the price of newly issued shares for the investor is executed dividing the amount of the investment by the number of new shares. *For example*: If the investment is €2 million and the number of new shares is 187,488, the price per new share is €10.67. The implied premoney valuation is 10.67 so the value of 300,000 shares equals €3201 million and the postmoney value of all 487,488 shares equals €5201 million.

It is important to point out that venture capitalists presume there will be dilution of their participations. To mitigate the effect of this dilution, the retention ratio is used to quantify the decreasing participation realized between the closing and exiting of the deal. In the previous example, if 20%–30% more capital is subscribed, then the participation of 38.46% will become 24.36% of the final equity capital and the retention ratio equal 64%. Therefore, to ensure an

**Table 18.1** Venture Capital Method Steps

|   | Steps | Formula Applied |
|---|-------|-----------------|
| 1 | Terminal value calculation | P/E or DCF methods |
| 2 | Future value of the investment | Investment $(1$ expected IRR$)^{\text{(expected time)}}$ |
| 3 | Percentage of shares | Future value of the investment/terminal value |
| 4 | Number of new shares to issue | (Existing shares $\times$ % shares)/(1% shares) |
| 5 | Value of new issued shares | Investment/number of new shares |

equivalent participation to the first investor, the actual percentage of the participation will be 60%; that is the ratio between the percentage of 38.36% and the retention ratio.

The formula of retention ratio is

$$\text{Retention rate} = \frac{\dfrac{\alpha}{1+\beta}}{1+\gamma} \qquad (18.5)$$

where

$\alpha$ is the percentage of equity capital subscribed by the investor at first issuing;
$\beta$ is the percentage of equity capital subscribed at second moment;
$\gamma$ is the percentage of equity capital subscribed at third moment (see Table 18.1).

# APPENDIX 18.1   COMPANY VALUATION: FINANCING THROUGH PRIVATE EQUITY

## The "Old Winery" Case: A Top Italian Winery

"Old Winery" is an Italian company operating within the winery sector and it is considered one of the top Italian winery worldwide. Old Winery is located in the South of Italy and has a very long tradition to produce white, red, and dessert wines. In 10 years Old Winery has been winning plenty of prizes and awards around the world for top wines. Old Winery is a family owned company and from 10 years about the 75% of sales is done through exports in Europe and in United States.

During 2017, the owners of Old Winery decide to look for a private equity investor to sustain growth and to plan in a long run an acquisition campaign. The motto is: "before growth, growth and growth, afterwards acquisitions."

The forecast for 4 years is based on the following assumptions coming from the business plan under the supervision of the advisors:

Profit and Loss Statement (Euros/000)

| | 2017 | 2018 | 2019 | 2020 |
|---|---|---|---|---|
| Sales | 49,860.00 | 52,756.00 | 56,698.00 | 61,721.00 |
| Operating costs | 39,379.00 | 40,910.00 | 43,782.00 | 45,714.00 |
| *EBITDA* | *10,481.00* | *11,846.00* | *12,916.00* | *16,007.00* |
| Depreciation | −1768.00 | −2305.00 | −2305.00 | −2388.00 |
| *EBIT* | *8713.00* | *9541.00* | *10,611.00* | *13,619.00* |
| Other income | – | – | – | – |
| Interest expenses | −300.00 | −36.00 | −36.00 | −36.00 |
| *EBT* | *8413.00* | *9505.00* | *10,575.00* | *13,583.00* |
| Taxes | −1648.00 | −4074.00 | −4378.00 | −5710.00 |
| *Net income* | *6765.00* | *5431.00* | *6197.00* | *7873.00* |

To calculate the cash flow, the approach chosen is the cash flow for the firm. The main information coming from the balance sheet concerns the following data:

Inputs to Calculate the Cash Flow Statement (Euros/000)

| | 2017 | 2018 | 2019 | 2020 |
|---|---|---|---|---|
| (+) Depreciation | 1768.00 | 2305.00 | 2305.00 | 2388.00 |
| (−) Increase net working capital | −9788.00 | −4500.00 | −500.00 | −500.00 |
| (−) Capex | −3000.00 | −3975.00 | −1322.00 | −500.00 |

In addition, the net financial position is 10 million euros and the liabilities are made of 12.5 million euros of debt and 8 million euros of equity; on the asset side, Old Winery has assets for 12 million, which are old villas and manors nowadays not used for promotions and special events.

The main comparables on the market comes not only from Italy but also from foreigners top wines producers because the wine market is international. The data are the following:

| | Beta | EV/sales | EV/EBITDA | D/E |
|---|---|---|---|---|
| Mondavi (US) | 0.73 | 6.2 | 26 | 9.45 |
| Beringer (US) | 0.94 | 5.5 | 22.9 | 5.25 |
| Southcorp (AUS) | 1.02 | 8.5 | 24.9 | 8.25 |
| Bodegas (SP) | 0.89 | 8.5 | 26.7 | 8.35 |
| Campari (ITA) | 1.23 | 6.7 | 24 | 7.35 |
| Antinori (ITA) | Not listed | 4.9 | 26.9 | 7.85 |

To evaluate the company for the PE investment, one should consider that: the risk free rate is 1.25% (calculated as 5-year Italian Government bonds); the return on market investment is estimated at 7.75%; the expected holding period is 4 years; the $g$ growth rate is estimated at 0.25%; the corporate tax is 35%.

## Solution

Here follows the inputs (Table 18.2) as presented in the above text.

Inputs to compute the cash flow statement (€/000): data presented in the business plan (Table 18.3):

Comparable companies' inputs (Table 18.4):

**Table 18.2** Profit and Loss Statement

|  | 2017 | 2018 | 2019 | 2020 |
|---|---|---|---|---|
| Sales | 49,860 | 52,756 | 56,698 | 61,721 |
| Operating costs | −39,379 | −40,910 | −43,782 | −45,714 |
| EBITDA | 10,481 | 11,846 | 12,916 | 16,007 |
| Depreciation | −1768 | −2305 | −2305 | −2388 |
| EBIT | 8713 | 9541 | 10,611 | 13,619 |
| Other income | − | − | − | − |
| Interest expenses | −300 | −36 | −36 | −36 |
| EBT | 8413 | 9505 | 10,575 | 13,583 |
| Taxes | −1648 | −4074 | −4378 | −5710 |
| Net income | 6765 | 5431 | 6197 | 7873 |

**Table 18.3** Business Plan

|  |  |  | 2017 | 2018 | 2019 | 2020 |
|---|---|---|---|---|---|---|
| (+) | Depreciation |  | 1768 | 2305 | 2305 | 2388 |
| (−) | Increase in the working capital | (−) | 9788 | 4500 | 500 | 500 |
| (−) | Capex | (−) | 3000 | 3975 | 1322 | 500 |

**Table 18.4** Comparables' Data

|  | Beta | EV/Sales | EV/EBITDA | D/E |
|---|---|---|---|---|
| Modavi (US) | 0.73 | 6.2 | 26 | 9.45 |
| Beringer (US) | 0.94 | 5.5 | 22.9 | 5.25 |
| Southcorp (AUS) | 1.02 | 8.5 | 24.9 | 8.25 |
| Bodgas (SP) | 0.89 | 8.5 | 26.7 | 8.35 |
| Campari (ITA) | 1.23 | 6.7 | 24 | 7.35 |
| Antinori (ITA) | Not listed | 4.9 | 26.9 | 7.85 |

**Table 18.5** Cash Flow Statement

|  |  | 2015 | 2016 | 2017 | 2018 |
|---|---|---|---|---|---|
| (+) | EBIT | 8713 | 9541 | 10,611 | 13,619 |
| (−) | Income taxes | −1648 | −4074 | −4378 | −5710 |
| (+) | Depreciation | 1768 | 2305 | 2305 | 2388 |
| (−) | Increase net working capital | −9788 | −4500 | −500 | −500 |
| (−) | Capex | −3000 | −3975 | −1322 | −500 |
|  | *Cash flow* | *−3955* | *−703* | *6716* | *9297* |

The aim of the private equity in this case is to compute the equity value through the formula (18.6):

$$\text{Equity} = \sum_{t=1}^{n} \frac{CF_t}{(1+\text{WACC})^t} + TV_n + (SA - M - NFP) \tag{18.6}$$

### Cash Flow

Starting with the EBIT, the cash flow for the period taken into consideration is being computed (Table 18.5).

### WACC

Following the steps in the WACC calculation, the following must be computed:

- Cost of debt net of tax     $i_d^* = i_d \times (1-t) = 1.56\%$
- $\beta$ unlevered     $\beta_u = \beta/[1 + (1-t) \times (D/E)] = 0.159337$
- $\beta$ relevered     $\beta^* = \beta_u[1 + (1-t) \times (D/E)^*] = 0.32116$
- Cost of equity     $i_e = r_f + \beta(r_m - r_f) = 3.34\%$
- WACC     $i_{WACC} = i_d^* \times (D/D+E) + i_e \times (E/D+E) = 2.25\%$

### Terminal Value

Computation of the terminal value (TV), using the following formula:

$$TV_n = \frac{\frac{CF_n \times (1+g)}{(\text{WACC} - g)}}{(1+\text{WACC})^n} = \frac{\frac{9297 \times (1+0.25\%)}{(2.25\% - 0.25\%)}}{(1+2.25\%)^4} = 425,482.50 \tag{18.7}$$

### Surplus Assets, Minorities, and NFP

$$(SA - M - NFP) = (12,000 - 0 - 10,000) = 2000 \tag{18.8}$$

### Equity Value

$$\text{Equity} = \boxed{\sum_{t=1}^{n} \frac{CF_t}{(1+\text{WACC})^t}} + \boxed{TV_n} + \boxed{(SA - M - NFP)} \tag{18.9}$$

$$\text{Equity} = \boxed{10,245.54} + \boxed{425,482.50} + \boxed{2000} = 437,728.04$$

# CHAPTER 19

# New Trends and Solutions in the Private Equity and Venture Capital Industry

## 19.1 INTRODUCTION

This chapter opens the fourth part of the book. This fourth and last part of the book is dedicated to new trends and solutions that arose over the past years in the private equity industry. As part of the financial industry, the private equity industry is changing at a very fast pace, *inter alia* following the recent global crisis. Despite the huge availability of liquidity in the market today, the players of the private equity industry are today particularly careful in the selection phase in order to concentrate their funds only on investments, which are more likely to produce the expected returns.

This particular attention entailed on a global base the tendency to extend the holding period of the investment. A study produced by Bain & Company at the beginning of 2017, showed that the holding period in buy out operations, accounting for the majority of the investment in the private equity business, was at its minimum level in 2007 and 2008 when it reached 3.6 and 3.3 years, respectively. In contrast, this trend reversed in more recent years, and the holding period reached its maximum level in 2014 when it was 6.1 years, to slightly decline in 2015 and 2016 when it was 5.3 and 5.2 years, respectively. These last levels are lower than the ones of 2014, but still these holding periods are much longer than the ones of the years in which the financial crisis was exploding. Again, this stands for the fact the industry is changing. As the industry is transforming, the techniques and strategies implemented also are transmuting at the same time.

In this chapter, the description of the different trends and solution will figuratively follow the life cycle of the company described in the first chapters. Thus, in the second section, the new tools dedicated to early growth companies will be illustrated, that is, incubators and accelerators. In the same section, a new way of funding young companies, that is, crowdfunding, will also be described.

The third section focusses on one of the ways for private equity investors to deal with the exit phase, that is, the secondary market. The fourth section deals with

Private Equity and Venture Capital in Europe. https://doi.org/10.1016/B978-0-12-812254-9.00019-X

a solution dedicated to mature companies that are ready to buy out another company, that is, the Special Purpose Acquisition Company (SPAC).

Last, the fifth section deals with impact investing, namely the investments made not only with the purpose of achieving economic returns but also with the purpose to have an "impact," namely a positive effect on the society.

## 19.2    INCUBATORS, ACCELERATORS, AND CROWDFUNDING

### 19.2.1    Incubators and Accelerators

In the first stage of the life of a company, there are two independent actors in the development of a newly born idea or newly founded company: incubators and accelerators.

They both have the common goal to boost the growth of start-up companies. Albeit frequently overlapped, despite their common goal and the role that is played toward start-up companies in the same moment of the life cycle, it can be observed that there exist some differences between them.

Accelerators usually provide an injection of money to the start-up company and they are structured in a way such that the start-up founding team can work with mentors of the accelerator. The mentorship program usually occur within a relative short period of time (around 6 months). The mentors can be venture capitalists, business angels, or professors that follow the company over a relative short period to help them deal with the problems that arise on the first years of activity.

The investment is not usually very big, as the real value added in being part of an accelerator is the access to the network of professionals that can help the company cope survive in the first years of activity, as they are the riskiest one. According to Eurostat, in Europe, more than a half companies die in the first 5 years of activity, making it very important for a young company to have mentorship in such a delicate time.

To express, in a direct way, what an incubator is, one should think of it as a laboratory. The incubator is an entity that interacts with entrepreneurs and with start-up companies and that offers to them services and mentorship with the main goal to kick-off the start-up's operations. Like in the case of the accelerator, there can be an equity injection at the beginning of the collaboration and in case there is one, this amount is not consistent and it is not the reason pushing a start-up company to be part of an incubator.

Incubators are usually owned and managed by either governments, public administration entities, or universities. Or, they may arise as the result of a partnership between a public and a private entity. As anticipated, the incubator plays the role of a laboratory in which managers, inventors, and entrepreneurs can work usually sharing the space with other start-ups for a time frame of 2–3 years. The incubator is in fact a physical place, and it is usually the first headquarters of a start-up company. In such site, the founding members can work freely and without worrying that their idea will be stolen.

REMEMBER: Which one of the golden rule of the seed investing is taken into consideration when the start-up operates in an incubator?

The incubators provide to the companies services such as

- assistance in the definition of the business plan,
- access to infrastructures,
- consultancy and mentoring on many different topics, such as general management, financial management, marketing, and implementation of the right informative systems,
- aid in the research and hiring of human capital,
- access to capital, both in a direct or indirect way. The direct access occurs when the injection of cash is made. The indirect access to financial resources occurs as during the period in which the start-up is incubated, the company gets ready under many different aspects that increase the likelihood that an investor finds it interesting.

All the above features are not necessarily acquired with an incubator, but also through other ways; however, the big advantage in doing this in an incubator is the reduced time frame in which this happens.

Broadly speaking, there exist two kinds of incubators:

- Nonprofit oriented incubators
- Profit oriented incubators

In the case of nonprofit incubators, profitability results come in the background as they prioritize social goals. In most cases, they are created on the initiative of public bodies (e.g., state-owned bodies, government, research centers) and are aimed at developing the territory, promoting entrepreneurship, and research.

In the case of profit incubators, they are mostly privately owned and they only have economic and financial targets and goals. This clearly affects the selection process and how the companies are mentored while at the incubator, which can decide either to ask for a fee to the start-up company or to participate in the share capital with a little stake.

Both for accelerators and for incubators, the teams have to pass an admission test. When applying for an incubator or for an accelerator, these are the factors that are taken into consideration:

- Business idea
- Team (whether the competences that are necessary to launch successfully that project can be found in the founding team)
- Scalability of the business idea (i.e., the ease of replicating that idea in large numbers)
- Technical feasibility
- Economic and financial feasibility

If the start-up can overcome these valuation steps, the incubator or the accelerator will follow the project, each of them according to their terms and different ways.

### 19.2.2    Crowdfunding

Crowdfunding is a recent financing source that is experiencing a huge development in recent years. As the name itself suggests, they are investments made in unlisted companies or projects by individuals who are neither institutional investors nor venture capitalists. Retail investors are able to donate in favor of a specific project via a web platform by specifying the amount they wish to donate. If this kind of investment is made in a company, this is typically in its early stage of activity and typically involves innovative businesses. However, such investments may also involve projects that have more of a "personal" nature, such as musical, literal, or art projects.

Crowdfunding platforms can be divided into different broad categories:

- Donation-based platform: These were the first forms of crowdfunding. They are widely used to finance artistic and musical projects as they require small sums. The duration of the time frame in which it is possible to donate is larger than the one of other forms.
- Reward-based platform: In these models, in return for monetary support, a reward is given to the donor. Within this model, there are two different types of operations, one is called "All or nothing" in which the target must be reached. In case the target is not reached, the collected amount up to that moment is not transferred. In the "Take It All" type, transactions to the beneficiary are also made even if the total target is not reached.
- Equity-based platforms: Through this category, donors become shareholders of the private company that is seeking for financing. As such, this type of crowdfunding is subject to legislative restrictions, both as for the maximum investment achievable and the maximum capital collectable by the company (see an example of Equity Crowdfunding in Box 19.1).

> ### BOX 19.1 THE X-RAYS ITALIAN START-UP THAT SMASHED CROWDFUNDING
>
> Xnext is an Italian advanced inspection technology company that provides in-line inspections with the patented and proprietary XSpectra unit.
>
> To date, XSpectra is the most advanced X-ray real-time quality control scanner capable to improve in-line quality controls and able to extend the application in all sectors where zero-defect is the expected goal, such as airport inspections, circular economy, and food contamination.
>
> Xnext systems are integrated in XSpectra. The technology is based on two patents and it is capable to analyze in few milliseconds the chemical–physical components of different materials to detect nonconformance of the product such as defects, foreign bodies or contaminants. XSpectra is not the X-rays machine, rather the "brain" of the machines that allows in-line production quality controls. When the product, that is being controlled, is illuminated from an X-ray source, XSpectra can precisely detect in real time the number of photons, as if it was taking its "fingerprint."
>
> As of today, there is nothing on the market such as XSpectra, as present inspection systems are capable to perform a two-level of energy analysis. XSpectra can reach up to 1024 levels of energy.
>
> The innovative technology used allows XSpectra to penetrate and inspect the material even if covered of glass, metal, or steel, guaranteeing, according to the company, a rate of 100% reliability. Ironically and simplifying, Bruno Garavelli, CEO of the company, says: "*to give an idea of the extent of the improvement in inspection brought by our invention you should think to the switch from Black and White TV to Ultra HD TV!*"
>
> XSpectra is not only innovative in what they do, but also in how they decided to raise financing. Despite disposing of quite a big share capital, in order to scale up, the management team decided to get funds from the ultimate beneficiaries of XSpectra: potentially everyone.
>
> In that sense, they launched an equity crowdfunding campaign in 2017.
>
> The management team decided to finance with crowdfunding, as in this way they would have been able to complete competitive technology development, increase high-tech technical resources, and provide the company with new laboratories and instrumentation to enhance the application technology development in other industries.
>
> The total capital collected with the equity crowdfunding was around 462,000 Euros, exceeding the preset budget of 250,000 Euros, with an overfunding of 184% and a maximum investment of 200,000 Euros. In addition to the positive success encountered in the market among retail investors, they crowdfunding campaign was also interesting for the nature of the 32 investors that agreed on subscribing the share capital: over 43% of the capital collected came from abroad (a record for Italian crowdfunding).
>
> Finally, shareholders' profile is all but homogeneous: among others, a multinational company, a university student, a businessperson, and a retail saver who aims at differentiating savings and activities.
>
> Dealing with many, and different by nature, shareholders is not easy. Hence, in addition to the scale up of the company, the young company had to manage the relations with the shareholders and change the communication strategy accordingly.

- Lending-based platforms: This latter partly derives from the increasing trend in microcredit and involves the investment of very modest amount of capital that the platform shares on several projects in a way such that it reduces the risks. It can be done with or without an intermediary; in the case without intermediary, it is called "peer-to-peer." At the same time it is also possible to lend money to companies, in this case it is called "peer-to-business"

## 19.3 SECONDARY MARKET

Despite the investment in private equity requires for its nature and purposes a holding period that can be defined as long term, it has been anticipated earlier in the chapter that there may be in the market a tendency to reduce this holding period. There are specialists in taking over stakes in private equity funds from investors that are interested in selling their shares before the fund ends. They are called secondary market operators.

The private equity secondary market (also often called private equity secondaries or, simply, secondaries) refers to the buying and selling of preexisting investor commitments to private equity and other alternative investment funds.

Through this operation, not only do sellers of private equity investments sell their investments in the fund but they also give up their remaining unfunded commitments to the funds. By its nature, the private equity asset class is illiquid, intended to be a long-term investment for buy-and-hold investors. For the vast majority of private equity investments, there is no listed public market. This may lead to think that it is not frequent to find a secondary buyer, however there is a robust and maturing secondary market available for sellers of private equity assets.

According to a Prequin study, in 2016, $28 billion were raised globally over 25 new funds in the secondary market and in the first quarter of 2017, six secondaries funds already raised a total of $13.6 billion; more than double the amount raised in the previous quarter ($5.8 billion), and a record amount for secondaries funds in any quarter. This denotes the rise in the importance of this new strategy of exit for some funds and of entry in the investment for other ones.

There are two different kinds of secondary operations:

(1) Transfer of limited partnership—LP transfer.
    It is the most common operation of secondary and consists in the transfer of one or more stake from a limited Partner to another investor (see Fig. 19.1).
    The buyer pays the agreed price for the stake and undertakes to pay in the future (outstanding commitment) according to the calling plan decided in the contract.
    The new investor can benefit from all future equity capital distributions as decided by the general partners in favor of limited partners. In this type of operations, there is no change in the fund management, that is, general partners. The managers are the same, although the fund ownership structure changes.

(2) Direct secondary or synthetic secondary.
    Direct secondaries (see Fig. 19.2) are sales transactions of direct investment portfolios in companies, traded on a single transaction, and generally involve different private equity assets excluded from the typical limited partnership structure.
    Many institutional investors, particularly financial institutions and large corporations, that operate in equity transactions, bring these direct investments into different companies. These portfolios are often

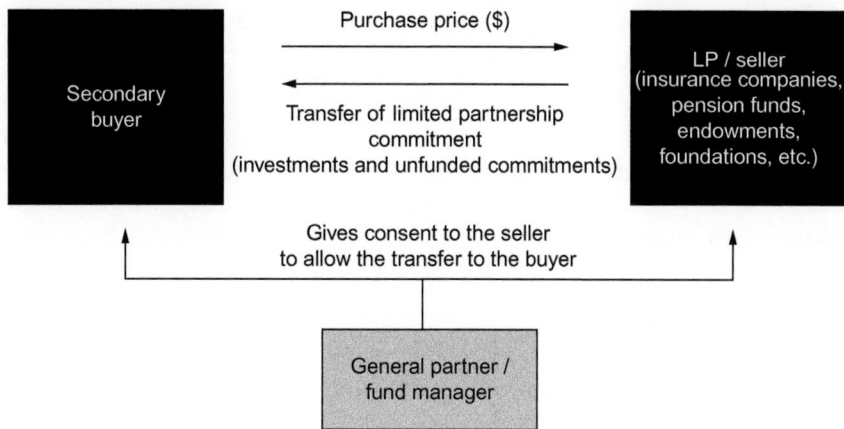

**FIG. 19.1** LP transfer.

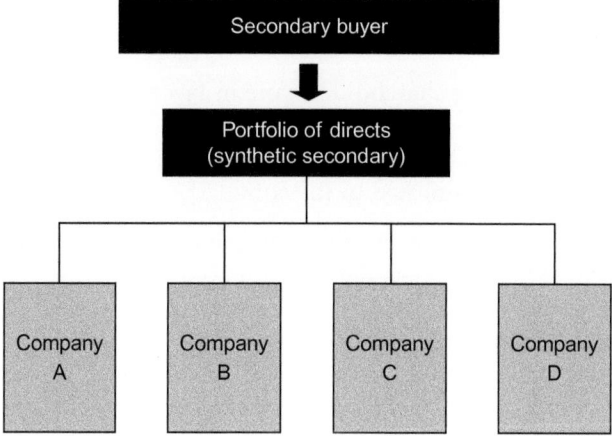

**FIG. 19.2** Direct secondary.

managed directly by a management team that, after the portfolio is sold, is released from the seller (the former owner) and gets involved by the new investor in the asset management of the portfolio. In the light of this, direct secondaries are more complex than LP transfers because they involve a due diligence (an entire portfolio is being transferred within this secondary).

## 19.4 SPAC

A SPAC is a listed investment vehicle, with the sole purpose of raising IPO funds in order to absorb and incorporate through a business combination a non-quoted operating company (target company). The SPAC's founders (i.e., the sponsors) are usually professionals that cumulated many years of good track record in the private equity world.

SPACs raise funds through the IPO of the so-called units, where the listed units are made up by one ordinary share and one warrant with an in-the-money strike price. The net proceeds deriving from the IPO are transferred in a trust or in an "escrow account" and they shall only be used when the business combination will be carried on. Despite the IPO, the sponsors usually keep for themselves 20% of the SPAC share capital.

The IPO process gives the SPAC an amount of capital that is enough to pursue the takeover of the target company. Then, after the IPO is successfully ended, the sponsor team of the SPAC begins to screen the market to find the potential target companies and they usually have from 18 to 24 months from the day of the IPO to close the business combination deal. If the SPAC does not receive approval for acquisition within deadline, it liquidates its trust to investors.

Once the potential target has been found, the business combination has to be approved, where the approval occurs only if:

- The majority of the shareholders vote in favor of that specific business combination,
- Dissident shareholders do not account for 20%–30% of the share capital (the threshold is indicated in the contract).

In case the assembly does not approve the business combination but the SPAC life has not come to an end yet, the SPAC can re-perform the search and hope to find another target company. If the time comes to an end and the SPAC has not found a target company yet, the shareholders can get the remaining funds available on a pro-rata basis. This amount may also be lower than the committed capital, as part of the funds may have been used to carry on the screening campaign.

On the contrary, if the SPAC finds the right target and the shareholders representing at least half of the share capital are in favor of the acquisition, they become shareholders of a listed target company. Dissident shareholders are provided with redemption rights (the right to convert shares into a pro-rata share of the proceeds in trust). Usually a cap to redeem shares is imposed in order not to jeopardize the closing of the acquisition.

The life cycle of a SPAC is represented in Fig. 19.3.

## 19.5 IMPACT INVESTING

The definition of impact investing remains, to date, a work in progress. Before defining impact investing, the definition of social innovation according to the European Commission should be given in order to understand the utter

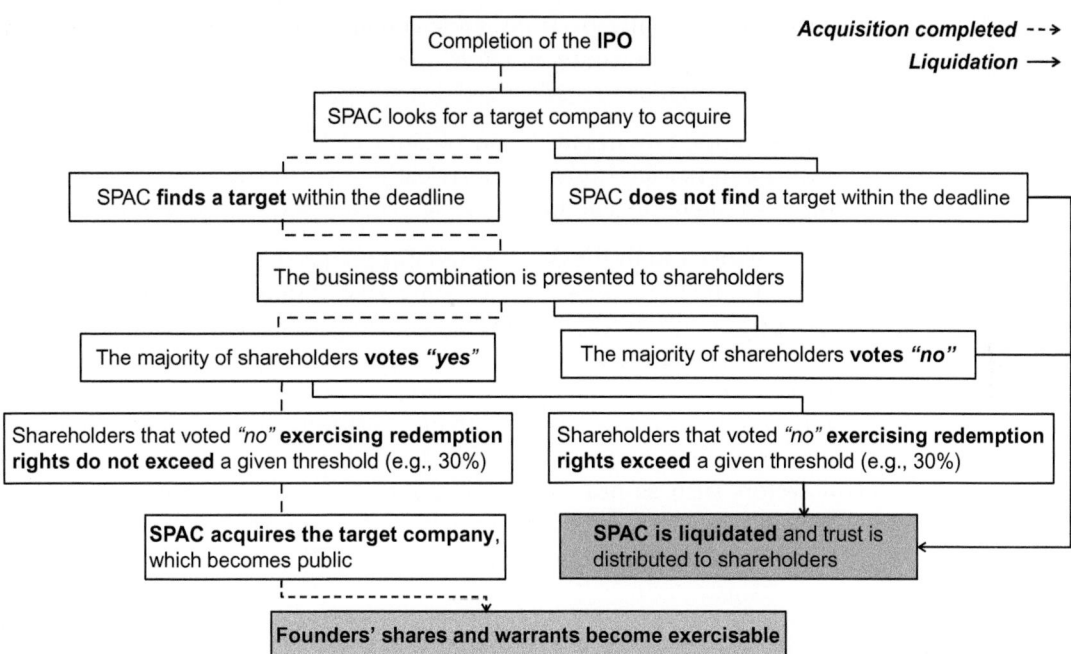

**FIG. 19.3** Life cycle of a SPAC.

meaning of this new trend in the market: "Social innovation can be defined as the development and implementation of new ideas (products, services, and models) to meet social needs and create new social relationships or collaborations. It represents new responses to pressing social demands, which affect the process of social interactions. It is aimed at improving human well-being. Social innovations are innovations that are social in both their ends and their means. They are innovations that are not only good for society but also enhance individuals' capacity to act."[1]

The demand of social needs has changed deeply (inequality, immigration, wealth divide, aging, digital divide, and globalization impact), however the offer, that should satisfy this demand, did not and it is yet unchanged. The offer of social services is mainly financed by the public sector and by some people willing to engage themselves in philanthropy. But this is not enough to fulfill the social needs, this is why in recent years a new trend spread in the financial market: Impact Investing, that is meant as an investment to create positive impact beyond financial returns.

The definition of impact investing is provided by Global Impact Investing Network (GIIN): "Impact investments are investments in companies, organizations, and funds with the intention of generating measurable social

---

[1]European Commission, Guide to Social Innovation, 2013.

and environmental impacts alongside a financial return. Impact investments can be made in both emerging and developed markets, and target a range of returns from below-market to market rate, depending on the circumstances."

The definition captures the blended nature of impact investing, as it is a mix of financial and social returns, but also clearly articulates the requirement for investors to be intentional in their efforts to generate social impact at the same time.

Many Scholars apply the venture capital approach to impact investments in that the target and the approach are the same. Like venture capital, an impact investing operator acts as an intermediary targeting young and privately held small firms, providing them with equity and with a hands-on approach. However, unlike venture capital, impact investing does not fund new technology-based solutions or ideas that still need to be transformed in a patent and eventually in an operating company but supports the development of social innovations in sectors such as healthcare, education, housing, and employment, hence towards those industries that may have a social impact (an example of Impact Investing in Europe is described in Box 19.2).

## BOX 19.2 OLTRE VENTURE—A EUROPEAN CASE OF IMPACT INVESTING

After a 20-year experience in venture capital and private equity, Luciano Balbo founded Oltre Venture in 2006. Oltre Venture is among the first European operators in impact investing.

Oltre Venture operates according to the venture capital model, combining financial resources, skills, proactive approach, and entrepreneurship.

The management team combines strong financial and managerial skills with a deep knowledge in the social work area. This combination and the "hands on" approach not only contribute to a qualified evaluation and selection of several investment opportunities, but also support an active growth of portfolio. Oltre Venture incubates and finances start-up companies by putting together entrepreneurs with competences within the social area and experienced managers who become the tutors of the enterprises' management team.

With Oltre I, the first fund, the firm raised €8 million that were invested in the following projects:

*PerMicro*—It is the first Italian microcredit experience. PerMicro set up 12 branches mostly in northern Italy, and thanks to the entrance in its capital structure by BNL (BNP Paribas Group), two branches were also opened in Southern Italy.

*Sharing*—Sharing is a social housing project and it has realized in Turin the most important temporary social housing project ever realized in Italy, in partnership with the municipality and other important local associations. In September 2011, a building composed by 183 apartments for a total of 470 accommodations was opened. The accommodations are meant for different users (students, relatives of in-patients coming from other cities, single mothers with children, young couples that cannot afford to pay rents at market level).

*Centro Medico Santagostino*—This medical center supplies medical care services in every medical area with excellent quality at affordable prices. It fills in the supply gap in the area of health services, which was supposed to be covered by the Health National System (mostly in the area of dental care and psychological assistance), offering services at prices slightly higher than the public sector, at a significantly higher quality level. The center is in constant growth and represents a novelty within the health sector.

In 2015, Oltre Venutre launched a second fund, Oltre II, and raised around €23 million.

# CHAPTER 20

# Strategies, Business Models, and Perspectives of Private Equity and Venture Capital

## 20.1 GENERAL OVERVIEW: A WORLD BETWEEN A LOST GOLDEN AGE AND UNCERTAINTY

After a 5-year period of overall economic growth and buy-out boom, for many countries last 2007–08 marked a clear inflection point in the global private equity environment. The golden age stands now behind and a new age of uncertainty starts, even for someone it has the sweet smell of opportunity. The lessons from the crisis 2007–08 in United States and in Europe with a turmoil on public debt and on the banking system amplify the concept of uncertainty and confirm uncertainty will be the mantra (or the status) for the next years. But opportunities always stay behind and the level of interest rates closed (or below) zero is a strong opportunity to leverage and its a stimulus to scan the market and to identify new asset classes as a target of investment.

While in 2008–09, with an estimated €200–300 billion in unsyndicated leverage loans on their books in 2008, it appears that banks were the first buyout players to suffer, nowadays banks are looking for investment generating a reasonable performance accordingly with the level of capital expenditure, which will represent the driver of all strategies and decisions within the banking system, at least in Europe. As bankers' attention moved from credit risk analysis to debt syndication many says they are reaping what they sowed. The credit crunch may have been triggered by the subprime mortgage problems but the consequences of a stricter capital adequacy regulation are deeper. In a short 5–7 years, the leading role of banks in the corporate banking and corporate finance market evolved dramatically: from principal lenders they became debt producer and broker, with a scale which is completely new. Financial structuring complexity has driven debt market participants to lose the sense of risk and driven to the great renaissance of the high-yield market. Private equity opponents blame big buyout partners and its true increased leverage multiples and loosened covenants can sound like a good thing for financial sponsors, that is more risk and less disciplined.

Private Equity and Venture Capital in Europe. https://doi.org/10.1016/B978-0-12-812254-9.00020-6

Apparently, the big buyout sector—supported by low interest rate—seems indeed the most exposed to risk and investors tend to oscillate between optimism and pessimism when asked about the credit crunch's effects. Some argued the end of large buyout era or the end of the golden age of private equity: but private equity always survive and it appears in different forms (from funds to club deals, to SPACs and even to crowdfunding) and with a high leverage again for top-quality deals. A large number of investors also fear the United States will be more affected—in case of another crisis—than other countries by a private equity downturn: in terms of capital deployment, fund investors hesitate between the worry of not having their money put to work fast enough and the fear of being too quickly deployed in less attractive and smaller deals. Most agree on the fact if the economic downturn were to affect operating companies, things could get really worst. While defaults rates remain at still historical lows, this may be simply the result of particularly weaker terms (i.e., few covenants, new repayment scheduling, etc.). Despite the big turmoil it is causing, the change in the leverage loan market conditions—thanks to the low interest rate—is also welcomed as a healthy and necessary correction by many market players, investors included too. It might be the end of the golden age but certainly not of the adventure of private equity. The players are simply being reminded that discipline and fair management are not old-fashioned European words, but pillars of competitive advantage for private equity and the financial system more generally.

Private equity investors are by ages long-term focused and its hard to find supporters of market timing approach. However, some investors both in Europe and in United States have clearly expressed concern about the future internal rate of return (IRR) as this new cycle starts and leading to an increased focus on investment strategies able to produce higher returns in less favorable economic environments. This means 2017 onwards asset allocation will be both defensive and offensive in the same time, looking for high standard of quality, well-suited pattern of investment and emerging potential targets of considerable interest. This approach will last for many years.

Nowadays investors agree that relevant performance will come from middle market and lower middle market players. Investors (and limited partners) are increasing their focus on teams capable of showing and demonstrating their value creation system. Europe and North America too offer significantly attractive and challenging opportunities with teams with proven experience in building strong private equity firms to invest through buy and hold approach, with a true "industrial touch" to their venture-backed companies. In the higher middle-market cluster, a number of teams target both privately held companies and listed companies; listed companies more and more appear as attractive targets for those larger middle-market buyout teams looking for undervalued companies to take private; great opportunities come out for private equity firms with track record in dealing with public companies, both in Europe and in the United States.

Even Europe and United States are offering very good opportunities, investors are in the same time adding attention (and money) to emerging markets as the next stop for fashionable performance. The different regions' growth rate and the little reliance on bank debt appear a convincing reason. Choosing the right private equity firms' teams is the key challenge in that area. A rising number of investors are starting to wonder whether the next bubble lies in China, India, or Korea. The Middle-East in another region where a number of family-owned investment teams have grown to become strong and experienced investors. However, some important challenges remain in these emerging markets, among which: the need of regulatory framework, a wider capital market, human resources, and political risks. For these reasons, Europe and United States still remain a preferable chance to invest because of the very strong capabilities of private equity firms' teams to live (and to survive) both in good and in bad times, like the 1998 Russian debt crises, the 2000 tech-internet bubble, September 11, the financial crisis 2007–09 and the sovereign debt crisis in Europe 2011–15 had clearly demonstrated.

Last, the new entries in private equity market are "Sovereign Funds." But while the visibility of this phenomena is quite new for the fundraising market, the actual sovereign funds investment activity is not. Some these players have been investing for many years and have grown to become very skilled and professional asset managing teams. But last 5 years proved other strong years for the secondary market too and for NPLs acquisitions due to banks crisis in Europe. It were the years confirming that the large majority of sellers accessed the market as part of natural portfolio management activities, even the power stays in the hands of buyers.

## 20.2 STRATEGIES AND BUSINESS MODELS OF PRIVATE EQUITY FIRMS

To analyze strategy within private equity firms its useful to identify some business models which are common in different countries in Europe. A FOP (focus-ownership-positioning) approach is helpful to distinguish:

- the focus of investment made by the private equity firm, related to the country/countries area of investment;
- the ownership of private equity firm, which conditions the style of investment and the long-term profit goals; and
- the positioning of the private equity firm on the market, related to the competitive strategy to select investment.

Focus, ownership, and positioning (FOP) are the three dimensions of a business model in private equity industry, in the sense every private equity firm is characterized by a different combination of the above-mentioned variables affecting the competitive strategy and profit results for investors.

## 20.2.1    The Focus of Investment

The focus of investment has a relevant impact on the scale, on the team and on the network, the private equity firm has to manage and to defend. The geographic area focus is the first step to identify a strategy and to build an organization; in comparison with other (even financial) services, private equity industry is totally "human and human network based": that means a process of diversification through geographic areas is quite difficult and it cannot be quick as skills are not so easy to be replied in other markets such as equipment, factories, and other tangible assets.

It is possible to distinguish three different choices of usage of the focus:

1. domestic focus,
2. international focus (i.e., pan-European or pan-American or pan-Asiatic focus), and
3. global focus.

The most common strategy in the world is domestic focused—if the size of the country is enough and makes it possible and rational—because of the natural linkage between the background of the management team and its expertise and the presence in the social and economic network. On the contrary, private equity firms following international or global focus are structured as a network, very similar to big consulting companies. Private equity firms following international or global focus can manage multicountries dimension into two different ways:

1. many funds investing in many countries (i.e., such as Permira, Apax partners, etc.) and
2. one fund (or more) for every country (i.e., like 3i, Blackstone, IFC, etc.).

Private equity firms following a global focus can act through both direct investment with many funds (the so-called "mega fund" strategy such as KKR) and direct investment in other funds (the so-called "fund of funds" strategy). Obviously, only the first one can be mentioned as a "pure" private equity strategy because of the capability to invest and to stay into venture-backed companies while the second one can be considered a financial strategy and not a "pure" private equity strategy.

The focus generates a sort of symmetry between the investment policy and the size of investment, by which private equity firms can be divided into three categories based on their size/average investment ticket:

1. Small-size players, investing between €1.0 and 5.0 million in each deal, typically small buyouts and expansion capital transactions; these players are in most cases all local, that is, based in the country of the management team;
2. Medium-sized players, investing between €5.0 and 20.0 million in each deal. Some of these players are sponsored by industrial companies or are connected to foreign financial institutions, even the majority of these vehicles are again local; and
3. Large private equity players, investing in equity tickets in excess of €20.0 million. Many of these are international or global private equity firms with widely available resources to invest but most of such players are also braches of global funds with an established presence in a country, if it is of relevant size.

## 20.2.2 The Ownership of Private Equity Firms

The ownership of the private equity firm is not neutral to strategy because it conditions both profit goals and style of management within investment. Using the ownership concept its possible to distinguish five different categories/strategic models of private equity firms:

1. banks (or financial institutions) owned,
2. corporate owned,
3. professionals owned (i.e., the so-called "independent" private equity firms),
4. government owned, and
5. private investors owned.

Banks- or financial institutions-owned private equity firms show as the origin a fund promoted from a financial institution willing to operate in the private equity market through a dedicated vehicle; its quite common in Europe because of the concept of the Universal Bank, aiming to create specific legal entities when the business is quite risky or quite relevant in term of capital expenditure such as the private equity case.[1] As a natural result, the activity of the banks-owned private equity firm is strictly related to the characteristic of the strategy of the financial group. The pros of this model are the brand name usage and leverage, the reputation effect, the support coming from the network of the financial group, the synergies with corporate lending, and the very high potential of fund raising. On the other hand, the cons are the potential divergence

---

[1]See Smith, R., Walter, I., "Governing the Modern Corporation," Oxford Press, 2006.

from a "pure" profit goal (i.e., the private equity sustain and subside the corporate lending) and the potential lack of an independent strategic view. Typically, banks-owned private equity firms are quite strong in the business of private equity whereas the financial know-how and expertise are more required and relevant for the competitive advantage than industrial knowledge and hands-on approach, that is, in buyouts and pure expansion financing.

Corporate-owned private equity firms show as the origin a fund promoted from a corporation aiming to operate in the private equity market or for profit and for sustaining the core industrial business. The nature of such private equity firms is strictly related to the characteristic of the strategy of the corporate group. The pros of this model are again the brand name usage and leverage (like in banks-owned private equity firms), the reputation, the network of the corporate group, the deep industrial knowledge, and the potential high capability to manage venture-backed companies. On the contrary, the cons are the potential low level of financial skills and the financial constraints coming from the corporate reputation: as an example, a downgrade of the corporation can generate a negative effect both on the fundraising and on the capability to raise money for each single deals. Typically, corporate-owned private equity firms are better performing and are well suited for private equity investment requiring industrial know-how and the presence through a strong hands-on approach such as seed financing, start-up, and early stage and restructuring financing.

Professionals-owned private equity firms take their origin from a fund promoted by a group of managers or professionals coming from industrial or consulting activity. As a result of it, the investment made by the firm are generally related to the previous sector of activity of professionals and aim to leverage the strong know-how of the managers. The pros of this strategic model are personal reputation of the managers, the strong network of the professionals, the very deep industrial knowledge, the potential high capability to manage venture-backed companies and a great sense of independence. On the other side, the cons are the absence of a strong organization behind, the youth (or the oldness) of managers and the lack of resources because of the absence of a banking or industrial group creating synergies. Typically, professionals-owned private equity firms excel through a pure hands on approach into private equity deals whereas using of leverage and financial capabilities are not so relevant. Medium-size and small-size equity tickets are quite common for this strategic model.

Government-owned private equity firms have as the origin a fund promoted by a governmental entity, also in joint-venture with other private investors and sometimes using a dedicated country law (i.e., like SBIC (Small Business Investment Companies) in the United States). The investment process is generally driven by the goals of the governmental entity, whereas the mix of profit and social return can have different balance and results. The pros of this strategic model are the possibility to reduce the expectation of IRR and to increase risk, the possibility to reduce the size of each equity investment and the easiest entrance in very risky sectors such as seed and start-up financing. Obviously, the cons of the model are the potential lack of top human resources, the divergence from a pure and explicit profit goal, the increasing of write offs and defaults, and the exposure to political cycle risk. Typically, government-owned private equity firms excel both through a geographic focus dedicated to emerging or developing countries and through a policy of joint-ventures with private investors to make easier the intervention into small-size equity tickets.

Private investors-owned private equity firms show the origin of a fund promoted by a family business or by a group of families to manage their wealth.[2] The nature of this last strategic model is related to investment which is generally driven by the goals of the family with the support of external managers they have in charge the management of the "family office." As a result of this definition, the pros of the model are the capability to manage with efficiency private wealth, the independence from the financial system and the usage of family network. On the contrary, the cons are the potential lack of top human resources, the divergence of opinion between family members, and the absence of a strong structure behind for professionals-owned private equity firms. Even the size and the reputation of the family owning the private equity firm could be relevant to characterizing the scope of the investment, a family office vocation generally leads the private equity firm to invest into equity ticket small- and medium-sized whereas the relevance of the family network gives a relevant advantage, such as for turnaround and family-buyouts.

## 20.2.3 The Positioning on the Market

The positioning of the private equity firm on the market is a crucial decision for every fund with whatever focus or ownership. The positioning means to identify the cluster(s) to invest money and to allocate resources in the portfolio. The asset allocation and the identification of market positioning generate consequence in terms of need of dedicated human resources and of knowledge required. This means positioning is a medium-long term choice of asset allocation, quite difficult to be changed weather in terms of high costs to sustain to change the managerial team. The positioning issue can be distinguished into many groups (i.e., "strategies" involving the positioning itself), which highlight different solutions to manage the asset allocation:

1. specialization within stage,
2. specialization within sector,

---

[2]See Caselli, S., Gatti, S., "Banking for Family Business," Springer Verlag, 2005.

3. specialization within areas,
4. specialization through an incubator approach, and
5. specialization through an alternative approach.

The case of the specialization within stages is the most common strategy in the world, followed and implemented by any focused or owned private equity firm. This specialization means the private equity firm chooses to allocate the portfolio in one of the stages of development of the firm and, as a natural consequence, the private equity firm recruits human resources and create knowledge only on this cluster. The potential benefit of diversification is reduced but the fund takes advantage from the deep control of the business. The specialization within stages is also driven from the presence on the market of different "business communities" and jobs profiles inside every stage which makes simpler the combination of management-business-investment.

The specialization within sector is not as common as a private equity firm strategy. In this case, the strategic model means the private equity firm chooses one industrial sector and it recruits human resources and it creates knowledge on it. Typical examples are biotech, telecoms, fashion, etc. Also in this case, the potential of diversification is strongly reduced but the fund takes an advantage from the deep control of the sector itself. The specialization within sectors is typically driven from the background of the managers and their relationship in the sector but, compared with the specialization within stages, the risk is higher because the fund allocate the whole amount of money into one sector only and it implies a bigger exposure at risk in case of economic downturn or changes of the competitive pattern for the sector itself.

The specialization within areas is a strategy typical of global funds aiming to enter and to stay in new markets. In this case, the strategy means the private equity firm chooses one area and invests in whatever sector and stage belonging to the area itself. The potential of diversification is extremely high—even linked to the size of the geographic area chosen by the private equity firm—but the fund takes great risk because of the very limited knowledge about the firms and of the evolution of the country in case of entry strategy. The specialization within areas is typically driven from the gamble on the development of a country, both for profit goals and for other goals and its quite common for government-owned private equity firms operating at international or at global level.

Specialization through an incubator approach is a strategy related to seed and to start-up investment and it tries to reduce the trade-off between risk and return which is dramatically high in the above-mentioned stages and, sometimes, not sustainable for a profit oriented investor. An incubator strategy is qualified from the offer from the private equity firm of an infrastructure (i.e., plants, machinery, real estate, technology, etc.) and of the knowledge for the development of ideas and research projects that the single entrepreneur/ inventor would not be able to face and to manage without a strong enhancement and support. That means the private equity firm reduces the costs for the new ventures and has a stronger control on the results and on the potential return. The infrastructure, that is the incubator, is of course an investment for the fund, but its made to have positive results and more sustainable risk-return profile.

Specialization trough an alternative approach is an emerging strategy nowadays, related to a big and a new quest for investment in alternative business. An alternative strategy is not driven simply from a profit goal but from the wish of private equity firm to develop a "new vision," sometimes related to social and mutual goals. For these reasons the target of alternative funds are social services, Employment opportunities for weak groups of people, arts, social-health services, social housing, protection of nature, etc. The common rationale of investment is to take an advantage from activities not (or badly) managed from the government to produce both profit and social return. More and more the new concept is also called "Venture Philanthropy" and its sustained by a greater number of investors—mostly high net worth individuals—looking both for new frontiers of investment and for a sustainable and socially performing usage of money (Box 20.1).

## 20.3 MANAGING THE VALUE CHAIN OF PRIVATE EQUITY FIRMS

The combination of the three sides coming from the FOP model can generate multiples options and choices to implement strategy for private equity firms. Even the future and the perspectives of private equity and venture capital will be examined in last section of this chapter (i.e., an exam of possible winning and losing strategies for the future), the focus now is to find the characteristics a private equity firm has to identify and to have for matching an efficient business model with the different choices made by the focus, the positioning and the ownership.

To analyze the spectrum of characteristics of a private equity firm, its useful to apply the traditional model of the Value Chain, designed by Michael Porter in 1985 because of the great coherence with the equity investment business. As well known, the value chain scheme distinguishes primary activities and support activities inside the organization of a specific firm. The primary ones are essential to produce and deliver the product, whereas the support ones enhance the process giving empowerment through firm infrastructure, human resource

## BOX 20.1 WHAT IS VENTURE PHILANTHROPY? (EVPA WORKING DEFINITION 2006)

Venture philanthropy is an approach to charitable giving that applies venture capital principles, such as long-term investment and hands-on support, to the social economy. Venture philanthropists work in partnership with a wide range of organizations that have a clear social objective. These organizations may be charities, social enterprises, or socially driven commercial businesses, with the precise organizational form subject to country-specific legal and cultural norms. As venture philanthropy spreads globally, specific practices may be adapted to local conditions, yet it maintains a set of widely accepted, key characteristics. These are:

1. High engagement: venture philanthropists have a close hands-on relationship with the social entrepreneurs and ventures they support, driving innovative and scalable models of social change. Some may take board places on these organizations, and all are far more intimately involved at strategic and operational levels than are traditional nonprofit founders.
2. Tailored financing: as in venture capital, venture philanthropists take an investment approach to determine the most appropriate financing for each organization. Depending on their own missions and the ventures they choose to support, venture philanthropists can operate across the spectrum of investment returns. Some offer non-returnable grants (and thus accept a purely social return), while others use loan, mezzanine, or quasi-equity finance (thus blending risk-adjusted financial and social returns).
3. Multiyear support: venture philanthropists provide substantial and sustained financial support to a limited number of organizations. Support typically lasts at least 3–5 years, with an objective of helping the organization to become financially self-sustaining by the end of the funding period.
4. Nonfinancial support: in addition to financial support, venture philanthropists provide value-added services such as strategic planning, marketing and communications, executive coaching, human resource advice, and access to other networks and potential founders.
5. Organizational capacity building: venture philanthropists focus on building the operational capacity and long-term viability of the organizations in their portfolios, rather than funding individual projects or programs. They recognize the importance of funding core-operating costs to help these organizations achieve greater social impact and operational efficiency.
6. Performance measurement: venture philanthropy investment is performance-based, placing emphasis on good business planning, measurable outcomes, achievement of milestones, and high levels of financial accountability and management competence.

*Source:* European Venture Philanthropy Association, EVPA.

management, technology development, and procurement. Both primary and support activities, variously combined together, are relevant to create value for the firm and to generate the competitive advantage, following a certain strategy that must be coherent with them (Fig. 20.1).

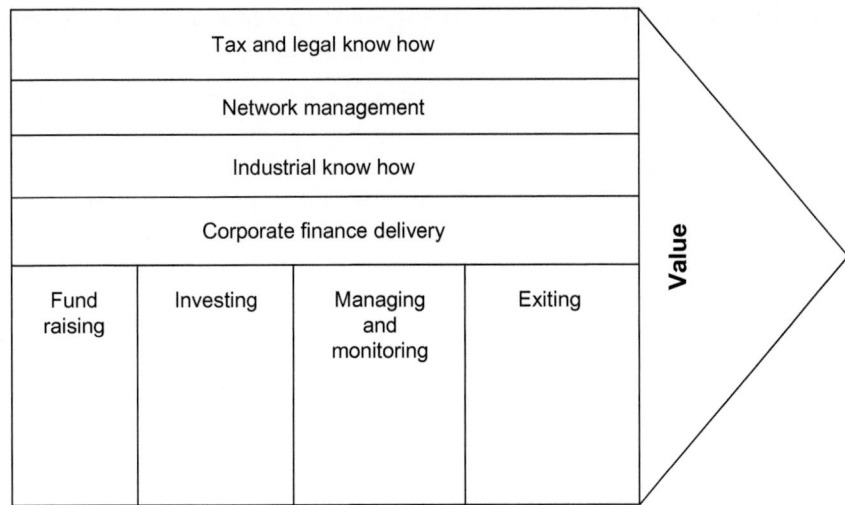

**FIG. 20.1** The value chain of private equity firms.

The same approach can be used for understanding the private equity firm and to measure the consistency of the chosen FOP. In this case, the primary activities can identified through the phases of the managerial process, as identified in Chapter 7 of the book: fundraising, investing, managing and monitoring, and exiting. On the other hand, the support activities can be identified through tax and legal know-how, network management, industrial know-how, and corporate finance delivery.

Tax and legal know-how is a fundamental competence for deal making because of the strong need of legal mastering both for execution of transactions and for corporate governance consulting support. Tax and legal moves from a pure add-on and peripheral around the core of equity investment to a relevant skill to dominate for a high-quality delivery process. Network management has a broad significance because the tools to manage the links and the connections within the economic system are multiples. Network management means, first of all, capability to interact with potential customers and suppliers of the venture-backed company, in order to give concrete advantages on cost and revenues side. But network management means to be the leader of a certain community too (i.e., chemical sector, IT sector, medical sector, etc.), relevant to recruit management, to run investment and to driver the proper lobbying activities. Industrial know-how becomes relevant not only to play a leading role within the venture-backed strategy but also to advice and to mentor the entrepreneurs to assume the right choices. Furthermore, industrial know-how is crucial to identify better potential acquirers to manage the exiting phase. Last, corporate finance delivery surrounds many private equity deals because both of the high involving of leverage and of the need to use M&A techniques to promote acquisitions to expand the venture-backed company.

The usage of the value chain must be done as a fundamental assessment of the robustness of private equity investment company profile and organization to follow a certain strategy and to face competition in the market with a sustainable return. In example, bank-owned and corporate-owned private equity firms can benefit a lot from the belonging to big groups in term of strong management of support activities such as networking and tax and legal as for primary activity such as investing and exiting. But while bank-owned private equity firms are quite strong for corporate finance delivery and fund raising, they do not have in most of cases industrial know-how. That means they cannot follow a hands-on strategy or, if they will, they have to insert reputable managers to fill this relevant gap. On the contrary, corporate-owned private equity firm show an evident advantage in the support activities of network and industrial know-how but they are quite weak into corporate finance delivery. And that means, a positioning in finance-intensive deal could be very dangerous if they do not assess a well-suited organizational solution to fill the gap. More generally, its obvious private equity firms internationally or globally focused multiply the option to master most (even all) of the primary and support activities enlarging the potential of competitive advantage but, on the contrary, they face the risk to lose the linkage with local network and community if the scale of investment were local and/or small- and medium-sized.

## 20.4   THE PERSPECTIVES AND THE DESTINY OF PRIVATE EQUITY AND VENTURE CAPITAL

The great capability and success of private equity and venture capital is to be able to change and to transform its own characteristic to find every time new and efficient (even creative) solution to sustain companies' liabilities. The 2007–09 and 2011–13 big financial crises marks a significant downturn in a certain usage of equity investment—mostly big buyouts, stock exchange, and profit driven—and it launches a global brainstorming about the future and the new destiny of private equity and venture capital.

The story (and perhaps, the future too) of private equity and venture capital suggests both strategies and business models are driven by a different combination of the three fundamental tools to create value in equity investment: multiples, leverage, and industrial growth.

Multiples are stock exchange driven and represent the explicit benchmark for entry and exit price for whatever equity transaction, leading from sublime opportunities like in 1999–2000 and 2005–06 to dramatic pitfalls like 2001–02 and 2007–08. Leverage is the oldest and the simplest tool to multiply the value the venture-backed company creates and, sometimes, the placing power combined with the certification effect coming from the private equity investor can introduce huge amount of debt, sustainable only at a certain level of interest rate. Industrial growth, that is, the earnings before interest, tax, depreciation, and amortization (EBITDA) growth, is the core variable of the venture-backed company's value creation even the most time consuming and energy absorbing to be managed and piloted by the managers and the private equity firm. Obviously, the usage and the combination of three variables depends from the cluster of private equity investment: in seed financing and, many times, in start-up EBITDA growth is the key variable to manage because both of the impossibility (in the seed case) and the strong constraints (in the start-up case) to raise debt and the very difficult usage of initial public offering (IPO) for the exit; on the contrary, in big buyouts both usage of leverage and multiples can be successfully used to create value for the equity investment. However, the combination of the three variables is related also to the strategy of private equity firms, to their style of management and to investors' expectation of IRR. For private equity and venture capital, the lesson learnt from 2007–09 financial crises is to come back to a strong usage of industrial growth because of the great fall both in multiples and in usage of leverage at a very cheap price.

If coming back to fundamentals, companies, and to a very enhancing hands-on approach are the sentences for the manifesto everybody fully agree and sign for the future. Its relevant to identify and forecast the options private equity firms can use for a successful future for the investors and for the economic system as a whole. These open options can be classified into the following groups:

- Big buyouts and mega-deals. Even the end of those transactions has been declared definitely that they will come back in the future. The economic turmoil leading to a credit crunch and to a strong de-leveraging of many structures and vehicles to invest makes today impossible to deliver big equity tickets to the market. But, very big transactions are a fundamental engine for the economic system when privatization, financing of infrastructure, and financing of large corporation becomes urgent and relevant. If in the past, big buyouts were born to restructure and to acquire big corporations and they later turn to a mindless usage for the only interest of investors, the wise use of private equity will come back on the stage when new campaign of privatization will be launched or the need of infrastructures, Government will be not able to finance, shall be financed by private investors. This new perspective will have in common with the past only the equity ticket size but not the aims and the approach mostly finance based and hands-off driven; but probably, also returns will be different as the time horizon of investment will be longer.
- Mid-cap transactions. They are the fuel for Europe, because of the great number in many leading countries. If the temptation (and the explicit

strategy many times) for private equity firms in the past was to use the same pattern for big deals to finance them, it will be necessary a wise come back to a clear focus on EBITDA growth, combined with a cautious and wise usage of leverage and of multiple when it makes sense in the company's perspectives. The needs of mid-cap companies are enlarging of variety of companies because they range from corporate governance restructuring, developing of internationalization, developing of R&D, and restructuring. The private equity firms intervention shall match a greater number of profiles and shall apply different format to solve companies' problems and needs. Private equity firms with an international focus could be of a great support if they will give and share their international network to sustain international development of the venture-backed companies and they will enhance technological transfer for a R&D process sustain. On the contrary, private equity firms with a domestic focus shall cooperate and integrate their offer with the corporate banking and corporate finance sector to give useful contribution to venture-backed companies.

— Small cap transactions. The financing of small and medium enterprises is the unsolved issue for private equity world. If from a logical point of view, many SMEs really need a private equity intervention to face a process of growth, their size make the equity investment not profitable for the private equity firms. That happens for very clear and reasonable facts: the time and the costs required to have due diligence and to run the whole process of investment (i.e., scouting, investing, managing and monitoring, exiting) are more or less the same independently from the company's size and the consequence is the need to fix a minimum threshold in term of sales by the private equity firms in order to reach a break-even for the profit; the probability to multiply EBITDA and variables relevant to calculate exit way price is lower than for bigger companies; to find a purchaser its difficult than for bigger companies again because of the niche and of the very specific activity of smaller companies. As a result of these facts, if SMEs required private equity intervention, for private equity firms is not profitable to do that and this leave many small firms in a steady state whereas the small size becomes the definitive size for the majority of companies. The solution to break this very dangerous loop can be identified only through a smart Government intervention, by which the policy is not of spending money but a wise participation to joint-ventures with private investors in which, from one side, the government fix the guidelines and activate controls and, on the other side, the private investors do their job carefully. But, what is relevant for the success is the fixing of an expected performance for the governmental investor and the transfer of the upside to the private investors; this multiplies the return for the private investor itself and makes sustainable the facing of fix costs and expenses even for small equity tickets.

— Seed and start-up. These businesses are the riskier ones and the very high-risk-return profile, combined sometimes with the need of a tremendous amount of money to launch research projects in seed cluster, avoid private investor to finance with the consequence of losing opportunities of growth and innovation for the economic system. In this case, only medium-long-term perspectives, a nonaggressive expectation of return and a disposal of a relevant amount of money are the key variables, which have to characterize private equity firms having a proactive and relevant role in these business. Till now, Sovereign Funds only seems to show those characteristics because of their very specific nature in which investors and managers are the same player and they are the Government of a single State. But the track record of investment in Europe of Sovereign Funds is not so long to judge clearly and it becomes urgent the finding of a solution coming from "pure" player belonging to private equity world. The governmental intervention again and the design of ad hoc rules seem to be the right solutions to enhance private equity firms intervention in these sectors.

— Venture philanthropy. These private equity firms decide to use the instrument of capital investment, even when such a thing implies its mere maintenance, as it is the best to satisfy the intermediate needs of social fragility.[3] In fact, they support the idea that different needs require different solutions. Whereas some needs (above all the extreme) necessitate public operations and/or donations, others (related to the social fragility) require market forms that match the economics to the social interest, and it is important to suit to the specific needs of the most adequate instrument. The intervention appeals to the so-called gray area of social fragility, part of which is an ever increasing range of population characterized by profound (yet not extreme) hardship. This hardship invests the basic needs such as housing, occupation, health, and interpersonal relations, specifically referred to uncertain work prospects, crises and problems of family, loneliness and lack of social contact, an increasing uncertainty about the future. Not being qualified for any Government Welfare programs, and similarly unable to access the free

---

[3]Venture Philanthropy suggests an innovative model of social investment, which is totally different from the to-date commonly known "ethical funds." Ethical funds generally identify the socially responsible funds on the basis of "exclusion criteria" (e.g., the choice to exclude from the investment-portfolio companies involved in armament, tobacco, or gambling activity) or simply selecting companies on the basis of "compliance" criteria by virtue of law and shareholder protection. Venture Philanthropy funds stays aloof from the above models offering a pro-active social investment, addressed to new experimental initiatives, and new modalities of intervention with a high impact social change and immediate results. This is a totally pioneering approach to most of the countries in Europe, part of the international trend promoted in the tradition of Venture Philanthropy, which offers strong pro-active operating models in support of sustainable organizations in terms of economic resources and skills. This standpoint comes out of the awareness that great skills and professionalism are required to satisfy the complex social needs; in particular, entrepreneurship and new operating models are needed. Along with the economic support the investors should provide professional back-up to promote projects and the organizations involved.

market's offer, this segment of population does not meet the proper needs. Venture philanthropy promotes new and more efficient models of social services to satisfy the new increasing segment of needs. These models provide market-like solutions and for this reason, they should be sustained by customers' contributions as well, matching in this way the social impact with the economic sustainability. The supported social enterprises are positioned in the intermediate market segment, in-between public and private, offering good-quality products and services at controlled prices. The promotion of these social enterprises needs two main factors: the presence of social entrepreneurs, able to entrepreneurially develop the idea/project and to supervise with efficient criteria the necessary financial resources for its implementation; the availability of private capital, that is "patient" and responsible, or rather the availability of investors, who believe in the concept of social responsibility of the wealth and are willing to promote it, by putting their capital at the disposal of innovative projects and accepting the concept of simple capital preservation at a high social return.

In future we will see that its not related simply to the open options the players in and out of the market will decide to use for implementing a private equity useful for the economic system but its based also on actions and decisions the policy makers will take. In the first part of the book, we have seen how policy makers intervention differ into many countries and how it was successful for the growth of private equity and venture capital in certain countries. Nowadays its not yet time for policy makers spending but a lot can be done with a smart usage of wisdom, power, and well-written rules. If the issue of regulation is on the stage now, the destiny of private equity and venture capital is not related to this story but to taxation rules and smart solutions/schemes to sustain the open options we have highlighted earlier. A durable and stable policy of taxation incentive to promote equity raising among small and medium enterprises, to sustain R&D and to invest abroad are the basic pillars for the growth; but it must be combined with a more incisive action that promote tax transparency (like for US limited partnership and SBIC) into private equity vehicles subject to their investment into sectors considered relevant/critical for a specific country. Moreover, a more aggressive policy of incentive for investors, it could be used to attract from off-shore relevant resources (they were produced in-shore) that could be used for private equity and venture capital to promote development and growth. But also, the quest of efficient joint-venture between public and private partners to balance risk and return will accelerate to intervention into small and medium transactions. And last, the challenge in Europe is related to the creation of efficient synergies between nonprofit and profit investors to grasp options of growth that otherwise will die into a gray area, which runs from the universities and research centers to go to small and potentially very big entrepreneurs.

# Glossary

**Accrued interest**  interest due securities or bonds since the last interest payment date.

**Acquisition**  process of taking control, possession, or ownership of a company, or a branch or part of it, by an operating company or conglomerate.

**Advisory board**  group of advisors external to a private equity group or company supplying different types of advices, from overall strategy to portfolio valuation.

**AIFMD**  alternative Investment Fund Managers Directive. It is a European Union Directive of 2011 issued to regulate *inter alia* hedge funds, and private equity and real estate activities.

**Allocation**  amount of securities assigned to an investor, broker, or underwriter during the offering process. The value of the allocation, due to the market demand, can be equal to or less than the amount indicated by the investor during the subscription process.

**Alternative assets**  nontraditional asset classes, which include private equity, venture capital, hedge funds, and real estate. Alternative assets usually have a higher risk profile than traditional assets but, at the same time, generate higher returns for investors.

**Amortization**  accounting procedure that gradually reduces the book value of an asset periodically charging costs to the income.

**Anchor investor**  an investor whose role is to attract other investors and capital when a fund is being launched.

**Angel financing**  capital for a private company from independent investors used as seed financing.

**Angel investor**  person (typically successful entrepreneurs often in technology-related industries) who provides backing to early-stage businesses or business concepts.

**Antidilution provisions**  contractual agreements that allow investors to maintain a flat share of a firm's equity despite subsequent equity issues. These provisions may give investors preemptive rights to purchase new stock at the offering price.

**Asset-backed loan**  typically supplied by a commercial bank, which is covered by asset collaterals, often consisting of guarantees supplied by the entrepreneurial firm or by the entrepreneur.

**Asset management company (AMC)**  financial institution regulated by EU laws and devoted to manage funds, both open and closed-end.

**Automatic conversion**  immediate conversion of an investor's privileged shares to ordinary shares at the moment of a company's underwriting, before an offering of its stock on an exchange.

**Average IRR**  arithmetic average of the internal rate of return.

**Balance sheet**  formal financial statement that shows the nature and amount of a company's assets, liabilities, and capital on a given date.

**Bankruptcy**  when debts incapacitate a company into discontinuing its business.

**BATNA (best alternative to a negotiated agreement)**  no-agreement alternative that indicates the course of action that parties, during a negotiation, will follow if the proposed deal is not possible.

**Best efforts** an offering in which the investment banker agrees to distribute as much of the offering as possible and return back to the issuer any no placed shares.

**Board rights** allowing an investor to be part of the Board of Directors of a company.

**Book value** stock value is defined based on the company balance sheet. The calculation consists of adding all current and fixed assets then deducting its debts, other liabilities, and the liquidation price of any preferred share. The result of this calculation is divided by the number of common shares outstanding obtaining the book value per each common share.

**Bootstrapping** the activity of financing a small firm by employing highly creative ways of using and acquiring resources without raising equity from traditional sources or borrowing money from banks.

**Bridge financing** limited amount of equity or short-term debt financing that is usually raised within 6–18 months of an anticipated public offering or private placement. This financing offers a "bridge" to a company until the next round of financing.

**Business judgment rule** legal principle that the Board of Directors has to respect during its activity. It consists of acting in the best interests of the shareholders. If the Board ignores this rule, it would be in violation of its fiduciary duties to the shareholders.

**Business plan** a document that explains the entrepreneur's idea and the market issues as well as business and revenue models, marketing strategy, technology, company profile, and the competitive landscape. It also describes future financial data.

**CAGR (compound annual growth rate)** year over year growth rate calculated on an investment using a base amount.

**Call option** owner's right to buy a security at a given price by a specific time period.

**Capital (or assets) under management** amount of capital available to a fund manager to invest.

**Capital call** approach to investors executed by venture capital firms when it has decided where to invest. The money usually has already been promised to the fund, but the capital call is the formal act of transferring the money.

**Capital gains** difference between an asset's purchase price and its selling price when the selling price is greater than the purchase price.

**Capitalization table** recaps the total amount of the different securities issued by a firm; it usually includes the amount of the financial resources raised from each source and the securities distributed.

**Capitalize** booking expenditures are considered as assets rather than expenses.

**Captive funds** venture capital firm owned by a bigger financial institution.

**Carried interest** portion of any gains realized by the fund without contribution to capital. Carried interest payments are widespread in the venture capital industry as an important economic incentive for venture capital fund managers.

**Cash position** amount of cash available to a company at any given moment.

**Claw back** obligation consisting of a promise made by the general partners that they will not receive a share greater than the fund's distributions. When the partners violate this rule, they have to return excess amount to the fund's limited partners.

**Closed-end fund** fund whose risk capital includes a fixed number of outstanding shares that are offered during an initial subscription period. After closing the subscription period, the shares are exchanged between investors in a regulated market.

**Closing** investment event occurring after the required legal documents are signed between the parties.

**Co-investment** syndication of a private equity financing operation or an investment realized by individuals next to a private equity fund in a financing round.

**Collar agreement** consists of conventional adjustments of the number of shares offered during a stock-for-stock exchange to account for price fluctuations before the completion of the deal.

**Committed capital** total amount of capital committed to a private equity fund.

**Committed funds or raised funds** capital pledged by investors equal to the maximum cash that may be requested or drawn down by the private equity managers. The difference between this amount and the invested funds most partnerships will initially invest only between 80% and 95% of committed funds, it may be necessary early in the investment to deduct the annual management fee used to cover the operation costs of a fund, and payback to investors usually begins before the final draw down of commitments has taken place.

**Common stock** security representing the base unit ownership of a company. In a public company, the stock is traded between investors on various public markets. The stocks entitle their owners to vote on the appointment of directors and other important events. Common stock owners receive dividends and an increase of the stock price creating capital gains. Common stocks do not include any performance guarantee and, in the event that a corporation is liquidated, their owners will be satisfied only after the repayment of secured and unsecured debts and of bonds and preferred stock, and only when the financial resources are available.

**Company buyback** repurchasing company shares by the original owners of the company from the venture capital firm.

**Consolidation (leveraged rollup)** investment strategy in which a leveraged buyout firm acquires companies in the same or complementary sectors to become the dominant player in the relative industry.

**Conversion ratio** number of shares of stock into which a convertible security may be converted.

**Convertible security** bond, debenture, or preferred stock that can be exchanged with another type of security, usually common stock, at a predefined price.

**Corporate charter** document outlining when a corporation is founded in order to set objectives and the goals of the corporation; it also includes the complete statement of what the corporation can and cannot do during its activity.

**Corporate resolution** official document reporting specific decisions taken by the corporation's Board of Directors.

**Corporate venturing** venture capital provided by in-house investment funds of large corporations to pursue their own strategic interests.

**Corporation** legal, taxable entity acknowledged by a state law; owners of the corporation are named stockholders or shareholders.

**Covenant** protective clause included in an agreement.

**Cumulative dividends** dividends that are accrued at a given rate until a predefined moment. Venture-backed companies use cumulative dividends because it allows them to conserve cash when the cash availability of the corporate is increased.

**Cumulative preferred stock** stock that contains the provision that if one or more dividend payments are omitted, the omitted dividends must be paid before the company pays dividends to the holders of common stocks.

**Deal flow** number of potential investments that a fund analyzes during a given period of time.

**Depreciation** expense booked to reduce the value of a tangible or intangible asset; if there is no cash expense, the free cash flow increases but reduces the value of the company income.

**Dilution** reduction in the shareholders' percentage ownership of a company caused by the issuance of new shares.

**Dilution protection** provision that changes the conversion ratio when there is a stock dividend or extraordinary distribution to avoid the dilution effect; it is usually applied to convertible securities.

**Director**  person appointed by shareholders to the Board of Directors. Directors select the president, vice president, and all other operating officers and have authority in the most important decisions regarding the corporate activity.

**Disbursement**  investments realized by funds in the companies included in their investment portfolio.

**Disclosure document**  describes the risk factors associated with an investment.

**Distressed debt**  corporate bonds of companies that have declared bankruptcy or will in the near future.

**Distribution**  disbursement of realized cash or stock to the limited partners of a venture capital fund at the moment of fund termination.

**Diversification**  dividing investments among different types of securities and companies operating in different industries and sectors.

**Dividend**  payments defined by the Board of Directors to be distributed among the shares outstanding. If there are preferred shares, it is usually a fixed amount; if there are common shares the dividend depends on the performances and the cash situation of the company and can be omitted in case of bad performance or when the directors determine to withhold earnings to invest in the development of the business.

**Down round**  issuance of shares at a later date and a lower price than previous investment rounds.

**Drag-along rights**  majority shareholder, right that obligate the minority shareholders to sell their shares when the majority wishes to execute the selling of the participation.

**Dual income taxation (DIT)**  taxation mechanism used to enhance equity issuing through a tax rate reduction in proportion to the amount of equity.

**Due diligence**  process executed by potential investors to analyze and valuate the desirability, value, and potential of an investment opportunity.

**Early stage**  life cycle phase of a company that has completed its seed stage and reports minimal revenues with no positive earnings or cash flows.

**EBITDA (earnings before interest, taxes, depreciation, and amortization)**  measure of cash flow calculated as revenue—expenses without considering tax, interest, depreciation, and amortization. EBITDA indicates the cash flow of a company because the exclusion of interest, taxes, depreciation, and amortization allows the analysis of the amount of money that a company creates.

**Economies of scale**  economic principle that states as the volume of production increases, the unit cost of producing decreases.

**Elevator pitch**  presentation of an entrepreneur's idea, business model, company solution, marketing strategy, and competition delivered to potential investors. This presentation should not take more than a few minutes or the duration of an elevator ride.

**Employee stock option plan (ESOP)**  plan organized by a company reserving a certain number of shares for purchase and issuance to key employees. Such shares serve as an incentive for employees to build a long-term value for the company.

**Employee stock ownership plan**  trust established by a company to purchase stock on behalf of its employees.

**Equity kicker**  option assigned to a private equity company allowing it to purchase shares at a discounted price.

**Evergreen promise**  agreement made by a company that agrees to pay an employee's salary for a number of years the day after he is employed or 10 years after.

**Exercise price**  price at which an option or a warrant can be exercised.

**Exit strategy**  method available to private equity funds to liquidate their investments and achieve the maximum possible return. The method chosen depends on exit climates such as market conditions and industry trends and specific characteristics of the deal and the investor.

**Exiting climates** conditions that influence the viability and attractiveness of various exit strategies.

**Exit** way in which private equity firms obtain a return on their investment. Private equity returns generally consist of capital gain realized with the sale or flotation of investments. Exit methods include a trade sale, quotation on a stock exchange, a share repurchase by the company or its management or a refinancing of the business, and a secondary purchase of the company to another private equity.

**Factoring** procedure in which a firm can sell its accounts receivable invoices to a factoring firm, which pays a percentage of the invoices immediately, and the remainder (minus a service fee) when the accounts receivable are actually paid off by the firm's customers.

**Finder** person who specializes in arranging transactions.

**Flipping** strategy of buying shares during an IPO and selling them immediately to gain a profit.

**Flotation** when a firm's shares start trading on a formal stock exchange its price is subject to flotation as per the dynamics between offer and demand of the market.

**Follow-on funding** investment realized by a private equity firm that has already invested in a particular company in the past and then provides additional funding at a later stage.

**Founders' shares** shares owned by the company founders.

**Free cash flow** cash flow of a company available to service the activity of the firm.

**Fully diluted earnings per share** earnings per share calculated as if all outstanding convertible securities and warrants have been exercised.

**Fully diluted outstanding shares** number of shares representing the total company ownership including common shares and current conversion, exercised value of preferred shares, options, warrants, and other convertible securities.

**Fund age** age of a fund (expressed in years) from its first takedown to the time an IRR is calculated.

**Fund focus** area in which a venture capital fund is specialized.

**Fund of funds** fund that specializes in distributing its investments among a selection of private equity funds. These types of funds are specialized investors and have existing relationships with firms.

**Fund size** total amount of capital committed by the investors of a venture capital fund.

**GAAP (generally accepted accounting principles)** common group of accounting principles, standards, and procedures accumulated from the combination of standards set by public authorities and accepted accounting standards.

**Gatekeeper** specialists advising institutional investors in their private equity allocation decisions.

**GDRs (global depositary receipts)** receipts for shares from a foreign company; these shares are traded in capital markets around the world.

**General partner (GP)** partner in a limited partnership that is responsible for all management decisions of the partnership.

**General partner contribution** amount of capital that the fund manager contributes to its own fund similar to a limited partner. This is the way that limited partners choose to ensure that their interests are aligned with those of the general partner.

**Golden handcuffs** provisions that incentivize employees to stay with a company. One type of golden handcuffs includes employee stock options that are assigned several years after that the employee has worked for the company.

**Golden parachute** provides employees, usually upper management, a large payout upon the occurrence of certain control transactions such as a certain percentage share purchase by an outside entity or when there is a tender offer for a certain percentage of a company's shares.

**Hedge of hedging** reducing the fluctuation of the price by taking a position in futures equal and opposite to an existing or anticipated cash position. This practice can also include shorting a security similar to one in which investor has a long position.

**Holding company** corporation that owns the control of other companies through the participation (usually majority participation) to their risk capital.

**Holding period** duration of the investment realized by an investor. It begins on the date of the deal closing and ends on the date of exit from the investment.

**Hurdle rate** internal rate of return that a fund must achieve before its general partners, or managers, can receive an increased interest in the management of the fund. If the expected rate of return of an investment is below the hurdle rate, the investment is not closed.

**Incubator** investor specializing in business concepts or new technology financing and development. An incubator usually provides physical space, legal services, managerial advice, and/or technical needs.

**Initial public offering (IPO)** process of sale or distribution of a corporate stock to the public for the first time. IPOs are often an opportunity for the existing investors as well as for venture capitalists to realize important economic returns on their original investment.

**Institutional investors** organizations specializing in professional investments insurance companies, depository institutions, pension funds, investment companies, mutual funds, and endowment funds.

**Intellectual property** intangible assets such as patents, copyrights, trademarks, and brand name.

**Internal code of activity** agreement that rules the activity of a Closed-end Fund and the relation between the AMC and the Investors. It has to receive the approval of the Supervisor.

**Investment firm** financial institution regulated by EU laws (i.e., Banking Directive) and committed to giving money through loans, by investing in equity, and selling payment services. The investment firm cannot collect money from deposits (i.e., like a bank), and it is supervised at different levels.

**IRA rollover** reinvestment of money received as a lump sum distribution from a retirement plan. Reinvestment may consist of the entire lump sum, or a portion.

**IRR (internal rate of return)** how venture capital funds measure their performance. Technically, an IRR is a discount rate that is the rate at which the present value of a series of investments is equal to the present value of the returns on those investments.

**Issue price** price per share paid for a series of stocks at the issuing date. This value is used for cumulative dividends, liquidation preference, and conversion ratios.

**Issued shares** amount of shares that a corporation has sold.

**Issuer** organization issuing or proposing to issue a security.

**J-curve effect** represents the returns generated by a private equity fund during the holding period of the investment. Following the usual dynamics of this type of investment, the private equity fund will initially receive a negative return and, when the first liquidations are realized, the fund returns start to rise.

**Key employees** professional managers hired by the founder to run the company.

**Later stage** fund investment phase that involves investors in the financing of the expansion of a growing company.

**Lead investor** member of a pool of private equity investors with the biggest participation in the deal. Usually in charge of the operation and in the management and control of the overall deal.

**Leveraged buyout (LBO)** it occurs when an investor acquires the controlling stake in a corporate equity through a complex investment operation financed with a combination of equity and borrowed funds. The acquiring group uses the target company's assets as collateral for the loans subscribed. Repayment of the loans is realized using the cash flow generated by the acquired company.

**Limited partner** investor participating in a limited partnership without taking part in the management of the partnership. A limited partner has limited liability and, usually, has priority over the general partners during liquidation of the partnership.

**Limited partner claw back** clause usually inserted in private equity partnership agreements that protects the general partner against future claims if he becomes the subject of a lawsuit. A fund's limited partners pay for any legal judgment imposed upon the limited partnership or the general partner.

**Limited partnerships (LPs)** organization established between general partners, who manages a fund, and limited partners, who invest money but with limited liability and without being involved in the day-to-day management activity of the fund. Usually, the general partner receives a management fee and a percentage of the profits or of the carried interest. The limited partners receive income, capital gains, and tax benefits.

**Limited partnership agreement (LPA)** agreement, written and signed in a contract, between the limited partners and the general partners to regulate both duties and rights and the private equity activity managed by the general partners.

**Liquidation** activity of converting securities into cash or the sale of the company assets to pay off debts. In a corporation liquidation, investors holding common shares are satisfied only after repayment of the claims raised by secured and unsecured creditors, bonds owners, and preferred shares holders.

**Liquidation preference** in a corporate liquidation it represents the amount per share that a preferred stockholder receives prior to the distribution of the amount per share to holders of common stock. It is usually defined as a multiple of the issue price, and there may be multiple types of liquidation preferences as different groups of investors buy shares in different series.

**Liquidity event** occurs when venture capitalists realize a gain or loss by exiting their investment. The most common exits are IPOs, buy backs, trade sales, and secondary buyouts.

**Lock-up period** period of time stockholders agree to waive their right to sell their shares. This clause is used when investment banks underwrite IPOs to ensure their support during market negotiation. Shareholders usually involved in lock-up are management teams, and directors of the company as well as strategic partners and large investors.

**Lump sum** one-time payment of money as opposed to a series of payments made over time.

**Management buyout (MBO)** financing from private equity companies to enable current operating management to acquire or buy the majority of the company they manage.

**Management fee** compensation paid by the fund to the general partner or the investment advisor based on the management activity of a venture fund.

**Management team** group of people who manage the activities of a venture capital fund.

**Mandatory redemption** an agreement between the investor and the company financed that gives the investor the right to require the corporation to repurchase some or all of his shares at a defined price and at a certain future time. It can occur automatically or may require a vote of the preferred stockholders with redemption rights.

**Market capitalization** total value of all outstanding shares. It is computed by multiplying the number of shares by the price per share current in the public market.

**Merchant banking** focuses on giving advice about financing, merger and acquisition, and equity investments in corporations.

**Merger** combining two or more companies into one larger corporate.

**Mezzanine financing** corporate financing immediately prior to a company's IPO. Investors taking part in this financing activity have lower risk of loss than the investors who invested in an earlier round.

**MiFID** markets in Financial Instruments Directive. It is a European Union Directive of 2004 issued to regulate the investment service activities.

**Mutual fund (also open-end fund)** allows investors to subscribe as many shares as they require. As money flows in, the fund grows. Open-end funds sometimes exclude new investors but, at the same time, the existing investors continue to increase their investment in the fund. When an investor wants to sell his participation, he usually sells his shares back to the fund

**Narrow-based weighted average ratchet** prevents the antidilution of the participations in a corporation. It reduces the price per share of the preferred stock of investor 1 if the issuance of new preferred shares to investor 2 are priced lower than the price investor 1 originally paid.

**NASDAQ** market provides participating brokers and dealers with price quotations on securities traded over the counter by the automatic process of information management.

**NAV (net asset value)** value of all investments in the fund divided by the number of outstanding shares of the fund.

**NDA (nondisclosure agreement)** agreement signed by two or more parties to protect the privacy of their activities and ideas when disclosing them to each other.

**Net financing cost (also cost of carry)** difference between the cost of financing the purchase of an asset and the asset's cash yield. With positive net financing cost the yield earned is greater than the financing cost; negative carry happens when the financing cost exceeds the yield earned.

**Net income** net earnings of a corporation after deducting all costs faced by the company during the execution of its business such as production costs, employees' salaries, depreciation, interest expense, and taxes.

**Net present value (NPV)** method of valuation that uses the actual value of future cash inflows subtracting future cash outflows.

**New issue** stock or bond that is offered to the public for the first time.

**NewCo** newly organized company used in LBOs.

**Noncompete clause** agreement signed by employees and management that states they will not work for competitors or establish a new competitor company for a defined period of time after termination of employment.

**NYSE (New York Stock Exchange)** founded in 1792, it is the largest organized public securities market in the United States.

**Open-end fund (also mutual fund)** allows investors to subscribe as many shares as they require. As money flows in, the fund grows. Open-end funds can exclude new investors but, at the same time, the existing investors can continue to raise their investment in the fund. When an investor wants to sell his participation, he usually sells his shares back to the fund.

**Original issue discount (OID)** bond or debt-like instrument discounted from the par value. This tool generates unfavorable tax effects because the IRS considers this cash flow as a zero coupon bond upon which tax payments are due annually.

**OTC (over-the-counter)** securities market in which dealers who may or may not be members of a formal securities exchange operate. The over-the-counter market is conducted through telephone contacts.

**Outstanding stock** amount of shares of a company owned by the investors equal to the amount of issued shares deducted by treasury stock.

**Over-subscription** during a public offering of shares, this happens when the demand for shares exceeds the offer. In private equity deals, this occurs when a deal has a great demand due to the company's growth opportunities.

**Over-subscription privilege** occurs when shareholders have the right to subscribe any shares that have not been purchased.

**Paid-in capital (also cumulative takedown amount)** committed capital transferred by a partner to a venture fund.

**Participating preferred** occurs when a preferred stock entitles the holder to the stated dividend and to additional dividends on a specified basis over the payment of dividends to the common shareholders. Preferred stock gives the owner the right to receive a predefined sum of cash, which is usually the original investment plus accrued dividends, if the company is sold or the subject of an IPO.

**Participation** sharing rights and duties of ownership of company securities with other investors.

**Partnership** legal entity in which each partner shares the profits, losses, and liabilities. Each member is responsible for the applicable taxes to its share of profits and losses.

**Partnership agreement** contract agreed and signed between investors and a private equity company for the duration of the private equity investment.

**Pay to play** an existing investor's right to participate in the next investment stage.

**PIV (pooled investment vehicle)** legal entity that collects different investor capital and manages it following a specific investment strategy.

**Placement agent** company specializing in locating investors that want to invest in a private equity fund or company securities. Using a placement agent allows the fund partners to focus on management activities.

**Poison pill** allows an owner to purchase shares in his company at a discounted price. This security is issued to make external takeover difficult.

**Pooled IRR** calculated as an aggregate of different IRRs based on a pool of cash flows.

**Portfolio companies** firms included in the investment portfolio of a private equity fund.

**Postmoney valuation** valuation of a company realized just after a round of financing.

**Premoney valuation** valuation of a company realized before a phase of the investment. This amount is defined by using different valuation models.

**Preemptive right** allows a shareholder to acquire an amount of shares in a future offering at current prices to maintain her percentage of ownership at the same level before the offering.

**Preference shares** shares of a firm that assigns the owner special rights over ordinary shares, such as the first right to receive dividends and/or capital payments.

**Preferred dividend** dividend paid to the owners of preferred shares.

**Preferred return** minimum return that has to be realized before a carry is permitted. A hurdle rate of 15% means that the private equity fund must achieve a return of at least 15% per annum before it can share the profits realized.

**Preferred stock** class of preferred shares. These securities can pay dividends at a specified rate and have priority in the payment of dividends and the liquidation of assets. Usually, venture capitalists invest in companies through preferred stock.

**Private equity** equity shares of companies that are not listed on a public exchange. Exchange of the participation in private equity is realized between buyers and sellers outside of the marketplace.

**Private investment in public equities (PIPES)** investment realized in a public company by a private equity fund.

**Private placement** sale of a security directly to a limited number of investors.

**Private placement memorandum (also offering memorandum)** official document explaining the terms and characteristics of securities offered through private placement.

**Private securities** not traded on a public exchange market and their price is fixed through negotiations realized between seller or issuer and buyer.

**Prospectus** written document containing information needed by an investor to make an informed decision. A prospectus must report any material risks and information according to the relevant laws and rules defined by regulatory agencies or authorities.

**Put option** gives its owner the right to sell a security at a predefined price during a certain period of time.

**Re-capitalization** reorganization of the risk capital of a corporation to improve the total value of the capital. It can be an exit strategy for private equity investors.

**Redemption**  right or obligation that pushes the company into repurchasing its own shares.

**Reorganization**  consists of critical changes in the equity structure of a company; for example, all shares converted to common stock or reducing the number of shares.

**Right of first refusal**  the owner has the right to refuse the closing of a proposed contract.

**Rights offering**  offering the right to purchase additional shares, usually at a discount price, to existing shareholders. These rights can be transferable so the owner can monetize their value on the trade market.

**Risk**  possibility of suffering losses on an investment; the sources of risk include inflation, default, politics, etc.

**Secondary funds**  used to purchase investment portfolios from other private equity funds providing liquidity to the original investors.

**Secondary market**  market where participations are traded to private equity funds.

**Secondary sale**  selling participations held by private equity funds to other investors.

**Securities and exchange commission (SEC)**  independent, nonpartisan, US market agency responsible for protecting investors; maintaining fair, orderly, and efficient markets; and facilitating capital information. The SEC checks up on participants in the securities market and it is concerned primarily with promoting the disclosure of important market-related information, maintaining fair dealing, and protecting against fraud.

**Seed money**  first capital investment in a start-up company. It is usually realized through loan or preferred stocks or convertible bonds or common stocks. Investors providing seed money are Angel Investors and early stage venture capital funds.

**Seed stage financing**  funding the initial state of a company's growth (see also Seed Money).

**Senior securities**  preferred stocks and bonds that entitle their owner with preferential claim over other investors on a firm's earnings and also during liquidation or bankruptcy.

**Shell corporation (also special purpose acquisition companies; SPACs)**  a corporation without any assets or business. It is usually organized to go public and then acquire existing businesses.

**Small business investment company (SBIC)**  special vehicle used to invest in private equity and regulated by a special US law (Small Business Investment Act, 1958). SBIC is a perfect joint venture between private and public investors with fiscal advantages.

**Special purpose vehicle (SPV)**  special corporation founded by a company to realize special financial deals; for example, LBO or M&A operations.

**Spin out**  company established by becoming independent of an already existing division or subsidiary of a firm. Private equity investors finance this activity by providing the necessary corporate financial funds.

**Statutory voting**  process of selecting members of the Board of Directors that gives shareholders one vote per each share owned and the ability to cast these votes for each of the candidates.

**Stock options**  owner ability to purchase or sell, at a defined price, the underlying securities during a prefixed period of time. It is also used as incentive for employees and managers.

**Strategic investors**  Investors that add value to the deals they realize due to industry and personal skills and services that assist companies in raising additional capital. They also support the business activity of the company in which they have invested.

**Subscription agreement**  investor request to join a limited partnership that has to be approved by the general partner.

**Sweat equity**  ownership of shares in a company that is assigned in front of supplying work rather than investment of capital.

**Syndicate**  group of underwriters, brokers, or dealers selling securities.

**Syndication** group of investors that offers funds for a particular deal; led by a lead investor who coordinates the deal and represents the group's members.

**Tag-along rights/co-sale rights** protection for minority shareholders that gives them the right to include their participation in any sale of the controlling shares at the same price offered to majority shareholders.

**Takedown schedule** plan, in terms of timing and size, of the contributions in the risk capital that has been agreed upon by the limited partners of a venture fund.

**Tender offer** offer made to the shareholders to purchase their shares.

**Term sheet** list of terms that investors have to accept when taking part in an investment.

**Thin capitalization (thin cap)** taxation mechanism that creates incentive to reduce the use of leverage through the reduction of deductible interest rate costs in proportion to the leverage.

**Time value of money** economic principle that assumes a different value of money during different times, looking both forward and backward.

**Trade sale** sale of the participation in risk capital of a firm to another company.

**Venture capital trust (VCT)** special vehicle used to invest in private equity and regulated by a special British law (Venture Capital Trust Act, 1997). The VCT is a vehicle listed on the London Stock Exchange where the investors are mostly retail.

**Voluntary redemption** allows a company to repurchase a part or all of the investor's shares at a predefined time. The purchase price is the issue price plus cumulative dividends.

**Voting right** assigned to stockholders allowing them to vote on company affairs.

**Warrant** security entitling the holder to buy an amount of common stock or preferred stock at a defined price for a period of time. Warrants are usually linked to a loan, bond, or preferred stock.

**Write-off** used to reduce or cancel the value of an asset. It reduces profits by changing the value of an asset to expense or loss.

**Yield** expressed as percentage calculated by dividing the gross dividend by the share price. It represents the annual return on an investment from interest and dividends, excluding capital gains.

# References

Abbot, S., & Hay, M. (1995). *Investing for the future.* London: FT Pitman Publishing.

Achleitner, A.-K., & Kloeckner, O. (2005). *Employment contribution of private equity and venture capital in Europe.* EVCA research paper.

Aghion, P., & Bolton, P. (1992). An incomplete contracts approach to financial contracting. *The Review of Economic Studies, 59*(3), 473–494.

AIFI (Associazione Italiana degli Investitori Istituzionali nel Capitale di Rischio). (2000). *Guide to venture capital.* Milan.

AIFI (Associazione Italiana degli Investitori Istituzionali nel Capitale di Rischio). (various years). *Development capital.* Milan: Guerini & Associati.

AIFI (Associazione Italiana degli Investitori Istituzionali nel Capitale di Rischio). (various years). *The Italian venture capital and private equity market.* Periodic reports, Milan.

Altman, E. I., & Hotchkiss, E. (2005). *Corporate financial distress and bankruptcy.* Hoboken, NJ: John Wiley and Sons.

Arnott, R., & Stiglitz, J. (1991). Moral hazard and nonmarket institutions: Dysfunctional crowding out or peer monitoring? *The American Economic Review, 81*(1), 179–190.

Assogestioni. (1999). *Mutual investment trusts.* Data and statistical guide, Milan.

Axelson, U., Strömberg, P., Jenkinson, T., & Weisbach, M. S. (2009). *Leverage and pricing in buyouts: An empirical analysis.* Available from: https://ssrn.com/abstract=1344023.

Baeyens, K., Vanacker, T., & Manigart, S. (2006). Venture capitalists' selection process: The case of biotechnology proposals. *International Journal of Technology Management, 34*(1–2), 28–46.

Bain and Company. (2017). *Global private equity report 2017.*

Balboa, M., & Martí, J. (2003). *An integrative approach to the determinants of private equity fundraising.* Available from: https://ssrn.com/abstract=493344.

Bank of England. (1999). *Practical issues arising from the Euro.* June. London.

Bank of England. (2000). *Finance for small firms: A seventh report.* London.

Bank of Italy. (1999). *Guidelines for banking supervision.* Circolare n. 229–21.4.99.

Bank of Italy. (from 2000a, various years). *Annual report, Rome.*

Bank of Italy. (from 2000b, various years). *Statistical bulletin, Rome.*

Barney, J. B., Busenitz, L. W., Fiet, J. O., & Mosel, D. D. (2001). New venture teams' assessment of learning assistance from venture capital firms. *Journal of Business Venturing, 18.*

Barry, C. B., Muscarella, C. J., Peavy, J. W., III, & Vetsuypens, M. R. (1990). The role of venture capital in the creation of public companies. *Journal of Financial Economics, 27.*

Bascha, A., & Walz, U. (2001). Convertible securities and optimal exit decisions in venture capital finance. *Journal of Corporate Finance, 7,* 285–306.

Basel Committee on Banking Supervision. (2013). *Consultative document. Capital requirements for banks' equity investments in funds.*

Bassi, I., & Grant, J. (2006). *Structuring European private equity.* London: Euromoney Books.

Beatty, R. P., & Ritter, J. R. (1986). Investment banking, reputation, and the underpricing of initial public offerings. *Journal of Financial Economics, 15.*

Benjamin, G. A., & Margulis, J. B. (2005). *Angel capital: How to raise early stage private equity financing.* John Wiley and Sons.

Benveniste, L. M., Erdal, S. M., & Wilhelm, W. J. (1998). Who benefits from secondary price stabilization of IPOs? *Journal of Banking and Finance, 22.*

Berger, A. N., & Hannan, T. H. (1997). Using measures of firm efficiency to distinguish among alternative explanations of structure-performance relationship. *Managerial Finance, 23.*

Berger, A. N., & Udell, G. F. (1998). The economics of small business finance: The roles of private equity and debt markets in the financial growth cycle. *Journal of Banking and Finance, 22.*

Berglöf, E. (1994). A control theory of venture capital finance. *Journal of Law, Economics, and Organization, 10,* 247–267.

Bester, H. (1987). The role of collateral in credit markets with imperfect information. *European Economic Review, 83.*

Bhave, M. P. (1999). A process model of entrepreneurial venture creation. *Journal of Business Venturing, 9.*

Bhidè, A. (1999). Developing start-up strategies. *The entrepreneurial venture* (2nd ed., pp. 121–137). Boston, MA: Harvard Business School Press.

Billingsley, R. S. (1995). Corporate financial decision making and equity analysis: An overview. In *Vol. 1995, No. 4. AIMR conference proceedings* (pp. 1–4): Association for Investment Management and Research.

Black, B. S., & Gilson, R. J. (1998). Venture capital and the structure of capital markets: Banks versus stock markets. *Journal of Financial Economics, 47,* 243–277.

Block, Z., & MacMillan, I. (1993). *Corporate venturing.* Boston, MA: Harvard Business School Press.

Blundell-Wignall, A., & Atkinson, P. (2010). Thinking beyond Basel III. *OECD Journal: Financial Market Trends, 2010*(1), 9–33.

Bond & Pecaro Inc. (2000). *Cyber valuation, internet business trends, analysis and valuation, New York.* Boston, MA: Harvard Business School Press.

Brav, A., & Gompers, P. A. (2003). The role of lock-ups in initial public offerings. *Review of Financial Studies, 16,* 1–29.

Brealey, R. A., & Myers, S. C. (2000). *Principles of corporate finance.* New York: McGraw-Hill.

Bruyat, C., & Julien, P. A. (2000). Defining the field of research in entrepreneurship. *Journal of Business Venturing, 14.*

BVCA. (1996). *Guide to venture capital.*

BVCA. (2016). *BVCA private equity and venture capital report on investment activity 2015.*

Bygrave, W. D., Hay, M., & Peeters, J. B. (1999). *The venture capital handbook.* Financial Times Management.

Byrne, M., & Bruen, M. (2009). *Accounting for private equity funds. Critical concepts, clear direction.* PwC.

Cairns, J. C., Davidson, J. A., & Kisicevitz, M. L. (2002). The limits of bank convergence. *The McKinsey Quarterly Journal, 2.*

Campioni, E., & Attar, A. (2003). Costly state verification and debt contracts: A critical resume. *Research in Economics, 57*.

Canals, J. (1997). *Universal banking. International comparison and theoretical perspectives*. Oxford: Clarendon Press.

Casamatta, C. (2003). Financing and advising: Optimal financial contracts with venture capitalists. *Journal of Finance, 58*(5).

Caselli, S. (2005). The competitive models of corporate banking and the relationship towards SMEs. *Small Bus. 1*.

Caselli, S. (2006). Dependent or independent? The performance contribution of board members in Italian venture-backed firms. *Journal of Corporate Ownership & Control, 4*(3).

Caselli, S., & Gatti, S. (2004). *Venture capital. A euro-system approach*. Berlin/London: Springer-Verlag.

Caselli, S., & Gatti, S. (2005). *Structured finance. Techniques, products and market*. Berlin/London: Springer-Verlag.

Caselli, S., & Gatti, S. (2006). Long-run venture-backed IPO performance analysis of Italian family-owned firms: What role do closed-end funds play? In G. N. Gregoriou, M. Kooli, & M. Kraussl (Eds.), *Venture capital: A European perspective*: Elsevier.

Caselli, S., Gatti, S., & Perrini, F. (2009). Are venture capitalist a catalysts for innovation or do they simply exploit it? *European Financial Management Journal, 1*.

Chapman, S. (1992). *The rise of merchant banking*. Happshire, London: Gregg Revivals.

Chevalier, J., & Ellison, G. (1997). Risk taking by mutual funds as a response to incentives. *Journal of Political Economy, 105*(6), 1167–1200.

Christiansen, C. M. (1991). *The innovator's dilemma*. Boston, MA: Harvard Business School Press.

Christofidis, C., & Debande, O. (2001). *Financing innovative firms through venture capital*. European Investment Bank Sector Paper.

Cochrane, J. H. (2005). The risk and return of venture capital. *Journal of Financial Economics, 75*(1).

Copeland, T., Koller, T., & Murrin, J. (2000). *Valuation—Measuring and managing the value of companies*. New York: Wiley.

Credit Suisse First Boston. (2001). *European technology—A game of two halves*. Internal report, January, London.

Cressy, R., Malipiero, A., & Munari, F. (2007). Playing to their strengths? Evidence that specialization in the private equity industry confers competitive advantage. *Journal of Corporate Finance, 13*.

Csikszentmihalyi, M. (1991). *Creativity: Flow and the psychology of discovery and invention*. New York: HarperCollins.

Cumming, D. (2004). The determinants of venture capital portfolio size: Empirical evidence. *Journal of Business, 35*.

Cumming, D. (2008). Contracts and exits in venture capital finance. *Review of Financial Studies, 21*(5), 1947–1982.

Cumming, D., Siegel, D., & Wright, M. (2007). Private equity, leveraged buyouts and governance. *Journal of Corporate Finance, 13*.

Cumming, D., & Walz, U. (2010). Private equity returns and disclosure around the world. *Journal of International Business Studies, 41*(4), 727–754.

Damodaran, A. (1994). *On valuation—Security analysis for investment and corporate finance*. New York: Wiley.

Damodaran, A. (1999a). *Applied corporate finance—A user's manual*. New York: Wiley.

Damodaran, A. (1999b). *The dark side of valuation: Firms with no earnings, no history and no comparables*. NYU Working Paper No. FIN-99-022. Available from: https://ssrn.com/abstract=1297075.

Damodaran, A. (2000). *Investment valuation: Tools and techniques for determining the value of any asset*. New York: Wiley.

Degeorge, F., & Zeckhauser, R. (1993). The reverse LBO decision and firm performances, theory and evidence. *Journal of Finance, 48*.

Demiroglu, C., & James, C. M. (2007). *Lender control and the role of private equity group reputation in buyout financing*. Available from: https://ssrn.com/abstract=1106378.

Desmet, D., Francis, T., Hu, A., Koller, T., & Riedel, G. (2000). Valuing dot coms. *McKinsey Quarterly, 1*(Spring).

Diamond, D. (1989). Reputation acquisition in debt markets. *Journal of Political Economy, 97*.

DRI-WEFA, NVCA. (2001). *Economic Impact of venture capital*. Washington DC, October.

Drucker, P. F. (1989). *The practice of management*. London: Heinemann Business Paperbacks.

EBAN. (2015). *European early stage market statistics*.

Eiglier, P., & Langeard, E. (1991). *Servuction. Le marketing des services*. Paris: McGraw-Hill.

Engel, D., & Keilbach, M. (2005). *Firm level implications of early stage venture capital investments. An empirical investigation*. ZEW discussion paper 22-05.

European Commission. (2002). *Enterprises in Europe*. 8th report, Bruxelles.

European Commission. (2013). *Guide to social innovation*.

European Commission. (2016). *Fiscal sustainability report 2015*.

European Information Technology Observatory. (2000). *The millennium edition*.

EY. (2000). *Convergence. The biotechnology industry report. Millennium edition, New York*.

EY. (2007). *Guide to financing for growth*. John Wiley & Sons.

EY. (2016a). *Annual report on the performance of portfolio companies, IX*.

EY. (2016b). *Worldwide corporate tax guide 2016*.

EY. (2016c). *Worldwide personal tax and immigration guide 2016–17*.

Fama, E. F. (1980). Agency problems and the theory of the firm. *The Journal of Political Economy, 88*.

Fama, E. F. (1991). Efficient capital markets. *Journal of Finance, 46*.

Fama, E. F., & Jensen, M. C. (1983). Separation of ownership and control. *Journal of Law and Economics, 26*.

Fenn, G. W., Liang, N., & Prowse, S. (1995). *The economics of private equity market: Vol. 168*. Board of Governors of the Federal Reserve System Staff Studies.

Financial Times. (1999). *The venture capital handbook*. London: Financial Times.

Foster, R., & Kaplan, S. (2001). *Creative destruction: Why companies are built to last underperform the market and how to successfully transform them*. New York: Currency/Doubleday.

Fried, V. H., & Hisrich, R. D. (1994). Toward a model of venture capital investment decision making. *Financial Management, 23*.

Fruhan, W. E. (1979). *Financial strategy—Studies in the creation, transfer and destruction of shareholder value*. Homewood: Irwin.

Gardella, L. A. (2000). *Selecting and structuring investments: The venture capitalist's perspective*. Charlottesville, VA: Reading in Venture Capital, Association for Investment Management and Research (AIMR).

Gartner, W. B., Starr, J. A., & Bhat, S. (2000). Predicting new venture survival: An analysis of anatomy of a start-up cases from Inc. Magazine. *Journal of Business Venturing, 14*.

Geisst, R. C. (1995). *Investment banking in the financial system.* Englewood Cliffs/London: Prentice Hall.

German Association of Biotechnology Industries. (1998). *Valuation of biotech companies, Berlin.*

Gervasoni, A., & Sattin, F. L. (2000). *Private equity and venture capital.* Guerrini e Associati.

GIIN. (2016). *Impact investing trends. Evidence of a growing industry.*

GIIN. (2017). *Annual impact investor survey* (7th ed.).

Gilder, G. (2000). *Telecosm.* New York: The Free Press.

Goldsmith, R. W. (1969). *Financial structure and development.* New Haven: Yale University Press.

Gompers, P. A. (1995). Optimal investment, monitoring and the staging of venture capital. *The Journal of Finance, 50.*

Gompers, P. (1996). Grandstanding in the venture capital industry. *Journal of Financial Economics, 42.*

Gompers, P. A., & Lerner, J. (1996). The use of covenants: An empirical analysis of venture partnership agreements. *Journal of Law and Economics, 39.*

Gompers, P. A., & Lerner, J. (1999). *What drives venture capital fundraising?* (No. w6906). National Bureau of Economic Research.

Gompers, P. A., & Lerner, J. (1999). *What drives venture capital fundraising?* W.P. 6906, NBER Series, Cambridge, MA.

Gompers, P. A., & Lerner, J. (2000). *The venture capital circle.* MIT Press.

Gordon Smith, D. (2005). Control and exit in venture capital relationships. In *Law and economics workshop*: University of California at Berkeley.

Gorman, M., & Sahlman, W. A. (1989). What do venture capitalist do? *Journal of Business Venturing, 4.*

Grabenwarter, U., & Weidig, T. (2005). *Exposed to the J-curve, understanding and managing private equity fund investments.* Euromoney Books.

Groh, A. P., & Gottschalg, O. (2006). *The risk-adjusted performance of US buyouts.* Groupe HEC.

Gupta, A. K., & Sapienza, H. J. (1992). Determinants of venture capital firms ' preferences regarding the industry diversity and geographic scope of their investments. *Journal of Business Venturing, 7.*

Hackbarth, D., Hennessy, C., & Leland, H. (2007). Can the trade off theory explain debt structure? *Review of Financial Studies, 20.*

Hambrick, D., & Schecter, S. (1983). Turnaround strategies for mature industrial product business units. *Academy of Management Journal, 26,* 231–248.

Hamel, G. (2000). *Leading the revolution.* Boston, MA: Harvard Business School Press.

Hannan, T. H. (1991). Bank commercial loan markets and the role of market structure: Evidence from surveys of commercial lending. *Journal of Banking and Finance, 15.*

Harris, M., & Raviv, A. (1991). The theory of capital structure. *Journal of Finance, 46*(1), 297–355.

Harvey, C., Lerner, J., Schoar, A., Fung, B., & Irwin, S. (Eds.), (2008). *Encyclopedia of alternative investment.* London: Chapman Hall.

Haspeslagh, P. C., & Jemison, D. B. (1991). *Managing acquisition. Creating value trough corporate renewal.* The Free Press.

Hayes, S., & Hubbard, P. (1990). *Investment banking.* Boston, MA: Harvard Business School Press.

Heifetz, R. (1994). *Leadership without easy answers.* Cambridge, MA: Belknap Press.

Hellmann, T. (2006). IPOs, acquisitions, and the use of convertible securities in venture capital. *Journal of Financial Economics, 81,* 649–679.

Hellmann, T., Lindsey, L., & Puri, M. (2007). Building relationships early: Banks in venture capital. *The Review of Financial Studies, 21*(2), 513–541.

Hellmann, T., & Puri, M. (1999). *The interaction between product marketing and financing strategy: The role of venture capital.* Research paper 1561, Research paper series Stanford: Stanford University. May.

Hellmann, T., & Puri, M. (2000). *Venture capital and the professionalization of start-up firms: Empirical evidence.* Research paper 1661, Research paper series Stanford: Stanford University.

Hellwig, M. (1991). Banking financial intermediation and corporate finance. In A. Giovannini & C. Mayer (Eds.), *European financial integration.* Cambridge: Cambridge University Press.

HM Revenue & Customs (HMRC). (2016). *Venture capital trusts statistics: An official statistics release.*

Holthausen, R. W., & Larcker, D. (1996). The financial performance of reverse leveraged buyouts. *Journal of Financial Economics, 42*(3), 293–332.

Hunt, D. (1995). What future for Europe's investment banks? *Mc-Kinsey Quarterly Review, 1.*

Ibbotson, R. G., & Ritter, J. R. (1995). Initial public offerings. *Handbooks in Operations Research and Management Science, 9,* 993–1016.

Impact Investing Lab, SDA Bocconi. (n.d.). *Public private collaborations for social ImpactCreation.* Position paper.

Impact Investing Lab, SDA Bocconi, Vecchi, V., Casalini, F., Caselli, S. (n.d.). *Impact investing as a societal refocus of Venture Capital. The perspective of mature economies.* Position paper.

Inderst, R., & Mueller, H. (2004). The effect of capital market characteristics on the value of start-up firms. *Journal of Financial Economics, 72.*

Invest Europe. (1999). *Private equity fund structures in Europe.* Zaventem: Internal Publication.

Invest Europe. (2001a). *Guide lines.* March. www.evca.com.

Invest Europe. (2001b). *EVCA mid year survey of Pan-European private equity and venture capital.* Press release, Helsinki, 17th October.

Invest Europe. (2005). *Employment contribution of private equity and venture capital in Europe.*

Invest Europe. (2008a). Annual survey of Pan-European private equity & venture capital activity 2007. In *EVCA yearbook.*

Invest Europe. (2008b). Pan-European private equity & venture capital activity report. In *EVCA yearbook 2008, Bruxelles.*

Invest Europe. (2010). *Private equity fund structures in Europe. An EVCA Tax & Legal Committee special paper.*

Invest Europe. (2014). *Essential work 2014–2019. Private equity's contribution to building European businesses.*

Invest Europe. (2015). *Professional standards handbook.*

Invest Europe. (2016). *Central and eastern European private equity statistics 2015.*

Invest Europe. (2017). *2016 European private equity activity.*

Invest Europe—European Venture Capital Association. (various issues). *Yearbook.*

Invest Europe. (n.d.). *Guide to private equity and venture capital for pension funds.*

Invest Europe—PwC. (1996). *The economic impact of venture capital in Europe.* September.

Invest Europe—PwC. (1997). *The economic impact of venture capital in Europe.* Zaventem.

Jackson, E. T., & Associates Ltd. for the Rockefeller Foundation. (2012). *Accelerating impact. Achievements, challenges and what's next in building the impact investing industry.*

Jain, B., & Kini, O. (1995). Venture capitalist participation and the post-issue operating performance of IPO firms. *Managerial and Decision Economics, 5.*

Jarrow, R. A., Maksimovic, V., & Ziemba, W. T. (1997). Handbooks in Operations Research and Management Science Volume 9 Finance. *Journal of the Operational Research Society*, 48(10), 1042.

Jeng, L., & Wells, P. (2000). The determinants of venture capital funding: Evidence across countries. *Journal of Corporate Finance, 6*.

Jensen, M. C. (1986). Agency costs of free cash flow, corporate finance, and takeovers. *American Economic Review, 76*.

Jensen, M. C., & Meckling, W. H. (1976). Theory of the firm: Managerial behavior, agency costs and ownership structure. *Journal of Financial Economics, 3*.

Kanniainen, V., & Keuschingg, C. (2004). Start-up investment with scarce venture capital support. *Journal of Banking and Finance, 28*.

Kaplan, S. (1989a). Campeau's acquisition of federated—Value destroyed or value added. *Journal of Financial Economics, 25*(2), 191–212.

Kaplan, S. (1989b). The effects of management buyouts on operating performance and value. *Journal of Financial Economics, 24*(2), 217–254.

Kaplan, S., & Schoar, A. (2005). Private equity performance: Returns, persistence and capital flows. *Journal of Finance, 60*(4), 1791–1823.

Kaplan, S. N., & Strömberg, P. (2000). *How do venture capitalists choose investments.* Working paper 121 (pp. 55–93). University of Chicago.

Kaplan, S. N., & Strömberg, P. (2002). Financial contracting theory meets the real world: An empirical analysis of venture capital contracts. *Review of Economic Studies, 70*(2), 281–315.

Kaplan, S. N., & Strömberg, P. (2004). Characteristics, contracts, and actions: Evidence from venture capitalist analyses. *Journal of Finance, 59*(5), 2173–2206.

Keeton, W. R. (1996). Do banks mergers reduce lending to business and farmers? New evidence from tenth district states. Federal Reserve Bank of Kansas City. *Economic Review, 81*.

Kellogg, D., & Charnes, J. M. (2000). Real options valuation for a biotechnology company. *Financial Analysts Journal, 3*.

Koller, T. (2001). Valuing dot coms after the fall. *McKinsey Quarterly, 2*.

Kortum, S., & Lerner, J. (2001). Does venture capital spur innovation? In *Entrepreneurial inputs and outcomes: New studies of entrepreneurship in the United States* (pp. 1–44): Emerald Group Publishing Limited.

KPMG. (2015). *2015 global tax rate survey.*

Kraus, A., & Litzenberger, R. H. (1973). A state-preference model of optimal financial leverage. *Journal of Finance, 28*.

Kuhn, R. L. (1990). *Investment banking, the art and science of high-stakes deal making.* New York: Harper & Row.

Leithner & Co. PTY. (1999). *The internet and value investing.* Internal report, Brisbane.

Lerner, J. (1994). The syndication of venture capital investments. *Financial Management, 23* (3 (Autumn)).

Lerner, J. (1995). Venture capitalists and the oversight of private firms. *Journal of Finance, 50*.

Lerner, J. (1999). The government as a venture capitalist: The long-run effects of the SBIR program. *Journal of Business, 72*(3), 285–297.

Lerner, J. (2000). *Private equity and venture capital—A casebook.* New York: Wiley.

Lerner, J., Schoar, A., & Wong, W. (2005). *Smart institutions, foolish choices? The limited partner performance puzzle.* MIT Sloan Research Paper, No. 4523-05.

Levin, J. S. (1994). *Structuring venture capital, private equity and entrepreneurial transaction.* Chicago, IL: CCH Inc.

Lewis, M. (1999). *The new thing*. New York: Norton & Company.

Liaw, K. T. (1999). *The business of investment banking*. New York: John Wiley & Sons.

Ljungqvist, A., & Richardson, M. (2003a). *The cash flow, return and risk characteristics of private equity (No. w9454)*. National Bureau of Economic Research.

Ljungqvist, A., & Richardson, M. P. (2003b). *The investment behavior of private equity fund managers*. Available from: https://ssrn.com/abstract=1295177.

Llewellyn, D. T. (1992). Financial innovation: A basic analysis. In H. Cavanna (Ed.), *Financial innovation*. London: Routledge.

Llewellyn, D. T. (1999). *The new economics of banking*. Amsterdam: Société Universitaire Européenne de Recherches Financières.

London Stock Exchange. (1999). *TECHMARK, The technology market. London*.

Lorenz, T. (1985). *Venture capital today*. Cambridge: Woodhead-Faulkner.

MacMillan, I. C., Kulow, D. M., & Khoylian, R. (1988). Venture capitalists' involvement in their investments: Extent and performance. *Journal of Business Venturing, 4*.

MacMillan, I. C., Siegel, R., & Subbanarasimha, P. N. S. (1985). Criteria used by venture capitalists to evaluate new venture proposals. *Journal of Business Venturing, 1*.

Mason, C. M., & Harrison, R. T. (2000). The size of the informal venture capital market in the United Kingdom. *Small Business Economics, 15*.

Mauboussin, M. J., & Hiler, B. (1999). *Cash Flow.com—Cash economics in the new economy*. Internal report New York: Credit Suisse First Boston Corporation. March.

Mauboussin, M. J., Regan, M. T., Schay, A., & Fisher, A. M. (2000). *Wanna be GE?* Internal report New York: Credit Suisse First Boston Corporation. February.

McBride, A. S., & McBride, R. G. (2001). *The vital role of investor relations. Strategic Investor Relations*. Summer. www.iijournals.com.

Mccue, J. (2000). Telecommunications and the new economy. In *Lucent Client Success and Partner conference, Doral, 30th October–2nd November, Florida*.

McNamee, M. (2001). America's future—Investment plays 27th August. *Business Week*.

Megginson, W. L., & Weiss, K. A. (1991). Venture capitalist certification in initial public offerings. *The Journal of Finance, 46*(3).

Meyers, S. C., & Miluf, N. S. (1984). Corporate financing and investment decisions when firms have information investors do not have. *Journal of Financial Economics, 13*.

Michaelson, J. C. (2002). *Restructuring for growth: Alternative financial strategies to increase shareholder value*. McGraw-Hill Professional.

Millan, I. C., & Zeman, L. (1987). Criteria distinguishing successful ventures in the venture screening process. *Journal of Business Venturing, 2*.

Miller, M., & Modigliani, F. (1963). Corporate income taxes and the cost of capital: A correction. *American Economic Review, 3*.

Modigliani, F., & Miller, M. (1958). The cost of capital, corporate finance, and the theory of investment. *American Economic Review, 3*.

MSDW. (1999). *Entrepreneur workshop—Exit strategies [Proceeding of the conference, 31 May, London]*. www.ms.com.

Murray, G., & Marriott, R. (1998). Why has the investment performance of technology-specialist European venture capital funds been so poor? *Research Policy, 27*.

Myers, S. (1984). The capital structure puzzle. *Journal of Finance, 39*.

Myers, S. C., & Howe, C. D. (1997). *A life-cycle financial model of pharmaceutical R & D. Program on the pharmaceutical industry*. Sloan School of Management, Massachusetts Institute of Technology.

Myers, S., & Majluf, N. (1984). Corporate financing and investment decisions when firms have information that investors do not have. *Journal of Financial Economics, 13.*

Nikoskelainen, E., & Wright, M. (2007). The impact of corporate governance mechanisms on value increase in leveraged buyouts. *Journal of Corporate Finance, 13,* 511–537.

Norman, R. (1984). *Service management: Strategy and leadership in service business.* Chicago, IL: Wiley & Sons.

NVCA (National Venture Capital Association). (various issues). *Yearbook, Annual economic impact of venture capital study,* USA.

Office of the Business Operations Officer. (2016). *Small Business Investment Company (SBIC) program overview.*

Ooghe, H., Manigart, S., & Fassin, Y. (1991). Growth patterns of the European venture capital industry. *Journal of Business Venturing, 6.*

Peek, J., & Rosengren, E. S. (1996). Small business credit availability: How important is the side of lender? In A. Saunders, & I. Walter (Eds.), *Financial system design: The case for universal banking.* Burr Ridge: Irwin Publishing.

Phalippou, L., & Gottschalg, O. (2008). The performance of private equity funds. *The Review of Financial Studies, 22*(4), 1747–1776.

Porter, M. E. (1980). *Competitive strategy. Technique for analysing industries and competitors.* New York: The Free Press.

Porter, M. (1985). *Competitive advantage.* New York: The Free Press.

Poterba, J. (1989). Venture capital and capital gain taxation. In L. Summers (Ed.), *Tax policy and the economy:* MIT Press.

Povaly, S. (2007). *Private equity exits: Divestment process management for leveraged buyouts.* Berlin/Heidelberg: Springer-Verlag.

Pratt, S. E. (1983). *Guide to venture capital.* Wesley Hills, MA: Capital Publishing Corporation.

Preqin. (2015). *Preqin special report: Private equity secondary market challenging the illiquidity myth.*

Preqin. (2017). *Secondary market update, Q1 2017.*

PwC. (1999). *Corporate finance.*

Rappaport, A. (1997). *La strategia del valore. Le nuove regole di creazione della performance aziendale.* Milan: Franco Angeli.

Ravid, S. A. (1988). On Interactions of production and financial decisions. *Financial Management, 3.*

Reid, G. C. (1992). *Venture capital investment.* London: Routledge.

Reid, G. C., & Smith, J. A. (2003). Venture capital and risk in high-technology enterprises. *International Journal of Business and Economics, 2.*

Reston, J. Jr. (1998). *The last apocalypse: Europe at the year 1000 A.D.* New York: Doubleday.

Robberts, M., & Bhidè, A. (Eds.), (1999). *The entrepreneurial venture.* Boston: Harvard Business School Press.

Robbie, K., & Wright, M. (1997). *Venture capital.* New York: Dartmouth Publishing.

Robbie, J., Wright, S., & Chiplin, M. (1999). Funds providers' role in venture capital firm monitoring. In *Management buy-outs and venture capital:* Edward Elgar Ltd.

Rock, K. (1986). Why new issues are underpriced. *Journal of Financial Economics, 15.*

Ross, S. A. (1977). The determination of financial structure: The incentive-signalling approach. *The Bell Journal of Economics,* 23–40.

Rybczynsky, T. M. (1996). Investment banking: Its evolution and place in the system. In E. Gardner & P. Molineux (Eds.), *Investment banking. Theory and practice.* London: Euromoney Books.

Sahlman, W. A. (1990). The structure and governance of venture-capital organizations. *The Journal of Financial Economics, 27.*

Sahlman, W. A. (1999). *The entrepreneurial venture.* Boston, MA: Harvard Business School Press.

Santomero, A. M., & Babbel, D. F. (1997). *Financial markets, instruments and institutions.* Chicago, IL: Irwin Publisher.

Sapienza, H. J., Amason, A. C., & Manigart, S. (1994). The level and nature of venture capitalist involvement in their portfolio companies: A study of three European countries. *Managerial Finance, 20.*

Saunders, A., & Walter, I. (1994). *Universal banking in the United States. What could we gain? What could we lose?.* Oxford University Press.

Schefczyk, M., & Gerpott, J. T. (2000). Qualifications and turnover of managers and venture capital financed firm performance: An empirical study of German venture capital investments. *Journal of Business Venturing, 16.*

Schumacher, E. F. (1973). *Small is beautiful.* London: Blond & Brigger.

Schwartz, E. S., & Moon, M. (2000). Rational pricing of internet companies. *Financial Analysts Journal, 3.*

Schwienbacher, A. (2002). *An empirical analysis of venture capital exits in Europe and in the United States.* University of California at Berkeley. Working paper.

Schwienbacher, A., Hege, U., & Palomino, F. (2003). *Determinants of venture capital performance: Europe and United States.* RICAFE working paper n. 1.

Shleifer, A., & Summers, L. (1988). Breach of trust in hostile takeovers. In A. J. Auerbach (Ed.), *Corporate takeovers: Causes & consequences*: University of Chicago Press.

Silver, A. D. (1994). *The venture capital sourcebook.* Chicago, IL: Probus.

Simon, H. (1989). *Price marketing.* Amsterdam: North Holland.

Simpson, I. (2000). *Fundraising and investor relations.* EVCA Association.

Sirri, E., & Tufano, P. (1992). *The demand for mutual fund services by individual investors.* Harvard Business School. Working paper.

Slatter, S. (1984). *Corporate recovery: Successful turnaround strategies and their implementation.* Penguin.

Slatter, S., Lovett, D., & Barlow, L. (2006). *Leading corporate turnaround.* San Francisco, CA: Jossey-Bass.

Smith, A. J. (1990). Corporate ownership structure and performance, the case of management buyouts. *Journal of Financial Economics, 27.*

Smith, R. C., & Walter, I. (1997). *Global banking.* Oxford: Oxford University Press.

Stein, J. C. (1989). Efficient capital markets, inefficient firms: A model of myopic corporate behavior. *Quarterly Journal of Economics, 104,* 655–669.

Stewart, G. B. (1991). *The quest for value—The EVA management guide.* New York: Harper Business.

Storey, D. J. (1991). The birth of new firms—Does unemployment matter? A review of the evidence. *Small Business Economics, 3.*

Strahan, P. E., & Weston, J. P. (1998). Small business lending and the changing structure of the banking industry. *Journal of Banking and Finance, 22.*

Timmons, J. A., & Bygrave, W. D. (1992). *Venture capital at the crossroads.* Boston, MA: Harvard Business School Press.

Titman, S., & Wessel, R. (1988). The determinants of capital structure choice. *Journal of Finance, 43* (1), 1–19.

Tobin, J. (1984). *On the efficiency of the financial system.* Lloyds Bank review. July.

Townsend, R. M. (1979). Optimal contracts and competitive markets with costly state verification. *Journal of Economic Theory, 21.*

Tyebjee, T., & Bruno, A. (1984). A model of venture capitalist investment activity. *Management Science, 30.*

Van Osnabrugge, M., & Robinson, R. J. (1999). *Financing entrepreneurship: Business angels and venture capitalists compared.* Division of Research, Harvard Business School.

Van Osnabrugge, M., & Robinson, R. J. (2000). *Angel investing.* Boston, MA: Harvard Business School.

Venture Capital Report. (1998). *Guide to private equity & venture capital in the UK & Europe.* London: Pitman Publishing.

Venture Economics. (1988). *Exiting venture capital investments.* Wellesley, MA.

Venture Economics. (1996). *Pratt's guide to venture capital sources.* New York: SDC Publishing.

Venture Economics. (2001). *Venture edge.* Spring.

Venture One Corporation, PricewaterhouseCoopers. (2001). *The PricewaterhouseCoopers money tree survey in partnership with venture one.* August, San Francisco.

Venzin, M. (2009). *Building an international financial services firm.* London: Oxford Press.

Vesper, K. H. (1989). A taxonomy of new business ventures. *Journal of Business Venturing, 4.*

Walker, D. (2007). *Disclosure and transparency in private equity London.* Consultation document BVCA.

Wall, J., & Smith, J. (n.d.). *Better exits.* Price Waterhouse Corporate Finance—EVCA.

Walraven, N. (1997). *Small business lending by banks involved in mergers.* Board of Governors of the Federal Reserve, Finance and Economics Discussion Series, n. 25.

Walter, I. (1998). *Global competition in financial services.* Cambridge: Harper & Row Ballinger.

Ward, J. (1987). *Keeping the family firm healthy. How to plan for continuing growth, profitability and the family leadership.* San Francisco, CA: Jossey-Bass.

Wetzel, W. E. (1981). Informal risk capital in New England. In K. H. Vesper (Ed.), *Frontiers in entrepreneurship research.* Wellesley, MA: Babson College.

Wilson, J. W. (1986). *The new venturers. Inside the high-stakes world of venture capital.* Addison-Wesley.

Winborg, H., & Landstrom, J. (2000). Financial bootstrapping in small businesses: Examining small business managers' resource acquisition behaviors. *Journal of Business Venturing, 16.*

World Economic Forum. (2008). *The globalization of alternative investments, the global economic impact of private equity report 2008.* Vol. 1. Working paper.

World Economic Forum. (2013). *From the margins to the mainstream. Assessment of the impact investment sector and opportunities to engage mainstream investors.*

World Economic Forum (2015a). *The future of financial services. How disruptive innovations are reshaping the way financial services are structured, provisioned and consumed—Prepared in collaboration with Deloitte.*

World Economic Forum. (2015b). *The Future of FinTech. A paradigm shift in small business finance.*

World Economic Forum. (2016). *Alternative investments 2020. The future of capital for entrepreneurs and SMEs.*

Zingales, L. (2000). In search of new foundations. *Journal of Finance, 55.*

# Index

Note: Page numbers followed by $f$ indicate figures, $t$ indicate tables, $b$ indicate boxes, and $np$ indicate footnotes.

CPI Antony Rowe

Chippenham, UK

2018-01-23 11:11